THADDEUS STEVENS

BOOKS BY RALPH KORNGOLD

Robespierre and the Fourth Estate

Saint-Just

Citizen Toussaint

Two Friends of Man

The Story of William Lloyd Garrison and Wendell Phillips and Their Relationship with Abraham Lincoln

Thaddeus Stevens

A Being Darkly Wise and Rudely Great

RALPH KORNGOLD

was born in Warsaw and brought up in Amsterdam, but came to the United States when he was nineteen. After a succession of jobs as bank clerk, insurance agent, cowboy, and teacher of French, he went to France to devote himself to the writing of *Robespierre and the Fourth Estate,* considered the definitive work on the Jacobin leader. This biography was published in the United States in 1941 and was translated into seven languages. With the outbreak of World War II, Mr. Korngold returned to this country, where his very successful biography of Toussaint L'Ouverture, *Citizen Toussaint,* was published in 1944. His next historical study, *Two Friends of Man* (1950), dealt with William Lloyd Garrison and Wendell Phillips and their relationship to Lincoln. Mr. Korngold now makes his home in Chicago.

THADDEUS STEVENS

A Being Darkly Wise and Rudely Great

RALPH KORNGOLD

HARCOURT, BRACE AND COMPANY
NEW YORK

first edition

LIBRARY OF CONGRESS CATALOG CARD NUMBER: 55-9381

PRINTED IN THE UNITED STATES OF AMERICA

FOR PIRI—MY WIFE

FOREWORD

If one mentions Thaddeus Stevens to the average American one is likely to receive a questioning look. Few have ever heard of him. Those who have, have a vague recollection that he was a Civil War figure—a senator or a representative—who during the war was a "thorn in Lincoln's side" because of his insistence on "extreme measures," and during Reconstruction was responsible for the spoliation of the South by the carpetbaggers. The term "vindictive" is generally associated with his name. Even so, however, the popular ignorance about him is surprising, since his importance on the stage of history is recognized by his severest critics.

James Albert Woodburn, onetime professor of American history and politics, in Indiana University, has said: "Thaddeus Stevens was the dominant figure in the American Congress during this notable period. It may reasonably be claimed that no more masterful leader ever directed the politics and legislation of the House of Representatives . . . and it may be said that for a part of this decade he led both the House and the nation by the sheer force and energy of his mind and will." [1]

Richard Nelson Current, professor of history in the University of Illinois, has written that Stevens "had exerted more influence upon American legislation, during the decade of conflict, than any other person in the United States! . . . War taxes, tariffs, greenbacks,

[1] From *The Life of Thaddeus Stevens* by James Albert Woodburn, copyright 1913, 1940. Quoted by special permission of the publishers, The Bobbs-Merrill Company, Inc., preface.

transcontinental railroads, 'forty acres and a mule,' the Thirteenth, Fourteenth, and Fifteenth Amendments, the reconstruction acts, the impeachment proceedings—these things and many more were largely his handiwork." [2]

Samuel Bowles, famous editor of the Springfield (Massachusetts) *Daily Republican,* wrote when news of Stevens's death reached him: "To the great mass of the loyal people of the country, the sudden event will cause regret, and to many, a profound grief. He was one of the few individuals on whom during the great revolution which we have been passing through, now for ten years, momentous events really hinged. . . . The new era of American nationality felt his powerful clutch and impetus, and his mark will remain on our Constitution and policy longer than that of Webster, of Clay, or even of Calhoun, the three traditional demigods of the Washington Olympus." [3]

A foreign observer, Georges Clemenceau of France, American correspondent of the Paris *Le Temps* during the Reconstruction period, wrote to his paper: "Thaddeus Stevens is dead. For nearly eight months the country has been expecting the end of the desperate struggle which this extraordinary man has waged against age, grief and disease which he knew was incurable. The nation has lost in him a great citizen, and the Republican party one of its most distinguished leaders. . . .

"The revolution which he so greatly desired, and which he supported with such enthusiasm, was practically completed, so he could die without too many regrets. He will stand out with Garrison, Wendell Phillips, Sumner and Lincoln, as one of the most interesting figures of the second American revolution." [4]

William Lloyd Garrison, Wendell Phillips, and Charles Sumner have fallen into almost as much disrepute as Stevens and are as little remembered. Of the political leaders of that time Lincoln alone has retained his hold on popular favor. It may well be by way of compensation that admiration for him far exceeds that which he

[2] From *Old Thad Stevens—A Story of Ambition* by Richard Nelson Current, copyright 1942. Quoted by special permission of the publishers, The University of Wisconsin Press, p. 317.

[3] Springfield *Daily Republican,* Aug. 13, 1868.

[4] From *American Reconstruction* by Georges Clemenceau, copyright 1928. Quoted by special permission of the publishers, The Dial Press, Inc., pp. 224-227.

enjoyed during his lifetime. When one considers how many rose to everlasting fame during the War for Independence, it is strange to find the stage of history so deserted politically during the Civil War period. Had the art of leadership so greatly deteriorated during the intervening years?

The scarcity of outstanding political personalities during the struggle for the preservation of the Union is more apparent than real. It is the nature of that struggle which is responsible for the neglect and even disrepute into which all but Lincoln have fallen. Apart from being a political leader Lincoln possessed qualities and characteristics that have endeared him to the American people. Others—especially Thaddeus Stevens, by far the ablest and most resolute of the Northern leaders—have been adversely affected by the fact that they were leaders in a struggle in which American was fighting American. During the War for Independence, a leader could be as fiercely patriotic as he chose without injuring his popularity either then or later. Samuel Adams was often intemperate and vituperative in his denunciations of the British, yet is fondly remembered. Thomas Paine advocated confiscation of the property of English loyalists, yet has not forfeited our admiration. But Thaddeus Stevens, who in language reminiscent of Danton's called upon the people of the North to smite the rebels and advocated confiscation of the property of disloyal slaveholders, does not evoke the enthusiasm of a reunited nation. Yet so confirmed a partisan of the South as Claude G. Bowers could not help acknowledging that "whatever may be said in criticism, he was the vitalizing force in the House and energized the whole country." [5] A man who had done so during the War for Independence would have become the darling of the American people for all time to come!

"The victors forget, the vanquished remember," Winston Churchill has written. When victors and vanquished are citizens of the same country it is but natural that those who remember should exercise greater influence upon public opinion than those who forget. I believe it was the late Professor James G. Randall who wrote: "In song and story it is the South that has won the decision at Appomattox." Not only in song and story. The movies and ad-

[5] From *The Tragic Era* by Claude G. Bowers, copyright 1929. Quoted by special permission of the publishers, Houghton Mifflin Co., p. 72.

vertising have been equally affected. *History and historical biography have not remained immune.*

2

"In whatever direction we look," Henry Adams wrote in 1894, "we can see no possibility of converting history into a science without bringing it into hostility toward one or more of the most powerful organizations of the era." Most historians are loath to come into conflict with such organizations, and history suffers as a consequence. Periodical reappraisal of history's judgments is therefore indispensable if history is to fulfill its scientific mission. The fact that those who "remember" are powerfully organized may well be responsible for the fact that such reappraisal of Civil War and Reconstruction history as has taken place has been in the nature of a more complete surrender to the very forces that have striven to corrupt the history of that era.

That Lincoln was the most sympathetic figure of the war period requires no argument, but a comparison of his and Stevens's political programs with measures adopted during the war leads to the inevitable conclusion that political leadership came from the Capitol rather than from the White House. Lincoln's program was rejected, Stevens's adopted, and Lincoln finished by praising what he had previously opposed. As for Reconstruction—"The Southern people are just what we would be in their situation," Lincoln said in 1854 in his Peoria speech. At the conclusion of armed hostilities they were what the existence of slavery in their midst, the misrule of their governing class, four years of war and of Confederate propaganda, and the bitterness of defeat had made them. To have lost sight of this when considering their reintegration into the Union would have meant to compromise the country's future.

No greater libel can be uttered against Lincoln than that he would have approved the Reconstruction program President Johnson sought to foist upon the country. Had Lincoln lived to witness the postwar attitude of the former rebels toward the Union, toward Southern loyalists and freedmen, toward the new Louisiana constitution he had praised in his last speech, there can be no doubt that he would have discarded his wartime Reconstruction experiment, as Congress felt obliged to discard its Wade-Davis plan.

Stevens conceived and introduced the Fourteenth Amendment to the Constitution, designed to prevent the former rebels from taking advantage of the presence in the South of four million nonvoting Negroes to exercise a disproportionate influence in the government they had sought to destroy. He proposed a Reconstruction plan that did not call for the immediate enfranchisement of the freedmen and was as just and reasonable as it was practical. His proposals were defeated by the intransigence of the South, the legalism of conservative Republicans, and the obstructionist tactics of President Johnson.

After that there remained only two courses open to him: The South could have been readmitted with an increased representation in the House and the Electoral College—with the practical certainty that the federal government would pass into the hands of former rebels and Copperheads at the next presidential election, or the immediate right of suffrage could be conferred upon the freedmen. No man worthy to be styled statesman could have chosen the former course. In choosing the latter Stevens acted upon the principle so ably enunciated by Lincoln in 1864, in his letter to A. G. Hodges: "By general law life *and* limb must be protected; yet often a limb must be amputated to save a life; but a life is never wisely given to save a limb."

Stevens had no other choice. So eminent a scholar and historian as John W. Burgess—onetime professor of political science and constitutional law, and dean of the faculty of political science, in Columbia University—could offer no other alternative than the one Conservative Republicans had rejected: placing the Southern states under territorial government, as Stevens had proposed.[6] In condemning him for taking the only course left open to him history has obviously succumbed to influences foreign to its scientific mission. The blame should have been placed where it belonged—on the Conservative Republicans for rejecting Stevens's original plan, on Southern politicians, and on President Johnson for defeating ratification of the Fourteenth Amendment, which would have made possible the re-

[6] *Reconstruction and the Constitution, 1866-1876* by John W. Burgess, copyright 1902. Charles Scribner's Sons, preface.

integration of the South into the Union without the concomitant of immediate suffrage for the freedmen. Stevens predicted that the South would refuse to ratify the amendment and pleaded that ratification be confined to the loyal states only. His warning and his plea were not heeded.

3

I have been able to add but little to what is already known concerning Stevens's career before the war. It is to his career during the war and Reconstruction that I have devoted four of the five years I have labored on this volume. I have been sparing with footnotes. When adequate indications have been given in the text, I have omitted them. In the first two parts of the book, in which I have broken no new ground, the reader will find few footnotes to distract him.

I wish to express my appreciation to Dr. Allan Nevins, chairman of the History Department in Columbia University, who took time off from his manifold duties to read two important chapters, and made valuable suggestions. Also to Dr. Stanley Pargellis, librarian of the Newberry Library in Chicago, who so graciously put the facilities of the library at my disposal, and to Mrs. Bess Finn, reference librarian at the library, who has been most helpful. My friend Dr. Ralph Newman, owner of the Abraham Lincoln Book Store in Chicago, likewise deserves my thanks. Finally and especially I wish to thank my wife, Piri Ozer Korngold, to whom this book is dedicated, for her invaluable assistance.

The subtitle of the book, "A Being Darkly Wise and Rudely Great," is a quotation from Alexander Pope's *An Essay on Man*, Stevens's favorite poem.

RALPH KORNGOLD

Chicago, Illinois
October 1949-October 1954

CONTENTS

PART FOUR · The Struggle with Johnson

PART ONE

LAW AND POLITICS

CHAPTER I
Boyhood

In the spring of 1786 a train of covered wagons and men and boys on horseback wound its laborious way through the hill country of northeastern Vermont. The wagons were filled with women, children, and household gear, for these were migrants from Essex County, Massachusetts, come to Vermont with the intention of settling in Caledonia County, near the town of Danville. A young married couple, Joshua and Sarah Stevens, were members of the migrating party. He was a powerfully built young man who prided himself on his prowess as a wrestler, but liked hard liquor better than hard work. He was not ill-equipped to make a living, being a surveyor as well as a shoemaker and handy with hammer and saw, but preferred fishing, hunting, and carousing to any other occupation. Sarah, whose maiden name was Morrill, was quite a different sort. She was small of stature, neat, industrious, a devout Baptist, and a capable nurse as well as a good housekeeper.

Arrived at their destination, the young couple bought a farm and for several years things went tolerably well. In 1790 a son was born to them whom Sarah named after her husband. That same year the town council hired Joshua to resurvey the town, which he did to their satisfaction, correcting several errors in the original survey. On April 4, 1792, a second son was born whom they named Thaddeus, after Thaddeus Kosciusko, Polish patriot and engineer who rendered valuable service in the War of the Revolution. When a worthless individual sires a remarkable offspring gossip often has it that he was not the real father. There has been such gossip about the paternity of Lincoln. Stevens having been born with a clubfoot, and it having been discovered that clubfooted Charles Maurice Talleyrand de Périgord, French diplomat and statesman, visited America in the early 1790's, the rumor spread that he was Stevens's putative father. It has since been established that Talleyrand did not visit America until at least two years after Stevens's birth.

A third son, Abner Morrill, was born two years later, and a fourth, Alanson, three years thereafter. After the birth of his fourth son Joshua began staying away from home more and more frequently and contributed little to the support of the household. Sometime in the early part of the new century he disappeared altogether. There was a rumor that during the War of 1812 he enlisted and was killed in battle.

2

With the aid of her sons Sarah tilled the rocky farm and added to her income by nursing the sick, though much of the latter she did gratuitously. There was no school at Danville, but she taught the boys reading from the Bible. Thad, whose infirmity made a special claim upon her affection, proved so apt a pupil that she began cherishing the hope he might become a Baptist minister. When he was twelve she took him on a visit to relatives in Massachusetts. Among the places they visited was Boston—hardly a metropolis at that time, but possessing some fine residences and public buildings that may well have impressed the boy and have aroused his ambition.

He was thirteen when an epidemic of spotted fever swept Vermont. Many people in Danville and the surrounding countryside contracted the disease, and Sarah was busy night and day with her nursing. Thad expressed the desire to help, and since he was not much use on the farm, she consented. He proved so capable and conscientious that she would often leave him in charge of one patient while she went to look after another. Thus at an early age he saw much of poverty and affliction. In later life he never idealized the poor, but he developed a profound sympathy for want and suffering, which did not remain unnoticed by his more discerning critics.

3

A short distance from Danville, amidst wooded hills, lies the pleasant town of Peacham. The town possessed what Danville sorely lacked—a school, known at the Caledonia County Academy. About the year 1807, Sarah sold the farm and moved to Peacham, so her boys could have the benefit of the school. The academy was a two-story wooden structure, the lower part of which, used mainly for religious purposes, consisted of a vestibule and an assembly hall, while the upper was fitted out as a classroom. There was only one teacher and about a hundred pupils, ranging in ages from five to twenty. A monthly tuition fee of twenty-five cents was charged.

Stevens was not happy in school. His infirmity set him apart. He could not participate in many of the games. One of his schoolmates has said that "boys would laugh at him boy-like, and mimic his limping walk." It requires little imagination to realize the effect this must have had upon him. He developed a tartness of speech and a combativeness of manner which remained with him throughout life. It is strange that so many of his critics should have failed to realize that this was a defense mechanism, which far from revealing his true character has tended to obscure it. The famous German-American leader Carl Schurz, who not only knew him well, but interviewed many people in Lancaster who had known him most of their lives, showed uncommon comprehension when he wrote in his *Reminiscences:* "Mr. Stevens' discourse was apt to make him appear as a hardened cynic . . . indifferent whether he gave pain or pleasure. But now and then a remark escaped him—I say 'escaped him,' for he evidently preferred to wear the acrid tendencies of his character on the outside—which indicated that there was behind his cynicism a rich fund of human kindness and sympathy. This was strongly confirmed by his neighbors at Lancaster. They had no end of stories to tell about the protection he had given to fugitive slaves, sometimes at much risk and sacrifice to himself, and of the many benefactions he had bestowed with lavish hand."

He discovered early in life the satisfaction to be derived from reading and from solitude. Often, in summer, he would take a book, go out into the hills, lie down in some secluded spot and remain there for hours reading or meditating. He was, however, by no means a weakling. Notwithstanding his infirmity there were two kinds of sport at which he excelled—swimming and horseback riding. As a young man he used to boast that he could easily duplicate Lord Byron's feat of swimming the Hellespont. Yet he remained essentially lonely, and the loneliness strengthened the bond between him and his mother. His love for her remained a mellowing influence throughout his life. An acquaintance has said that when in his old age he spoke of his mother, "all the harsh lines of his countenance appeared to give place to the tenderness of a child."

4

Stevens remained at the academy four years and learned some things rather well, but not to write legibly. When he became a member of Congress constituents who wrote to him begged him to dictate his reply, since otherwise they might be unable to decipher it. "If thee could write so I could read it I would be very willing to know what thy opinion is," a Quaker friend wrote to him.

His graduation from the academy in 1811 was attended with an occurrence until then unheard of in the annals of the institution. It appears probable that he was the instigator.

The rules of the school provided that there should be "an annual exhibition" at which members of the graduating class and a few others were expected "to recite pieces selected by the preceptor and submitted to the inspection of the prudential committee." In keeping with Puritan tradition, tragedies, comedies, and theatricals of any kind were barred, and there was the further stipulation that there was to be "no performance by candlelight." The year Stevens graduated he and twelve others revolted against the regulation. They not only failed to put in an appearance at the graduation exercises, but staged a theatrical performance by candlelight!

The trustees were somewhat at a loss how to deal with the culprits. Since most of them belonged to the graduating class, about the only punishment that could be visited upon them was withholding their certificates. They finally decided that the rebels must sign "articles of submission," declaring they regretted their insubordination and would comply in the future. The latter was meaningless as far as the graduates were concerned, but outraged dignity insisted upon the formula. Stevens and ten others signed, two refused.

CHAPTER II

The Student

After his graduation from the academy Stevens entered Dartmouth. He had not been there long before he managed to become involved in some difficulty sufficiently grave to result in his expulsion. Its exact nature is not known. It could not have been of too serious a nature since he was later readmitted. In the meantime he entered the University of Vermont.

His expulsion from Dartmouth seems to have had a sobering effect upon him. A few months later he wrote to an aunt in New Hampshire that one of the professors had pronounced his conduct to be "perfectly unexceptionable." Entirely "unexceptionable" it was not. A stubborn citizen of Burlington believed it to be his right to pasture his cow on the university campus. Stevens and a few other students decided to play a prank upon him, which to their consternation resulted in the animal's death. The inquiry that followed pointed the finger of suspicion at a student who had had no part in the affair. When Stevens and his fellow pranksters realized that an innocent man might become involved, they went in a body to the owner of the cow and confessed their guilt, offering to make restitution. He must have been an unusual man, for, impressed by their conduct, he not only withdrew the charges, but declined their offer of reimbursement. Stevens did not forget. When he began making money at the law he sent the man a check in full payment of the cow and a gold watch and chain.

His ambition at first took a literary turn. He concocted a tragedy entitled *The Fall of Hellenic Liberty,* in which eleven of the fourteen characters were generals. Faculty and students were sufficiently impressed to arrange a staging at the university auditorium. It may well be that while watching the performance Stevens became disillusioned about his literary ability, for there is no record of any further attempt on his part to seek literary laurels.

In 1812 came the war with England. The federal government requisitioned the university buildings and the student body scattered. Stevens applied for readmission to Dartmouth and had the satisfaction of being accepted.

2

When after Stevens's death Dartmouth requested his college roommate, Joseph Tracy, to furnish a biographical sketch of his former colleague, Tracy declined and wrote: "I would not honestly write such a sketch as it would be expedient to publish in the 'Dartmouth.' . . . He was then inordinately ambitious, bitterly envious of all who outranked him as scholars and utterly unprincipled."

Stevens was a man about whom few people could remain neutral. He was either greatly liked or fiercely disliked. James Albert Woodburn, who at the beginning of this century made extensive inquiries about him among his fellow townsmen in Lancaster, has written: "Few men were more generally beloved by their friends and neighbors than Thaddeus Stevens." Indeed, it appears that he was more popular at Lancaster than Lincoln was at Springfield. When in 1860 he stood for Congress he polled 12,964 votes against a combined vote of 470 for his Whig and Democratic opponents. Congressman Oliver J. Dickey of Pennsylvania said after Stevens's death: "No man ever died more deeply mourned by his constituents than Thaddeus Stevens." Yet James G. Blaine may have been right when he wrote: "Towards his own race he seemed often to be misanthropic." Two notes found among his papers serve to corroborate this. One reads: "Learn to rely through life upon your own unaided efforts. Trust not the professions of friendship which will everywhere greet you so long as you do not need them, but whose hollow sycophancies will be apparent in your first hour of adversity." And the other: "When you have passed through the romantic period of your existence, and found your warm sympathies and ardent hopes all chilled and blasted; and the milk of human kindness which flows in your breast is in danger of being curdled by the cold ingratitude of those upon whom you have continually bestowed nothing but benefactions, you will learn to appreciate the truth of the remark 'That he is a happy man who has one true friend; and he is more happy who never has need of a friend.' "

Nevertheless he formed a friendship at Dartmouth with a young preceptor, Samuel Merrill, who hailed from Peacham. They shared dislikes as well as likes, college fraternities being among the former. After Merrill left Dartmouth to become preceptor at Dr. Perkins's Academy at York, Pennsylvania, Stevens wrote him a letter which might be considered a partial corroboration of Tracy's criticism. The epistle contained the following acrid remarks: "Charles Leverett has entered into the service of the aristocracy, in the capacity of scullion; and it is expected as a reward for his services he will be knighted; that is elected Phi Betian. Those fawning parasites who are grasping at unmerited honors, seem for once to have blundered into the truth, that they must flatter the nobility or remain in obscurity; that they must degrade themselves, or others will not exalt them."

3

Stevens graduated from Dartmouth in August, 1814. In his commencement address he argued that the unequal distribution of wealth was necessary to progress. He may have drawn on his recollections of what he had seen and heard when aiding his mother in nursing the sick, poor as well as rich, when he said that "if the lofty mansion sometimes becomes the habitation of costly excess, the hovel and the cabin are as frequently polluted by the gratification of baser passions."

When he returned to Peacham he was offered and accepted the post of teacher at the academy. He was a born teacher. When he was a famous lawyer at Lancaster he conducted a veritable law school, mainly for his own entertainment. His attitude toward his colleagues in Congress was often pedagogic, sometimes amusingly so. During the year he taught at the academy he founded the Juvenile Library Association, to which more than half a century later he was to bequeath a thousand dollars. But he had no intention of remaining in a profession where a respectable kind of poverty is the rule rather than the exception. He had no hankering for luxury, but hated poverty with its restrictions and humiliations. The richest man in Peacham was "Judge" John Mattock—lawyer, banker, and influential politician. Stevens knew that Mattock had become the last two by virtue of his success at the law. He paid a visit to the "Judge" and obtained permission to "read" law in his office. Henceforth, when not at the academy, he could be found in Mattock's office, poring over law books or discussing politics with the lawyer, who was a confirmed Federalist.

He and Merrill continued to correspond. In one of his letters Stevens wrote: "Friend Sam, I assure you, you can hardly conceive the anxiety your friends feel for you, in that distant country. Considering you exposed to the invincible charms of those fair Dutch wenches, with their dozen pair of petticoats they are really afraid that you will lose your heart and get lost, with Goodie Twiller's ladle, in one corner of their pockets; that filthy lucre will induce you to become the son-in-law of some Ten Breeches; and then we shall despair of seeing you again." The letter contained this hint: "If you know of any vacancies and should assist me without trouble to yourself, you would do me a favor."

It appears unlikely that a mental image of the "fair Dutch wenches" was responsible for his desire to migrate to York in Pennsylvania. Peacham with its five hundred inhabitants and the sparsely settled country roundabout were not a promising field for the practice of law, notwithstanding Mattock's success. Moreover, much as he loved his mother, their outlook upon life differed so widely that it was difficult for him to remain living with her without making her unhappy. It is not without significance that although he remained a bachelor all his life he never asked her to come and keep house for him. She was deeply religious, he was a skeptic. She had a strict code of morals, he was by no means an ascetic.

There are differences of opinion regarding Stevens's religious convictions, as there are about Lincoln's. He believed in a Supreme Being, but cared little about doctrinal religion. It is doubtful if he believed in a life after death. When death was near he wrote jestingly to a friend: "If you come after me, just knock and I will have it opened." Jeremiah Black, attorney general in Buchanan's cabinet, has written that Stevens's mind, "as far as his obligation to God was concerned, was a howling wilderness." But what is a public man's "obligation to God"? Is it not to defend the weak and oppressed against the strong and tyrannical? Were the virtuous upholders of slavery, of whom Black was one, fulfilling that obligation? Assuredly Stevens did better than they. He was, moreover, as we shall see, exceedingly charitable. No one who came to him for help went away empty-handed, and he often sought out want and suffering in order to alleviate them. Although not belonging to any church, he generously aided religious institutions, Catholic as well as Protestant. Many an underpaid minister of religion was cheered by an unsolicited donation from the man whom his enemies called an atheist. "Your $10 came to hand. Thanks. God bless you. When will you give yourself heart and soul? The Lord hasten the day," wrote one. He did not like to hear religion ridiculed and once cut short the fulminations of an atheist with the words: "My mother was a soft-shell Baptist and held the Ten Commandments to be good law and the Sermon on the Mount as orthodox. I am one of her poor disciples. Good morning, sir."

All this, however, did not satisfy his mother. She worried about his spiritual welfare and after he left home often sent him religious admonitions, such as, "Thaddeus, you have been taught the Scriptures from a child, which is able to make you wise in Salvation." That there was some reason for her uneasiness is evident from the following letter Stevens received in February, 1865, when he had little more than three years to live, from his clerical friend Jonathan Blanchard:

> At present in every part of the United States, people believe that your personal life has been one prolonged sin; that your lips have been defiled with blasphemy, your hands with gambling, and your body with women. . . . Now you owe it to yourself and your mother's God, to leave some means of correcting this belief, if false, or to show that you have always condemned and despised yourself on account of these besetting sins!
>
> I have a strange hope that you are not to be lost . . . but as I have studied you this last quarter of a century, you seem to me to have been at times able to say, "With the mind I myself serve the laws of God, but with the flesh the law of sin"; that, as I do, you really loathe and despise yourself on account of sins. The good you have done the country (and

none have done more, if so much) is no offset for vices such as I have named above. . . . What makes bad governments is bad and sinful men. If there were no vile men there could be no bad government.

But if . . . even now, you will go to Christ, he has all the power in Heaven and earth and can make your scarlet sins white! I have loved and followed you with a strange fascination. I have prayed and do still pray for you with a terrible earnestness, and now I bid you farewell.

Stevens meekly replied: "Probably as between us and our Creator, all of us are somewhat deficient. I know I am deplorably so. But as to my fellowmen, I hope so to live that no one shall ever be wronged or suffer on my account."

4

Merrill wrote that he was moving to Indiana. He had recommended his friend as his successor and believed the recommendation would be accepted. In due time Stevens was notified of his appointment, packed his belongings, and departed for York.

The town had an Old World appearance. There were rows of red-brick, white-shuttered houses, each with a stone step and a knocker. On market days one saw Quakers, Mennonites, Dunkers, Amish—the men in clerical black and broad-brimmed hats, the women in gray Mother Hubbards and poke bonnets, the children miniature facsimiles of their elders. A German dialect was frequently heard in the streets. The rolling country roundabout was in keeping with the town—neat, orderly, prosperous. Foreign as it all seemed, it was an integral part of the varied American scene: after the Revolution the Congress of the United States had for nine months met in the York courthouse.

One of Stevens's colleagues at Dr. Perkins's Academy, the Quaker Amos Gilbert, has said of him that he was "one of the most backward, retiring and modest young men I have ever known." The judgment is principally interesting because it differs so widely from that of Joseph Tracy, who knew him only a year or two earlier.

Thad resumed the reading of law in his spare time at the law office of David Cossett, and the following summer was ready for admission to the bar. A difficulty arose. The members of the York County Bar had adopted a rule (apparently for his especial benefit) that no one could be admitted who had not devoted at least one year wholly to the study of law. It was not an insurmountable obstacle. Across the state line was Bel Air, county seat of Hartford County, Maryland. Cossett knew a lawyer there who was willing to sponsor Stevens. So, toward the end of August, 1816, Thad, dressed in his best, mounted a hired horse and set out for Bel Air to take the bar examination.

The ordeal took place in the dining room of the local hostelry. Behind a table, covered with green baize for the occasion, sat Judge Theodore Black, flanked on either side by a fellow member of the examining committee. The Judge informed Stevens that before questioning could commence, "there must be two bottles of Madeira on the table, and the applicant must order it in." Stevens complied, the wine was poured, and questioning began. What law books had he read? He replied that he had read Blackstone, Coke upon Littleton, a work on pleading, and Gilbert on evidence. Three more questions were asked. When he had finished explaining the difference between executory devices and contingent remainders, Judge Black said: "Gentlemen, you see the young man is all right. I will give him a certificate." His colleagues nodded assent, whereupon the Judge told Stevens that when the certificate was delivered it was customary for the recipient to order two more bottles of Madeira. The wine was brought, Stevens was handed the certificate, clinked glasses with the committee and was invited to sit in at a card game known as "fiploo." He had come to Bel Air with forty-five dollars in his pocket; he departed with three dollars and fifty cents.

He had decided to return to York by way of Lancaster, so he might appraise that town as a possible location for his law office. The decision well-nigh cost him his life. A bridge in course of construction over the Susquehanna seemed safe to cross. Stevens proceeded to do so at a trot, and the next moment saw a gaping hole in the planking. Too late to rein in! He gave his horse the spurs and leaped to safety.

He did not settle in Lancaster—at least not yet. The town awed him. It seemed so large, prosperous, sophisticated.

CHAPTER III

The Lawyer

Gettysburg, county seat of Adams County, Pennsylvania, had a heterogeneous population of about a thousand—Scotch, Irish, Germans, French, Dutch, and Negroes. In the center of town was the courthouse square—paved with cobblestones and called the "Diamond" by the inhabitants—and in the center of the square, the courthouse, surmounted by a belfry with a finial consisting of a gilt ball and an arrow. Turnpikes from Philadelphia and Baltimore joined at Gettysburg into a road to Pittsburgh, and red-painted lumbering stagecoaches, trains of white-topped wagons, and droves of cattle were a frequent sight in the square. Pigs roamed the linden-shaded streets, and in the summer the odor of pigsties and the pungent smell of tanneries pervaded the air.

It was upon this town, in the neighborhood of which nearly half a century later the fate of the Confederacy was to be decided, that Stevens's choice fell. He took lodgings at the McClellan House (now the Gettysburg Hotel), on the square, and rented a small brick building adjoining the hostelry to serve as office. It was customary for a lawyer seeking admittance to practice at a local bar to get a colleague to sponsor him, but he ignored convention and himself made application. Soon after, he hung out his shingle and inserted a card in the local paper informing the public that "Thaddeus Stevens, Attorney at Law . . . will give diligent attention to all orders in the line of his profession."

Clients were slow in coming. The few that came had small collection cases which the established lawyers scorned to handle and referred to him with the words: "There is a lame young lawyer by the name of Stevens in town, who, if you ask him, may attend to your case." His meager savings dwindled rapidly. When winter came he had to economize on the firewood and sat shivering in his office, reading what books he had or was able to borrow. He fell behind in his office rent and had difficulty meeting his board bill. There came a time when he said to an acquaintance that he "could hold out no longer and must select a new location." And then, suddenly, fortune smiled upon him.

2

On a small farm a short distance from town lived James Hunter, a bachelor in his early thirties. He was considered simple-minded, but nobody believed him to be dangerous although he was apt to be quarrelsome when under the influence of drink. He tended his plot of land and occasionally hired out to neighboring farmers. In the early summer of 1817 he was ordered arrested for nonpayment of a debt. When Heagy, the constable, came to fetch him, he refused to come along peaceably. The officer thereupon called his son Henry to aid him and he was forcibly taken to the lock-up.

Shortly after his release Hunter was hired to help another man mow grass in a meadow. As he went into the meadow with his scythe he recognized the mower as Henry Heagy. He had been drinking that morning and the sight of the young man who had helped drag him off to jail infuriated him. Nevertheless he set to work, but rage continued to seethe within him. Sometime later, when Henry was resting, leaning on his scythe, he suddenly saw a blade flash before his eyes and the next moment fell to the ground, blood gushing from a gaping wound in his throat. A week later he died.

Indignation in Gettysburg and the surrounding country was such that a lynching was feared. Popular anger subsided and the law was allowed to take its course, but none of the established lawyers cared to incur the hostility of the populace by defending the slayer. This was another case to which the "lame young lawyer" was welcome. Stevens took the case without hesitation.

On the day of the trial the Diamond was crowded with horses and wagons. People had come from miles around to witness the proceedings. The courtroom was packed to suffocation. There was considerable speculation concerning the plea the young lawyer would make. In a case of that kind an insanity plea was then a rarity. When Stevens rose to address the jury there was a hostile murmur, but he had not been speaking long before people found themselves listening intently. In those days lawyers addressing a jury either shouted at the top of their voices and gesticulated wildly or indulged in pompous oratory. Stevens spoke in a conversational manner and made few gestures. He used no legal verbiage, quoted few authorities, but what he said made sense. He pointed out that Hunter was far from normal. No one who knew him but would agree that although his body was that of a man, his mind was that of a child. Had a child committed the crime would the jury vote to hang him? The safety of society demanded that he be confined for the rest of his natural life; but when a man admitted to be irrational has killed, should rational men retaliate by killing him? "Vengeance is mine; I will repay, saith the Lord." In the eyes of a just Providence such retaliation might appear worse than the crime itself.

Years later, when a member of the Pennsylvania Legislature, Stevens spoke and voted against capital punishment. Throughout his legal career he refused to be associated in the prosecution of any case involving the death penalty. Conviction must therefore have lent force to his argument. No plea, however logical, could have saved Hunter. The sentiment of the community demanded that he be hanged and he was hanged. But months later people discussed the plea Stevens had made and the general opinion was that no lawyer in town could have done nearly as well.

3

The change in Stevens's fortunes came with astonishing rapidity. He no longer lacked clients. A year after Hunter's trial he was able to buy a house on fashionable Chambersburg Street, valued at $2,500, and to acquire a fine saddle horse. During the succeeding years he appeared in practically every important case in Gettysburg and was occasionally called to assist in cases tried in York or Lancaster. Nine years after he had opened his law office, he was the largest individual holder of real estate in the county. That his legal ability was extraordinary has been attested by so bitter a political opponent as Jeremiah Black, who said that Stevens had "no equal as a lawyer at the American bar." Alexander K. McClure, famous publicist and lawyer, has written of him: "I have known many of our great lawyers who were great advocates or great in the skillful direction of a case, but he is the only man I can recall who was eminent in all the attributes of a great lawyer." His success was as great before the higher courts as before juries. Between 1821 and 1830 he tried ten cases before the state supreme court and won all but one.

Congressman George W. Woodward, Democrat from Pennsylvania, has said that Stevens "loved Pope's *Essay on Man* more than Siderfin's *Reports*. . . . I think he relied more upon the reasons, than upon the authorities of the law." He seldom quoted authorities. Once when he came into the courtroom and found opposing counsel entrenched behind a barrier of legal tomes, he looked at him quizzically and inquired: "What are all these books for?" Congressman Oliver J. Dickey of Pennsylvania has claimed that Stevens "never took or used notes of the evidence, the speeches of opponents, or the rulings of the court, trusting wholly to memory that never failed him." James G. Blaine confirms this, saying: "His memory of facts, dates and figures was exact, and in argument he knew the book and chapter and page for reference."

The combativeness he had acquired as a boy was at times in evidence in the courtroom as it was later in the legislature and in Congress. Usually it took the form of biting sarcasm. "He was a lucky lawyer who managed to get through a case with him without being laughed at," Woodward has said. Judges were not immune. Once when a judge warned him that he was running the risk of being arraigned "for manifesting contempt of court," he replied: "Manifesting contempt, your Honor? Sir, I am doing my best to conceal it."

There is, however, evidence to the effect that the combativeness was occasional rather than habitual. McClure, who saw him in action in court probably more often than any man who has written about him, has testified that "he was one of the most courteous men at the bar whether associate or opponent. He was especially generous in his kindness to young members of the bar, unless they undertook to unduly flap their fledgling wings, when they were certain to suffer speedy and humiliating discomfiture."

CHAPTER IV

Man of Property

Stevens had reached his middle thirties. An attack of typhoid fever had left him completely bald, a deficiency he tried to remedy by wearing a reddish-brown wig. It must have served its purpose rather well, for when he was a member of Congress, a feminine admirer was deceived to the extent of asking him for a lock of hair. With his usual cynicism he removed the wig and invited her to help herself. A portrait of him painted by Jacob Eichholtz when he was about forty, shows a long-headed, full-cheeked, pleasant-faced man, with a ruddy complexion, aquiline nose, hazel eyes, and well-formed mouth and chin. He was nearly six feet tall, broad-shouldered and deep-chested. He dressed well, in the somewhat florid fashion of the day, and while he walked with a cane, his friend Merrill assures us that he was "only a little lame."

He had prospered and owned houses and lands. Some fifteen miles from Gettysburg, near South Mountain, he owned, in partnership with one James D. Paxton, an iron and charcoal business named Maria Furnace, after Paxton's wife. Two other members of the firm had prudently withdrawn, for the furnace never paid and was finally abandoned. A much larger furnace, known as Caledonia Furnace or Caledonia Iron Works, was constructed in the meantime, but many years were to pass before it became profitable. Stevens was not devoid of business sense, but had too many irons in the fire. With his law practice and politics occupying nearly all his time, he had to leave the management of the business to his partner, who was incompetent, to say the least. Stevens was wont to refer to the ironworks as his "sinking fund," by way of saying that he sank into it most of the money he made at the law.

2

When Stevens's will was opened it was found to contain this clause: "I bought John Shert's [Schulz's] property at sheriff's sale at much below its value. I want only my own. All except $300, the proceeds and interest I direct shall be returned to the estate." He apparently wished to make restitution of something not justly come by. This gives color to the charge that in private as well as in public life he occasionally deviated from a strict code of ethics.

A charge made by those who prefer to believe the worst of him concerns a certain James Dobbin, a superannuated lawyer who had ruined himself financially and in other ways by dissipation, and whose property, including a law library, was sold by the sheriff. It has been claimed that a prospective purchaser came to consult Stevens regarding the advisability of offering two thousand dollars for the property. Stevens is said to have advised against it, mentioning liens and other encumbrances, only to buy the property himself at the auction for six hundred dollars. That Dobbin sued Stevens for having made him the victim of "legal fraud" and won the case before a jury is true, but it is likewise true that the state supreme court reversed the finding and exonerated Stevens. Stevens's friends have claimed that after the court's decision he offered to turn the property over to Dobbin for what it had cost him if the old lawyer could find a buyer willing to pay more.

It has been further charged that Stevens—by now president of the Borough Council and attorney for the Directors of the Poor—became angered when he heard that Dobbin went about saying he had been defrauded, and had him committed to the almshouse, where the poor fellow died. Stevens's friends have denounced this as a particularly cruel libel. They have claimed that Dobbin had become a derelict, and that Stevens, taking pity on him, proposed to the Directors of the Poor that he be allowed to resign and Dobbin be appointed in his place. He would continue to do the work, but Dobbin was to draw the salary. His proposal was accepted and the old lawyer was given an office and living quarters at the almshouse. Stevens had the law library formerly belonging to Dobbin moved to the office. The old man went about boasting that he had displaced Stevens and continued to charge that he had been defrauded. When told of this Stevens merely shrugged and said that Dobbin was "a half-lunatic who fancies a thousand things that have no existence."

3

That Stevens was uncommonly charitable, especially toward the old, admits of no doubt. When years later he moved to Lancaster he bought, at sheriff's sale, a two-family house with the intention of using it for office as well as residential purposes. When, however, the octogenarian former owner begged him to be allowed to remain living in the house with his wife and daughter until the end of his days, Stevens did not have the heart to refuse him. When ten years later the old man died the two women claimed the right of occupancy. This was more than Stevens had bargained for. Not wishing to institute ouster proceedings himself, he wrote to his friend John B. McPherson, president of the Gettysburg Bank, to do so on his behalf. He wrote to McPherson: "He and his wife and daughter did occupy the main house up to last spring, when the old man being dead I desired to take possession. The She Devils now claim to live there during the woman's life who was 20 years younger than her husband. I get often such return for the kindness I extend to others; and it serves me about right."

An old German whom he furnished with a home for life was more appreciative and wrote effusively: "In the very Hon. Mr. Stevens are concealed all the qualifications that can constitute a noble Gentleman—a good man, and a father. I have experienced him. Oh! that I were in person before him, the Hon. sir, I would press that kind hand of him, into my hand, out of excessive affection—like a son."

He was especially kind to those laboring under a physical handicap. When late in life he hired a private secretary, he chose one lame, like himself. "He is crippled, but smart," he used to say. Dr. Henry Carpenter of Lancaster has testified that Stevens paid him "a handsome fee" for curing the son of a poor Quaker woman of a disease of the knee joint, and told him: "Now, doctor, if you come across any poor boy that is deformed and disabled in his limbs in any manner, take him in hand and relieve him and I will pay you well." Misfortune of any kind touched a sympathetic chord within him. Walking one day down Pennsylvania Avenue in Washington with a friend, he saw an old woman weeping. He stopped and asked what ailed her. She told him that she had lost her market money—seventy-five cents. "Well!" Stevens exclaimed. "It so happens I have just found a five dollar bill. You might as well have it." So saying, he took a bill from his pocket, stuffed it into the old woman's hand and walked away.

Congressman Godlove S. Orth of Indiana, reared and educated in Gettysburg, said on the floor of Congress after Stevens's death: "He was the almoner of Gettysburg during my residence there." E. B. Callender, Stevens's earliest biographer, has written that when "the Commoner" died, "they found among his effects bills and notes to the extent of a hundred thousand dollars, which he never pressed for payment, knowing that the makers needed the money more than he." James G. Blaine, with whom he was not particularly friendly, has written: "He was fond of young men, invited their society, encouraged and generously aided them. He was easily moved by the distress of others. He was kind, charitable, lavish with his money in the relief of poverty."

Even a rebuke contained in a letter found among his papers bears testimony to his reputation for generosity. It reads: "I must say from your reputed generous nature I expected more prompt attention on behalf of the widow."

4

Stevens seldom went visiting. The comfortable class in Gettysburg, especially those with marriageable daughters, would have been glad to receive him, but his baldness added to his lameness made him shun women who might have matrimonial designs. He apparently believed that any woman who might want to marry him would do so for reasons that had little relation to love. He hunted the fox and the deer in company with other leading citizens and spent many an evening at the Indian Queen, playing euchre, whist, or poker. He played to pass the time, indifferent to gain or loss, but so habitually that he acquired the reputation of being an inveterate gambler. His inherent kindness manifested itself even at the gaming table. One evening a young Irishman, who was about to be married and had saved five hundred dollars for a honeymoon journey, insisted on playing with him and promptly lost his savings. The following evening the luckless young man called on his betrothed to tell her about the misadventure. She consoled him, saying: "Never mind. I have some money of my own, sufficient to pay all expenses." Years later she told him that Stevens had called on her the morning after the game, had given her the money he had won and had made her promise not to tell her betrothed, "so it will be a lesson to the young man."

He was never a heavy drinker, but kept a well-stocked wine cellar for the entertainment of his friends. One bitterly cold winter evening when he entertained several of his cronies, wine and other spirits flowed freely. The cashier of the Gettysburg Bank, a particular friend of his, became so befuddled that when it was time to depart two others had to support him. They left him in the vestibule of his house. Here, in the morning, he was found dead.

When the news reached Stevens he was deeply affected. He sat for a while thinking, then, armed with a hatchet, he went down into the wine cellar. The startled Negro servants heard the splintering of wood and the crash of glass and earthenware as their employer smashed every cask, every bottle and jug the cellar contained. He did not touch strong drink again until in his old age the doctor prescribed small doses of wine. When war broke out he offered prizes to officers of companies organized in the county who would sign a pledge to abstain from intoxicating liquors while in the army.

CHAPTER V

Anti-Mason

William Morgan of Batavia, New York, was a man of no particular importance. He was an itinerant stonecutter and bricklayer, contentious and fond of strong drink. Yet he was the direct cause of the birth of a political party of national scope.

He had been a member of the Masonic order, but had quarreled with the brethren of the mystic tie and thirsted for revenge. Uncommonly literate for one of his occupation, he wrote a book in which he revealed secrets he had solemnly sworn never to divulge. He gave it the inoffensive title of *Illustrations of Masonry* and offered it to Thurlow Weed, politician and publisher of a newspaper at Rochester, New York. Weed was not interested, but Morgan found other backers, and his book was in process of publication when things began happening to him.

On September 11, 1826, he was walking down the street at Batavia when he was placed under arrest for the alleged theft of some articles of clothing belonging to an innkeeper. He was taken to Canandaigua, booked for theft, and released, only to be rearrested and jailed for a debt of $2.69. The following day the debt was paid, but as he was leaving the prison he was seized, thrown into a carriage, and driven at breakneck speed in the direction of Fort Niagara. Nobody ever saw him again. The general opinion was that he had been kidnaped by members of the Masonic order, killed, and his weighted body thrown intc the Niagara River.

Although George Washington, Benjamin Franklin, and other

Founding Fathers had been Freemasons, and Andrew Jackson and Henry Clay belonged, the order had not escaped criticism. Its English origin was cited together with the claim that it was creating "secret titles of nobility." Others charged that it made use of a ritual in which symbols of Christianity figured sacrilegiously and wine was quaffed from a human skull. In 1821 the Presbyterian Church Synod of Pittsburgh had declared Freemasonry "unfit for professing Christians." It was further claimed that Masons were sworn to uphold each other even when crime was involved. The Morgan case appeared to confirm the most damaging of these charges. When Masons believed to have been guilty of the kidnaping were arrested and put on trial, officers and fellow members of the order did their utmost to obstruct justice. The accused were found guilty, but since in the absence of the *corpus delicti* murder could not be proved, the punishment was light. This together with the attitude of those connected with the order, aroused public resentment to an unprecedented degree. Protest meetings were held throughout the state. Petitions were circulated. Pamphlets recounting real or imaginary misdeeds attributed to the order, and demanding its instant suppression, were eagerly bought.

The astute Thurlow Weed watched the turmoil and a plan ripened in his mind. The Federalist party to which he had hitched his fortunes was languishing and appeared to be dying. Andrew Jackson and the "Van Burenites" had captured the public imagination. Why not let the old party die and organize a party based on the Masonic issue? It was, to be sure, an ephemeral issue, but when one had captured the offices other issues could be given precedence. He talked the matter over with his friends and the result was the organization of an Anti-Masonic party that polled 27,000 votes in 1827 and more than double that number the following year.

The United States has since witnessed the growth of a secret society that for a while threatened the overthrow of democratic institutions. The principles of Freemasonry bear no resemblance to those of that ill-famed organization, but unscrupulous and designing men can pervert the noblest of causes. Such men appear to have insinuated themselves at that time into places of power in the Masonic order. As neither the Federalist nor the Democratic party cared to take up the issue, it is not surprising that the Anti-Masonic party should have spread rapidly from state to state and have obtained the support of such luminaries as John Quincy Adams, John Marshall, William Henry Seward, Amasa Walker, Richard Rush, and a host of others, including Thaddeus Stevens.

2

Stevens, aggressive by nature, was well suited for the arena of politics. He was a Federalist by conviction, having been schooled in the principles of that party by the jovial John Mattock, in whose office at Peacham he had commenced the study of law. In Adams County, Pennsylvania, that party's organization was, however, in the hands of men who had dominated it for years and who did not feel in the least disposed to share their influence with a newcomer. Had Stevens regarded politics merely as a means of satisfying personal ambition, he might have been tempted to join the Democrats. In 1827 he had heard the voice of the tempter. He happened to be associated in the trial of a case at the York County courthouse with James Buchanan, who combined an impressive appearance with an opportunism that took little account of principles. He had been a Federalist, but having seen Jackson's star rise on the horizon decided to follow it in the hope it would lead to greener pastures. It led him ultimately into the White House. During a recess in the trial he and Stevens went for a walk in the country. Tiring a little they sat down on a rail fence. Buchanan told Stevens about his intention to join the Democratic party and advised him to do the same. Stevens did not take his advice. In politics he was often ruthless and sometimes indulged in questionable practices, but he was true to his convictions and possessed a hard core of idealism, which, however, did not include Jacksonian principles.

That same year the Anti-Masonic movement invaded Pennsylvania. By 1828 Weed's Anti-Masonic *Enquirer* had subscribers throughout the state, and a paper devoted to the party's principles had been launched in Lancaster. The people of southeastern Pennsylvania were peculiarly susceptible to that sort of propaganda. Quakers, Mennonites, Dunkers, Amish, Dutch-Reformed, Scotch Presbyterians—devotees of primitive or Puritanical Christianity—disliked organizations that were shrouded in mystery and indulged in "popish" rites. Stevens, too, was susceptible. At Dartmouth he had been opposed to college fraternities, believing they fostered class distinctions. In college his poverty had relegated him to the ranks of those whom the fraternities snubbed; now, however, his social standing in the small community was of the highest. It is therefore to his credit that one of his principal reasons for opposing secret societies was that he considered them undemocratic. As for the Masonic order, he believed it to have degenerated into a conspiratorial organization whose real purpose was to acquire power, political and economic, for a select group, by fair means or foul.

In the fall of 1829 Stevens called a meeting of opponents of secret societies at the Gettysburg courthouse. It was well attended and resulted in the organization of the Anti-Masonic party of Adams County. The keepers of the Federalist citadel in the county were chagrined to see their followers desert to Stevens, but there was little they could do about it. He solidified his influence by launching a weekly—the Anti-Masonic *Star*—which appeared regularly until years later he moved to Lancaster. Soon the Democratic *Sentinel* was referring to him as "the great luminary of Antimasonry in Adams County, within whose orbit all the lesser planets of the new system revolve and reflect the light he dispenses." That same fall Joseph Ritner, former speaker of the legislature, stood for governor on the Anti-Masonic ticket and Stevens carried Adams County for him. When in February of the following year the Anti-Masonic state convention met at the state capital, a Harrisburg newspaper referred to Stevens's presence as "an event of great significance in Pennsylvania." In the fall of 1830 the party polled 54,000 votes in the state, electing six congressmen, four state senators, and twenty-seven state representatives. Although holding no political office Stevens had become a power in the political life of the state.

3

"My son, we hear you are ingaged in the anti-misonick cause. I think it is a good cause, but a dangerous won, because it creates enemyes."

Thus faultily, but with motherly solicitude, old Mrs. Stevens wrote to her favorite son. She was right. It did create enemies. All that had ever been alleged against him was now repeated with suitable embellishments. It was at this time that the most damaging version of the Dobbin case gained circulation. When the body of a colored girl in a pregnant condition was found in a neighboring wood, there were sly insinuations that a certain bachelor known to be a "nigger-lover" might be responsible.

In June, 1831, Stevens was invited to speak at an Anti-Masonic rally in Hagerstown, Maryland. He went on horseback and made a fighting speech. Royal Arch candidates, he said, were required "to extricate each other from every difficulty whether right or wrong," and "to keep each other's secrets, murder and treason not excepted." He charged that Freemasons "robbed justice of its due and honesty of its rights," by making "signs of distress" to officers of the court and to jurymen, members of the order. "How can the evil be destroyed? Refuse to trust Masons with any office of profit or trust, until they are shorn of their locks and become like other men. . . . We want no hireling forces. Those who address themselves to this warfare must do it from love of country."

When Jacob Lefever, publisher and editor of the Gettysburg *Compiler* and a leading Freemason, received an account of Stevens's speech from his Hagerstown correspondent, he published it without revision, although it contained the following libelous comment: "Any men who attempt to change our course, must come to us with pure hearts and clean hands. If they talk to us of crimes and murder, we must know that *they have no blood on their skirts.* If a change in politics or religion be their object, we must have assurance that they are honest. Those must not come, in whose wake is heard the wail of the widow and the orphan, or rioting in the spoils of the unfortunate."

Two months after the appearance of the libel, Lefever was sentenced to three months in jail and a fine of fifty dollars. Governor Wolfe, a member of the order, promptly pardoned him. A civil suit launched by Stevens dragged on until 1834, when he was awarded damages of $1,500. He obtained judgment for the amount, but offered to vacate it if Lefever would furnish the name of the author of the libel and would testify against him. The editor manfully refused and his property was sold by the sheriff. The buyer was Stevens, but after buying the property he returned it to its former owner and assigned the unsatisfied portion of the judgment to Lefever's wife.

4

During its short but turbulent existence the Anti-Masonic party made a contribution of doubtful value to American politics. It was the first political party to nominate a presidential candidate by the convention method. The convention met in Baltimore in 1831. Twelve states were represented and men of national prominence attended. Stevens made what many considered the most effective speech. His influence was already such that for a while it seemed the convention might have to adjourn without nominating anyone unless it consented to name his choice—John McLean, associate justice of the Supreme Court. When McLean asked that his name be withdrawn, Stevens insisted that he be drafted. William H. Seward, Stevens's roommate at the hotel, finally managed to persuade him to throw his support to William Wirt, a distinguished lawyer who had played an important role in the prosecution of Aaron Burr.

At the presidential election the following year the Anti-Masonic party made a poor showing, carrying only Vermont. Jackson's popularity, the rise of the Whig party and the fact that two-thirds of the Masonic lodges had disbanded and the remainder had cleaned house, spelled the doom of the party. After the election it virtually gave up the ghost everywhere except in Pennsylvania, where Stevens's tireless energy and dissension in the Democratic party kept it alive long after it had lost all reason for existence. Stevens was elected to the legislature on the Anti-Masonic ticket in 1833 and re-elected six times.

5

Stevens's career as member of the Pennsylvania Legislature was a curious mixture of the good and the bad, the sublime and the ludicrous, true statesmanship and questionable politics. On various occasions he gave a demonstration of that peculiar talent for irony and invective that later made him feared in Congress. Once when a colleague interrupted him with the remark: "Mr. Speaker, the gentleman from Adams neither sees nor understands the consequences of this bill," he shrugged and replied: "Oh, very likely, very likely, Balaam's ass saw the angel when his master did not." At another time, when a Democrat made a personal attack upon him, he rose and said: "Mr. Speaker, it will not be expected of me to notice the thing which has crawled into this House and adheres to one of the seats by its own slime." He usually sat in the legislative chamber with his feet upon his desk and got into the habit (which later in Congress served to augment his fame) of making sarcastic remarks in an undertone, yet loud enough for those around him to hear and be amused.

He wasted a great deal of time and energy fighting Masonic windmills, sublimely indifferent to the fact that the public no longer cared. Santayana's definition of a fanatic as "one who redoubles his efforts after he has forgotten his aim" fits Stevens on the Masonic issue. He became known as the "Archpriest of Anti-Masonry." As late as 1836, almost three years after Thurlow Weed had given up anti-Masonry as a lost cause, Stevens made the amazing declaration that the people would soon perceive "there was no other question than Masonry and Anti-Masonry."

Early in 1834 he managed to get a committee appointed, with himself as chairman, to investigate "into the evils of Masonry." The opposition countered by securing the appointment of a committee to investigate "into the evils of Anti-Masonry." He had intended to summon Governor Wolfe and other prominent Masons as witnesses, but the power of subpoena having been denied him, his committee had to content itself with bringing in a report that was little more than a propaganda document. The opposition's report was no more enlightening.

His opportunity came in the fall of 1835. As a result of dissension in the Democratic camp, a combination of Whigs and Anti-Masons elected Joseph Ritner governor and seventy-two members of the lower house out of a total of one hundred. The Democrats retained control of the senate, but on a joint vote would be outnumbered. The victory had little relation to Anti-Masonic doctrine, but Ritner, who was wax in Stevens's hands, said in his inaugural address: "The people have willed the destruction of all secret societies, and that will cannot be disregarded."

The day after the legislature convened Stevens asked leave to present a bill entitled, "An Act to suppress Secret Societies bound together by Secret and Unlawful Oaths." Permission was granted and a committee appointed, with him as chairman, to prepare the bill. Four days later he presented a report and petitions asking for an investigation into the evils of Masonry, with power "to send for persons and papers." A Democrat derisively suggested the appointment of a committee "to inquire into the evils of gambling, with power . . . to have before them one Stevens, a notorious gambler." Notwithstanding all efforts to thwart him, Stevens got what he wanted.

Masonic leaders became alarmed. For the first time the power of a sovereign state was to be arrayed against the order. A conference of Masonic bigwigs decided on passive resistance as the best policy. Witnesses called to testify refused to be sworn, refused to answer questions, but declaimed volubly about the unconstitutionality of the proceedings. Most of the newspapers sided with the Masons. The committee was called the "Star Chamber" and Stevens was referred to as the "Chief Inquisitor." When he brought the defiant witnesses before the bar of the house and asked that they be committed for contempt, the Whigs refused to follow him. The recalcitrants were discharged by a vote of fifty to forty-three.

Stevens had lost, this time conclusively. He did not appear to realize it and refused to give up the struggle. "I will go home again in a minority," he declared, "and call again and again upon the people and will either succeed in crushing that polluting order, which will maintain itself by trampling on the best interests of the country, or will go down to the grave never faltering in a righteous cause."

CHAPTER VI

Champion of Education

The urge to aid others to cultivate their minds was one of the most admirable traits of Stevens's character. When barely out of college he founded the Juvenile Library Association in Peacham. In Gettysburg he placed his considerable collection of books at the service of his fellow townsmen. He resigned as president of the Gettysburg Borough Council so he might serve on the school board. In 1832 he helped secure a charter for Pennsylvania (now Gettysburg) College, founded by the Lutherans. He permitted the college to erect a building on land belonging to him, which he subsequently deeded to the institution for a nominal sum.

During his first term in the legislature he introduced a bill calling for an appropriation of eighteen thousand dollars for the benefit of the college. Institutions of higher learning were scarce in the state and he considered it important that the college should not deteriorate for lack of funds. The bill was unpopular with his constituents, hard-working farmers who believed people who wanted their children to become "scholars" should bear the cost themselves. Stevens's Democratic colleague from the county, Samuel S. Patterson, made a speech protesting against the measure. When he had finished, Stevens rose to reply.

Those agreeing with his colleague, he said, "apparently deemed it of much more importance that mudholes in their roads should be filled up, so their horses may get dryshod to the mill, than that the rubbish of ignorance should be cleared from the intellects of their children. . . . If a bill had been brought into the House to improve the breed of *hogs,* there would have been no opposition, but when a measure was brought forward to improve the breed of *men,* the scales were produced and the dollars first laid in." He pronounced this personal declaration of independence: "In matters of doubtful propriety or of mere local concern the will of our constituents should be obeyed, but not in matters of interest to the entire state, the rightfulness of which could not be doubted." If his constituents wished to punish him for this, that was their privilege. "I know of no one whose sacrifice would be less regretted, whose immolation would break fewer ties." He had been called ambitious. Well then, let it be known that his ambition did not consist "in the desire to be the idol fools, and his noblest enjoyment the propagation of folly." Turning to Patterson he added: "Demagogues might note it for future use and send it on the wings of the wind to the ears of every one of my constituents."

Patterson accommodated and the Anti-Masonic organization of Adams County promptly notified Stevens that if he did not withdraw the bill, he would be retired to private life. His reply was characteristic: "Painful as it is, if such must be the consequences of bestowing a blessing on your children, *let it come.* Pardon me, therefore, if I tell you that I cannot obey your orders. I will not sacrifice posterity to selfish view. . . . I will withdraw from active part in your political discussions. And if it be necessary to the well-being of our country, dear to me as are my friends and constituents, I shall withdraw from your county to some place where the advocates of Anti-Masonry may still be the advocates of knowledge." He signed the letter: "Your faithful if not obedient servant, Thaddeus Stevens."

This manifestation of moral courage was no isolated occurrence in Stevens's political career. In Congress as well as in the legislature he repeatedly risked his political future by unflinching loyalty to his convictions. His colleague James K. Moorhead of Pennsylvania said of him after his death: "Always in advance of public opinion he constantly antagonized it with a valor and boldness unequaled. Usually political leaders ascertain the current and drift of public sentiment and accommodate themselves to it. . . . He formed his own opinion and acted on his own conviction." [1]

[1] Quotations from speeches made in Congress in honor of Stevens after his passing

Stevens's bill carried, and grateful Pennsylvania College elected him member of its board of trustees—an honorary post he held until his death. Nothing came of the threat to retire him to private life. He was re-elected, and during his second term in the legislature achieved what was perhaps the greatest triumph of his career.

2

Except in Philadelphia there were at that time no free public schools in Pennsylvania. Parents wishing to educate their offspring but unable to bear the cost could have them admitted free by making a declaration of pauperism. As few self-respecting people cared to do this, thousands of children received no schooling. During Stevens's second term in the legislature a bill was introduced by a joint committee of both houses to extend the Philadelphia system to the entire state. Stevens was heartily in favor of the measure, as was his political adversary Governor Wolfe, Democrat and Freemason. It is therefore not surprising that the bill should have passed the house with only one dissenting vote.

Then, however, the taxpayers were heard from.

It was an almost unanimous chorus of protest. What! Were they going to be taxed to pay for the education of the children of the improvident or slothful? And what purpose would it serve to educate the children of paupers, except to make them unfit for their proper station in life? The unwed and the childless asked why they should be required to pay for the education of other people's children any more than for their food and clothing. Quakers, Mennonites, Lutherans, Dutch-Reformed, and Catholics, who had schools of their own, raised the cry of double taxation. Farmers—not always those in poorest circumstances—said their children were needed on the farm, so why should they pay for something they had no intention of using? In the fall election many legislators who had voted for the measure were defeated. Those re-elected had with few exceptions promised to vote for repeal.

Stevens was among the exceptions. He had been advocating free public schools for over a decade. At public functions he was wont

are from *Memorial Addresses on the Life and Character of Thaddeus Stevens, delivered in the House of Representatives, Washington, D. C., December 17, 1868.*

to propose this toast: "Education! May the film be removed from the eyes of Pennsylvania, and may she learn to dread ignorance more than taxation." He had made his campaign for re-election on the free public school issue. The result was a triumph for the man, not for his principles: he was re-elected, but more than three-fourths of his constituents signed a petition, circulated throughout the state, for the repeal of the Free Public School Act. When the document was presented to the legislature it bore some thirty-five thousand signatures. Counterpetitioners had been able to muster scarcely twenty-five hundred.

Governor Wolfe stood his ground gallantly. He publicly declared that he would veto repeal. Democratic party managers warned him that this meant political suicide and would be useless anyway since repeal would pass over his veto. The senate passed the substitute measure restoring the *status quo ante* with only eight dissenting votes. Members of the house, elected annually, hence more responsive to the popular will, were expected to vote repeal almost unanimously. Everybody considered the matter as good as settled.

Everybody but Stevens.

He was in Philadelphia on legislative business when the substitute bill was voted in the senate. He hurried back to Harrisburg, where his colleague from Adams County, McSherry, gave him a discouraging report. He had just heard from their constituents. They were more determined than ever that the bill should be repealed. It was the same throughout the state. He advised Stevens either to vote for repeal or to abstain from voting.

Stevens had formed the habit of thrusting out his lower lip when displeased or defiant. It gave him a petulant and belligerent air. As he grew older the protruding lower lip became a set feature. Together with his clubfoot it has been cited by one of his critics as an outward sign of inner deformity. He must have thrust out his lip more than ordinarily when he told his colleague that he had no intention of giving up the struggle.

Then as now, practical politicians undoubtedly would have said that considering the circumstances, no speech, however logical or eloquent, could have changed the outcome. Stevens himself must have been surprised at the effect his words produced. He delivered the speech with the aid of only a few notes, but at the request of numerous colleagues later reconstructed it, and it appeared in pamphlet form. Extracts from it, printed on silk, were presented to him by his admirers. The conviction that rang in his voice must have greatly added to the force of the argument, for he had not been speaking more than a few minutes when news spread through the building that something extraordinary was taking place in the house. Senators and public officials came running. All available standing room was quickly occupied. The following are a few of the most striking paragraphs of a speech about which it has been said that it produced an effect "second to that of no speech ever delivered in an American legislative assembly":

"The repealing act is, in my opinion, of a most hateful and degrading character. It is a re-enactment of the pauper law of 1809. It proposes that the assessors shall take a census and make a record of the *poor*. This shall be revised and a new record made by the county commissioners, so that the names of those who have the misfortune to be poor men's children shall be forever preserved, as a distinct class, in the archives of the county. The teacher, too, is to keep in his school a *pauper* book and register the names and attendance of poor scholars; thus pointing out and recording their poverty in the midst of their companions. Sir, hereditary distinctions of rank are sufficiently odious; but that which is founded on poverty is infinitely more so. Such a law should be entitled, 'An Act for Branding and Marking the Poor, so that they may be known from the Rich and Proud.'

"Many complain of this tax, not so much on account of its amount, as because it is for the benefit of others, not for themselves. This is a mistake; it is for their own benefit, inasmuch as it perpetuates the government and insures the due administration of the laws under which they live, and by which their lives and property are protected. Why do they not urge the same objection against all their taxes? The industrious, thrifty, rich farmer pays a heavy county tax to support criminal courts, build jails, and pay sheriffs and jail keepers, and yet probably he never has, and never will have, any direct personal use of either. He never gets the worth of his money by being tried for a crime before the court, or being allowed the privilege of the jail on conviction, or by receiving an equivalent from the sheriff or his hangman officers! He cheerfully pays the tax which is necessary to support and punish convicts, but loudly complains of that which goes to prevent his fellow-being from becoming a criminal, and to obviate the necessity of those humiliating institutions.

"This law is often objected to because its benefits are shared by the children of the profligate spendthrift equally with those of most industrious and economical habits. It ought to be remembered that the benefit is bestowed, not upon the erring parents, but the innocent children. Carry out this objection, and you punish the children for the crimes or misfortunes of their parents. You virtually establish castes and grades, founded on no merit of the particular generation, but on the demerits of their ancestors; an aristocracy of the most odious and insolent kind—the aristocracy of wealth and pride.

"I know that there are some men whose whole souls are completely absorbed in the accumulation of wealth, and whose avarice so increases with success, that they look upon their very children in no other light than as instruments of gain—that they, as well as the ox and the ass within their gates, are valuable only in proportion to their annual earnings. According to the present system the children of such men are reduced almost to an intellectual level with their co-laborers of the brute creation. This law will be of vast advantage to the offspring of such misers. If they are compelled to pay their taxes to support schools, their very meanness will induce them to send their children to them to get the worth of their money. Thus it will extract good out of the very penuriousness of the miser.

"I have seen the present chief magistrate of this Commonwealth violently assailed as the projector and father of this law. I am not the eulogist of that gentleman; he has been guilty of many deep political sins. But he deserves the undying gratitude of the people for the steady, untiring zeal which he has manifested in favor of common schools. . . . I trust that the people of this State will never be called upon to choose between a supporter and an opposer of free schools. But if it should come to that, if that should be made the turning point on which we are to cast our suffrages, if the opponent of education were my most intimate personal and political friend, and the free school candidate my most obnoxious enemy, I should deem it my duty, as a patriot at this moment of our intellectual crisis, to forget all other considerations, and I should place myself unhesitatingly and cordially, in the ranks of him whose banners stream in light!

"Those who have failed of re-election on this issue have been passed by only for the moment. They had earned the approbation of all good and intelligent men more effectually by their retirement than they could ever have done by retaining popular favor at the expense of self-humiliation. They have fallen between the powers of light and darkness; but they fell, as every Roman mother wished her sons to fall, facing the enemy with all their wounds in front. . . . Instead of flattering the people and prophesying smooth things, it is the duty of faithful legislators to create and sustain such laws and institutions as shall teach us our wants, foster our cravings after knowledge, and urge us forward in the march of intellect.

"Sir, I trust that when we come to act on this question, we shall take lofty ground—look beyond the narrow space which now circumscribes our vision—beyond the passing, fleeting point of time on which we stand—and so cast our votes that the blessing of education shall be conferred on every son of Pennsylvania—shall be carried home to the poorest child of the poorest inhabitant of the meanest hut of your mountains, so that even he may be prepared to act well his part in this land of freemen, and lay on earth a broad and solid foundation for that enduring knowledge which goes on increasing through eternity."

When Stevens finished speaking the chamber rang with cheers and applause. Before he began his speech he had offered a substitute amendment that strengthened and enlarged the Free Public School Act. Now, from all parts of the hall, there were cries of "Vote! Vote!" His amendment carried by a two-thirds vote amidst tumultuous applause. Governor Wolfe sent a message to Stevens asking him to come and see him. As Stevens entered the governor's office, Wolfe rushed forward to meet him and threw his arms about him. A short time later the senate rescinded its previous action and concurred with the house.

Comments by contemporaries leave no doubt about the impression the speech produced. The correspondent of the American *Daily Advertiser* declared himself incapable "to give even an outline of this magnificent production." Colonel John W. Forney wrote in the Philadelphia *Press* that "Those who were almost ready to take the life of Thaddeus Stevens a few weeks before, were instantly converted to his admirers and friends." The Pennsylvania *Reporter,* a Democratic newspaper which in the past had bitterly assailed him, declared: "We feel assured that a more powerful effort of oratory was never listened to within the walls of this or any legislative hall." Alexander Harris, a contemporary historian by no means friendly to Stevens, wrote that the speech had "a magical effect upon the sentiments of the members. . . . All without distinction, whether enemies or friends, acknowledged the overpowering superiority of it. . . . This speech ranks the author henceforth as one of the first intellects in Pennsylvania."

Stevens considered his oratorical effort on behalf of free public schools "the crowning utility" of his life. Once, in a sentimental mood, he remarked that he would feel amply repaid "if a single child, educated by the commonwealth, should drop a tear of gratitude on my grave." Three weeks before his death, when Alexander K. McClure came to visit him, he found him in a pessimistic mood. "My life," he said, "has been a failure. With all this great struggle of years in Washington, and the fearful sacrifice of life and treasure, I see little hope for the Republic." Then, however, his face brightened and he said: "After all, I may say that my life has not been entirely vain. When I remember that I gave free schools to Pennsylvania, my adopted State, I think my life may have been worth living." And after a meditative pause: "That was the proudest effort of my life. It gave schools to poor and helpless children of the state." A few months after his death Representative Henry L. Cake of Pennsylvania said on the floor of the House: "But for him Pennsylvania would have been, perhaps, the last of the old free states to establish an educational system based upon equal taxation. But for his example our seminaries of learning would have been inferior and few. Half a million young men and women within our borders are this day chiefly indebted to him for the blessings of a sound education. I freely acknowledge my own indebtedness."

Two years after Stevens had made his famous speech there were 3,400 free public schools in Pennsylvania, with a total of 150,000 pupils.

3

Stevens's interest in education never waned. In 1837, in the Pennsylvania Constitutional Convention, he urged that adults be not excluded from the free public schools. "I myself have been a teacher in New England. I have taught married men of thirty. I have taught persons of all ages between four and thirty. There is nothing in the Constitution so important, nothing which affects so deeply the good or evil of the country as this very subject of education."

There was no love lost between him and the citizenry of the District of Columbia, whose sympathy with the "peculiar institution" was notorious, but when in March, 1862, a bill was introduced in the House to establish free public schools in the District, Stevens gave it his unqualified support. "I care not," he said, "whether the people here are worthless; they have children who are to grow up and become men and women; and the more worthless the people are, the greater the necessity for taking care that their children are properly educated." The measure failed to pass, and a month before his death he introduced a bill "to establish a system of schools for the District of Columbia which shall serve as a model for similar institutions throughout the Union." When a young colleague in the House voted against a subsidy to a college in the District, Stevens said to him: "Young man, let me implore you in all your after life never to oppose any measure for the education of the people. Follow the advice and you will never regret it."

CHAPTER VII

The Bank and the "Tapeworm"

When in 1835 a combination of Whigs and Anti-Masons elected Joseph Ritner governor and gained control of the lower house of the legislature, Stevens emerged as the most powerful political figure in Pennsylvania. "Ritner the Farmer," as the new governor was often called, appears to have been entirely under his influence. It cannot be said that Stevens employed his power exclusively *pro bono publico*. His harassment of the Freemasons appears to have been mainly for the purpose of justifying the continued existence of the Anti-Masonic party. Other forms of his political activity were even less to his credit. "Man in everything and everywhere is but patchwork and motley," Montaigne has said, and bade us remember that for the uses of man gold needs to be alloyed with baser metal.

By far the most important measure passed by the legislature when Whigs and Anti-Masons came into power was the Bank Bill. The charter of the United States Bank, whose headquarters were in Philadelphia, expired in 1836. The stockholders had applied for its renewal as early as 1832, but when renewal had been voted by Congress it was vetoed by President Jackson, archenemy of the bank. The bank's president, Nicholas Biddle, thereupon decided to obtain a Pennsylvania state charter. As long as the Democrats were in power in the commonwealth it was useless to press the matter, but when Whigs and Anti-Masons swept into office negotiations were promptly begun. Stevens did most of the negotiating.

As soon as the legislature convened, Ner Middlesworth, speaker of the house, appointed a Committee on Banks composed of Stevens's followers. The committee wrote to Biddle that having been informed of the bank's desire to obtain a charter, they wished to receive particulars regarding the terms he was prepared to offer. Biddle communicated the terms he and Stevens had negotiated and urged prompt action. The matter was then referred to the Committee on Inland Navigation and Internal Improvements, of which Stevens was chairman. Eleven days later Stevens introduced a bill entitled, "An Act to repeal the State Tax on Real and Personal Property, and to continue and extend the Improvement of the State by Railroads, and other purposes." "And other purposes" meant granting a charter to the United States Bank, all the rest was bait for taxpayers and legislators.

The bill specified that the bank was to be granted a thirty-year charter, during which period its profits were not to be taxed. In consideration of this the state was to receive a bonus of two million dollars; a loan of six million at a low rate of interest; $675,000 for public improvements; $500,000 for its free public school system during the year 1837 and $100,000 annually thereafter. The measure repealed the state tax on real and personal property, which was certain to find favor with the taxpayers, but of which one of Stevens's critics has said that it "completely unbalanced the financial sense of the commonwealth." The legislators were put in a receptive mood by appropriations for public works, judiciously distributed, about which another critic has said that "If the legislators had not been bribed privately, they had been bribed publicly in the house."

When the bill had been read, an obtuse Whig inquired if all this meant granting a charter to the United States Bank. Stevens curtly replied that it did, whereupon the member exclaimed: "That will never do!"

"Won't it?" queried Stevens with some of the dictatorial arrogance that later characterized his rule in Congress. "All you have to do is to take your seat and vote for it."

Stevens had no difficulty piloting the bill through the house. In the senate the Democrats were in the majority, but Stevens did not appear worried. When the vote was taken eight Democrats voted for the measure. As three of them had previously spoken against it the cry of bribery was raised. Passage was deferred until the matter had been investigated by a joint committee of both houses. No evidence of corruption was found, which some said was natural enough since Stevens was chairman of the committee.

2

It had for a long time been Stevens's ambition to connect Gettysburg with the outside world by means of a railway. The ambition was not devoid of self-interest. A railway passing Maria Furnace would lower the cost of transportation for that unprofitable enterprise and augment the value of Stevens's extensive real-estate holdings in the vicinity of the ironworks. Gettysburg, however, was ringed in by mountains, making the construction of a railway difficult as well as costly. Private capital had shied away from the project. In the Bank Bill Stevens had earmarked $200,000 for the construction of the Gettysburg Railway. Some of the Whigs had joined the Democrats in protest, but Governor Ritner had made it clear that he would not sign the bill if any change were made in the appropriations.

Stevens saw to it that work on the project commenced with the least possible delay. A survey was ordered, and at the cost of a considerable detour the railway was made to pass close to Maria Furnace. Winding in and out among the mountains the road turned on itself four times. From Gettysburg to Waynesboro by turnpike was twenty-two miles. If and when the railway began functioning it would be thirty-five miles by rail. Stevens's political enemies managed to obtain a copy of the survey, labeled it Stevens's "Tapeworm" and used it as a campaign document in the fall election of 1836, which turned out badly for Stevens and his followers. The Democrats regained control of the house and Stevens himself lost his seat, though only by fourteen votes.

Determined to demonstrate that his defeat had been due to overconfidence, Stevens, a month after his defeat, became a candidate for delegate to the Constitutional Convention, which was to meet in Harrisburg the following year to revise the state constitution. He decided to take no chances. There were some two hundred men at work on the railway. Few of them were permanent residents of the county or even of the state, but by taking advantage of a technicality of the election law Stevens had them qualify as voters. The contractors assisting, all voted for him. He was elected delegate to the convention by a substantial majority.

When the new legislature convened the Democrats pounced upon the Gettysburg Railway project with gusto. A committee was appointed to visit Gettysburg and investigate the matter. Stevens, who was in Harrisburg at that time, wrote to John B. McPherson of the Gettysburg Bank: "Let no foolish engineers of the neighborhood be talking. You know how to drug the committee." McPherson did his best, but to no avail. The committee reported that they found "an isolated work . . . beginning in the woods and ending nowhere, and passing through a barren waste without fertility, presenting the general features of an American Sahara." They recommended that "all operations be immediately suspended." By skillful political maneuvering Stevens managed to keep the work going for another year, and in October, 1837, was re-elected to the legislature.

Finally, however, work on the railway was discontinued. The last shovelful was dug, the last workman departed. Nature set to work repairing the ravages man had made. Several narrow clefts dug in the hills were, however, not obliterated. A quarter of a century later one of these became a death trap for a detachment of the Confederate army during the Battle of Gettysburg.

In 1842 the state advertised the unfinished railway for sale. The Harrisburg *Keynote* exulted: "Bargain! Ho! Bargain! The Tapeworm for sale! . . . The moral and political career of its illustrious patron is not more full of twistings, windings and contortions than is this most extraordinary of all projects, ancient and modern."

CHAPTER VIII

Foe of Slavery

There are some interesting analogies between the careers of Thaddeus Stevens and Abraham Lincoln. One is that while both detested slavery, both were guilty—Stevens in 1821, Lincoln in 1847—of appearing in court on behalf of a slaveholder against a fugitive slave woman. Lincoln's case was more serious, since it involved the liberty not only of the woman, but of her six children, and since it was known that her Kentucky owner wished to sell her in the deep South. Lincoln, however, lost his case, while Stevens won his.

Two circumstances may serve to explain, if not excuse, Stevens's misstep. The Missouri Compromise had just been concluded. While negotiations were in progress Thomas Jefferson wrote to John Holmes: "This momentous question like a fire bell in the night, awakened and filled me with terror. I considered it at once the knell of the Union." Might it not be that Stevens was similarly affected and felt that nothing must be done to aggravate the situation? This is one possibility; another is that he succumbed to temptation, this being his first opportunity to argue a case before the state supreme court. The facts in the case were as follows:

Charity Butler, a slave woman belonging to a Maryland slaveholder, had been leased to a Marylander who was in the habit of spending the summer with his family in the pleasant mountain country near Gettysburg. Charity always went along as a nursemaid. The Pennsylvania Emancipation Act provided that a slave transported into the state and kept there six months became free. Charity had never spent six consecutive months in Pennsylvania, but if her various sojourns were added up would be able to qualify. The Emancipation Act being ambiguous on this matter she sued for her freedom. Stevens argued that the lawmakers intended continuous residence, even if they had not specifically said so. The court agreed, and Charity was sent back to bondage in Maryland.

Careful research has failed to reveal any other blemish on Stevens's antislavery record. Congressman Godlove S. Orth of Indiana, reared and educated in Gettysburg, said on the floor of the House after Stevens's death that when news of the arrest of a fugitive slave would reach Thad, "he invariably volunteered his services to defend the alleged fugitive; and it is among the reminiscences of the neighborhood that he seldom failed to secure the freedom of his clients." Orth has given the following account of how Stevens freed a slave in Maryland at considerable personal sacrifice:

Thad had been "but a few years at the bar." His practice was growing and he urgently needed additional law books. He put three hundred dollars in his pocket—equivalent to several times that amount today—mounted his horse and rode off to Baltimore. In the course of the journey he reined in before a wayside inn where he had often stayed. A young mulatto named John, whom Stevens knew to be the white proprietor's son, came to greet him and took charge of the visitor's mount. Sometime later, hearing a woman weep in the hall, Stevens went to look. The woman, a free mulatto servant, told between sobs that her husband, who was a slave, was going to be sold.

"Who and where is your husband?" Stevens asked.

"Why, Massa Stevens, he is the boy who took your horse to the stable."

The young lawyer went to remonstrate with the proprietor, finally offering him one hundred and fifty dollars for the slave. The man would not hear of it and Stevens said wrathfully: "Aren't you ashamed to sell your own flesh and blood!" The hotel proprietor replied sullenly: "I must have money and John is cheap at three hundred dollars."

Stevens put down the money, manumitted the slave, and rode home without the coveted law books.

2

There had been a time when there was considerable sentiment among slaveholders for gradual emancipation, and antislavery societies were tolerated in some of the slave states. When, however, the cotton gin made the keeping of slaves far more profitable, that sentiment gave place to a desire for expansion of slave territory and for the reopening of the African slave trade. Although slaveholders and their immediate families were only a small minority—about one-sixth of the South's white population—they had managed to secure almost absolute control of state, county, and local governments. In South Carolina no man could be elected to the legislature or to Congress unless he owned at least ten slaves. They moreover controlled all sources of information and ruthlessly suppressed any attempt to enlighten the people about the disastrous effect of slavery upon the economy of the South. Henry J. Raymond, founder and editor of the New York *Times,* an ultraconservative Republican, wrote in 1860 in an open letter to William L. Yancey: "Freedom of speech, freedom of opinion, freedom of political action, are more thoroughly stifled and extinguished in the South than in Austria and Russia, or the most absolute despotism on the face of the earth."

Since the Constitution forbade the federal government to interfere with the South's domestic institutions, and since it was almost equally impossible for men of good will in the South to make themselves heard, the situation seemed well-nigh hopeless. In the fourth decade of the nineteenth century, however, Northern men and a few freedom-loving Southerners who had taken refuge in the North, began to exert pressure upon the South by means of antislavery publications. They hoped to arouse the North to a comprehension of the horror of slavery, in the belief that this was bound to affect the South. They tried, moreover, to arouse public opinion in the South by sending antislavery literature to people in the slave states. No one will pretend that what they wrote and said was always wise—often, indeed, it was not—but it is interesting to note that those who criticized them were generally men who themselves did nothing, either wise or unwise, to correct a situation that should have been repugnant to anyone who took the Declaration of Independence seriously. Their activities alarmed and angered the slaveholders and they demanded that their state authorities do something about it.

Thus it happened that the governor of Virginia sent a letter to several of his Northern colleagues, requesting that measures be taken to prevent the appearance of such "seditious and incendiary publications." Governor Ritner of Pennsylvania, one of the recipients, turned the letter over to the legislature, where it was referred to the Judiciary Committee, whose chairman was Stevens.

Until the outbreak of the rebellion Stevens recognized unequivocally the constitutional right of the slaveholders to keep Negroes in bondage in the slave states. But he was unalterably opposed to the extension of the institution into free territory and believed Congress had the constitutional right to abolish slavery in the District of Columbia. He was, moreover, a firm believer in freedom of speech and of the press. So, on May 30, 1836, he presented a report, of which he was the author, acknowledging that "slaveholding states alone have the right to regulate and control domestic slavery within their limits," but claiming that "Congress possesses the constitutional power, and it is expedient, to abolish slavery and the slave trade within the District of Columbia." [1] The committee, he wrote, could not concede "that individual freemen are, or can be prohibited from discussing the question of slavery in all its bearings upon the morality, religion and happiness of a people and the expediency and duty of abolishing it by constitutional means." They therefore denied "the right of Virginia or any other State to claim from us any legislation to suppress publications criticising slavery." If a citizen had the right to attempt to prove that the usury laws of New York or Pennsylvania were "immoral and unjust and injurious to the peace and happiness of the respective States," why deny him the right to criticize the laws regulating Negro slavery in Virginia or Mississippi? "His arguments may be weak, foolish and false, but it would be tyranny to prohibit their promulgation."

The legislators found the report embarrassing. Its adoption would offend powerful proslavery interests in Philadelphia, its rejection

[1] Professor Richard Nelson Current, in his volume *Old Thad Stevens* (pp. 33-34), writes: "He agreed with the Virginians that Congress had no constitutional power to abolish slavery and the slave trade, either in the District of Columbia or in the Southern States." This was not Stevens's position on the slavery question either then or at any other time.

would displease the Quakers, numerous in Pennsylvania. When McElwee, leader of the Democrats, moved "indefinite postponement" it was immediately recognized as a way out of the dilemma. Henceforth, however, Stevens came to be regarded as the leading antislavery advocate in the commonwealth.

3

The Reverend Jonathan Blanchard was a young man in his middle twenties. He was a graduate of Lane Theological Seminary and had come to Pennsylvania as an agent of the American Anti-Slavery Society. In February, 1837, he was in Harrisburg, where he became acquainted with Stevens. Stevens's defeat for re-election to the legislature the previous fall had made him wonder whether the days of the Anti-Masonic party were not numbered. He and Blanchard were discussing this one day when the young minister remarked: "Mr. Stevens, if you can turn your Anti-Masons into Abolitionists, you will have a party whose politics will not bleach out. The slaveholders will not 'possum' like the Freemasons, but will die game."

Stevens looked at him quizzically, produced forty dollars and handed them to him with the words: "Take that and go down to Adams County and lecture, and if they Morganize you, we'll make a party out of it." As the young man hesitated to accept the proffered bank notes, he added: "Never mind. I am twenty-one in such things and know they can not be done without money."

The following month Blanchard went to Gettysburg, obtained the use of the courtroom and attempted to deliver an antislavery lecture. The attempt was a failure. Encouraged by one Judge McLean, men and boys jeered, whistled, stamped their feet, threw superannuated eggs and decayed vegetables until the speaker was forced to stop. When he had been silenced, McLean and another prominent citizen delivered harangues against abolition and resolutions were passed condemning agitation of the slavery question.

Blanchard wrote to Stevens giving an account of his experience. He had not been "Morganized," but had, it appears, been roughly handled before reaching the hotel. Stevens hastened to Gettysburg and called a meeting at the courthouse. McLean and the young ruffians who had prevented Blanchard from speaking were present, but knew better than to repeat their performance. Blanchard was to write: "Giving his words as a report of his speech without the overwhelming, crushing looks and intonations, seems like pointing to a shivered tree as a description of a thunderstorm." He quoted Stevens as saying: "McLean has said: 'We have no slaves here. Why come and disturb our borough with a discussion of slavery?' So human liberty is to become a local question, to be discussed only in particular localities—is it? A Universalist comes here preaching *universal salvation* and denying the faith of the orthodox and you listen to him quietly and do not molest him, but if a man comes to speak of *universal liberty,* you answer him with violence and rotten eggs! Shame! Shame!! Shame!!! What true freeman would not blush at such behavior on the part of those calling themselves freemen?"

McLean hastily left the hall. A resolution favoring freedom of speech carried unanimously.

4

Stevens's election as delegate to the Constitutional Convention had aroused uneasiness among proslavery interests. To counteract his influence an organization was formed known as the Friends of the Integrity of the Union. Shortly before the opening of the Constitutional Convention the group called a convention of its own in the Harrisburg courthouse. Over seven hundred delegates attended and things were progressing smoothly when a murmur of consternation swept through the hall. Down the center aisle, tall, limping, and saturnine, came Thaddeus Stevens.

Delegates from Adams County had been chosen at a secret conclave. Stevens had ridiculed the secrecy in his paper and had written that the proposed convention was "in favor of the integrity of the chains of the slaves, rather than of the 'Integrity of the Union.' " Blanchard, however, had prevailed upon him to attend the gathering, and with his usual expertness in such matters, he had experienced little difficulty in being substituted for one of the delegates. His presence soon made itself felt, but hardly to the satisfaction of the sponsors.

Soon after Stevens's arrival a clerical delegate from Pittsburgh—who, as it later developed, was soliciting money for the purpose of launching a proslavery newspaper—rose and said: "Born, sir, in Tennessee, raised in Kentucky, I am an exile from my native state on account of slavery; yet I have come to this convention ready to peril my all in the cause of the Union." He had no sooner finished than Stevens rose to speak. Blanchard, present as a spectator, thus described the scene: "In an instant every spitbox was kicked and rattled. Hundreds hissed and mouths that did not hiss groaned and howled. It was bedlam uncapped. For a moment I was stunned; then I looked at Mr. Stevens. He turned with calm haughtiness around and looked that storm of howls in the face. Then, with an emphasis utterly indescribable, above the uproar, he said, 'Mr. President, we're not slaves here in Pennsylvania, and if (slowly and solemnly), sir, the attempt is made to make us such, there are some in this Court House who will make resistance enough to let Pennsylvanians outside know the doom that awaits them."

The minatory tone of his voice, his glowering looks, his reputation for being a man not to be trifled with, awed the delegates into silence. "One could hear the clock tick," wrote Blanchard. Turning toward the man who had spoken with such pathos about the sufferings he had endured for the sake of the Union, Stevens said in his best satirical manner: "I deeply sympathize with my respected friend in all he has done and suffered in the cause of the glorious Union. Indeed, sir, so moved am I at beholding him an exile from his native state, driven out by slavery, that I am ready to join the convention in a vote of reprobation of that foul institution which drives men from their homes as exiles in distant states."

A few men snickered, then burst into laughter. The laughter spread. The next moment all or nearly all had joined in. After that Stevens virtually took over the convention. He kept the delegates amused by witty sallies and by mimicking some of the speakers in so comical a fashion that time after time the delegates were convulsed with laughter. When a resolution was introduced denouncing antislavery agitation, he did not combat it, but offered a quotation from the Declaration of Independence as an amendment. As few cared to vote against an amendment of that nature, it carried, rendering the resolution meaningless. He neutralized another proslavery resolution by appending a quotation from the Pennsylvania Bill of Rights. "The proceedings," wrote Blanchard, "turned into a farce and broke up in laughter."

5

Stevens's leadership at the Constitutional Convention, which assembled at Harrisburg in May, 1837, was disappointing. The Whig–Anti-Masonic combination commanded a majority of only one over their Democratic opponents. The closest co-operation between the allies was therefore indispensable. At the beginning Stevens's tactics left little to be desired. "Who has not delighted with the precision, accuracy, and effect of our evolutions under his drill, throughout the election of officers?" a Whig wrote enthusiastically. Even the Democrats could not withhold admiration. "The highest state of party discipline I ever saw in my life!" exclaimed one. Stevens, whom they referred to as the "drill master," managed to get his entire slate of officers elected, from chairman to assistant doorkeeper. Later, however, his leadership became erratic.

It will be recalled that when during the investigation of the Masonic order he had wished to have the recalcitrant witnesses committed for contempt, the Whigs had refused to follow him. Some blamed the defeat of the coalition in the fall of 1836 on that ill-starred investigation. It was therefore a mistake to try to revive the Masonic issue by proposing a constitutional amendment barring secret societies. A Whig member remarked: "I appeal to my friend from Adams County whether we were not sufficiently rebuked at the last October election for public interference in such concerns." Stevens did not insist, but later in the proceedings made an even more serious blunder. He introduced a motion to the effect that cities, irrespective of size, should be limited to six representatives in the house, as otherwise four or five counties might rule the state. To bolster up his argument he quoted Jefferson's none too sage remark that "great cities are sores on the body politic." Stevens's proposal was impolitic, since many of his Whig followers were from Philadelphia and Pittsburgh. The Whig leader William R. Meredith sprang to his feet and assailed him in intemperate language, calling him "the Great Unchained from Adams," whose "broad front, stertorous voice, and impudent looks and action, form the true basis of his greatness." Stevens replied in kind. After this he could no longer count on undivided support from the Whig delegates.

As the convention progressed many delegates dropped out and

were replaced by others. A financial panic accompanied by a business depression and widespread unemployment was plaguing the country. Radical Democrats—the Loco-Focos—gained the upper hand in the convention. Stevens did not understand their language. He was a manufacturer and the representative of a farming constituency. He had the reputation of being good to his workmen and often kept his factory going for their sake when it would have been cheaper for him to have closed it. But he lived in an age when *laissez faire* was the watchword of the statesman and when so notable a social reformer as John Bryce opposed sorely needed factory legislation. As the Loco-Focos began to press their demands his utterances took on an increasingly antilabor ring. This reached its climax when the radicals sought to deprive Negroes of the right to vote.

As a general rule labor at that time was not sympathetic toward the Negro. White workingmen feared emancipation would result in an influx of Negro labor from the South, affecting wages and working conditions. Free Negroes trying to earn a living often met with abuse and violence. That hostility now manifested itself in the convention. The old state constitution guaranteed the right of suffrage to all men of twenty-one or over. The Democrats wished to restrict it to white men. Stevens opposed this energetically and managed to defeat the proposal. Soon after, the convention adjourned temporarily. It reconvened not in Harrisburg, but in Philadelphia, where Loco-Foco influence became even stronger. Stevens, discouraged, often absented himself. The Democrats took advantage of one of his absences to have the suffrage clause reconsidered, and Pennsylvania Negroes lost the right to vote. When the delegates were invited to sign the new state constitution, Stevens refused.

Thad's experience at the Constitutional Convention may well have been responsible for the extraordinary effort he was to put forth to prevent a Democratic victory at the coming gubernatorial election. While he had much to gain personally by a defeat of the Democrats, principle too was involved. Many of their utterances at the convention seemed to him to presage on the one hand a social revolution, on the other a setback for the cause of the Negro.

CHAPTER IX

Buckshot War

On December 17, 1868, Congressman George W. Woodward, Democrat from Pennsylvania, referring to what in the history of that state became known as the Buckshot War, said on the floor of the House: "The late Mr. Dallas, our then minister at the court of St. Petersburg, told me he was annoyed by daily notes from the whole diplomatic circle anxiously inquiring for the news from Harrisburg." The central figure in that noisy but bloodless conflict, echoes of which apparently reverberated far beyond the frontiers of the United States, was Thaddeus Stevens.

The executive officers of Pennsylvania were elected every three years. Ritner had been elected governor in 1835, when Whigs and Anti-Masons had also gained control of the house, which they lost the following year. Since then, however, they had obtained a majority in the senate. The fall of 1838 had now arrived, when it would be decided whether the Whig–Anti-Masonic combination would regain control of the house or would lose the governorship and other executive offices. Stevens was their political strategist upon whom they relied to lead them to victory. If he succeeded his reward would be a United States senatorship. He must have felt fairly confident of success, for he had wagered a large sum—some claimed $100,000—on the result. The tactics he used to gain the coveted prize are no ornament to his reputation.

He had Ritner appoint him member of the Board of Canal Commissioners and was promptly elected chairman of that body. In June,

1838, he set out on what he cynically referred to as a "missionary tour" of the state. The missionary work consisted of calling on contractors engaged on public works and getting them to contribute liberally to Ritner's campaign fund. They were, moreover, required to enlarge their working force around election time and to take whatever measures were necessary to make sure the men voted for Ritner and other coalition candidates. He is said to have suggested that getting them to bet on Ritner was as good a way as any to insure their political fealty. While these charges have been made by Stevens's enemies, there is reason to believe that they contained a fair amount of truth. Such methods were commonly used by politicians at that time, and Stevens was no political purist. Indeed, in the political atmosphere then prevailing in Pennsylvania a purist would have been a lamb among wolves. Stevens's principal Democratic opponent, Thomas B. McElwee, was a man who stopped at nothing. This, however, did not prevent Democratic leadership from being righteously indignant about Stevens's tactics. They spoke of "heaven-daring frauds," called Ritner a "damned Dutch hog" and Stevens a "monster of iniquity." They had, however, an important advantage which Stevens appears to have underestimated: times were hard; there were thousands of unemployed. When this happens around election time it is generally fatal to the party in power.

2

The counting of the ballots had barely begun when it became evident that the Democratic candidate for governor, David R. Porter, was likely to be the victor. This became a certainty as further returns came in. The vote for representatives to the legislature was, however, more satisfactory, so Stevens did not give up hope. Whigs and Anti-Masons controlled the senate. If they managed to regain control of the house, it might be possible to contest Porter's election. Success or failure hinged on the returns from Philadelphia County, and success in the county on the vote of a district known as Northern Liberties, where dwelt a conglomeration of social outcasts notorious for selling their votes to the highest bidder. Since the Whigs had more money to spend Northern Liberties had gone Whig by a comfortable majority. There were, however, difficulties to overcome.

Of the seventeen members of the Board of Election Returns of Philadelphia County ten were Democrats. The ten pronounced themselves shocked at reports of corruption at Northern Liberties and ruled that returns from the district should not figure in the result. The Whig members disagreed, held a meeting of their own and sent the complete returns to the sheriff, to be certified and forwarded to Thomas H. Burrowes, secretary of state and chairman of the Whig Central Committee. The sheriff, a loyal Whig, understood the urgency of the matter. He lost no time in certifying the returns and sending them to Harrisburg by special messenger. In the meantime the Democratic members of the board debated whether or not to bypass the sheriff. They finally did so, which was an infringement of the election law and put them at a disadvantage. When their messenger arrived at Harrisburg he was told that certified returns from the county had already been received and sealed.

Stevens and Burrowes now put their heads together. In his capacity of secretary of state Burrowes announced that the only legal returns from Philadelphia County were those certified by the sheriff. In his capacity of chairman of the Whig Central Committee he issued a statement to the "Friends of Governor Ritner" in which he challenged Porter's election, saying that "there is a strong possibility of malpractice and fraud in the whole transaction, which it is our duty peacefully to resist and fully expose. . . . But, fellow citizens, until the investigation is made, let us treat the election of the ninth instant as if we had not been defeated, and in that attitude abide by the results."

Burrowes's letter—which, it was charged, had been written by Stevens—resulted in an outburst of popular indignation beyond anything the leader of the coalition had anticipated. His hope that the excitement would have subsided by the time the legislature met was not fulfilled. Shortly before December 4, when the legislature was to convene, the cry, "On to Harrisburg!" reverberated through Democratic strongholds in Philadelphia. Hordes of rough-looking men piled into railway carriages of trains chartered for the occasion, determined to show the "Archconspirator" Stevens that the people could not be trifled with. Stevens has given the following description of the invaders:

The most respectable of them—the "Captains of Ten," were keepers of disorderly houses in Kensington. Then came journeymen butchers, who were too worthless to find regular employment—next professional boxers who practiced their pugilistic powers for hire and low gamblers who infest the oyster cellars of the suburbs. A portion of them consisted of a class of men whose business you would hardly understand—dogkeepers who in Spring Garden and Southwark, raise and train a ferocious breed of dogs, which they fight weekly for wages and for the amusement of the "indignant people." Their troop was flanked by a few professional thieves and discharged convicts. These men gathered up from the dens and hovels, were refitted with such cast-off clothes as their employers could command and hired at fifteen dollars the head and freight to come to Harrisburg, instruct the legislators in their duties and *protect their rights.*

Stevens had in the meantime not been idle. He intended to rely on political strategy rather than on a display of force. Realizing, however, that force might be necessary to keep the invaders in check, and that the sheriff, a Democrat, could not be relied upon, he had instructed the contractors to send their brawniest men to Harrisburg. He had summoned the Whig and Anti-Masonic members of the legislature—senators as well as representatives—to the capital several days in advance and had given them precise instructions. He had prepared several measures he intended to rush through and had picked the man he wanted for speaker. To guard against the eventuality of a member of the opposition absconding with the Bible, so the speaker could not be sworn, he had provided himself with a pocket Bible. Thus prepared he calmly awaited the fateful day.

3

The house convened on December 4, 1838, at eleven o'clock in the forenoon. The scene resembled scenes in the French National Assembly during the Revolution, when the Paris mob invaded the building to demand action against aristocrats and traitors. Legislators had to force their way through, for not only the gallery, but the corridors and the aisles were densely packed. Stevens experienced less difficulty than most of his colleagues. There was something intimidating about the tall, scowling, limping, bewigged man. People made way before him as if suspecting him of possessing some occult, satanic power. When he reached his seat, however, he noticed that special attention had been given him by the Democratic leaders. "My seat," he wrote, "had the honor of being guarded by eight or ten of the most desperate brawlers in Kensington. . . . Most of them wore coats with outside pockets in which their hands were generally thrust and, as I afterwards satisfactorily ascertained, were armed with double-barreled pistols, bowie-knives and dirks. Men of similar description and similarly accoutred occupied the platform around the speaker's desk."

The clerk, a Democrat, ignored the invaders and called the house to order. Secretary of State Burrowes handed him the sealed returns. He broke the seal and proceeded to read the names of those composing the house. When he reached Philadelphia County, a Democrat rose and declared that returns from that county were false. He produced a paper which, he claimed, was a copy of the true returns. The clerk asked the house if both sets of returns should be read. A motion to that effect having been made, he put it to a vote, pronounced it carried, read both sets of returns from Philadelphia, then proceeded with the remainder of the list.

A murmur swept through the hall as Stevens rose to speak. It was the duty of the house, he said, to elect a speaker and to swear in those named in the official returns. When the house had been organized those wishing to contest any of the seats could do so by presenting a petition to the house, which would be "referred to a committee selected by lot according to the Act of 1791, whose report is final and conclusive." This, he declared emphatically, was the only legal procedure. Then he made the following apparently conciliatory proposal: He saw no objection, he said, to the election of *two* speakers—one elected with the aid of the official, the other with the aid of the unofficial returns from Philadelphia County. Both could occupy the platform "until the law decided between them."

There was a murmur of surprise. Whigs and Anti-Masons wondered about Stevens's concession regarding the speakership. As for the Democrats, "Beware of the Greeks bearing gifts!" must have occurred to some. Since, however, the Whig–Anti-Masonic majority was small, a committee selected by lot might easily contain a majority of Democrats, especially as they would have a speaker of their own to keep a watchful eye on the drawing. After a few minutes' deliberation they accepted Stevens's proposal. Whigs and Anti-Masons now elected Thomas S. Cunningham speaker, while the Democrats chose William Hopkins. There was now not one house, but two. Both adjourned, each voting to meet at a different hour the following day.

It was not until after adjournment that Democratic leaders realized they had been outmaneuvered. It was not the "law" that would decide which house should be recognized, but the senate. Recognition of the "Cunningham House" by the senate would mean recognition of all its members as legally elected, precluding any further contest. And in the senate Whigs and Anti-Masons had an undisputed majority! By proposing the dual speakership Stevens had succeeded in transferring the contest from the house to the senate.

4

When it dawned on the Democratic leaders that they had been duped, their fury knew no bounds. It has been claimed that McElwee's first reaction was to have Stevens assassinated. The plan was either abandoned or miscarried. There were measures to be taken of greater practical value. The principal thing necessary was to gain time. The senate was to meet at four o'clock that afternoon. If that body could be prevented from taking action on recognition—not only that afternoon but for a sufficient length of time thereafter—the situation could still be saved. Individual senators could be "persuaded" to vote for recognition of the "Hopkins House." McElwee had various ways of "persuading" people, one of which is said to have been ferreting out secrets in their private or public lives and threatening exposure.

News that Stevens's conciliatory gesture had revealed itself a clever maneuver that might spell Democratic defeat reached the grogshops where McElwee's followers were priming themselves. Soon crowds of men appeared in the street shouting that before the day was over Stevens's body would be at the bottom of the Susquehanna. A well-wisher called on Stevens in his room in Wilson's Hotel and begged him to remain indoors as otherwise he would surely be killed. Stevens replied that he had promised Charles E. Penrose, presiding officer of the senate, to be present at the opening session and meant to keep his promise. A contemporary observer has written that at the height of the excitement Stevens appeared unperturbed and acted "with the most perfect coolness and deliberation."

He managed to reach the senate chamber unmolested and together with Cunningham, speaker of the "Cunningham House," stationed himself in front of the fireplace. Later they were joined by Penrose and by several others, for soon after the opening of the session the presiding officer and his assistants were pushed off the platform by McElwee and his henchmen. The scene that unfolded before their eyes resembled, even more than the one in the house that morning, the tumultuous scenes of the French Revolution. Aisles and gallery were packed by a noisy, raffish-looking crowd. Speeches were made that would have done credit to Marat during the Reign of Terror. A certain Charles Brown was frantically applauded when he declared that the revolution was on, the Constitution had ceased to exist and that it was time for the people to take possession of the government. "Are you ready," he cried, "in order to defend your rights, of which you have been robbed by Stevens, Burrowes and Company, to drench the Senate chamber with the best blood of the State?" "We are!" roared the crowd. Taken aback by the promptness and eagerness of the response to what apparently had been merely a rhetorical flourish, the speaker blurted out: "I hope not!"

Not all the speeches, however, were disingenuous. Some genuinely reflected the desperate condition of the unemployed and the despair of tradesmen ruined by the financial panic and the business depression. The *laissez-faire* policy of the Whigs offered no remedy for this. Not that the Democrats had a remedy. They were in power in Washington when the panic began and were turned out of office in 1840 because of their inability to cope with it. But in Pennsylvania Whigs and Anti-Masons held the executive offices and received the blame.

Gas lamps had been lighted, adding to the weirdness of the scene. The organized disorder was accomplishing what it had been meant to accomplish. It was obvious that no action other than that demanded by McElwee would be possible unless sufficient force were on hand to maintain order. To remain and listen to the harangues served no purpose for Stevens and his friends, but exit was blocked by a solid mass of men. One of those who had joined Stevens by the fireplace tried a door back of the platform. It was unlocked and gave into a committee room. He motioned to the others, and unnoticed amidst the uproar they went into the room, opened a window and one by one lowered themselves to the ground.[1]

5

That evening Stevens conferred with Governor Ritner. The obese, phlegmatic Governor hesitated to call out the militia. He feared the men might refuse to obey orders—might even side with the mob. The most Stevens was able to prevail upon him to do was to call upon the civil authorities "to exert themselves to restore order to the utmost of their power," and upon the military force of the commonwealth "to hold themselves in readiness to repair to the seat of government."

On the morning of December 5 the "Hopkins House" met in the legislative chamber, and in the afternoon the "Cunningham House" —called "Stevens' Rump" by the Democrats—assembled in the parlor of Wilson's Hotel. That same day a mob, armed with a cannon, marched upon the state arsenal. A catastrophe was averted when the official in charge, claiming to act on orders from Stevens, made an agreement with the leaders of the mob that arms should not be delivered to either side. As soon as Stevens heard of this he issued an open letter in which he denied having given anyone the right to negotiate in his name. "I should deem it disgraceful to treat with the rebels on any subject," he wrote.

As the situation was growing increasingly tense, Ritner appealed to the commander of United States dragoons stationed at Carlisle to come and restore order. The commander referred him to Washington. President Van Buren, a staunch Jacksonian, declined to intervene. Finally, on December 8, Ritner notified General Paterson, commander of the state militia, to bring his force to the capital. Paterson issued an order to his men "to assemble in winter uniform,

[1] Almost exactly two years later, on December 5, 1840, Democrats in the Illinois Legislature, wishing to vote resumption of specie payments by Illinois banks—a measure Lincoln and other Whig members opposed—took the precaution of locking the doors of the legislative chamber, so as not to be balked by lack of a quorum. Lincoln and several other Whigs escaped through a window. Herndon has written that "Mr. Lincoln always seemed willing to forget" the incident. Stevens's exit through a window came to plague him during his congressional career.

with knapsack, provided with thirteen rounds of buckshot, cartridge, etc.," thus giving currency to the term "Buckshot War."

Light is thrown on the character of Stevens's principal adversary by the account of Colonel Pleasanton of a confession made to him by McElwee on January 20, 1839. Being under the impression that Paterson's force was to be carefully screened, so as to consist entirely of Whigs, it had been McElwee's intention to wreck the train on which the soldiers were to arrive by the removal of several rails. At the same time a mine was to be exploded "and the whole body of them blown into the air together." McElwee claimed to have personally purchased three barrels of gunpowder for that purpose. He had abandoned the plan when discovering that the men were "not all of one party" and many Democrats would be killed.

Paterson restored order in the city, but not at the capitol. Ritner, still fearing a mutiny, had instructed him to "permit no officer or private in uniform or armed to enter within the enclosure in which the State Capitol stands." Crowds in the senate gallery were therefore still able to aid Democratic filibustering by noisy demonstrations. In the meantime McElwee's agents were at work on several wavering senators. There were rumors of bribery and of blackmail. Yet, on December 19, the senate voted that the "Hopkins House" was "not a House of Representatives legally constituted," but stopped short of recognizing the "Cunningham House." Finally, on December 25, the blow fell. By a vote of seventeen to sixteen the senate recognized the "Hopkins House."

Stevens remained defiant. In an open letter to his constituents he wrote that while his Whig and Anti-Masonic colleagues had "determined to submit to the mortifying necessity and enter the illegal house," he himself had no intention of doing so. "I find no difficulty in choosing my own course in selecting between an association with successful insurgents or withdrawing from office. Such voluntary association would sanctify or at least palliate their treason." At a mass meeting in Gettysburg his constituents expressed their faith in him, but requested that he attend the next session, as his presence in the legislature could be "of service to the commonwealth." He replied that he owed too much to "the kindness and steady confidence of the people of Adams County to disobey their wishes. I shall therefore conquer my repugnance to it and enter the house at the adjourned session."

He reckoned without McElwee.

6

Among Stevens's acquaintances in Gettysburg was a certain Mr. Young at whose house he occasionally dined. Young had an unmarried daughter who made the mistake of allowing an admirer greater privileges in courting than is customarily considered prudent and proper, and who as a consequence gave birth to a child. Stevens had barely returned to Harrisburg to fulfill his promise to his constituents when word reached him that he had been indicted for bastardy and that Young had brought civil suit against him.

The great and near-great are not free from human frailty. Benjamin Franklin cheerfully admits in his *Autobiography* that he "got a naughty girl with child." After Stevens's death a man who had known him in his middle years wrote in the Cincinnati *Commercial:* "Far back in his forties he is remembered as a ladies' man of the type of Henri Quatre, lusty and merry. He was a bold rake and fond of flirtation." However that may be, one of Stevens's biographers who has left no stone unturned to place him in the worst possible light, has felt constrained to admit that Stevens's involvement in the affair was due to the machinations of McElwee. Stevens, in a letter to his friend John B. McPherson, gives the following information about the matter:

> I have been informed, from a quarter which I could hardly think misinformed that five men in Gettysburg had often . . . visited Mr. Young and urged him to bring suit against me, some of them assuring him that he could recover $20,000, and offering to back him with money. That prosecution, while it annoys me, will compel me to prove things in my defense which I greatly regret. I pretend to no prudish sanctity, but the pretense in the case referred to is so perfectly false, that I shall show beyond doubt that the girl was courted—and worse than merely courted by a man who turned out to be married at that time—and that too just nine months before the birth of the child. So far from being a seducer, I swear to God I have never yet learnt (except from description) the meaning of maidenhead! Nevertheless I wish this cursed matter were ended. But I shall never made advances. I shall carry on the war in the

same spirit in which it has been begun, and regret it more for the sake of the weak girl—the instrument of her father's cupidity—than for my own.

The indictment was eventually dismissed and the civil suit dropped, but not before they had served McElwee's purpose. Hardly had Stevens taken his seat in the house than the Democratic leader introduced a motion that a committee be appointed to investigate "whether he [Stevens] has, if duly elected, not forfeited his seat by misconduct." It is not without significance that several Democrats not only voted with the Whigs and Anti-Masons against the motion, but presented a written protest.

Stevens refused to appear before the committee, whom he informed that he could not "admit the intellectual, moral and habitual competency of McElwee, his compeers, coadjutors and followers to decide a question of decency and morals." The committee wisely decided to let decency and morals take care of themselves, but reported that Stevens, "having resigned his office, is not entitled to a seat in the house," and recommended a special election to fill the vacancy. Stevens accepted the challenge and wrote in a letter to his constituents: "Both my inclination and my interest require me to retire from public life. But I will not execute that settled intention when it will be construed into cowardice or despondency. . . . I present myself to you as a candidate to fill that vacancy which was created to wound my and your feelings. I do not want to receive a party nomination from my friends. The question now to be decided is above party consideration, and would be disgraced by sinking it to the level of a party contest."

He was triumphantly re-elected.

CHAPTER X

President Maker

Although no longer a power in the government of Pennsylvania, Stevens remained a figure of importance in party politics. The Anti-Masonic party, while maintaining a separate identity in parts of the state, had now virtually merged with the Whigs. In the fall of 1839 Stevens expected to head the Pennsylvania delegation to the Whig National Convention in Harrisburg and at the same time to seek re-election to the legislature on the Anti-Masonic ticket. He abandoned the latter intention on receipt of an autograph letter from William H. Harrison—one of the aspirants to the Whig presidential nomination—soliciting his support at the convention and promising him a cabinet appointment in the event of victory at the polls.

In his volume *Our Presidents and How We Make Them* Alexander K. McClure relates that during the convention Francis Granger of New York showed Stevens a letter he had received sometime before from Winfield Scott—a leading aspirant to the nomination—suggesting that assurances be given to antislavery forces in the Empire State concerning his stand on the slavery question. The letter was confidential, which, however, did not deter Granger from entrusting it to Stevens. The head of the Pennsylvania delegation paid a visit to the Virginia delegation at their headquarters, and before leaving managed to drop the letter where it could not possibly escape notice. It was found and read, ruining Scott's chances and resulting in Harrison's election.

Stevens did yeoman work during the famous "Log Cabin and

Hard Cider" campaign from which Harrison emerged victorious. Feeling certain of the promised appointment, he took no further action but confidently awaited Harrison's summons. Then one day the list of cabinet appointments appeared in the newspapers, with his name conspicuous by its absence.

2

He was nearing the half-century mark with his political fortunes at a lower ebb than they had been for years. President-making had not turned out satisfactory either for him or for his party. Harrison died a month after his inauguration and his successor, John Tyler, played into the hands of the Democrats. Nevertheless, Stevens resolved to try again. The man whom he decided to groom for the high office was none other than Winfield Scott. In October, 1841, he wrote to the General suggesting the possibility of his nomination in 1844 and requesting biographical material "as the best way to present your claim to the people." If Scott knew of the role Stevens had played at the Harrisburg convention, he gave no inkling of it. He sent what Stevens had asked and wrote: "I see evidence of your power in many and important quarters. . . . I hope to do nothing that may not be for the best; and in matters not involving principle, I shall always be found sufficiently docile and practicable." This was welcome assurance, even though Stevens had experienced to his sorrow that assurances from presidential aspirants had to be taken at a discount. He was busy laying the foundation for Scott's nomination when he received two letters from Ohio which attempted to steer him into a different channel. One was from Salmon P. Chase, the other from his friend Jonathan Blanchard.

Chase was some sixteen years younger than Stevens, an able lawyer, a fine figure of a man, and an enemy of slavery. He was at this time a member of the Liberty party, to which Blanchard likewise belonged. It was at Blanchard's request that in April, 1842, he wrote to Stevens inviting him to join, at the same time explaining the difference between the party and the abolition movement. "Abolition," he wrote, "seeks to abolish slavery everywhere. The means which it employs are of a moral nature—arguments, persuasion, remonstrance and the like. The Liberty party seeks to abolish slavery wherever it is within the reach of the constitutional action of Congress; to restrain slavery within the slave States and to deliver the government from the slave power." He predicted that unless these steps were taken slavery would burst its confines and "stalk at large through the country." Blanchard's letter contained the following appeal: "I am anxious that you should employ the extraordinary power with which God has endowed you for the furtherance of righteousness and justice on this wretched earth. You are utterly unfit to make speeches on the common miserable topics of political life."

Stevens knew that James G. Birney, the Liberty party's candidate for president in 1840, had received only six thousand votes. The party might eventually attract a larger following, but only if the slaveholders seriously threatened invasion of free territory. Thus far, however, they seemed willing to abide by the Missouri Compromise. A political party dedicated to the task of preventing something that to the average man did not appear at all imminent seemed to him premature. He allowed six weeks to pass, then wrote to Blanchard: "I need not say to you how entirely my views and wishes accord with your own in the object you have in view. The only question is as to the means most likely to accomplish it. I have believed that could best be done by declining, *as yet,* to organize a distinct political party." He told Blanchard about his correspondence with Scott, who, he assured his friend, if not an outspoken opponent of slavery, had no sympathy with the institution. Winning with him would, he felt, be of greater advantage to the cause of freedom than going down to defeat "with a still more thorough anti-slavery man."

3

It was not only Stevens's political fortunes that were at a low ebb. His financial loss from wagers he had made on Ritner's election had been considerable and the business depression had well-nigh ruined his iron business. In the spring of 1842 he was on the verge of bankruptcy. Indeed, his partner, James D. Paxton, insisted there was no way out of the difficulty except to take advantage of the bankruptcy law. Stevens would not hear of it. He wrote to Blanchard: "I have failed for ninety thousand dollars. I know of no way out of such things than to pay the uttermost farthing. I may be forced to take advantage of the bankruptcy laws in the next world, but I will never do so in this."

Hitherto he had allowed Paxton a free hand in the management of the ironworks, now he took charge himself with his customary vigor. He asked the creditors for an extension of time, promising that if it were granted all would be paid in full. They accepted, but Paxton demurred. He had no intention, he said, of slaving for years for the benefit of the creditors. Stevens now sold most of his other property, paid Paxton twenty thousand dollars for his share of the business and assumed the entire indebtedness himself. Realizing, however, that for some time to come he would have to rely mostly on his law practice to meet his financial obligations, he decided to seek a broader field for his legal talents. Having already a number of important clients in Lancaster, he moved in April, 1843, to the small manufacturing city whose bustle and apparent sophistication had awed him as a young man. Gettysburg would, however, often see him on court days.

CHAPTER XI

Lancaster

When Stevens moved to Lancaster the town had some eight thousand inhabitants and was growing apace. In the succeeding decade its population more than doubled. Its factories produced a variety of objects, large and small—locomotives and railroad cars, plows and threshing machines, carriages and wagons, umbrellas and combs, stoves and hats, rifles and distilled liquors. A canal and a railroad served to carry these products to Philadelphia and Baltimore and thence to many places at home and abroad. The courthouse, on Courthouse Square, was situated on an elevation over which arched, at right angles, the town's two principal streets, King and Queen. Both were paved and were lined with neat, red-brick, white-shuttered houses. Surrounding the town were rich farm lands where wheat, barley, corn, buckwheat, and potatoes grew in abundance.

It has been related in a previous chapter that soon after his arrival in Lancaster, Stevens acquired, at sheriff's sale, a two-family house on South Queen Street. It was an unpretentious red-brick structure of two stories and an attic. He had allowed the octogenarian former owner to continue to occupy the larger unit, and fitted out the smaller for himself as office and living quarters. When the old man died the living quarters were moved to the main dwelling. The house was furnished in the somewhat gloomy, tasteless fashion of the period. One of the upstairs rooms was fitted out as a library, where Stevens often read late into the night.

His law practice prospered from the beginning. Bankers, manufacturers, and merchants were eager to secure his services. His colleagues in the profession had a high opinion of his legal talents. When a case had to be appealed it was seldom that the lawyer in charge did not advise his client to engage Stevens as associate counsel. His professional standing may be judged from the fact that when Chief Justice John B. Gibson of the state supreme court died, Stevens was chosen to deliver the obituary before the court, notwithstanding the fact that the deceased had been a Democrat and a Freemason. It has been estimated that his annual income from the practice of law in Lancaster exceeded fifteen thousand dollars, easily equivalent to four times that amount today. During his first six years in his new location he was able to pay all but thirty thousand dollars of his indebtedness.

Sometimes as many as ten young men "read" law in Stevens's office. It was customary for lawyers of established reputation to charge for that privilege, but Stevens was never known to turn away a student because of inability to pay. A note in answer to a student's application reads: "Have room. Take students. Terms $200. Some pay—some don't." The note is characteristic of the man—laconic, gruff, to the point, the gruffness ill-concealing an underlying generosity of character. Of no man can it more truthfully be said that his bark was worse than his bite. One of his students has related that when he came to apply, Stevens asked him several questions, then said gruffly: "You better forget about the law." The young man's face fell, but brightened when Stevens added: "You have too honest a face to be a lawyer." Young people have an intuition about character often blunted in later life. The fact that Stevens's students loved him and nearly all became his devoted disciples speaks strongly in his favor. Usually one or more of the students boarded at the house. When Stevens's brother Morrill, a country doctor, died, his sons, Thaddeus and Alanson, came to live with their uncle.

2

Stevens found it considerably more difficult to carve out a place for himself in the political life of Lancaster County than to become its leading lawyer. As once in Adams County the Federalist leaders had rebuffed his efforts to share influence with them, so now the Whig leaders adopted a similar attitude. Remembering how he had outmaneuvered the former by organizing the Anti-Masonic party of Adams County, he decided to resuscitate that party in his new location. That at so late a date he should have succeeded even to a moderate extent seems extraordinary, but the effort only served to demonstrate that the Whigs of Lancaster County were able to elect their candidates without the help of the Anti-Masons.

Grooming Winfield Scott for the presidency likewise produced no results. In 1844 the Whigs nominated Henry Clay. Stevens suspected Clay and Webster of responsibility for Harrison's breach of faith and showed no interest in the campaign. He even advised some of his followers to support James G. Birney, the Liberty party candidate. When news of this reached Whig national headquarters it created considerable uneasiness. The slavery issue had gained importance as a result of the Southern demand for the annexation of Texas. Stevens had a large following throughout the state not only among Anti-Masons, but among opponents of slavery. His defection might easily cost Clay the electoral vote of Pennsylvania. It was not long before Whig leaders in Lancaster County received orders to conciliate him at any cost.

But he was too shrewd a man to allow himself to be easily conciliated. He met the advances with cold indifference. Finally Clay himself sent him a message to the effect that if he would give him his support, "redress would be made for past wrongs." This apparently meant that if Clay was elected President, Stevens could count on a cabinet appointment. Vague as was the promise, his political future was now so uncertain that he felt he could not afford to disregard the opportunity and plunged into the fray. How valuable a campaigner he was may be judged from what occurred at a monster rally in Philadelphia, where he and Webster spoke simultaneously from platforms erected on opposite sides of a large camping ground. At first Webster had the larger audience, but as repeated bursts of cheering and applause attested Stevens's success, Webster's listeners began to desert until the balance was greatly in Stevens's favor.

3

Henry Clay is known in history as the "Great Compromiser." There are issues, however, that cannot be compromised. The annexation of Texas appeared to many to be one of these. The Whig party was divided on the issue. Most Northern Whigs opposed annexation; the great majority of Southern Whigs favored it. Seeing no possibility of compromising the matter, and needing the support of both factions, Clay decided to agree with both. He told his Northern followers that annexation was "a measure compromising the national character . . . dangerous to the integrity of the Union," then wrote to a friend in Alabama that if elected he would not oppose annexation, since he considered slavery a transitory evil, while annexation would be a permanent good. Unfortunately for him the letter became public, whereupon many opponents of annexation decided to vote for the Liberty party candidate. As a result Clay lost the electoral vote of New York and Michigan, and with it the presidency.

Stevens was opposed to annexation. Had Clay been elected and had Thad become a member of his cabinet, their association would undoubtedly have been brief. Stevens would have resigned rather than have supported a policy that meant increased power for the slaveholders. Yet the result of the election must have been a severe blow to him. The fact that a Lancasterian whom he had come to regard as a bitter political adversary was invited by President-elect James K. Polk to become his secretary of state must have added to his feeling of frustration. The man so favored was none other than James Buchanan, with whom many years before he had sat on a rail fence outside the town of York and who had advised him to join the party of Jackson. Buchanan, too, had remained a bachelor. He lived in the company of his niece, the beautiful Harriet Lane, on an estate called "Wheatland" a short distance from town. It has been claimed that once, at a reception given by Dr. Henry Carpenter, who was Buchanan's physician as well as Stevens's, the future President unintentionally snubbed Stevens by failing to notice his proffered hand, and that thereafter they were not on speaking terms. This, however, is contradicted by the fact that in 1850, when Stevens was a member of Congress, Buchanan asked him to recommend his nephew for an appointment to West Point, if he could do so "consistently with the duty you owe to your political friends." Stevens promptly complied.

CHAPTER XII

Lydia Hamilton Smith

Stevens employed a housekeeper and one or two maids. In Lancaster he had a succession of housekeepers, white and colored, none of whom proved satisfactory. In 1848 a colored widow of thirty-five, Lydia Hamilton Smith, was recommended to him. She lived in Harrisburg and was the mother of two boys, William, aged twelve, and Isaac, aged five. Her husband, a Negro carpenter, had died soon after the birth of the second child. Stevens remembered having known Lydia in Gettysburg, before her marriage, and to have been favorably impressed. He communicated with her and engaged her. She went to live with her boys in a small building back of his house, bringing her furniture with her. When William grew older she was assigned a bedroom in the house. She remained with Stevens until his death.

Lydia was a light mulatto with comely features and straight hair. She is said to have been of Creole origin and was a devout Catholic. She was small of stature, well-formed, extraordinarily neat, modest and courteous. Stevens found her an ideal housekeeper, loyal, honest, capable. The editor of the Union Spring *Times,* an Alabama newspaper, who during Reconstruction came to Lancaster to interview Stevens, described her as "a neat, tidy housekeeper who appears to be as polite as well-trained Negroes generally are." Stevens addressed her as Mrs. Smith and showed her the consideration a white woman in her situation would have considered her due. When he grew old and infirm and she undertook the task of nursing him in addition to her other duties, he left it largely to her judgment what callers should be admitted. To this the Alabama editor gave an invidious interpretation: "The mulatto manages his household in Lancaster and Washington. She receives or rejects visitors at will, speaks of Mr. Stevens and herself as 'we,' and in all things comports herself as if she enjoyed the rights of a lawful wife." Since this contradicts what has already been quoted, he apparently obtained the additional information from his Democratic colleagues in Lancaster, who were hardly unprejudiced witnesses.

There exists a letter written by Lydia to Stevens's nephew, Thaddeus, when Stevens was on his deathbed, in which she addresses the young lawyer as "Dear Thad." One of Stevens's biographers considers this "a degree of familiarity unusual even to-day between a mere servant and an adult member of the household." [1] Lydia, however, was not a "mere servant," but a trusted housekeeper and nurse who had known the young man since boyhood. Had she been white her manner of addressing him would under the circumstances not have been considered unusual. Since Stevens tolerated no racial distinction in his household it is difficult to see why this form of address for his young nephew should be considered undue familiarity.

In his will, Stevens gave Lydia the choice of a cash payment of five thousand dollars or an annuity of five hundred for life. She was to be allowed to remain in the house at Lancaster for one year after his death, and as several pieces of furniture belonging to her had been placed in the main dwelling, her word was to be taken "without further proof" as to which were hers. Lydia outlived her employer by sixteen years, dying in 1884, at the age of seventy-one. She lies buried beside her two sons in St. Mary's Catholic Cemetery in Lancaster. An inscription on her tombstone informs the visitor that she was "for many years the trusted housekeeper of Honorable Thaddeus Stevens."

2

The above is all that is known with certainty regarding Stevens's relationship with Lydia. There exists no reliable evidence justifying the assumption that she was his mistress as well as his housekeeper.

[1] Alphonse B. Miller, *Thaddeus Stevens,* p. 13.

In February, 1850, the *Lancasterian,* a Democratic newspaper, hinted that Stevens's sympathy with the Negro race was due to "what has been whispered by the tongue of scandal." It may well have been the tongue of Democratic politicians, for Carl Schurz and James Albert Woodburn, who interviewed many of Stevens's acquaintances and neighbors, failed to record any such insinuations. In June, 1867, the editor of the Alabama newspaper, whose interview with Stevens was reprinted in the New York *World,* wrote:

Radicals have a good deal to say about the close relationship some of the former slaves bear to their masters. They tell the Southern people that numbers among their servile class are too yellow to be white, and too white to be black. It is horribly unkind to their great leader and master. In the city of Lancaster, nigh upon the pure city of Philadelphia, Thaddeus Stevens has for years lived in open adultery with a mulatto woman, whom he seduced from her husband, a full-blooded negro. . . . I only mention the fact that the ultra-supersanctimonious saints of the African Ascendancy may get the beam out of their own eyes before they gouge mercilessly at the motes of others.[2]

Granted that this was actionable, is the fact that Stevens failed to bring suit proof of the existence of an irregular relationship? He could easily have proved the falsity of the accusation that he had seduced Lydia from her husband, while his accuser would have been hard put to prove that she was his mistress, assuming the charge to have been true. A favorable verdict would, however, not have convinced those who wished to believe the worst of him and the trial would have given the charges nationwide publicity. For Lydia's sake as well as his own he did well in ignoring the attack.

The article in the Union Spring *Times* was followed a month later (July, 1867) by an attack in the Lancaster *Intelligencer.* Stevens had agreed to purchase a lot in a local cemetery, but canceled the agreement on learning that Negroes were refused burial there. He subsequently acquired a lot in Martin Schreiner's Cemetery, where no such regulation existed. The Lancaster *Express* commented that

[2] It is an interesting coincidence that while this attack was being made on Stevens, the following appeared concerning Thomas Jefferson in the London *Morning Star* of June 22, 1867: "Jefferson scorched it [slavery] with his fiery invectives, but such was the difference between his profession and his practice that after his death one of his own children was sold on the auction block."

this was proof of the sincerity of Stevens's convictions. The *Intelligencer* replied editorially:

Nobody doubts that Thaddeus Stevens has always been in favor of negro equality, and here, where his domestic arrangements are so well known, his practical recognition of his pet theory is perfectly well understood. . . . There are few men who have given to the world such open and notorious evidence of a belief in negro equality as Thaddeus Stevens. A personage, not of his race, a female of dusky hue, daily walks the streets of Lancaster when Mr. Stevens is at home. She had presided over the house for years. Even by his own party friends, she is constantly spoken of as Mrs. Stevens, though we fancy that no rite of Mother Church ever gave her a right to it. It is natural for men to desire to sleep their last with those they loved in life. If Thaddeus Stevens insists on being buried side by side with the woman he is supposed to have taken to his bosom, it is entirely a matter of taste. But why did he not purchase a lot in an African burying ground at once? There no white man's bones would have jostled his own, and she who has long been his most intimate associate might have been gathered to his side without exciting public scandal.

The following general denial of the charges was made by Stevens in a letter to his friend W. B. Mellins, September 14, 1867:

I received your letter of the 8th inst., containing a printed libel from the Union Spring *Times:*

In the course of my life, I have received a very large number of such attacks. Perhaps no man in the State has received more slanders or been charged with more vices, or malignant crimes than I have. It has been my misfortune for forty years to be the bitter object of attack by violent politicians. I have seldom noticed them—never contradicted them—unless they affected my moral character aside from politics, or was required by the interest of others. You tell me that this charge may influence your next election. Hence I notice it. I have already denied a part of it on application from a distant State. The rude doctrines ascribed to me by the fellow who wrote them, I pass over with a general denial of their accuracy. As to the domestic history, I have only to say, that the whole is totally without foundation, except so far as follows:

From the time I began business (forty odd years ago) I have kept house, through the agency of hired servants, having no female relations. Those servants were of various colors, some white, some black, others of intermediate colors. My inquiry was only into their honesty and capacity. They have resided with me for various periods, from one month to fifteen years, generally more than one at a time, indeed I believe always so. I believe I can say that no child was ever raised, or, so far as I know, begotten under my roof. Sometimes husband and wife have worked. The one for me, and the other for another, generally at the same time cohabiting together on Saturday night. But I believe none of these ever became pregnant at that time.

This is a longer disclosure than, I believe, I have ever made before of my private affairs. These calumnies and worse, have been frequently published all around me by fellows living within sight of my door. I know of no one who has believed one of them, or scarcely pretended to believe them. Having no ambition for office, no aspirations for fame, I have not found it pleasant to turn aside to encounter the offensive odor of diseased dog secretions.

Few men who choose to remain bachelors are ascetics. We can take it for granted that in his younger days Stevens had intimate relations with women. But that Lydia, a devout Catholic with whose confessor he was on the best of terms, was one of these, appears improbable. Unless his considerate treatment of her and his failure to bring suit for slander are regarded as proof, there is nothing on which to base the accusation.

PART TWO

CONGRESSIONAL INTERLUDE

CHAPTER I

Stevens Goes to Washington

The year 1849: Texas had been annexed; the war with Mexico fought and won. California and what is now New Mexico, Arizona, Nevada, Utah, and parts of Colorado and Wyoming—some nine hundred thousand square miles—had been added to the Union.

The previous fall Stevens had been elected to Congress by the Whigs, polling 9,500 votes to 4,500 for his Democratic opponent. When he received the nomination the Lancaster *Intelligencer* had commented: "We have ascribed the nomination of Mr. Stevens to the homage awarded to commanding intellect, but . . . yet more patent reason exists at the bottom. *He is the sworn enemy of the South*—avowedly selected as a champion able and willing to 'worry' the representatives from beyond Mason's and Dixon's line."

The statement was true only if one identified the South with the slaveholding oligarchy, composed, according to the census of 1850, of fewer than 200,000 slaveholders. President Eisenhower's secretary of defense, Charles Wilson, is reported to have said: "What is good for General Motors is good for the country," but no historian would be so rash as to claim that what was good for the slaveholders was good for the common people of the South. In his second rejoinder to Douglas at Peoria, Lincoln was to say: "Slave States are places for poor white people to remove from, not to remove to. New Free States are the places for poor people to go to and better their condition." The question at issue between the North and the South was whether slavery should be permitted to expand to free territory.

The poor whites of the South needed a place "to go to and better their condition" even more than the poor white people of the North, who had no slave labor to compete with.

At this particular time the slaveholders considered *their* interests greatly endangered. They had confidently expected that the territory ceded by Mexico would be open to slavery, or that, at the very least, the Missouri Compromise line would be extended to the Pacific. But now California, whose population had grown by leaps and bounds following the discovery of gold, was applying for statehood with a constitution excluding slavery. What made the situation particularly alarming to the slaveholders was that antislavery sentiment was growing in the North and was affecting both major political parties. In 1846 a Northern Democrat, David Wilmot of Pennsylvania, had introduced in the House what became known as the Wilmot Proviso, barring slavery from all territory ceded by Mexico. A House in which Democrats predominated had passed the proviso, which however had been defeated in the Senate. In 1848 antislavery Whigs and Democrats had combined with Liberty party men in a Free-Soil party, which in the fall of that year had polled nearly three hundred thousand votes for its presidential candidate, Martin Van Buren, and had sent two senators and thirteen representatives to Congress. Their platform not only demanded the exclusion of slavery from territory where it had never existed or had ceased to exist, and its banishment from the District of Columbia, but also the prohibition of the interstate slave trade. State after state in the North was, moreover, enacting personal liberty laws, making it increasingly difficult to reclaim fugitive slaves. In fine, the slaveholders felt grievously put upon, and the word secession, which their representatives had been wont to utter at the slightest provocation, took on a grave and sinister significance.

It was at this critical period that Stevens was elected to his first term in Congress.

2

The Washington of that day—a city of some forty thousand inhabitants—was a curious mixture of the urban and the bucolic. Imposing public edifices looked down on broad unpaved streets, where, in winter, carriages and wagons often became mired over their hubs, and from which in summer clouds of fine dust were churned up by wheels and horses' hoofs. For some unaccountable reason houses were not numbered. Geese and hogs roamed about at will. There were some eight thousand Negroes, most of them free, but a slave pen and an auction block were in evidence on one of the principal streets. It was not uncommon to see a coffle of manacled slaves driven down Pennsylvania Avenue by a man on horseback wielding a whip.

The majority of white Washingtonians had proslavery sympathies. Now that slavery had again become a burning issue they crowded the galleries at the opening sessions of Congress, applauded the champions of the institution and jeered at its critics. Stevens did not allow this to remain unrebuked. During a debate concerning an appropriation for the District he was to say: "This town is a pauper on the nation. We make their sewers and everything else, and we feed them, in order that, at the opening session, they may come here and hiss if freedom is mentioned, and applaud if slavery is mentioned. Before I will vote anything not absolutely necessary for this town, they must reform their manners. I should hate to starve them; but if they got so lean that, at the opening session, they cannot howl or hiss, so much the better."

He had taken lodgings in one of Washington's numerous boardinghouses and had been pleased to discover that one of his fellow boarders was Associate Justice John McLean. Wendell Phillips, who was not given to understatement, has said of McLean that he had "made more pro-slavery law on the bench than all pro-slavery judges put together," but Stevens appears to have had a peculiar predilection for him. The jurist had been his candidate for president at the National Convention of the Masonic party and would be so again at the Republican National Conventions of 1856 and 1860.

When not in the House or in committee, Stevens was to spend most of his time reading. James G. Blaine has written: "He was disposed to be taciturn. A brilliant talker, he did not relish idle and aimless conversation. He was much given to reading, study and reflection, and to the retirement which enabled him to gratify his tastes. As was said of Emerson, Mr. Stevens loved solitude and understood its uses." In the congressional library there is a partial record of the books he borrowed. By far the greater number deal with history—ancient as well as modern—and biography. Parliamentary and international law and pedagogics were likewise among his favorite studies. He had little taste for fiction, but was fond of Shakespeare and of Cervantes's *Don Quixote*. There were always a few books on his night table, and when sleep would not come, he would light a candle and read.

Opponents of slavery were seldom invited by the Washington *beau monde*, but Stevens did not mind. The city was well provided with luxurious gambling houses, enabling him to indulge in his favorite pastime. Once when he visited one of these in the company of the clerk of the House, luck was against him. His companion urged him to bet on the ace. "I'll stake my reputation it will win this time," he declared with assurance. Stevens put a stack of chips on the ace and lost. "Martin," he remarked dryly, "you owe me a quarter."

Blaine has related that he once saw Stevens coming down the stoop of a fashionable gambling establishment. They had just exchanged greetings when a Negro preacher approached Stevens and solicited a contribution toward a church he was building. Stevens, whom fortune appeared to have favored, took a roll of bills from his pocket, peeled off one hundred dollars and handed it to the minister while remarking to Blaine: "God moves in a mysterious way his wonders to perform."

CHAPTER II

The Compromise

Congress convened on December 3, 1849, in an atmosphere surcharged with excitement. In the preceding Congress there had been violence and threats of violence. Both major political parties had a proslavery and an antislavery wing. Neither could command a majority without the aid of the Free-Soilers. Taking advantage of this the Free-Soilers were determined to vote for no man for speaker upon whom they could not rely to give them representation on important committees. Stevens was one of their favorites. When his name was placed in nomination the venerable Joshua Giddings of Ohio rose and said that he and his friends were willing to vote for him "without other pledges than his antecedent opinions and acts." Most Whigs, however, considered him too extreme. He received only twenty-seven votes.

Speeches made by the Southerners left no doubt concerning their intentions. "I do not hesitate to avow before this House and the country that if by your legislation you seek to drive us from California and New Mexico, and to abolish slavery in this District, thereby attempting to fix a national degradation upon half the states of this confederacy, *I am for disunion,*" declared Robert Toombs of Georgia. Richard K. Meade of Virginia made the damaging admission that Virginia had "a slave population of half a million, whose value is chiefly dependent on Southern demand. . . . If slavery is abolished in the District and prohibited in the Territories, I trust to God that my eyes have rested upon the last Speaker of the House of Representatives."

After three weeks of impassioned debate, during which violence was with difficulty averted, a resolution was adopted permitting the election of a speaker by a plurality vote, and Howell Cobb of Georgia was chosen. During the contest for the speakership representatives from the North, Democrats as well as Whigs, had shown themselves sufficiently firm. Soon after, however, many of them began to waver. Toward the end of December a motion to table a resolution to bar slavery from all territory ceded by Mexico—a reaffirmation of the Wilmot Proviso—was lost by a vote of 105 to 71. Five weeks later a similar motion carried. Eighteen Democrats and fourteen Whigs had changed sides, others abstained.

2

Stevens had remained silent during the debate concerning the speakership, but when he saw the breakup of the antislavery forces, he decided to make an attempt to rally them by firm and unequivocal speech. On February 29, 1850, he obtained the floor and said, in part:

"Mr. Clingman in opening the debate on behalf of human bondage, notified us that unless Congress submitted to settle the slavery question according to Southern demands, there should be no legislation, even to the passage of the ordinary appropriation bills necessary to sustain the government. I doubt not that before he ventured upon so high a threat, he had full assurances from a sufficient number of Southern gentlemen to carry it into effect.

"Here, then, we have a well defined and palpable conspiracy to disorganize and dissolve [the Government]. I doubt if there is another legislative body in the world where such sedition would not be followed by prosecution and punishment. But in this glorious country, where two thirds of the people are free, we can say anything within these walls or beyond them with impunity, unless it be to agitate in favor of human liberty—that is aggression!

"While I announce my hostility to slavery in every form and every place, I also avow my determination to stand by all the compromises of the Constitution. . . . Some of these compromises I greatly dislike, and were they now open for consideration, they should never receive my assent. But I find them in the Constitution, formed in difficult times, and I would not disturb them. By these compromises, Congress has no power over slavery in the States. I greatly regret that it is so, but I know of no one who claims the right, or desires to touch it, within the states. But when we come to form governments for territories acquired long after the formation of the Constitution, and to direct new states, whose only claim for admission depends on the will of Congress, we are bound so to discharge that duty as shall best contribute to the prosperity and glory of the nation. Does slavery contribute to either of these? Is it not rather subversive of them? Let us first view it in the light of political economy.

"Slave countries never can have an intelligent and industrious yeomanry. . . . The white people who work with their hands are ranked with the other laborers, the slaves. Their minds and conduct generally conform to their condition. . . . The soil occupied by slavery is much less productive than a similar soil occupied by freemen. Men who are to receive none of the wages of their labor do not care to multiply its fruits. The land being neglected becomes poor and barren. . . . Take Virginia. She has a delightful climate; a soil naturally fertile. She is intersected by the noblest rivers. Her hills and mountains are filled with rich minerals and covered with valuable timber. Her harbors are among the best in the world. At the time of the adoption of the Constitution, she was the most populous state—her population was double that of New York. It was the boast of her statesmen that she was *prima inter pares*. What is she now? The population of New York is more than double—I think the next census will show nearly treble hers. Her land, cultivated by unwilling hands, is unproductive. Travel through the adjoining states of Ohio and Pennsylvania, and you will see that the land produces more than double as much as the same kind of land in Virginia. In the free states new towns are everywhere springing up and thriving. . . . In Virginia there is scarcely a new town within her whole borders. Her fine harbors are without ships except from other ports; and her seaport towns are without commerce and falling to decay. Ask yourself the cause, sir, and I will abide the answer."

He referred to the statement of Meade of Virginia that the value of the Old Dominion's "half million slave population was chiefly dependent on Southern demand" and said: "In plain English, what does it mean? That Virginia is now only fit to be the breeder, not the employer of slaves. That she is reduced to the condition that her proud chivalry are compelled to turn slave-traders for their livelihood! Instead of attempting to renovate the soil, and by their own honest labor compelling the earth to yield her abundance; instead of seeking for the best breed of cattle and horses to feed on her hills and valleys and fertilize the land, the sons of that great state must devote their time to selecting and grooming the most lusty sires and the most fruitful wenches to supply the slave barracoons of the South! And the gentleman pathetically laments that the profits of this genteel traffic will be greatly lessened by the circumscription of slavery. This is his picture, not mine.

"I am opposed to the diffusion of slavery, because confining it within its present limits will bring the states themselves to its gradual abolition. . . . Confine the malady, surround it with a cordon of freemen so that it cannot spread, and in less than twenty-five years every slaveholding state in the Union will have a law upon its statute books for its gradual and final extinction."

Referring to the oft-repeated argument that slavery was solely the concern of the South, he said: "I trust that it may be so decided by impartial history and the unerring Judge, that we may not be branded with that great stigma. But could we hope for that justification if now, when we have the power to prevent it, we should permit this evil to spread over thousands of square miles now free? . . . Sir, for myself, I should look upon any Northern man, enlightened by Northern education, who could directly or indirectly permit it to spread over one rood of God's free earth, as a traitor to liberty and a recreant to God."

He referred to a boast made by Meade that though the slave states had been "in a numerical minority in the Union for fifty years, yet during that period we have managed to control the destinies of the Union," and commented: "I do not complain of this statement. It is both candid and true. But I cannot listen to the recital without feeling the burning blush on my countenance, that the North with her overwhelming millions of free men, has for half a century been tame and servile enough to submit to this arrogant rule. How often have these walls been profaned and the North insulted by insolent threats that if Congress legislated against the Southern will it would be disregarded, resisted to extremity and the Union destroyed? During the present session we have been more than once told amid raving excitement that if we dared to legislate in a certain way the South would teach the North a lesson. . . . You have too often intimidated Congress. You have more than once frightened the tame North from its propriety and found dough-faces enough to be your tools. . . . I trust that now, when the great battle between liberty and slavery comes to be fought on this floor there will be not an accursed Achan in this whole camp of the representatives of freemen."

The New York *Tribune* characterized Stevens's speech as "one of the most forcible and telling expositions of Free Soil doctrine of the session." *The Freeman,* of which Whittier had once been the editor, called it "the best anti-slavery speech ever made in Congress." The Free-Soilers published two hundred thousand copies in pamphlet form. The speech was widely quoted and discussed in the Northern press. The only reply it ever received in Congress was a torrent of abuse. In June of that year Stevens was able to say on the floor of the House without fear of contradiction: "I do not remember one of the numerous gentlemen who have referred to my remarks who has attempted to deny any of the facts or refute one of the arguments. They have noticed them only to vituperate their author."

3

While all this was taking place in the House, in the Senate Henry Clay had introduced his "Omnibus Bill," that aimed at settling the principal differences between the two sections. California was to be admitted as a free state. All the rest of the territory ceded by Mexico was to be given territorial government "without the adoption of any restriction or condition on the subject of slavery." The debt of Texas was to be paid and her eastern boundary fixed. The slave trade (but not slavery) was to be prohibited in the District of Columbia. The Fugitive Slave Act of 1793 was to be replaced by a more drastic law. Congress was to declare formally that it did not possess the power to interfere with the interstate slave trade.

On March 7, 1850, Webster made his famous speech in support of Clay's "Omnibus Bill." When Stevens read the speech (which Webster thought it prudent to revise before sending copies to newspapers in Massachusetts) he growled: "I could cut his damned heart out!" To a friend he wrote: "The North will yield and the South will triumph." On June 10, 1850, he again took the floor. Although considering the battle lost, he wished to make it plain to the representatives of the slaveholders that there were men in the North whom they had failed to intimidate and that the struggle would continue.

He had not been particularly concerned about the attacks Southern representatives had made upon him, but when Thomas Ross, Democrat from his own state, took up the cudgels for the slaveholders he had felt his anger rise. Having no better arguments at his disposal than his Southern colleagues, Ross, too, had resorted to personalities. Referring to Stevens's speech he had said that "language so offensive, and impudence so unblushing has never been heard or seen in any respectable assembly of men. . . . Pennsylvania knows that member, and with deep humiliation she acknowledges the acquaintance."

Stevens began with a mild rebuke to his Southern colleagues, who had "indulged in abuse to the total neglect of reason." He did not, he said, intend to retaliate in kind. If he cared to use such weapons, he could "find them any day by entering the fishmarket. However, I beg these respectable fish ladies to understand that I do not include my colleague from Pennsylvania among those whom I deem fit to be their associates. I would not so degrade them. There is in the natural world a little, spotted, contemptible animal which is armed by nature with a foetid, volatile, penetrating virus, which so pollutes whoever attacks it as to make him offensive to himself and to all around him for a long time. Indeed, he is almost incapable of purification. No insult shall provoke me to crush so filthy a beast!" He checked himself, then added: "But this is more than I intended to say." Turning to the presiding officer, he assured him that he would "never again be betrayed into a similar digression, even to brush off these invading vermin."

There were few after this sufficiently rash to trade insults with him.

He satirized the claim of the slaveholders that the slaves were content with their lot:

"Gentlemen on this floor had repeatedly asserted that slavery was a moral, political and personal blessing; that the slave was free from care, contented, happy, fat and sleek. Comparisons have been instituted between slaves and laboring free men, much to the advantage of slavery. . . . Well, if this be so, let us give all a chance to enjoy this blessing. Let the slaves who choose, go free; and the free who choose, become slaves. If these gentlemen believe there is a word of truth in what they preach, the slaveholders need be under no apprehension that they will ever lack bondsmen. Their slaves would remain and many freemen would seek admission to this happy condition. We will not complain if they establish societies in the South for that purpose—abolition societies to abolish freedom. Nor will we rob the mails to search for incendiary publications in favor of slavery, even if they contain seductive pictures, and cuts of those implements of happiness, hand-cuffs, iron yokes and cat-of-nine tails."

He paid his respects to the Reverend Hilliard of Alabama, who had quoted the Bible in defense of slavery: "These reverend parasites do more to make infidels than all the writings of Hume, Voltaire and Paine. If it were shown that the Bible authorized, sanctioned and enjoined slavery, no good man would be a Christian."

A Southerner interrupted, asking if it was not true that New England had at one time permitted slavery. "She was very wicked. She has long since repented. Go ye and do likewise!" Stevens shot back.

He assailed Senator James M. Mason's Fugitive Slave Act, incorporated by Clay in his "Omnibus Bill." The act obliged citizens, on pain of heavy fine, to assist the authorities in the arrest of such fugitives: "The distinguished gentleman from Kentucky [Clay] wishes further to make it the duty of all bystanders to aid in the capture of fugitives; to join the chase and run down the prey. This is more than my constituents will ever grant. They will strictly abide by the Constitution. The slaveholder may pursue his slave among them with his own foreign myrmidons, unmolested, except by their frowning scorn. But no law that tyranny can pass will ever induce them to join the hue and cry after the trembling wretch who has escaped from unjust bondage."

He paid his respects to the South and to Clay and Webster in these words:

"I do not reproach the South. I honor her courage and fidelity. Even in a bad, a wicked cause, she shows a united front. All her sons are faithful to the cause of human bondage, because it is *their* cause. But the North—the poor, timid, drivelling North—has no such united defenders of her cause, although it is the cause of human liberty. Even her own great men have turned her accusers. . . . She is offered up as a sacrifice to propitiate Southern tyranny—to conciliate Southern treason. . . . In this crisis of the fate of liberty, if any of the renowned men of this nation should betray her cause, it were better that they had been unknown to fame. It need not be hoped that the brightness of their past will dazzle the eyes of posterity or illumine the pages of impartial history."

4

If there ever was a time when the expansionist ambitions of the slaveholders might have been checked without serious danger of secession it was in the fateful year 1850. "In 1850," Professor Allan Nevins has written, "hundreds of thousands who ten years later would think of themselves as Southerners still thought of themselves simply as Americans." [1] Had President Zachary Taylor not died suddenly all might have been well. Although born in Virginia, reared in Kentucky, and a resident of Louisiana, where he owned a plantation and three hundred slaves, the old warrior was a staunch unionist and firmly opposed to slavery expansion. Even after his death his influence was sufficiently great to bring about the rejection of Clay's "Omnibus Bill." But with Millard Fillmore in the White House and Webster secretary of state, the friends of the compromise decided to try again. They introduced the bill piecemeal. Although they now had the support of the administration to aid them instead of having its opposition to overcome, patronage, bribery, and intimidation proved necessary to obtain the passage of some of the compromise measures.

Stevens kept up the fight. When the Texas bill came up for discussion he again took the floor. The bill provided for the payment of ten million dollars to Texas for the relinquishment of its claim on the greater part of New Mexico. Texas bonds had been selling at ten to fifteen cents on the dollar, at which price they had been

[1] From *Ordeal of the Union* by Allan Nevins, copyright 1947. Quoted by special permission of the publishers, Charles Scribner's Sons, vol. I, p. 377.

accumulated by crafty politicians in Texas and other Southern states. They were expected to go to par as soon as the measure passed. Horace Greeley has related in his *Recollections* that after the death of a Western senator conclusive proof was found that he had been paid thirty thousand dollars in Texas bonds for his vote in favor of the bill. Others in the Senate and in the House were bribed or allowed themselves to be intimidated by threats of secession. "Civil war and bloody desolation were the mildest figures garnishing their discourses," said Stevens. He was opposed, he said, "to buying peace from armed rebels. If any state or portion of a state choose to place themselves in military array against the Government of the Union, I am for trying the strength of the Government of the Union. I will not be persuaded by any intimation of spilling of blood. If blood is to be spilt, by whose fault is it to be spilt? Pass this bill and instead of repose it will be the fruitful mother of future rebellion, disunion and civil war."

When the Fugitive Slave Bill came up for discussion he moved that it be tabled. Frederick W. Seward has written in his *Reminiscences:*

> I happened to be in the Congressional Library that morning, when I saw many Northern members coming in, one by one, and aimlessly strolling about. Inquiring of one what was going on in the House, I was told that the Fugitive Slave Law was about to be voted on. Those were the "dodgers," who did not want to vote for it, nor dare to vote against it. I hurried to the House gallery, in time to find Thaddeus Stevens on his feet, and sarcastically moving that the Speaker "send one of his pages to inform the members that they can return with safety, as the slavery question had been disposed of"! [2]

5

One of Stevens's biographers has written that none of his predecessors "has taken adequately into account the simple fact that he [Stevens] was, above everything else, a man of politics seeking always to get and exercise the power of public office." [3] That Stevens loved power is true, and to this might be added that he sometimes used questionable means to obtain and to hold it. But the

[2] From *Reminiscences of a War Time Statesman and Diplomat,* pp. 83-84. Quoted by special permission of the publishers, G. P. Putnam's Sons.

[3] Current, *op. cit.,* p. iii.

matter is far less simple than his critic supposes. Much as he loved power he preferred to lose it rather than to sacrifice any of his fundamental principles. We have seen him risk his political future in the Pennsylvania College and free public school matters. We have seen him openly avow his antislavery principles when others, more prudent or more calculating, waited until opposition to slavery had become a promising political issue. In persisting in his opposition to the compromise Stevens risked not only his political future, but his interests as an ironmaster.

The long and bitter struggle in Congress was injurious to business. This, combined with the fact that the two most prominent Whig leaders, Clay and Webster, favored compromise, had convinced the Whigs of Pennsylvania and of Stevens's own district that the measures were desirable. Moreover, Southern Whigs had promised to help raise the tariff if Northern Whigs would support the compromise measures. In Pennsylvania a high tariff was considered so indispensable to the welfare of the state that Democrats agreed with Whigs on the matter. And no industry in Pennsylvania stood more in need of tariff protection than the iron industry, which suffered greatly from British competition. Furnaces that burned charcoal, like the Caledonia Iron Works, were especially handicapped. Yet Stevens persisted in his opposition to the compromise. The editor of the Lancaster *Intelligencer,* a paper claiming to be politically independent, voiced the opinion of Whigs and Democrats alike when he spoke of Stevens as "a bold and reckless politician who follows the bent of his own inclinations without regard to the wishes of the people. He takes his position and adheres to it, not caring a fig whether it pleases or displeases his constituents." This is strange conduct for one who "above everything else" seeks "to get and exercise the power of public office."

CHAPTER III

Stevens Joins the Republican Party

Stevens was re-elected to Congress, but with a greatly reduced majority. He did not distinguish himself during his second term. Like most antislavery Whigs he felt profoundly discouraged. He took little interest in the proceedings and was often absent. President Fillmore and his cabinet were, however, sufficiently shortsighted to feel gratified at the success of the compromise. William A. Graham, a member of the cabinet, wrote in a letter: "I think the settlement of the last session [of Congress] and the firm course of the Administration in the execution of the fugitive slave law have given a new lease to slavery, and property of that kind has not been so secure for the last twenty-five years."

Presented with an opportunity of making "property of that kind" somewhat less secure, Stevens was prompt in taking advantage of it.

Edward Gorsuch, a Baltimore slaveholder, had learned that two of his slaves, who had escaped some three years earlier, were living with a mulatto named William Parker near the village of Christiana, a Quaker settlement not far from Lancaster. Gorsuch and his son journeyed to Philadelphia, obtained a federal warrant for the arrest of the fugitives, and accompanied by a United States deputy marshal arrived at the two-story stone house occupied by Parker and his friends. Arrest, however, proved no easy matter. Parker's house was one of a number of houses in the neighborhood occupied by Negroes. The fugitives barricaded themselves in the upper story, and Parker having blown a trumpet, Negroes armed with a variety of weapons came swarming from all directions. Several who had firearms joined the fugitives in the upper story.

Confronted with the opposition of half a hundred armed Negroes there obviously was not much the three white men could undertake. Before long, however, other white men arrived, and the deputy ordered them to aid in the arrest. The new Fugitive Slave Law made it mandatory to obey the order on pain of heavy fine. The new arrivals, however, were Quakers, opposed to slavery and all its works. They refused to obey, and their spokesman, Castner Hanway, said to Gorsuch: "The sooner you leave the better, if you would prevent bloodshed." The slaveholder, seeing the deputy was loath to risk entering the house, called on his son to follow him and bounded up the stairway. Shots rang out. Gorsuch fell over dead; his son was seriously wounded.

Had the country been invaded by a foreign enemy the outcry could hardly have been worse. Friends of the compromise called the Christiana riot treason, rebellion, conspiracy against the government! Castner Hanway and three other white men were arrested, as were a score of Negroes. The charge against them? Nothing less than treason—conspiracy to make war upon the government of the United States!

The trial took place before Judge Grier, in the federal court in Philadelphia. It was the first trial in a higher court under the new Fugitive Slave Law and the proceedings were eagerly watched by friends as well as enemies of the compromise. Stevens had charge of the defense, but fearing his prominence as an enemy of slavery might prejudice the jury, he had John M. Reid, Free-Soil Democrat from Philadelphia, play the more conspicuous role. It was he, however, who planned the strategy of the defense, and it was his argument before the court that secured the right for the defense to introduce evidence showing that free Negroes had been kidnaped in that part of Pennsylvania by men representing themselves to be officers of the law.

In his instructions to the jury Judge Grier denounced agitators who preached disobedience of the law, but directed acquittal, saying the case did not rise to the dignity of a conspiracy to wage war upon the government.

Gorsuch had not died in vain. Following the trial, the Fugitive Slave Act became a dead letter in Pennsylvania.

2

Clay had died. Webster had died. The Whig party was dying. Clay, who claimed to have been its founder, had inflicted a mortal blow upon it with his compromise. In 1852 the Whig candidate for president, Winfield Scott, carried only four states. Following the election the party rapidly disintegrated. Notwithstanding this, Stevens would have had little difficulty in being nominated and elected, but made it known that he did not care to return to Washington and threw his support to one of his friends. He was in a mellow mood when in March, 1853, he rose in the House and said: "It is more than probable that hereafter I shall never meet any member here or elsewhere officially, and I desire to part with no unfriendly feelings towards any of them."

After his return to Lancaster he devoted himself to his law practice, his iron business, and his two nephews. He sent the elder, Thaddeus, to an academy in Pennsylvania and thence to Dartmouth. The younger, Alanson, who had not much taste for study, having received an elementary education, became assistant to John Sweeney, manager of the ironworks. Stevens's correspondence with his elder nephew shows that he took his responsibility toward his charges seriously. In 1853 he wrote to him: "I fear indolence is your besetting sin, for sin it is. . . . I trust you will raise your energies and do honor to yourself. . . . *Never* taste intoxicating drink—a little is folly—much is crime." The following year, when the young man had apparently got into some scrape, he wrote: "I have read your letter with pain. It is grievous to lose your relatives by death. But it is more painful to see them disgraced and worthless men. . . . I must say that until you have redeemed yourself from disgrace I have no desire to see you." He soon relented and when the young man became a lawyer, took him into partnership in his law office.

The remark "it is grievous to lose your relatives by death" referred to his mother, who had died that year. He mourned her sincerely. Once, in a reminiscent mood, he said to a friend: "I really think the greatest satisfaction of my life resulted from my ability to give my mother a farm of two hundred and fifty acres, and a dairy of fourteen cows, and an occasional bright gold piece, which she loved to deposit in the contributors' box of the Baptist Church, which she attended. . . . Poor woman! The very thing I did to gratify her most hastened her death. She was very proud of her dairy and fond of her cows; and one night going to look after them, she fell and injured herself, so that she died soon after."

3

No amount of sophistical reasoning can obscure the fact that Clay's and Webster's compromise meant the abandonment of the principle not to make any additional territory available to slavery. Nor can it obscure the fact that it endangered the Missouri Compromise. Much of the territory which was to be given territorial government "without the adoption of any restriction or condition on the subject of slavery" was above the prolongation of the Missouri Compromise line, which, it had been agreed, slavery was never to cross. The consequences of this policy now made themselves felt. In 1854 Stephen A. Douglas introduced the Kansas-Nebraska Bill, which, having passed Congress, swept away the Missouri Compromise line, throwing an immense empire open to slavery. The immediate result was the organization of the Republican party. Antislavery Whigs and Democrats united with Liberty party men and Free-Soilers to stop the onward march of slavery.

Stevens now came out of his political retirement. He was one of a score of men who in 1855 met in Fulton Hall in Lancaster to form a Republican county organization. The following year he was a delegate to the Republican National Convention in Philadelphia that nominated John C. Frémont for president. He did not favor Frémont's nomination. His candidate was John McLean. The Know-Nothings—haters of Catholicism and of immigrants—had considerable influence in Pennsylvania, Indiana, and Illinois. Without their aid the three states could not be carried by the Republicans. Although Frémont was an Episcopalian, he was popularly believed to be a Catholic. Stevens was no religious bigot and personally would not have cared had the candidate been a Catholic. But he did not think it wise to risk the support of the Know-Nothings, and made an able speech in favor of the nomination of McLean. "I have never heard a man speak with more feeling and in more persuasive accents," Lincoln's friend Elihu B. Washburne has testified. When an Ohio delegate produced a letter from McLean asking that his name be withdrawn, Stevens proposed that the jurist be drafted. Whether the Republicans would have won in 1856 had his advice been followed is problematical. It is a fact, however, that had Pennsylvania, Indiana, and Illinois gone Republican, victory would have been theirs.

4

Stevens did not sulk. He threw himself wholeheartedly into the campaign. Indeed, it might be said that his enthusiasm was somewhat excessive. There is in existence a letter written by him to the chairman of the Republican State Committee, in which he says: "I negotiated with the leading American [Know-Nothing] editor of York who was doing much mischief. . . . He was to change his course and have $350. I have advanced $50 of it. As I have already expended $4000 in securing presses I have resolved to go no further. Now if your friends could send $300 it would secure York County—If not it must slide. It is mortifying to need money for the public and not have it."

"The end justifies the means" is not regarded as good ethics, yet when of two evils one chooses the lesser, it usually means consenting to what one knows to be evil in order to avoid a greater evil. Lincoln said once: "Much as I hate slavery, I would consent to any extension of it rather than see the Union dissolved, just as I would consent to any great evil to avoid a greater one." Who will say that to consent to the extension of slavery is more ethical than to bribe editors in an attempt to prevent its extension?

In 1858 Stevens decided to return to Congress, and had no difficulty in obtaining the Republican nomination. In trying to force Kansas to become a slave state and in permitting the *de facto* reopening of the African slave trade, President Buchanan had worked into the hands of the slaveholders to such an extent that Stevens now regarded him as a personal enemy. "If saying that he is the *meanest* man that has ever occupied the Presidential chair brings him displeasure, *then I will say it,*" he declared during the campaign. Buchanan on his part left no stone unturned to bring about his defeat. Stevens wrote to Salmon P. Chase: "The only difficulty is that I am ahead of the people in Anti-Slavery. . . . Mr. Buchanan is very busy aiding to defeat me. The Gov't's money will do much in a population like ours, but I do not think they can succeed."

He was elected by an impressive majority.

CHAPTER IV

Renewed Struggle in Congress

Stevens must have felt confident that this time his stay in Washington would be a lengthy one. He decided not to remain in the boarding-house, but rented a modest dwelling at 219 South B Street, behind the Capitol, and sent for Lydia to come and keep house for him.

Strained as had been relations between the North and the South at the commencement of his first term in Congress, the tension now was nearly as great. Many things had happened in the interval that had embittered the North—the enforcement of the new Fugitive Slave Law, the passage of the Kansas-Nebraska Act, the struggle in Kansas, the assault upon Charles Sumner by Preston Brooks of South Carolina, the Dred Scott decision, the attempt of the Buchanan administration to make Kansas a slave state despite the opposition of an overwhelming majority of the settlers, the *de facto* reopening of the African slave trade. The North fairly reeled under the blows. The slaveholders, on their part, felt disturbed about the formation and rapid growth of the Republican party, the desertion of Douglas, John Brown's raid on Harpers Ferry, and—judging by the debate in Congress—apparently most of all by the endorsement by prominent Republicans of a book written by a North Carolina poor white, Hinton Rowan Helper.

Helper's book, *The Impending Crisis of the South,* was crudely written, but contained many irrefutable charges that made the rulers of the South squirm. It was, moreover, the passionate outcry of a man belonging to a class that had suffered nearly as much from the effects of slavery as had the slaves themselves—the poor whites, the "mudsills" of the South, nearly three-fourths of the white population in some of the slave states, yet helpless politically and suffering greater deprivation than many of the slaves. "We have endured much," wrote Helper, addressing himself to the slaveholders; "slaves only of the most despicable class would endure more. An enumeration or classification of all the abuses, insults, wrongs, injuries, usurpations, and oppressions, to which you have subjected us would fill a larger volume than this. Out of our effects you have long since overpaid yourselves for your negroes; and now, Sirs, you *must* emancipate them—speedily emancipate them, or we will emancipate them for you!"

The blunt-spoken Helper had no love for the Negro. Like most poor whites he felt an unreasonable resentment against the race that was the innocent cause of the ruin and degradation of his own class. But unlike most of that class he put the blame where it belonged—on the slaveholders—without, however, sufficiently understanding that they, too, were the victims of a system that had taken root in the South with the assistance of many Northerners. Making ample use of the census of 1850, compiled under the supervision of a learned Southerner, J. D. B. De Bow, he had no difficulty in demonstrating the pernicious effect of slavery upon the economy and cultural development of the South. He showed to what extent the slave states had fallen behind the free states in industry, in agriculture, in the material and intellectual well-being of the mass of their citizens, in all that constituted civilization. He bolstered his arguments by quotations from illustrious Southerners who had eloquently pleaded for the gradual abolition of the institution.

The fact that Helper was a Southerner, that his book was written in language the common man could understand, that it did not appeal for sympathy for the Negro but addressed itself to the self-interest of Southern nonslaveholders, made it a powerful propaganda document. The slaveholders were quick to realize this and its sale was forbidden in the South. In the North, however, it had an immediate success. Published at a time when the people of the North were aroused by the attempts of the slaveholders to extend their domain, it was admirably suited to bolster up resistance to such extension and to gain recruits for the Republican party. A compendium was prepared for general distribution, and Horace Greeley, Thurlow Weed, William Cullen Bryant, John Jay, and many others of note—including seventy Republican members of Congress—signed an appeal for funds to distribute a hundred thousand copies. The governor of New York headed the subscription list with a donation of one hundred dollars.

2

The Thirty-sixth Congress assembled on December 5, 1859. Neither the Republicans nor the Democrats were in the majority. There was a group known as South Americans and another known as Anti-Lecompton Democrats who held the balance of power. The former, mainly composed of Southern Know-Nothings and Whigs, agreed with the Republicans on some important issues, such as the tariff, but not on slavery; the latter was composed of followers of Stephen A. Douglas, who had broken with the administration about its attempt to force slavery upon Kansas. The Republicans, the largest political group, nominated for speaker John Sherman of Ohio; the Democrats nominated Thomas J. Bocock of Virginia. Stevens placed in nomination a candidate of his own—Galusha A. Grow of Pennsylvania, law partner of David Wilmot of the famous Wilmot Proviso. It was a complimentary gesture, and Grow withdrew after the first ballot. No sooner had the nominations been made than James B. Clark of Missouri, holding in his hand the manuscript of a prepared speech, rose to speak. Stevens, who from the beginning of the session appears to have assumed leadership of the Republicans, raised a point of order. Nothing, he said, was in order except balloting for speaker or a motion to adjourn. Clark pocketed his speech, but introduced a motion to the effect that no member who had endorsed Helper's book, which he termed "hostile to the domestic peace and tranquillity of the country," was "fit to be Speaker of the House." Both Republican candidates having endorsed the book, the fat was in the fire. The debate that followed, interrupted now and then by futile balloting, was to last for nearly two months.

Early in the debate Clark had an opportunity to read extracts from Helper's opus. After the reading John S. Millson of Virginia declared that one who had "lent his name and influence to the propagation of such writings, is not only unfit to be Speaker, but not fit to live." Sherman mildly explained that when he signed the letter of endorsement he had not read the book, but had relied on the judgment of previous signatories. Lawrence M. Keitt of South Carolina vehemently declared that all the South wanted was its rights, "but as God is my judge, I would shatter this Republic from turret to foundation before I would take a tittle less."

Stevens rose again and insisted that "until the House is organized it is not competent for the Clerk to entertain any question except that of proceeding with the election of the Speaker or on a motion to adjourn. . . . Not that I blame the gentlemen from the South for taking the course they do, although I deem it untimely and irregular. Nor do I blame them for the language of intimidation—for using the threat of rending God's creation from turret to foundation." In repeating Keitt's bombast he succeeded in making it sound so comical that the House burst into laughter. He waited until the laughter had subsided before making the statement that led to the first violent scene of the session.

"All is right with them," he said, "for they have tried it fifty times and fifty times they have found weak and recreant tremblers in the North who have been affected by it, and who have acted from those intimidations. They are right, therefore, and I give them credit for repeating with grave countenances that which they have so often found to be effective when operating upon timid men."

What was there in these words that kindled the wrath of the Southerners? Did they resent the irony, the intimation that their threats were empty bluster, which unfortunately they were not? Or was their anger due to a feeling of frustration, to the realization that threats had lost their potency, that they had cried wolf too often? Whatever the reason, there was an angry growl from the Southerners. William A. Crawford of Georgia sprang to his feet and advanced toward Stevens, fists clenched, face distorted with rage. A half-dozen of his Southern colleagues, looking equally belligerent, followed in his wake. But before they could reach the aged leader they were confronted by a bearded giant, who, arms folded, legs firmly braced, planted himself in front of Stevens. It was Roscoe Conkling of New York, six feet four, broad-shouldered and barrel-chested. He shook a lock of reddish-blond hair across his forehead with a defiant toss of his head and awaited the assault. It did not come. The chivalry retreated, Crawford shouting that the Republicans were abolitionists in disguise. "All we want," he cried, "is a square and manly avowal of your sentiments that our people may not be deceived. Do this and my life upon it, you will see no cowardly shrinking from the maintenance of every constitutional right to which our people are entitled."

Stevens had remained unperturbed and had not moved an inch. When the excitement had subsided he remarked with a humorous twinkle, the nearest thing to a smile that ever illumined his severe features: "That is the way they *used* to frighten us. Now you see exactly what it is, and what it has always been." He shrugged the incident off as "a momentary breeze," but the following day a Douglas Democrat, referring to it during a speech, said: "A few more such scenes and we will hear the crack of the revolver and see the gleam of brandished steel."

Lucius Lamar of Mississippi accused the Republicans of not being "guiltless of the blood of John Brown and his co-conspirators and the innocent men, the victims of their vengeance. . . . The Fathers had put the negro into the Constitution as an institution of property, and when that Constitution is violated I war upon your government; I am against it. I raise the banner of secession, and I will fight under it as long as the blood flows in my veins." Turning toward Stevens he added: "I almost tremble for the South when I recollect that the opposing forces will be led by the distinguished hero of the Buckshot War. However gloomy the catastrophe, his saltatory accomplishments will enable him to keep out of any difficulties in which he may be involved. I understand that he gave in a conspicuous way a practical illustration of peaceable secession."

3

During one of the numerous roll calls Stevens surprised his Republican colleagues by voting for John C. Gilmer of North Carolina, the largest slaveholder in Congress. It appears to have been a tactical move. Gilmer was an old-line Whig, leader of the South American party. Since there did not exist the remotest possibility that he would receive the required number of votes, Stevens apparently thought it advisable for a few Republicans to vote for him, since it might induce the South Americans to reciprocate by helping to elect a Republican. A number of Republican newspapers, however, expressed their astonishment and were of the opinion that Stevens owed the party an explanation. This gave him an opportunity for the exercise of his quaint sense of humor. He rose on a question of personal privilege and said that in this matter he had departed "from the general rule of obeying party decrees, which requires some explanation, as I see from a paper I sent to the Clerk's desk to be read." He would, therefore, be obliged if the clerk would now read the article he had marked.

"The paper is printed in German, and the Clerk cannot read it," exclaimed the puzzled official.

"Then I postpone my remarks till the Clerk can read it," said the solemn-faced Stevens, while a wave of laughter swept the House.

When the speechmaking and balloting had lasted a month, George W. Anderson of Missouri, an administration Democrat, said he wished to make an appeal in the interest of the country, whose credit was being endangered by the failure to pass the necessary appropriations. He invited both minority parties each to select a committee of three to meet that night at the Capitol with a committee selected by the Democrats and together "agree upon a full organization of the House, from Speaker to doorkeeper." Stevens rose and said he regretted the gentleman had not found it expedient to extend his patriotic invitation to the Republicans. He congratulated him, however, on his attempt to give reality to something hitherto regarded as a fable, "that happy family described in the *Prairie,* where the prairie wolf, the owl and the rattlesnake lived together in harmony in a hole. When they get together in this hole to-night I hope there will be no biting." This was greeted with laughter and applause. He proposed that the speaker be elected by a plurality vote, but the proposal did not find favor with the Democrats.

Tempers were becoming frayed. There were some violent scenes. At one time a challenge to a duel was flung by a Southerner to a Northern Democrat, but Stevens relieved the tension by his proposal that the gentlemen fight it out with dung forks. At another time a Douglas Democrat, during a verbal assault upon a Southern colleague, made a movement that caused a pistol to drop from his breast pocket. Southerners being under the impression that he had meant to draw it rushed upon him, while others hastened to his defense. Floor and gallery were in an uproar. The sergeant at arms appeared with the mace and the tumult was stilled.

In the course of the seemingly endless debate, Thomas Corwin of Ohio, who had nominated Sherman, said that in a climate where slave labor was the only kind that could be employed profitably, he was willing to admit its necessity. Such a statement from a leading Republican shocked Stevens profoundly. It virtually conceded the Southern contention that slavery was not morally wrong and that, if an evil at all, it was, in a hot climate, an unavoidable evil. Stevens repudiated that contention. On January 25, 1860, he took the floor with the intention of defining the principles of the party in clear and unmistakable language. Except for an awkward beginning it was one of the best speeches of his career.

4

He began by saying that he meant to address himself to the gentlemen of the Democratic party. By this, he said, he meant "the Democrats of the South—the others are mere parasites."

Clement L. Vallandigham of Ohio interrupted. He objected, he said, to the gentleman's "offensive language." Stevens replied he regretted not to have had foreknowledge of what the gentleman would approve. He was willing, he said, to withdraw the term "parasites" and substitute "satellites." The gentleman could hardly deny the accuracy of that term, since the Northern Democrats "revolved, of course, around the larger body, as according to the laws of gravitation they must." This was received with laughter. He paid his respects to President Buchanan, whom he charged with responsibility for the inability of the House to organize itself: "The distinguished gentleman who occupies the executive at this moment is a politician as well as a statesman. He has long believed, and I doubt not still believes, that the true way to aid the increase of the Democratic Party North, is for the South to frighten people into the belief that if they venture to elect a Northern man with Northern principles, the Union is to be dissolved and all their industrial and pecuniary interests sacrificed."

He predicted the failure of Buchanan's strategy, saying that as far as he was concerned he meant to remain firm even "if the House were not organized till the crack of doom," and believed his Republican colleagues would do the same. Then came the portion of his speech that many consider the ablest exposition of the party's principles made by any man of that period:

"Before I take my seat I will give an answer, plain, temperate and true, to all the allegations by stating what I consider the principles of the Republican Party. I would have no man vote under false pretenses. In my judgment Republicanism is founded in love of universal liberty, and in hostility to slavery and oppression throughout the world. Undoubtedly, had we the legal right and the physical power, we would abolish human servitude and overthrow despotism in every land that the sun visits in its diurnal course. But we claim no right to interfere with the institutions of foreign nations, or with the institutions of the sister States of this Republic. We would wish that Russia would liberate her serfs, Austria her oppressed subjects, Turkey her minions, and the South her slaves. But the law of nations gives us no authority to redress foreign grievances, and the Constitution of the United States gives us no power to interfere with the institutions of our sister States. And we do deny now, as we have ever denied, that there is any desire or intention, on the part of the Republican Party, to interfere with those institutions. It is a stern, an inflexible, a well-recognized principle of the Republican Party, that every law must be obeyed till it is either repealed or becomes so intolerable as to justify rebellion.

"But, sir, while we claim no power to interfere between foreign sovereignties and their subjects, there is no law to prevent our sympathizing with the oppressed of Italy, Turkey, or with the crushed souls of America; and, as we shall ever vindicate this liberty of speech, no earthly power shall prevent our giving utterance to such sentiments and denouncing such wrongs whenever we deem it proper. Sir, while we claim no power to interfere with any institution in the States, yet where the law of no State operates, and where the responsibility of government is thrown on Congress, we do claim the power to regulate and the right to abolish slavery. . . .

"Now, sir, the Territories, the District of Columbia, the navy yards, and the arsenals have no legislative bodies but Congress; and it is our purpose to provide in the exercise of our legislative duty for preventing the extension of slavery into free soil under the jurisdiction of the general government. I do not in this remark desire to shun the question. I do not found this remark on exclusion by climate, or latitude, or soil. My hostility to slavery is of a higher character, I trust, than that. If it was not, there would be no kind of necessity for the existence of the Republican Party at all. If I believed that slavery was right in itself, and it might be permitted in places where certain labor was or was not useful, I can not see what principle the Republican Party could stand upon. The whole ground is yielded, and this Republican Party, is a nuisance, and this agitation is a crime, in my judgment."

Regarding the abolition of slavery in the District of Columbia he said:

"Now sir, we agree with Clay and Webster and the other fathers of our earlier day, that while we have the power to abolish slavery in the District of Columbia, the time for its exercise is a question of expediency about which, I have no doubt, many men on this side of the House differ. I believe that most of us agree that that time has not yet arrived, nor do I see the period, for the present, when it will; but when it can be safely and justly abolished it is the purpose of Republicanism to do so.

"Now, sir, these are the principles of the Republican Party. Let those who approve them aid in their propagation. Let those who condemn these principles oppose us. For ourselves, we have resolved to stand by them until they shall become triumphant; and we cheerfully submit them to the judgment of our fellow countrymen, to the civilized nations of the earth, and to posterity."

5

Stevens's straightforward, yet temperate address made a favorable impression. Jere Clemens of Virginia rose and said: "The gentleman from Pennsylvania has, with a frankness and manliness which I admire, laid down the program of the Republican Party." He wished to know, however, what stand Stevens and his party meant to take regarding the Fugitive Slave Law. Stevens replied that as far as he was concerned, he considered the law unconstitutional and hoped the time would soon come when its constitutionality could be tested, but that as long as it remained on the statute books he meant to obey it. Moreover, since the Constitution gave the slaveholders the right to reclaim fugitive slaves, he would not object to "a fair law giving the South the opportunity to reclaim their slaves."

Clemens continued his interrogation. Had not Stevens at one time said that it was the policy of his party "to encircle the Slave States of the Union with Free States as a cordon of fire, and that then slavery like a scorpion would sting itself to death?"

"If I did," Stevens replied, "it's in the books." He was of the opinion, however, that the gentleman was mistaken in ascribing the aphorism to him. He believed a colleague from New York had said something to that effect.

Clemens said it was his recollection the saying had originated with the gentleman from Pennsylvania. But no matter. Assuming that the Republicans were in possession of the power, patronage, and prestige of the presidency and controlled the army and the navy—assuming also that they excluded slavery from the territories, from arsenals, dockyards, and forts—would not a situation have been created that would compel slavery, like the proverbial scorpion, to sting itself to death?

Everybody in the House knew the answer to that question. The answer was—Yes! Would Stevens claim that with the power of the federal government in Republican hands and slavery irrevocably confined to the slave states, the institution could continue to flourish, or would he boldly reply that under those circumstances it would be doomed to extinction? He did neither, but said amidst general laughter: "I do not know, not being a prophet."

Thomas B. Florence, Democrat from Pennsylvania, rose and said he wanted to present to his colleague "a question of figures," which he might be able to answer, "because I know my colleague was once a schoolmaster."

"Yes," said Stevens, "I am proud to say I have taught several hopeful boys. I wish I had taught you too."

This provoked considerable merriment. Florence, somewhat discomfited, asked how the Democrats—a minority of ninety—could be blamed for the nonorganization of the House, when it took one hundred and sixteen to elect a speaker; and how did it happen that the gentleman possessed such intimate knowledge about what happened at the White House? Stevens replied: "If my friend and about five men would slip outside some day during the voting—get a little sick, or go out to get something to eat, or anything—we would then elect a Speaker. As to my intelligence about White House affairs, the gentleman must remember that the President is one of my constituents." There was renewed laughter, but this time Florence had an answer ready. "If the gentleman represents his other constituents no better than he does the President, there is little hope for him," he remarked.

The struggle for the speakership was drawing to a close. The Republicans realized that Sherman could not be elected and presented as their candidate William Pennington of New Jersey. He had not signed the controversial endorsement of Helper's book and was an old-line Whig who as governor of his state had urged the strict enforcement of the Fugitive Slave Law. So, on February 1, 1860, after nearly two months of incessant wrangling, the House finally organized. Sherman became chairman of the important Committee on Ways and Means, of which Stevens became a member.

During that session of Congress Stevens made a speech on the tariff which presented nothing new. When a demand was made for a larger appropriation for the army, so settlers could be given adequate protection from the Indians, he remarked: "I think there would be less danger upon our border if the white men were watched and the Indians protected; instead of the Indians being watched and the whites protected."

CHAPTER V

Secession

Stevens was a member of the Pennsylvania delegation to the Republican National Convention in Chicago that nominated Lincoln for the presidency. He went accompanied by his nephew Thad and wore a tall white hat, distinguishing mark of the delegation.

Most of his colleagues were pledged to vote on the first ballot for Simon Cameron, senator from their state and a member of the delegation. Stevens, for the third time in his political career, favored Associate Justice John McLean. Seward he considered out of the question for the same reason that four years earlier he had opposed the nomination of Frémont. Thurlow Weed's protégé was *persona non grata* with the Know-Nothings, whose help was indispensable for victory in Pennsylvania and Indiana. Governor Andrew Curtin and most of the delegation agreed with Stevens on the unavailability of Seward, but there existed a certain amount of uncertainty whether Lincoln or Edward Bates would be the final choice of the Pennsylvania delegates. Cameron took advantage of this to make a bargain with Lincoln's manager David Davis which netted him a place in the cabinet.

Stevens, together with several other members of the delegation, voted for McLean on the first two ballots, but on the third, decisive ballot, voted for Lincoln.[1] In 1848, Lincoln, returning from a speak-

1 Professor Current claims that Stevens voted for McLean on all three ballots. He presents no proof. In February, 1861, Stevens said on the floor of the House: "If he [Lincoln] is what I understood him to be when I voted for him, it is his intention to retake all the public property." Alexander K. McClure has written: "He [Stevens] voted

ing engagement in the East, where he had been campaigning for Taylor, wrote to Stevens: "I desire the undisguised opinion of some experienced person and sagacious Pennsylvania politician, as to how the vote of that state, for governor and president, is likely to go. In casting about for such a man I have settled upon you." Stevens had replied promptly and Lincoln had thanked him, but there had been no further intercourse between them.

Stevens threw himself wholeheartedly into the campaign, emphasizing in his speeches the slavery issue rather than the tariff. "He was one of Mr. Lincoln's most efficient supporters," John W. Forney has written. It appears that he cherished the ambition of becoming a member of Lincoln's cabinet. "In obedience to his invitation," wrote McClure, "I met him at Harrisburg, and found him more interested in reaching the Cabinet than I had ever known him in any of his political aspirations. . . . And the position he desired was that of Secretary of the Treasury." But in conformity with the bargain made by his manager, Lincoln, after much hesitation, appointed Cameron secretary of war.

That the President-elect should have hesitated about Cameron's appointment need not surprise us. The Pennsylvania Senator had an unsavory reputation. Jackson described him in a letter as "not to be trusted by any one in any way." Polk characterized him in his *Diary* as "a managing tricky man in whom no reliance is to be placed." Buchanan called him an "unprincipled rascal." He had been a Democrat until 1856, having, according to Polk, joined the Democratic party to serve "his own personal and sinister purposes." Stevens apparently believed he had joined the Republican party for the same reason. In obedience to party regularity he had supported him for the Senate in 1857, but to have him serve as a member of the cabinet at so critical a time was too much. In April, 1861, he gave the following explanation in the House of his attitude toward Cameron: "I, together with eight or ten others of my colleagues, waited on Mr. Lincoln and protested against his [Cameron's] appointment as a member of the Cabinet. We did not think that he had the capacity. We gave other strong reasons why he should not be appointed."

for Lincoln simply because it was not possible to nominate any other man more in accord with his convictions." (*Lincoln and Men of War Times,* p. 259.)

That Cameron did not have the capacity was fully demonstrated. What the "other strong reasons" were may be inferred from the fact that soon after Cameron had taken office, Stevens again called on Lincoln and said things about his Secretary of War that prompted the President to ask: "Why, Mr. Stevens, you don't think the Secretary would steal, do you?" "Well, Mr. President," Stevens replied, "I don't think he would steal a red-hot stove." This in some way came to the ears of Cameron, who called on Stevens and demanded that he accompany him to the White House and take back what he had said. Stevens promptly complied. When they stood before the President, Stevens said: "Mr. President, I told you the other day that Mr. Cameron would not steal a red-hot stove. I now take that back."

The cause of the Negro was, however, so close to Stevens's heart that when Cameron took a position in advance of his colleagues in the cabinet and of the President himself concerning the enrollment of Negroes as soldiers, Stevens became one of his supporters. He explained in the House: "He was in favor of employing fugitives from labor or service in the service of the United States. . . . I felt he was right, and I said here, and I stated everywhere, that I would support him so long as he pursued that course. . . . I told him further that I would look upon his past record as a blank sheet, and would judge him by his official conduct."

Stevens had no high opinion of the cabinet as a whole. James G. Blaine has written: "Thaddeus Stevens, with his accustomed sharpness of speech, said the Cabinet was composed of an assortment of rivals whom the President appointed from courtesy, one stump speaker from Indiana, and two representatives of the Blair family."

2

When Congress convened in December, 1860, South Carolina had already seceded and the Gulf states were inclining toward secession. Over the North brooded an atmosphere of impending disaster. Lincoln was in Springfield conferring with his advisers about cabinet appointments, but for the rest kept his own counsel. The country still had to rely on Buchanan for leadership. He appeared before Congress to deliver a message that, considering the gravity of the occasion, should have equaled the Declaration of Independence in loftiness of outlook and firmness of resolve. The document he produced was mischievous, contradictory, and confusing.

Having repeated the charges made by Southern extremists against the North and having pronounced them justified, he informed his listeners that "no single Act had ever passed Congress, unless the Missouri Compromise was an exception, impairing in the slightest degree the rights of the South to their property in slaves." This, however, did not prevent him from declaring that the "injured States, after having used all peaceful means to obtain redress, would be justified in revolutionary resistance to the government of the Union"—equivalent to saying that when a minority has exhausted all legal means to obtain what it desires it is justified in resorting to force. He then declared that South Carolina lacked that justification. Nevertheless, "after much serious reflection," he had "reached the conclusion that no power has been delegated to Congress, or to any other department of the Federal Government, to coerce a State into submission which is attempting to withdraw, or has already withdrawn."

Seward interpreted the message to mean that "a State had no right to secede unless she wanted to, and that the Government must save the Union, unless somebody opposes it." Stevens did not attempt interpretation, but when it was proposed to refer portions of the message to a committee, he voted against it, considering it unworthy of any consideration whatever.

3

That no leadership could be expected from the solemn-faced nonentity in the White House was apparent to all. The Senate and the House now took the matter in hand and appointed committees on conciliation, composed of members from both sections of the country. The Senate committee was composed of thirteen members, symbolical of the thirteen original states; the House committee had thirty-three, one from each state. Stevens called the House committee derisively the "Committee on Incubation." He believed there were matters a nation that valued its survival as a nation could not afford to compromise. The principal one of these was, in his opinion, rebellion by a disgruntled minority. He did, however, nothing to obstruct the efforts of his colleagues and even left Washington for a while. He wrote to Edward McPherson, son of his banker friend, who had been elected to Congress: "I do not care to be present while the process of humiliation is going on—Buchanan is a very traitor."

The Senate committee quickly became aware that, in the words of Blaine, "any agreement that could be reached would humiliate the North without appeasing or satisfying the South." The less realistic House committee managed to produce a report which received the approval of the majority of its members. The length to which Republicans were willing to go to appease the slaveholders borders on the fantastic. Charles Francis Adams, who in 1848 had been the Free-Soil candidate for vice-president, declared that rather than permit a breakup of the Union "every other cause should be sacrificed"! He proposed a Thirteenth Amendment to the Constitution that in its final form read: "No amendment shall be made to the Constitution which will authorize or give to Congress the power to abolish, or interfere, within any State, with the domestic institutions thereof, including that of persons held to labor or service by the laws of that State." This meant that slavery in the United States could not be constitutionally abolished so long as a single state objected. Since the foundation of the republic no slaveholders' representative had had the temerity to make such a proposal, yet it now passed both houses of Congress—133 to 65 in the House, 24 to 12 in the Senate. Eight Republican senators voted for it. What is more, Lincoln of the "House Divided" speech was to say in his inaugural address: "I understand a proposed amendment to the Constitution . . . has passed Congress, to the effect that the federal government, shall never interfere with the domestic institutions of the States, including that of persons held to service. . . . I have no objection to its being made express, and irrevocable."

Other proposals in the committee's majority report were for Congress to make a declaration that it was "highly inexpedient to abolish slavery in the District of Columbia unless with the consent of the States of Maryland and Virginia"; that the states be requested to repeal all personal liberty laws; that fugitive slaves be tried not in the state in which they were caught, but in the state from which they were supposed to have fled, which would have made it unsafe for any free Negro to reside in the North; that a law should be enacted providing that all offenses against slave property should be tried where the offense was committed. Since in some of the slave states it was considered an offense against slave property to say that slavery was morally wrong, Lincoln, among others, could have been extradited had he said concerning slavery in the South what he had said in the North. The committee further proposed that New Mexico (including Arizona) be admitted as a slave state, but the proposal failed to pass, notwithstanding the support of Seward and Cameron.

A minority report, known as the Crittenden Compromise, presented by five Southern members of the committee, called for no less than six constitutional amendments, which would have made slavery the most zealously guarded institution in the country, and might well have made the world wonder if the principal result of the American Revolution had not been to make the American continent safe for slavery.

If Republican victory did not prove slavery's greatest triumph it was no fault of the Republicans. Not only were they willing to make slavery perpetual by an irrevocable constitutional amendment—not only were they ready to make pledges to the slaveholders such as had never before been made, but in violation of pledges made in their platform they voted to admit the Territories of Dakota, Colorado, and Nevada without any restrictions on slavery whatever! "Never before in the existence of the Federal Government had its territory been so open, by Congressional enactment and by judicial decision, to the slave-holder as on the day that Abraham Lincoln assumed the office of President of the United States," wrote James G. Blaine. The slaveholders saved the day for liberty by their intransigence.

4

Stevens did not long remain absent from the scene. The previous year, speaking upon the death of an aged colleague from Pennsylvania, he had said: "It were perhaps more graceful for those who are conscious that age or infirmity had impaired their mental and physical powers, who find by repeated trials that they can no longer bend the bow of Ulysses, to retire and lay down the discus which they have not the strength to hurl."

Old age and infirmity were upon him, but he did not consider himself incapable of bending the bow of Ulysses or of hurling the discus. He was nearing threescore and ten, rheumatism plagued him, his face looked ravaged, his voice was hoarse; yet, in the midst of so many younger and more vigorous men, he was a tower of strength. In him burned an unquenchable flame of conviction and determination. He rejected all thought of compromise concerning an issue which, in his opinion, it was treason to raise. He believed Congress should occupy itself with stamping out rebellion, not with talk of compromise which, he felt, would either lead to nothing, or, what might prove even worse, would merely postpone the struggle, giving the rebels more time to prepare. "I think that this rebellion has not come an hour too soon," he was to say later. "Every humane and patriotic heart must grieve to see a bloody and causeless rebellion, costing thousands of human lives and millions of treasure. But as it was predetermined and inevitable, it was long enough delayed. Now is the appropriate time to solve the greatest problem ever submitted to civilized men." [2]

On December 31, 1860, he had introduced a resolution calling upon the President to inform the House concerning the condition of the forts, arsenals, and public properties in the vicinity of the city of Charleston; the measures taken to put the forts in a state of defense; the strength of the garrisons, and the orders given to reinforce them when it became evident that South Carolina intended to secede. Under the rules of the House the resolution, to be binding upon the President, had to pass by a two-thirds vote. Had it received the requisite majority the effect on future events might have been incalculable. It passed by a vote of 91 to 62, and undoubtedly contributed toward stiffening the attitude of the administration toward the secessionists.

On January 28, 1861, Roger A. Pryor of Virginia said on the floor of the House that no compromise could now save the Union. The following morning newspapers reported that South Carolina had rejected Virginia's proposal "to help formulate amendments to the Constitution for security of their rights." The Palmetto State had

[2] *Globe,* Jan. 22, 1862.

replied that she did not "deem it advisable to initiate negotiations when we have no desire or intention to promote the object in view," and that its separation was "final." That same day Stevens rose and delivered a speech that had the quality of Danton's "Dare! Dare! And dare again!" shouted to a wavering National Assembly during one of the darkest hours of the French Revolution. Congressman Henry L. Dawes of Massachusetts was to say after Stevens's death: "He was then an old man approaching seventy, on whose frame and voice time had already made sad inroads, but still standing erect and firm as a man of thirty-five." He began by apologizing for the huskiness of his voice, which, he said, was due to ill-health and might prevent him from being heard in all parts of the hall. So great already was his authority that scores of members left their seats and formed a ring around him, so they might miss nothing of what he had to say. Henceforth, whenever he rose to make an important speech the scene was repeated.

"I regret, Sir," he said, addressing himself to the Chair, "that I am compelled to concur in the belief stated yesterday by the gentleman from Virginia, that no compromise which can be made will have any effect in averting the present difficulty. . . . When I see these States in open and declared rebellion against the Union, seizing upon her public forts and arsenals, and robbing her of millions of public property; when I see the batteries of seceding States blockading the highways of the nation, and their armies in battle array against the flag of the Union; when I see, Sir, our flag insulted, and that insult submitted to, I have no hope that concession, humiliation and compromise can have any effect whatever.

"The question of the dissolution of the Union is a grave one, and should be approached without excitement, or passion, or fear. Homilies upon the Union, and jeremiads over its destruction, can be of no use, except to display fine rhetoric and pathetic eloquence. The Southern States will not be turned from their deliberate and stern purpose by soft words and touching lamentations. After the extent to which they have gone, it would do them no credit; condemnation which is now felt for their conduct, would degenerate into contempt. . . . The virtue most needed in time of peril is courage, calm, unwavering courage, which no danger can appall, and which will not be excited by indignation or revenge. . . . If such statesmen, governed by such qualities should be found at the head of this nation when danger comes, there can be no fear of the result."

Referring to Buchanan's statement that the federal government had no right to coerce a state that chose to leave the Union, he said: "It is time to decide whether this nation exists by the sufferance of individual States or whether it required a constitutional majority to absolve them from their allegiance. . . . If it should be determined that secession is a rightful act, or that there is no power to prevent it, then this Union is not worth preserving for a single day. Whatever disposition we may make of the present difficulty, fancied wrong will constantly arise and induce State after State to withdraw from the confederacy. If, on the other hand, it should be decided that we are *one people* and the government possesses sufficient power to coerce obedience, the public mind will be quieted, plotters of disunion will be regarded as traitors, and we shall long remain a happy and united people."

As immediate measures to be taken in the crisis he advocated depriving the rebellious states of national services; holding federal fortifications at all cost; if federal revenues cannot be collected, "abolish all laws establishing ports of entry and collection districts within the seceding States and prevent all vessels, foreign or domestic, from entering or leaving any of their ports."

He addressed this solemn warning to the South: "Let no Slave State flatter itself that it can dissolve the Union now and then reconstruct it upon better terms. The present Constitution was formed in our weakness. Some of its compromises were odious and have become more so by the unexpected increase of slaves. Now in our strength the conscience of the North would not allow them to enter into such a partnership with slavery. . . . *While we will religiously observe the present compact nor attempt to be absolved from it, yet if it should be torn to pieces by rebels, our next United States will contain no foot of ground on which a slave can breathe.*[3] Then we can boast of liberty. Then we can rise and expand to the full stature of untrammeled freemen and hope for God's blessing. Then the bondmen who break their chains will find a city of refuge."

To the assertion that the senators from his state, both of whom favored compromise, more truly represented the sentiment of the

[3] Italics added.

people of Pennsylvania, he replied: "Pennsylvania would go, as I would, to the verge of the Constitution and of her principles to maintain peace. But it is a libel on the good name of her virtuous people to say that she would sacrifice her principles to obtain the favor of rebels. I believe it to be a libel on her manhood to say that she will purchase peace by concessions to insurgents with arms in their hands. If I thought such was her character, I would expatriate myself. I would leave the land where I have spent my life from early manhood to declining age and would seek some spot untainted by the coward breath of servility and meanness."

PART THREE

THE STRUGGLE WITH LINCOLN

CHAPTER I

The "Natural Leader"

When Congress was not in session Stevens could be found in his law office in Lancaster. Thad, the elder of his two nephews, who had been admitted to the bar, now had charge of the office during his absence, while the younger, Alanson, was assistant to John Sweeney, manager of the ironworks. In the spring of 1860 when Stevens made an unexpected visit to the works, he and Sweeney were conversing outside when he noticed a thin veil of smoke rising from the chimney of a cabin he believed to be unoccupied.

"Anybody living there?" he asked.

Sweeney explained with some embarrassment that Alanson had "gone to housekeeping" there with a girl named Mary Primm. "Mr. Stevens said it was very bad behavior on the place," the manager later related; "that was all that was said on the subject, and Mr. Stevens remarked as we parted, 'Charge him with whatever he gets.' "

The affair was to have an unhappy ending. When after the fall of Fort Sumter Lincoln called for volunteers, Alanson enlisted for three months. In the autumn he returned to Caledonia, but it was not a joyful home-coming. One day he remarked moodily to a workman that he wished he had "got killed." The man asked him why. "Then I would be out of trouble," he said. Soon after, with a burst of energy, he recruited a company of volunteers and was off to war again.

In September, 1863, after the Battle of Chickamauga, Stevens received word that Alanson had been killed in action. Thad, who went to claim the body, wrote to his uncle: "Alanson was shot through the left breast. His body is in the hands of the enemy and I do not suppose it can be obtained."

2

News of the fall of Fort Sumter, followed by the news that Virginia had joined the Confederacy, reached Stevens in Lancaster. On April 19 a regiment of Massachusetts militia, passing through Baltimore on its way to Washington, was attacked by a mob. There were dead and wounded. That same day Stevens learned that Lincoln had proclaimed a blockade of the Confederate coast. The news worried him. To declare a blockade meant *de facto* recognition of the Confederacy: a nation did not blockade its own coast. In his opinion the President should have issued an order closing all Southern ports and have had the navy enforce that order. The result would have been the same, but no nation could then have recognized the Confederacy on the pretext that the United States had already done so. What was done could not be undone, but Stevens decided to go to Washington and have a talk with the President.

The Washington to which he returned was full of alarming rumors: Confederate cavalry was about to raid the city; suspicious-looking craft had been seen lurking on the Potomac; a mortar battery had been planted on the Virginia heights and a bombardment might be expected at any moment; a plot had been discovered to kidnap or to assassinate the President! Unionists felt comforted by the thought that the Massachusetts militia was encamped in the lobby of the Capitol, that "Cash" Clay, the fiery Kentucky abolitionist, was drilling a regiment in Willard's Hall, and that Kansas "Jayhawkers" under the command of the redoubtable Jim Lane were guarding the White House.

Stevens lost no time in calling on the President.

Those of Lincoln's contemporaries who have left descriptions of him have with few exceptions emphasized his homeliness, the awkwardness of his appearance, the ill-fit of his clothing. Nor, on first acquaintance, did his mentality appeal to men of intellect. Carl Schurz has written that Lincoln "occasionally spoke about important affairs of State with the same nonchalance—I almost say irreverence—with which he might have discussed an every-day law case in his office at Springfield, Illinois." Thoughtful men felt repelled by his inveterate habit of storytelling, especially as the stories were sometimes off-color.[1] Charles Francis Adams, wartime minister to Great Britain, after a first visit to the White House, was so unfavorably impressed that ever after he considered Lincoln unfit for the high office he occupied. It was only on closer acquaintance that the homeliness began to fascinate, as one might develop a taste for a tart but choice vintage, and qualities of heart and mind began to reveal themselves that evoked respect and admiration.

A portraitist or student of human nature would have been intrigued by the contrast between Lincoln and Stevens as the two sat opposite each other at the President's desk. If Lincoln was homely, Stevens in his old age was far from handsome. But John W. Forney, famous editor of the Philadelpia *Press,* has written that "no one who saw him could ever forget him." Rutherford B. Hayes wrote about him in a letter to his wife: "The only blemish in his puritanical, severe appearance was his brown wig." He looked like an angry eagle, with his hollow cheeks, his aquiline nose, his deep-set eyes, his firm-set mouth, his outthrust lower lip. The whole expression was one of severity and resolution. The student of human nature would probably have said that if prompt, forceful action was required, Stevens was the better man, if patience and forbearance were principally needed, Lincoln was by far the superior.

When the visitor had explained the difference between a blockade and an order closing the ports, the President said: "Well, that is a fact. I see the point now, but I don't know anything about the law of nations and I thought it was all right."

"As a lawyer, Mr. Lincoln, I should have thought you would have seen the difference at once," Stevens remarked.

"Oh, well," the President replied, "I'm a good enough lawyer in a western court, but we don't practice the law of nations there, and I supposed Seward knew all about it, and left it to him. But it's done

[1] *Reminiscences of Abraham Lincoln by Distinguished Men of His Time,* Allen Thorndike Rice, ed., pp. 485-486; Villard, *Memoirs,* vol. I, pp. 143-144.

now and can't be helped, so we must get along as well as we can." [2]

3

The Thirty-seventh Congress assembled in extraordinary session on July 4, 1861. No important battle had yet been fought. The disloyal governor of Missouri had been driven out by the Union Army. There had been small military successes in western Virginia and the upper Potomac, small reverses near Hampton Roads and near Washington.

James G. Blaine, describing the assembling of the Thirty-seventh Congress, wrote: "The natural leader, who assumed his place by common consent, was Thaddeus Stevens, a man of strong peculiarities of character, able, trained and fearless." Alexander K. McClure has written: "There were those around him in Congress much riper in experience in national legislation, for he had served but six years in the House when the war began, and four of these were nearly a decade before the rebellion; but when the great conflict came before which all the brave-hearted quailed, Stevens' supreme ability and dauntless courage made him speedily accepted by all as the leader of the popular branch of Congress."

Stevens was now chairman of the Committee on Ways and Means, which then also fulfilled the functions of what is now the Committee on Appropriations. Its chairman could rise at any time to discuss measures within the committee's jurisdiction and took precedence in the discussion of any other measure. He made use of his prerogatives to the utmost. "He was a born dictator in politics," McClure has written. When he wished to expedite a measure he would shut off debate by moving the previous question, call for suspension of the rules, or limit discussion to one hour—five minutes—one minute—once even half a minute! In the party caucus his word was law and he brooked no insubordination. When a colleague protested that his conscience would not permit him to vote for a party measure, he banged his fist on the table and shouted: "Conscience, hell! Throw conscience to the devil and stand by the party!" McClure speaks of his "iron will and ruthless mastery" in commanding a solid party vote

[2] New York *Herald*, July 8, 1867.

on measures to which many in the party objected. "I sat by him one morning in the House," he relates, "before the session had opened when the question of negro suffrage in the District of Columbia was about to be considered, and I heard a leading Pennsylvania Republican approach him to protest against committing the party to that policy. Stevens' grim face and cold grey eye gave answer to the man before his bitter words were uttered. He waved his hand to the trembling suppliant and bade him go to his seat and vote for the measure or confess himself a coward before the world. The Commoner was obeyed, for had disobedience followed, the offender would have been proclaimed to his constituents, over the name of Stevens, as a coward, and that would have doomed him to defeat."

No man can acquire and hold such power in a democracy unless he possesses to an extraordinary degree the confidence of the people. Stevens possessed qualities of intellect and character that made him peculiarly fitted to be a leader during a crisis. He had in the past sometimes misused those qualities. Now, unreservedly placed at the service of the country and the cause of human liberty, they proved invaluable. McClure has written: "Lincoln as President and Stevens as Commoner of the nation during the entire period of the sectional war assumed the highest civil responsibilities in the administrative and legislative departments of the government. While Lincoln was President of the whole people, Stevens, as Commoner, was their immediate representative and oracle of the popular branch of Congress when the most momentous legislative measures of our history were conceived and enacted." [3] McClure put his finger on the reason for the differences between Lincoln and Stevens when he wrote that *"Lincoln believed that he might best save the Union by saving slavery,"* while Stevens, from the beginning of the conflict, was *"the master-spirit of every aggressive movement in Congress to overthrow the Rebellion and slavery."* [4] Stevens believed there was a political as well as a military battle front on which hard blows could and should be struck. He believed the best and quickest way to crush the rebellion was to strike at slavery.

[3] McClure, *Lincoln and Men of War Times,* p. 255.
[4] *Ibid.,* pp. 93, 265.

4

Carl Schurz has said of Stevens's ability as a public speaker: "In the great French struggle his oratory would have outblazed Mirabeau." His speeches were short, to the point, enlivened by a tart, ironical wit. Charles Sumner remarked that no man could express more in fewer words or give "to language a sharper bite." James G. Blaine has written: "He spoke with ease and readiness, using a style somewhat resembling the crisp, clear sententiousness of Dean Swift. Seldom, even in the most careless moment, did a sentence escape his lips, that would not bear the test of grammatical and rhetorical criticism. He possessed the keenest wit, and was unmerciful in its use towards those whom he did not like. He illustrated in concrete form the difference between wit and humor. He did not indulge in the latter. He did not enjoy a laugh. When his sharp sallies would set the entire House in uproar, he was as impassive, his visage as solemn, as if he were pronouncing a funeral oration . . . a man who had the courage to meet any opponent, and who was never overmatched in intellectual conflict." Rutherford B. Hayes wrote to his wife: "He is witty, cool, full of and fond of 'sarcasms,' and thoroughly informed and accurate. He has a knack of saying things which turn the laugh on his opponent. When he rises everyone expects something worth hearing, and he has the attention of all. . . . He is leader."

He was impatient with men whose vanity prompted them to make needless display of oratory. Replying to James Brooks of New York, who had made a long prepared address replete with lengthy quotations from history and literature, he referred ironically to "the gentleman's elaborate speech, so full of literary and historical allusions, which in superficial scholars might look like pedantry, but in the learned gentleman are but the graceful overflow of a well-stored mind."

When displeased with an argument made by a colleague he often managed to spoil its effect by a satirical remark that provoked general laughter. Once when a member kept walking back and forth while making such an argument, Stevens interrupted him with the query: "Do you expect to collect mileage for that speech?" When Vallandigham of Ohio, explaining a call for a caucus made by the Democrats, attempted to be facetious by saying: "That call has been signed by thirty-five members of the House of Representatives, all of them able to read and write—no one made his mark," Stevens commented loud enough for all to hear: "Nor ever will!"

Stories about his wit, his quickness at repartee, his devastating sarcasm made the rounds of Washington, and witticisms uttered by him have often been attributed to others. When a member who had the peculiar habit of prefacing his remarks with an apology concerning their lack of importance asked Stevens to yield the floor, he obliged with the words: "I now yield the floor to the honorable gentleman from . . . who will make a few feeble remarks." Once when he came into the House during a debate concerning a contested seat, he asked a Republican colleague about the merits of the case. "They're both damned rascals," the man replied. "Which is *our* damned rascal," Stevens inquired. A member of the opposition who had indulged in personalities during a speech received this reply: "The gentleman who has just spoken need not fear that I will make an attack upon him. There are some reptiles so flat that the foot of man cannot crush them." The historian Alexander Harris, who was of a quarrelsome disposition and not on good terms with the Commoner, once met him on a narrow path leading through a rain-soaked field outside Lancaster. Planting himself squarely in front of Stevens he said belligerently: "I don't go out of the way for a skunk." "I do!" said Stevens and walked around him.

In the *Congressional Globe* of that period one frequently finds the following between parentheses: "Mr. Stevens from his seat made some remark inaudible to the reporter." It refers to the running commentary Stevens indulged in loud enough for those around him to hear and be amused. Congressman Justin S. Morrill of Vermont has written: "Never indeed was wit of all varieties, coarse and fine, exhibited in more bewildering confusion. He daily wasted in this private and semi-grotesque distribution of mirth, sense and satire, often indiscriminately among friends and foes, a capital sufficient, could it have been preserved, to rival almost any of the acknowledged masters among colloquial wits of this and possibly of any age."

CHAPTER II

The Great Commoner

Salmon Portland Chase, secretary of the treasury, appeared before Congress at the extraordinary session and gave an estimate of the government's expenses for the ensuing fiscal year. To the present generation, accustomed to having the government spend billions in peacetime, that estimate will seem surprisingly low. It proved as a matter of fact far too optimistic. To Stevens and his colleagues, however, it must have appeared formidable indeed, being more than four times the amount of the public debt and about five times the annual revenue during Buchanan's administration. Chase asked for $320,000,000. One-fourth of this (for ordinary expenses) was to be raised by taxation; the balance (for the financing of the war) was to be obtained by borrowing. The reason the Secretary did not recommend that a larger portion come from the pockets of the taxpayers appears to have been that the President as well as he felt convinced the war would be short. Why not wait until it was over and then tax the South as well as the North to pay the cost? Before a week had passed there came the disaster of Bull Run, and Washington saw the debris of what had been an army sweeping through its streets, but even this did not change the prevailing notion that the war would not last long.

Stevens was one of the few men in Congress who did not share the general opinion concerning the duration of the war. On July 24, 1861, he said: "I look upon it, as I have looked upon it ever since these States went deliberately into treason, as one which will be a protracted and bloody war. . . . I believe that the battles which are to be fought are to be desperate and bloody battles, and that they are to be numerous. I believe that many thousand valuable lives will be lost, and that millions of money will be expended." He did not agree with the administration's light taxing program: "The only question is whether this Government is prepared to meet all these perils and overcome them. If they are, they must submit to taxes which are burdensome: which the people at any other time, would not submit to for a moment, but which I believe they will now submit to." Realizing, however, the uselessness of trying to overcome the combined opposition of Congress and the administration, he did not insist. Time pressed. Buchanan had left an empty treasury and an impaired national credit. There was no money to pay the army. So he called his committee together and advised support of the administration's program. Three days after Chase had made his proposals Stevens presented his report. The following day he called up a bill authorizing the Secretary to borrow $250,000,000. He demanded suspension of the rules and limited debate to one hour. Vallandigham of Ohio was allowed to have his say without being vouchsafed a reply, then the gavel fell, the vote was taken, and the measure passed with only five dissenting votes. The Senate followed the example of the House.

When the Revenue Bill came up for discussion, Stevens did his best to raise the national revenue. Among the measures he favored was a direct tax on real estate. He deserves some credit for this, for not only was most of his capital invested in that form of property, but he represented one of the richest farming districts in the country and knew that his constituents would be displeased. Representatives from farming districts put up so determined an opposition that he was obliged to make important concessions, which greatly reduced the revenue he had hoped to raise by this means. Eventually an income tax was resorted to which in the last year of the war produced more revenue than had been obtained from all sources before the outbreak of hostilities. On August 5, less than three weeks after the Revenue Bill had been presented to the House, it became law, and Congress was ready to adjourn. "In no other session of Congress," James G. Blaine has written, "was so much accomplished in so brief a time."

2

Secretary Chase had contacted banks in New York, Philadelphia, and Boston, who agreed to lend the government $50,000,000 immediately and like amounts the fifteenth of October and of December. They were to receive three-year treasury notes bearing 7.3 per cent interest. The country was then on a gold basis and the total gold reserve of the contracting banks was only $63,000,000. The bankers expected, however, that the Secretary would allow the gold to remain in their vaults and would pay suppliers with bank notes or by check. They likewise expected that those receiving payment would not immediately draw out the amount in specie, but would be satisfied with bank credits. They even hoped to increase their supply of gold by selling the treasury notes to the public. None of these hopes was fulfilled. The Secretary—a hard money man if there ever was one—insisted on paying with specie. The suppliers did not redeposit the specie but hoarded it. The sale of treasury notes proved disappointing.

The banks paid the October installment of the loan, but in November something happened that aggravated the situation. An overzealous naval officer stopped the British steamer *Trent* and removed two Confederate commissioners, one accredited to Great Britain, the other to France. He brought them and their secretaries triumphantly to the United States, where they were interned at Fort Warren, in Boston Harbor. The people and even Congress applauded, but the British government and public became so incensed that fresh war clouds began to gather. The matter was finally adjusted, but in the meantime the administration had itself dealt a blow to the national credit. Secretary Chase had presented a report to Congress in which he had asked for huge appropriations, but had again recommended a wholly inadequate taxing program. When the December installment of the loan fell due, the banks refused to accept treasury notes as security. They demanded twenty-year 6 per cent government bonds, and would take these only at a discount of over 10 per cent. Chase was forced to comply and received less than $45,000,000 instead of the fifty he had expected. As a result of all this the public became alarmed and businessmen began drawing their money from the banks—not in bank notes, which they no longer trusted, but in specie. The banks, seeing their gold reserve shrinking rapidly, took drastic action. On December 28, 1861, all the banks in the country stopped specie payments and the Treasury had to follow suit.

3

The situation was one of the most alarming the country had ever faced. At home and abroad many feared national bankruptcy. The sum that had to be raised if military operations were not to come to a standstill appeared staggering. Chase had underestimated the expenses for the current fiscal year by $214,000,000. In addition to this he asked $475,000,000 for the fiscal year ending June 30, 1863. The revenue he estimated at $95,000,000, leaving over $600,000,000 to be appropriated. Demands on the Treasury were $2,000,000 per day. Gold and silver specie had ceased to circulate; they had become commodities. The only remaining medium of exchange was the notes of some sixteen hundred state banks, which, in the language of Stevens, were "merely local issues sadly depreciated and many so badly that they had little or no value at all."

It was evident that some plan had to be devised that would give the country a fairly stable currency without the aid of gold. The previous summer Secretary Chase had declared himself an avowed enemy of "irredeemable paper currency, than which no more fatally certain expedient for impoverishing the masses and discrediting the government can well be devised." Someone else, therefore, had to take the initiative. The chairman of the Ways and Means Committee did so unhesitatingly.

The "Old Commoner" or the "Great Commoner," as he was beginning to be referred to, was not wholly without experience in matters of finance. He had been for years director of the Gettysburg Bank, had been instrumental in securing a Pennsylvania charter for the United States Bank, and had done much legal work for banks in Lancaster. But he made no pretense to erudition on the subject. In 1864 he was to say: "I have no knowledge which would justify me in theorizing in financial matters," but added: "I have not much faith in theory against facts." If anyone imagines, however, that financial experts would necessarily have done better than he, let him consider the experience of the chairman of the Senate Finance Committee, William Pitt Fessenden.

When Stevens reported out his bill to authorize the government to issue legal-tender notes—that is to say, greenbacks, backed not by gold but by the nation's credit—Fessenden decided to get some expert advice on the subject. He wrote to two eminent financiers—James Gallatin and Morris Ketchum, both of New York—and asked them to favor him with their opinion. Mr. Gallatin wrote that it was a hare-brained scheme that would surely be the ruin of the country. Mr. Ketchum wrote that it was a wise measure, indispensable under the circumstances. The senator was still puzzling over this contradictory advice, when in walked Mr. Gallatin. He had become so disturbed about the impending ruin Stevens was about to unleash that he had thought it best to hurry to Washington and put some additional pressure upon the chairman of the Senate Finance Committee. Fessenden listened to him and then showed him the letter of Mr. Ketchum. Mr. Gallatin was pained as well as astonished and shortly after departed for New York.

The following morning the Senator received a telegram from him to the effect that he had changed his mind and now believed the measure to be "absolutely necessary." Fessenden felt relieved, but when he opened his morning mail he found a letter from Mr. Ketchum, who told him that he had changed his mind! Even then the Senator did not lose faith in financial experts and consulted several others, after which he told the Senate: "I declare here to-day, that in the whole number of learned financial men that I have consulted, I never have found any two of them who agree; and therefore it is hardly worth while for us to plead any very remarkable degree of ignorance when nobody is competent to instruct us."

4

Stevens's proposal, which had the backing of the majority of his committee, was for the government to issue $500,000,000 worth of twenty-year 6 per cent bonds, payable in gold at maturity, and $150,000,000 of legal-tender notes, convertible into bonds at the holders' pleasure. He took it for granted that when the bonds matured the country would be again on a gold basis. The interest on the bonds was to be payable not in gold, but in legal-tender notes or in whatever form of currency might be adopted. He believed that if proper precautions were taken, legal-tender notes would not depreciate in terms of gold: "The value of legal tender notes depends on the amount issued compared with the business of the country. If a less quantity was issued than the needed circulation, they would be more valuable than gold. . . . I do not think that any more would be needed than $150,000,000. The notes bear no interest. No one would seek them for investment. The money would soon lodge in large quantities with the capitalists and banks, who must take it. But the instinct of gain would not allow them to keep it long unproductive. . . . Where could they invest it? In United States loans at six per cent, redeemable in gold in twenty years, the best and most valuable investment that could be desired. The government would thus again possess such notes in exchange for bonds and again reissue them."

This was too optimistic. He underestimated the amount of legal-tender notes the country's business would require. Demand for labor and for commodities was bound to increase enormously as a result of the war. This meant an increase in wages and prices, which together with the greater volume of business was bound to require a greatly increased circulation. It is practically certain that the inelastic gold standard could not have survived such an increase. Professor R. E. Dewey informs us in his *Financial History of the United States* that on January 1, 1862, the banks of the country had but $87,000,000 in gold to meet an indebtedness of $459,000,000, of which nearly half was represented by bank notes. This means that the gold standard was not so much based on gold as on illusion. If one-fifth of the indebtedness were redeemed in gold, the other four-fifths would have had nothing except the bankers' promise to rely on. How much of a guarantee would depositors have had if the banks had doubled their circulation? Already, anyone who took a note issued by a state bank was assuming a risk. Assuredly Stevens was right when he claimed that legal-tender notes, backed by the resources and credit of the nation, were a far more reliable guarantee.

5

Stevens's proposal provoked a heated debate. Several substitute proposals were offered, including one by the minority of his committee.

Stevens closed the debate on February 6, 1862, with what Greeley's *Tribune* called a "smashing speech."

"This bill," he said, "is a matter of necessity, not of choice. No one would willingly issue paper currency not redeemable on demand and make it legal tender. It is never desirable to depart from the circulatory medium which by the common consent of civilized nations, forms the standard of value.

"The grave question is, how can this large amount be raised? Several modes of relief have been suggested; the most obvious is to borrow on Government bonds. That can only be effected by putting the bonds into the market to the highest bidder. But if sufficient to meet our wants up to the first of next December, or $700,000,000, were forced into the market, I have no doubt that they would sell as low as sixty per cent of their par value. It would require $1,500,000,000 of bonds to produce sufficient currency to carry the Government to the next fiscal year, a sum too frightful to be tolerated."

He repudiated the scheme of Roscoe Conkling to issue 7 per cent bonds redeemable in gold in twenty years and turn these over to the banks of New York, Boston, and Philadelphia in exchange for bank notes no longer redeemable in specie. "The banks would issue unlimited amounts of what would become trash and buy good hard money bonds of the nation. Was there ever such a temptation to swindle? If we are to use suspended notes to pay our expenses, why not use our own? Are they not as safe as the bank notes?"

Secretary Chase had proposed that the banks purchase government bonds with their depreciated currency, and leave them on deposit with the government, which would then supply the banks with an issue of notes to the full amount of the bonds. Two years later Chase's proposal became the basis of the National Banking Act. To one not a financier the proposal appears a piece of legerdemain designed to fill the pockets of the bankers. If government bonds were good as a guarantee for an issue of bank notes, why were they not equally good as a guarantee for an issue of government notes? Did the bonds gain in value by first being traded for irredeemable bank currency? And is it not obvious that if the government kept the bonds and with these as security issued notes for its own use, it would save millions of dollars in interest? Stevens saw through the scheme and exposed it.

He said in answer to Chase: "To the banks I can see the advantages. They would have the whole benefit of the circulation without interest, and at the same time would draw the interest on the Government bonds from the time they got the notes. . . . In other words, it would be equal to a loan, without interest, to the full amount of the circulation."

Champions of the creditor class were particularly opposed to the "legal-tender" clause in Stevens's proposal. If the notes were made "legal tender" they would have to be accepted in payment of all debts contracted when the country was on a gold basis. If they depreciated in terms of gold, the creditors would suffer. Stevens replied: "Gentlemen are clamorous in favor of those who have debts due them, lest the debtor should the more easily pay his debt. I do not much sympathize with such importunate money-lenders. . . . While these men have agonized bowels for the rich man's case, they have no pity for the poor widow, the suffering soldier, the wounded martyr to his country's good, who would have to receive these notes without legal tender, or nothing; and would have to give half of it to the Shylocks to get the necessaries of life. Sir, I wish no injuries to any, nor with our bill would any happen; but if they must lose, let it not be the soldier, the mechanic, the laborer and the farmer. . . . Unless this bill is to pass with the legal tender clause in it, it is not desirable that it should pass at all."

He had at first entertained some doubts regarding the constitutionality of legal-tender notes, but had brushed these resolutely aside. Granted that the Constitution did not specifically give the government the right to issue such notes, did that prove their unconstitutionality? "If nothing could be done by Congress except what is enumerated in the Constitution, the Government could not live a week." He dismissed the proposal of the minority of his committee with a few humorous sentences. Their report proposed that the notes be not made legal tender, but be redeemable in gold at the pleasure of the government instead of on demand. The notes were furthermore to be endowed with a quality no medium of exchange had ever been known to possess—they were to bear interest at 3.65 per cent! "Suppose," said Stevens, "a tailor, shoemaker or laborer were to take one of these bills, and in a week he should wish to use it in market, or store, or elsewhere, he must sit down and calculate the interest on the days he had it to find its value. This would be rather inconvenient on a frosty day. This currency would make it necessary for every man to carry an arithmetic or interest table with which to gage the value of the circulating medium."

He closed by expressing the ardent hope that the bill would pass. If it failed to do so he wished, he said, to resign from the committee and let someone else try.

The bill passed the House 93 to 59.

6

The sobriquet the "Great Commoner" the people bestowed upon Stevens is explicable only on the supposition that they believed him to be the champion of the common man—of the farmer, the mechanic, the laborer, the soldier, the sailor, the small businessman—as well as of the slave. They apparently thought so when they learned the provisions of his Legal Tender Bill. They hailed the measure with rejoicing. Here at last was a proposal to establish a national currency, backed by the credit and resources of the country. They were tired of the endless variety of state bank notes, of which nobody knew the real value even when the country was on a gold basis, and which were now more than ever discredited. Congratulations rained in upon the House from farmers and working people as well as from merchants and manufacturers. The Boards of Trade of Boston, New York, Philadelphia, Cincinnati, Louisville, St. Louis, Chicago, and Milwaukee gave the measure their unqualified endorsement, expressing the hope that the bill would pass the Senate unchanged. Senator Henry Wilson of Massachusetts declared on the floor of the Senate that the sentiment of the nation "approaches unanimity in its favor." But a small, powerful minority of bankers, brokers, and speculators opposed the bill. "They went to the Ways and Means Committee," Stevens was to write to his friend John Geiger, "and asked that the interest be payable in coin, leaving the principal as it was. The committee utterly rejected the absurd proposition of two currencies—two legal tenders—in the same empire and for the same commodities. The [bullion] brokers then resorted to the Secretary of the Treasury. He was more easily persuaded and went with them to the Senate Committee to urge the change. The Senate agreed and sent the bill so amended." Stevens's bill provided that the legal-tender notes should be receivable "for all salaries, debts and demands owed by the United States to individuals, corporations, and associations within the United States." The Senate drew a line through this and substituted that they should be receivable for "all claims and demands against the United States of whatever kind *except for interest on bonds and notes, which shall be paid in coin.*" The sinister meaning of the amendment was pointed out by Stevens on February 20, 1862.

"I approach the subject," he said, "with more depression of spirits than I ever before approached any question. . . . No act of legislation was ever hailed with as much delight by every class of people without exception, as the bill which we sent to the Senate. It is true there was a doleful sound came up from the caverns of the bullion brokers, and from the saloons of the associated banks. Their agents were soon on the ground, and persuaded the Senate to mangle and destroy what it had cost the House months to digest, consider and pass. They fell upon the bill in hot haste and so disfigured and deformed it that its very father would not know it. Instead of being a beneficent and invigorating measure, it is now positively mischievous. It has all the bad qualities that its enemies charged on the original bill, and none of its benefits. It now creates money, and by its very terms declares it a depreciated currency. It makes two classes of money—one for the banks and brokers, and another for the people. It discriminates between the rights of different classes of creditors, allowing the rich capitalist to demand gold."

He denounced the Senate amendment as class legislation in the interest of the rich:

"All classes of people shall take these notes at par for every article of trade or contract unless they have money enough to buy United States bonds, and then they shall be paid in gold. Who is that favored class? The bankers and brokers and nobody else! But how is the gold to be raised? It is to be raised in coin, which nobody holds but the large capitalists. Does anybody suppose that they will give that coin for such notes as we are now about to issue at par? They will compel the Government to give anything they choose, unless the Government consents to be dishonored.

"The first purchase of gold by the Government will fix the value of these notes, which we issue and declare to be legal tender. The sale will fix their value at 10, 15 or 25 per cent discount, and then every poor man, when he buys his supplies must submit to this discount, because you have said that that shall be the value of the very notes which you have made legal tender to him, but not a legal tender to those who fix the value of those very notes. . . . Was ever before such a machine got up for swindling the Government and making the fortune of the gold bullionists in a single year?"

He pointed out that it would require $60,000,000 in gold annually to pay the interest on the bonds—more than two-thirds of the gold reserve of all the banks in the country! The owners of the gold would sell it only at a substantial premium. "I trust I may be a false prophet, but if gold does not go up to two hundred per cent, my judgment is entirely at fault." They would then buy more hard-money bonds with the proceeds and so "clear by a single operation thirty per cent on their capital. The gold would automatically return to their coffers as interest on the bonds and the operation would be repeated. In three years a gold jobber could double his money—and that in time of war! If a financial system which produces such results be wise, then I am laboring under a great mistake."

Stevens's protest resulted in a demand for a conference between the House and the Senate. A conference committee was appointed, but the principal concession obtained was that import duties should be payable in gold, which would then be used to meet the interest on the bonds. Even if sufficient gold could have been collected in this manner, it would in no way have changed the harmful effect of the Senate amendment. The distinction created between legal tender and specie to the detriment of the former would have remained. Moreover, what difference did it make if businessmen went into Wall Street to buy gold with which to pay import duties, or the government went there to buy gold to pay interest? In either case the owners of gold would sell it for as much as they could get. In the summer of 1864, it took two dollars in legal tender to buy a gold dollar. It had been Stevens's aim to dispense with gold as a circulating medium for some time to come; the Senate amendment created a greater demand for that medium than had ever before existed!

There can be no doubt that the amendment was mainly responsible for the rise in the price of gold, as there can be no doubt that the rise stimulated the increase in the price of all other commodities. From the par of 1860 to the end of the war prices rose 217 per cent; wages—always slow to catch up with prices—only 143 per cent. Thus, at the conclusion of the war, the wage workers of the country were considerably worse off than they had been five years before, although business flourished and speculators waxed enormously rich.

CHAPTER III

Lincoln, the Negro, and Emancipation

It is impossible to understand the struggle that was now to develop between Stevens and his followers in Congress on the one hand, and Lincoln and some of his principal advisers on the other, without a thorough understanding of Lincoln's attitude toward the Negro and emancipation. That attitude is generally misunderstood, owing to the fact that, with few exceptions, Lincoln's biographers appear to have been anxious to obscure it rather than to clarify it. In this they have not acted in the spirit of Lincoln, whom Herndon quotes as having said, on one occasion: "Biographies as generally written are not only milseading, but false. . . . In most instances they commemorate a lie, and cheat posterity out of the truth. History is not history unless it is the truth." [1]

That Lincoln hated slavery and sincerely sympathized with the slave admits of no doubt, but there is ample evidence that he regarded the Negro as an inferior being whose integration into a white society on terms even remotely approaching equality was an impossibility. Considering the intensity of the prejudice then existing against free people of color, in the North as well as in the South, he entertained serious doubts whether emancipation would be of much value to the slave. He made no attempt to allay that prejudice, frankly admitting that he himself shared it. On October 4, 1854, he said in Peoria, Illinois: "Free them and keep them among us as underlings? *Is it quite certain that it will better their condition?* . . . Free them

[1] *Herndon's Lincoln* (edition annotated by Paul M. Angle), p. 353.

and make them politically and socially our equals? *My own feelings will not admit of this,* and if mine would, we well know that those of the great mass of whites will not. Whether this feeling accords with justice and sound judgment is not the sole question, if indeed it is any part of it. A universal feeling, whether well or ill founded cannot be safely disregarded." [2]

The condition of the free people of color was at that time so appallingly wretched that one might well have doubted if emancipation would be of much value to the slave. In the North as well as in the South it was exceedingly difficult for a free Negro to earn his bread by honest labor. If an employer took pity on him and engaged him, the chances were that white workmen would force him to leave. The number of free Negroes arrested for vagrancy or petty thievery was as a consequence disproportionately large. In the free states Negro children were not permitted to attend school with white children, and it was the exception rather than the rule that facilities were provided for their instruction. Segregation on public conveyances was practiced throughout the country.

In most Southern states it was forbidden to teach a free Negro to read or write. In Georgia the offense was punishable by a fine of five hundred dollars. In Virginia any justice of the peace could disband a school where free Negroes or their children were taught to read or write and could condemn each pupil to twenty lashes on the bare back. In Maryland a justice of the peace could order a free Negro's ears cut off for striking a white man even in self-defense. In Kentucky the offense was punishable by thirty lashes "well laid on." In all Southern and in most Northern states, including Illinois, free people of color could not vote, serve on a jury, or testify against a white man.

That political disability was in a large measure responsible for this unfortunate situation was generally acknowledged, but it was considered inadvisable to grant the free Negro civil rights. The *African Repository,* official organ of the American Colonization Society, summed up the situation in these words: "Whether we consider it with reference to the welfare of the state, or the happiness

[2] Italics added. Quotations from Lincoln's speeches and writings are from the *Works.* Indications for their identification will be given in the text.

of the blacks, it were better to have left them in chains, than to have liberated them to receive such freedom as they enjoy, *and greater freedom we cannot, must not give them.*" [3]

That Lincoln fully agreed with this is evident from his debate with Douglas at Charleston, Illinois, September 18, 1858, when he said in his opening speech:

"I will say that I am not, nor ever have been, in favor of bringing about in any way the social and political equality of the white and black races; that I am not, nor ever have been, in favor of making voters of the free Negroes, or jurors, or qualifying them to hold office, or having them marry with white people. I will say in addition that there is a physical difference between the white and black races, which, I suppose, will forever forbid the two races living together upon terms of social and political equality; and in as much as they cannot so live, that while they do remain together, there must be the position of the superiors and the inferiors; and that I as much as any other man, am in favor of the superior being assigned to the white man."

Not only was he opposed to granting the Negro civil rights, but he was in favor of turning the clock back. Since the foundation of the republic free Negroes had enjoyed the right of citizenship. When in 1787 the federal Constitution was ratified, free Negroes possessing other necessary qualifications, voted in New Hampshire, Massachusetts, New York, New Jersey, and North Carolina. The Dred Scott decision, besides declaring the Missouri Compromise of 1820 unconstitutional, made the pronouncement that a Negro could not be a citizen. In his rejoinder to Douglas at Charleston, only two years before his election to the presidency, Lincoln unequivocally declared his agreement with that part of the decision:

"Judge Douglas has said to you that he has not been able to get from me an answer to the question whether I am in favor of negro citizenship. . . . He shall have no occasion to ask me again, for I tell him very frankly that I am not in favor of negro citizenship. . . . My opinion is that the different States have the power to make a negro a citizen, under the Constitution of the United States, if they choose. The Dred Scott decision decides that they have not that

[3] *Af. Rep.*, vol. III, p. 197. Italics added.

power. If the State of Illinois had that power, I should be opposed to the exercise of it."

2

That so humane, tolerant, and justice-loving a man should have held such views would be well-nigh incomprehensible if we did not know that they were the outgrowth of a firmly rooted conviction that the two races could not live together in freedom under the same government—hence that free Negroes were merely sojourners in the United States and must eventually emigrate. "I yield to all that follows from necessity. What I would desire would be a separation of the white and black races," he said at Springfield, Illinois, January 29, 1859. He was not the only great man to hold that opinion. Thomas Jefferson has said: "Nothing is more certainly written in the book of fate than that these people are to be free. Nor is it less certain that the two races, equally free, cannot live in the same government. Nature, habit, opinion have drawn indelible lines of distinction between them. It is still in our power to direct the process of emancipation and deportation, peaceably. . . ." [4]

Many prominent men, Northerners as well as Southerners, agreed with Jefferson, and had banded together in the American Colonization Society whose aim it was to colonize free Negroes in Liberia, on the west coast of Africa, a territory acquired with that purpose in view. Henry Clay, idol of Lincoln's young manhood, was one of the society's vice-presidents. While slaveholders belonging to the organization were principally interested in ridding the country of the free people of color, whose presence they believed to be detrimental to discipline among the slaves, this was not true of the majority of the membership. Such confirmed antislavery advocates as Benjamin Lundy and William Lloyd Garrison were at one time members of the society. They and others sincerely believed that the greatest obstacle to emancipation was the problem of what should be done with the freedmen. They felt convinced that once it was demonstrated that free Negroes could be settled in large numbers in the land of their origin, gradual emancipation, by action of the slave states themselves, would quickly follow.

[4] *Writings,* vol. I, p. 49.

Lincoln, while not a member of the society, agreed with those of its members who saw in colonization the *sine qua non* of emancipation. He likewise agreed with the society's managers that as long as the free people of color remained in the United States little or nothing could be done to improve their wretched lot, and that in the meantime it was best to keep the two races as far apart as possible. In 1847 he favored the clause in the new Illinois constitution forbidding free Negroes to immigrate. On January 29, 1859, commenting in a letter to his friend Elihu B. Washburne on a speech made in Congress by his friend's brother C. C. Washburn, he wrote: "His objection to the Oregon constitution because it excludes free Negroes, is the only thing I wish he had omitted."

That in this matter also Lincoln was in favor of turning the clock back very considerably is evident from the following: The fourth article of the Articles of Confederation, which constituted the law of the land from the time of their passage in 1778 to the adoption of the federal Constitution, reads in part: "The better to secure and perpetuate mutual friendship and intercourse among the people of the different States in the Union, the free inhabitants of each of these States—paupers, vagabonds, and fugitives from justice excepted—shall be entitled to all privileges and immunities of free citizens in the several States." The delegates from South Carolina moved to amend by inserting the word *"white"* between *"free"* and *"inhabitants."* Only two states voted in the affirmative and the amendment was lost.[5]

Lincoln's conviction concerning the impossibility of integrating the Negro into American society must have been profound to have prompted him to disregard such important precedent.

It should be mentioned that on March 13, 1864, Lincoln wrote to Michael Hahn, first Free State governor of the reconstructed State of Louisiana: "Now, you are about to have a convention, which among other things, will probably define the elective franchise. I barely suggest for your private consideration whether some of the colored people may not be let in—as, for instance, the very intelligent, and especially those who have fought gallantly in our ranks. They would probably help, in some trying time to come, to keep the jewel of liberty within the family of freedom. But this is only a suggestion—not to the public, but to you alone." That the letter did

[5] *Elliot's Debates,* vol. I, p. 79.

not represent any firm conviction on his part is evident from the fact that a year later he summoned General Ben Butler to the White House for the express purpose of discussing with him the possibility of removing all the colored people, including those "who have fought gallantly in our ranks," to Liberia, or South America.[6]

3

Lincoln ardently desired to see slavery abolished, but being prudent and conservative by nature and realizing that undue haste might cause greater misery than it sought to cure, he wished to proceed with caution. He recognized that under the Constitution the federal government had no power to interfere with slavery in the slave states. Abolition of slavery, gradual or immediate, must therefore come by action of the slave states themselves. He believed, moreover, that it would create far less social disturbance and be cheaper in the long run if the slaveholders were compensated for the loss of their slaves. Since Northern businessmen and the North in general had profited and were still profiting from slavery, and Northern shipowners had aided in establishing the institution, he believed it but fair that the North should participate in the cost of freeing the slaves, hence that the federal government should give financial aid to any state wishing to abolish slavery.

He was opposed to immediate general emancipation for reasons easily understandable. Since he doubted the slaves would be benefited if after obtaining their freedom they remained in the United States, and was, moreover, firmly convinced that the two races could not live together in freedom in the same country, what more natural than that he should have been opposed to a form of emancipation which would have made colonization a hopeless task. How strong his conviction was concerning the undesirability of immediate emancipation may be judged from the fact that when already past forty he expressed the opinion that that form of emancipation would be a greater evil than slavery. On July 16, 1852, speaking at a memorial meeting in Springfield, Illinois, in honor of Henry Clay, he said that Clay "did not perceive, as I think no wise man can perceive, how it [slavery] could be at once eradicated without pro-

[6] Rice, *Reminiscences,* pp. 150-152.

·ducing a greater evil even to the cause of human liberty itself." He believed the North as well as the South would be disastrously affected by such a measure. "He considers that general emancipation will smother the Free States. Such are his precise words," wrote Count Gurowski, an intimate of the White House, to Governor John A. Andrew of Massachusetts.[7] Ben Butler has reported that Lincoln told him shortly before his death he feared there would be a race war in the South.[8]

It is obvious that to one believing as Lincoln did, gradual emancipation was bound to be as unsatisfactory a solution as immediate emancipation, *unless accompanied by colonization*. Henry Clay was entirely consistent when he said: "If the question were submitted, whether there should be either immediate or gradual emancipation of all the slaves in the United States, without their removal, painful as it is to express the opinion, I have no doubt that it would be unwise to emancipate them."[9]

In his speeches both before and after his election to the presidency, Lincoln seldom mentioned emancipation without at the same time mentioning colonization. In his oration on Henry Clay he said that if by any means the country could be relieved of "the dangerous presence of slavery, and at the same time the negroes could be restored to their long-lost fatherland with bright prospects for the future, and this so gradually that neither races nor individuals shall have suffered by the change, it will be indeed a glorious consummation." In his Peoria speech he said: "If all earthly power were given me, I should not know what to do as to the existing institution. My first impulse would be to free all the slaves, and send them to Liberia, to their own native land." Immediate general emancipation would, he realized, make colonization a hopeless undertaking: "If they were all landed in a day, they would all perish in the next ten days; and there are not surplus shipping and money enough to carry them there in many times ten days." He had, however, "high hopes" that it might be done "in the long run."

"The long run" meant gradually. How gradually would emancipation have to take place to enable colonization to keep pace with

[7] Gurowski to Andrew, May 7, 1862, *Andrew MSS*, vol. XIV, No. 22.
[8] Rice, *op. cit.*, pp. 150-152.
[9] *Af. Rep.*, vol. VI, p. 5.

it? Fitzhugh, one of the managers of the American Colonization Society, had said: "We have never supposed that the Society's plan would be accomplished in a few years; but on the contrary have boasted [sic] that it will demand a century for its fulfillment." [10] Lincoln was inclined to agree with this. In his rejoinder to Douglas at Charleston, Illinois, he said: "I do not suppose that in the most peaceful way ultimate extinction [of slavery] would occur in less than a hundred years at least." In December, 1862, he proposed emancipation over a period of thirty-seven years, but even if a place could have been found to colonize the emigrants, it is extremely doubtful if with the facilities then at the country's disposal colonization in an undeveloped region could have kept pace with the natural increase from births among the slave population.

On June 26, 1857, at Springfield, Illinois, Lincoln had deplored the fact that no political party was doing anything to promote colonization. It was a difficult task, he said, "but where there is a will there is a way, and what colonization needs most is a hearty will." There was no lack of a hearty will on his part. In his address at the opening of the first regular session of the Thirty-seventh Congress, December 2, 1861, he recommended that such slaves as were freed as a result of the first Confiscation Act, and free people of color willing to emigrate, should be colonized "at some place or places in a climate congenial to them." He was to make similar recommendations repeatedly during his term of office.

When in 1862 the District of Columbia slaves were freed, $100,000 was appropriated to colonize the freedmen. Later, on a motion by Stevens—himself no believer in colonization, but who wished to humor the President—$500,000 additional was voted. Lincoln undertook two colonization projects—at Ile à Vache, an uninhabited island off the coast of Haiti, and at the Chiriqui location on the Panamanian isthmus. It was his intention ultimately to settle five thousand Negroes on the island, and about five hundred were sent there. It soon developed, however, that Bernard Kock, who had recommended the location to him, was an unscrupulous adventurer who had indulged in gross misrepresentation. The island had remained uninhabited because it was unfit for human habitation.

[10] *Af. Rep.*, vol. VI, p. 5.

Yellow fever, malaria, poisonous snakes, and venomous insects plagued the colonists. More than a hundred died before the remainder were repatriated.

The Panamanian project had been proposed to the President by a group of speculators who owned coal deposits on the isthmus and needed laborers. On August 14, 1862, Lincoln summoned a number of colored men to the White House in the hope of enlisting their co-operation. Wishing to convince them that there was no future for their race in the United States, he said: "You are suffering, in my judgment, the greatest wrong inflicted on any people. But even when you cease to be slaves, you are yet far from being placed on an equality with the white race. You are cut off from many of the advantages which the other race enjoys. The aspiration of men is to enjoy equality with the best when free, but on this broad continent not a single man of your race is made the equal of a single man of ours. Go where you are treated best, and the ban is still upon you. I do not propose to discuss this, but to present it as a fact, with which we have to deal. I cannot alter it if I would."

The men departed saying they would think the matter over and eventually wrote that they considered the proposal "inexpedient, inauspicious and impolitic."

In the meantime Stevens had made inquiries, and on August 25, 1862, wrote to Secretary Chase that the region was "so unhealthy as to be wholly uninhabitable." He added this criticism of the President: "How unexpectedly the Pres't is applying our appropriation for a purpose never intended by Congress. I moved the appropriation of a half a million for general colonization purposes, but never thought new and independent colonies were to be planted—I intended it to aid in sending to Haiti, Liberia, and other places the liberated Dist. of Columbia slaves." [11]

Chase read the letter to Lincoln, who promised a thorough investigation. As a result of the inquiry the project was abandoned.

4

Soon after he issued the Emancipation Proclamation, Lincoln became convinced that the freedmen would not depart voluntarily.

[11] *Salmon P. Chase MSS,* Historical Society of Pennsylvania.

He concluded that the only remaining solution was *compulsory* colonization. No one who has studied Lincoln's character will doubt that he found it difficult to arrive at that decision and that in making it he had the welfare of the Negro no less than that of the white population at heart. Warnings that a race war was inevitable in the South and that the Negroes would be massacred were heard on all sides. On March 12, 1862, Garrett Davis of Kentucky, a staunch Unionist, had said in the Senate during the debate on the bill freeing the District of Columbia slaves (regarded by many as a prelude to general emancipation): "Whenever any power, constitutional or unconstitutional, assumes the responsibility of liberating slaves, where slaves are numerous, they establish, as inexorably as fate, a conflict between the races that will result in the exile or extermination of the one or the other. . . . The moment you re-organize the white inhabitants of those States as States of the Union, they would reduce those slaves again to a state of slavery, or they would expel them upon you or south of you, or they would hunt them like beasts, and exterminate them. . . . I know what I talk about. Mr. President, the loyal people of the slave States are true to this Union as any man in the Senate Chamber or in any of the free States: but never, never, will they submit . . . to have their slaves liberated and to remain domiciled among them; and the policy that attempts it will establish a bloody La Vendée in the whole of the slave States, my own included."

Lincoln saw in such utterances confirmation of his own fears.

After he had issued the preliminary Emancipation Proclamation it was natural that his thoughts should have dwelt with increasing frequency on colonization. They appear to have definitely turned to "deportation" of the freedmen as the only possible solution. "When he very reluctantly issued the preliminary proclamation in September 1862," wrote Congressman George W. Julian of Indiana, who although a follower of Stevens had a great affection for the President and had frequent talks with him, "he wished it distinctly understood that the *deportation* of the slaves was, in his mind, inseparably connected with the policy. Like Mr. Clay and other prominent leaders of the Whig party, he believed in colonization, and that separation of the races was necessary to the welfare of both." [12] In

[12] Rice, *op. cit.*, p. 61.

his message to Congress of December 1, 1862, Lincoln for the first time used the word "deportation" in connection with colonization.

Shortly before his death he sent for Major General Benjamin F. Butler, who has given the following account of the interview:

Lincoln doubted very much whether the negro and the white man could possibly live together in any other condition than that of slavery. . . . He was very much disturbed after the surrender of Lee . . . upon the question of what would be the result of peace in the Southern States as affected by the contiguity of the white and black races. Shortly before the time when Mr. Seward was thrown from his carriage and severely injured, being then in Washington, the President sent for the writer and said, "General Butler, I am troubled about the negroes. We are soon to have peace. We have got some one hundred and odd thousand negroes who have been trained to arms.[13] When peace shall come I fear lest these colored men shall organize themselves in the South, especially in the States where the negroes are in preponderance in numbers, into guerrilla parties, and we shall have down there a warfare between the whites and the negroes. In the course of the reconstruction of the Government it will become a question how the negro is to be disposed of. Would it not be possible to export them to some place, say Liberia, or South America, and organize them into communities to support themselves? . . . Your organization of the flotilla which carried your army from Yorktown and Fort Monroe to City Point, and its success show that you understand such matters. Will you not give this your attention, and, at as early as day as possible, report to me your views upon the subject." I replied "Willingly," and bowed and retired.

A short time later Butler presented calculations to the effect that "negro children will be born faster than your whole naval and merchant vessels, if substantially all of them were devoted to that use, can carry them from the country." [14]

Stevens expressed his views on colonization in general and compulsory colonization in particular in his speech of May 2, 1864: "I have never favored colonization except as a means of introducing civilization into Africa. Its effect upon slavery was injurious. It was a salve for the consciences of slaveholders and their advocates. As a means of removing the African from the country it was puerile. All the revenue of the United States would not pay for the trans-

[13] There were 178,975 in the army, about half of whom were fugitive slaves, and about 20,000 in the navy.

[14] Rice, *op. cit.*, pp. 150-152.

portation of one half their annual increase. The scheme of colonizing them in South America . . . was a very shallow vision. They were averse to removing from their native land; their forcible expatriation would be as atrocious a crime as stealing them in Africa and reducing them to bondage. Five hundred were lately seduced to go to an island near St. Domingo. Such as have not died in six months have been brought back at our expense. I hope this will be the last of the unwise and cruel schemes of colonization."

5

There are those who will point to certain encouraging signs in the relations between the races and will say that Lincoln's fears were exaggerated and his colonization schemes unwarrantable. Others, who see in such racial disturbances as have taken place at East St. Louis, Chicago, Atlanta, Washington, Detroit, and Cicero, and in the slaughter of the Jews in Central Europe, portents of what may yet be expected in the United States, will say that had colonization been practical, it might have been best for all concerned. *But the point is that various circumstances combined to render it wholly impractical.* So learned and so profound an admirer of President Lincoln as the late Professor James G. Randall speaks of its "utter impracticability." [15] Yet, impractical as it was, it could not have helped seriously influencing Lincoln's war and reconstruction policies. His deeply rooted conviction that the two races could not live together in freedom under the same government, and that unless a way was found to colonize the Negroes it was doing them and the country a disservice to free them, must have been mainly responsible for his reluctance to stop the enforcement of the Fugitive Slave Law, to issue the Emancipation Proclamation, and to employ Negroes as soldiers. So also his belief that there was no room for the Negro in the United States and that he must eventually emigrate serves to explain why so humane a man failed to include in his reconstruction plan a provision to give the freedmen a few acres of land, as was done by Alexander II of Russia when in 1861 he freed the serfs.

To fail to take these things into account in an appraisal of the differences between the President and Congress—between Lincoln

[15] Randall, *Lincoln and the South,* p. 90.

and Stevens—and sweepingly condemn Stevens and other leading Radical Republicans for their opposition to the President is to fail to take into account the prime cause of those differences. Lincoln's honorable place in history is secure, but he was not infallible. He was not always right and those who differed with him were not always wrong.

CHAPTER IV

First Blow at Slavery

That in the event of invasion or civil war the federal government had the constitutional right to interfere with slavery in the slave states was claimed on May 25, 1836, by a constitutional authority, former President John Quincy Adams, who said on the floor of Congress: "From the instant that your slaveholding States become the theatre of war, civil, servile, or foreign, from that instant the war powers of the Constitution extend to interference with the institution of slavery in every way in which it can be interfered with." It is evident from his letter of April 4, 1836, to his friend Solomon Lincoln of Hingham, Massachusetts, that he considered such interference a congressional as well as a presidential prerogative. He wrote: "I did not start the question whether in the event of a servile insurrection and war, Congress would not have complete unlimited control over the whole subject of slavery, even to the emancipation of all the slaves in the State where such insurrection should break out, and for the suppression of which the freemen of Plymouth and Norfolk counties, Massachusetts, should be called by acts of Congress to pour out their treasures and to shed their blood."

That to strike at slavery meant to strike at the heart of the rebellion is evident from the following passage from Jefferson Davis's *Rise and Fall of the Confederate Government:* "Much of our success was due to the much-abused institution of African servitude, for it enabled the white men to go into the army, and leave the cultivation of their fields and the care of their flocks, as well of their wives and children, to those who in the language of the Constitution, were 'held to service or labor.'" He might have added that thousands of slaves—it has been claimed one in five—were used in the preparation of war material or served as auxiliaries with the Confederate armies. Such auxiliaries—of whom there is no mention when the numerical strength of Confederate armies is given—were performing duties that in the federal armies were performed by enlisted men. They built fortifications, threw up entrenchments, felled trees, repaired roads, built bridges, and did other work ordinarily performed by engineering troops and pontoniers. They handled and transported supplies, chopped wood, acted as cooks and orderlies, and served as stewards and waiters in military hospitals. So valuable were they to the Confederate war effort, that when the Confederates retreated from Kentucky they took with them every slave they could lay their hands on. The Memphis (Tennessee) *Avalanche,* in its issue of September 30, 1861, gave this glimpse of the Negro auxiliaries: "Yesterday a procession of several hundred stout negro men marched through the streets of Memphis, in military order, under the Command of Confederate officers. A merrier set never was seen, shouting for Jeff Davis and singing war songs."

2

When on March 4, 1861, Lincoln delivered his inaugural address, the Confederate States of America had already been formed, with a president, a vice-president, and a provisional constitution. While one might still have cherished the hope that the Union could be preserved without the employment of armed force, the chances were all the other way. Yet, in his inaugural address, President Lincoln gave the following assurance to the slaveholders: "I have no purpose either directly or indirectly to interfere with the institution of slavery in the States where it exists. I believe I have no lawful right to do so, and I have no inclination to do so."

The assurance was given with the intention of deterring slaveholders in slave states still remaining loyal from using their influence to have their states join the rebellion. It may, however, have been a mistake to give that assurance without suitable qualification. A man is not deterred from grasping a hot poker by being made to believe that it will not burn him. When South Carolina seceded President Buchanan, on the advice of Attorney General Jeremiah S. Black, made a similar statement in his message to Congress regarding the employment of armed coercion. The result was discouraging: the Gulf states promptly seceded, and the general opinion was that Buchanan's pronouncement might well have been responsible. Lincoln's statement may not have influenced the slave barons of Virginia, Arkansas, Tennessee, and North Carolina to plunge their states into secession, but it was hardly of a nature to deter them from doing so.

Stevens appears to have felt that Lincoln's pronouncement was equivalent to a pledge not to make use of the most formidable weapon in the government's arsenal. He determined to disabuse the slaveholders at the earliest possible opportunity.

3

On July 22, 1861, the Union Army was routed at Bull Run. Alarmed by the defeat and hoping to strengthen the bond with the loyal border states, Congress passed the famous Crittenden Resolution. While the resolution did not question the government's right to interfere with slavery in time of armed rebellion, it assured the slave states that the war was not being fought for the purpose of "overthrowing or interfering with the rights or established institutions of those States, but to defend and maintain the supremacy of the Constitution and to preserve the Union with all the dignity, equality and rights of the several States unimpaired."

Stevens was one of two members of the House who voted against the Crittenden Resolution, the futility of which became quickly apparent. No sooner had it been voted than Congress proceeded to interfere with slavery after all. Participants in the Battle of Bull Run reported that thousands of slaves had been employed by the Confederates "in the construction of earth works, in driving teams, in cooking, in the general work of the Quartermaster and Commissary Departments, and in all forms of camp drudgery." Realizing the seriousness of this Congress took prompt action. A bill was introduced in the House which in its final form provided that any person who permitted a slave belonging to him to be used for any military or naval purpose "against the Government and lawful authority of the United States," forfeited his claim to that slave "any law of the State or the United States notwithstanding." An acrimonious debate followed. Burnett of Kentucky cried: "That amounts to a wholesale emancipation of the slaves in the seceding and rebellious States!" John J. Crittenden declared: "It has been conceded in all time, that the Congress of the United States had no power to legislate upon the subject of slavery within the States. Absence of all power of legislation in time of peace must be absence of the same power at all times. You have no power, by your Constitution, to touch slavery at all."

On August 2, 1861, Stevens rose to speak.

"We are told," he said, "that because the Constitution does not allow us to confiscate a certain species of property, therefore we cannot liberate slaves. Mr. Speaker, I thought the time had come when the laws of war were to govern our action; when constitutions, if they stood in the way of the laws of war in dealing with the enemy, had no right to intervene. Who pleads the Constitution against our proposed action? It is the advocates of rebels, of rebels who have sought to overthrow the Constitution and trample it in the dust; who repudiate the Constitution. Sir, these rebels, who have disregarded and set at defiance that instrument, are, by every rule of municipal and international law, estopped from pleading it against our action. . . . The law established in the days of Cicero—*Inter arma silent leges*—is a law that has been in force to the present time; and any nation which disregards that law is a poor, pusilanimous nation which submits its neck to be struck off by the enemy.

"When a country is in open war with an enemy, every publicist agrees that you have the right to use every means which will weaken him. Every measure which will enable you sooner to subdue him and triumph over him, is justified on your part. If we are justified in taking property from the enemy in war, when you have rescued an oppressed people from the oppression of that enemy, by what principle of philanthropy, can you return them to the bondage from which you have delivered them, and rivet again the chains you have once broken? It is a disgrace to the party that advocates it. It is against the principle of the law of nations. It is against every principle of philanthropy. I, for one, shall never shrink from saying, when these slaves are once conquered by us, 'Go and be free.' God forbid that I should ever agree that they should be returned again to their masters! I do not say that the war is made for that purpose. I did not like the resolution of the distinguished gentleman from Kentucky because it looked like an apology from us in saying what were the objects of the war. *Ask those who made the war what its object is. Do not ask us. Our object is to subdue the rebels.*

"But it is said that the South will never submit—that we cannot conquer the rebels—that they will suffer themselves to be slaughtered, and their whole country to be laid waste. *Sir, war is a grievous thing at best, and civil war more than any other; but if they hold this language, and the means which they have suggested must be resorted to,* if their whole country must be laid waste, and made a desert, in order to save this Union from destruction, so let it be.[1]

"If this war is continued long, and is bloody, I do not believe that the free people of the North will stand by and see their sons and brothers and neighbors slaughtered by thousands and tens of thousands by rebels, with arms in their hands, and forbear to call upon their enemies to be our friends, and to help us in subduing them; I for one, if it continues long, and has the consequences mentioned, shall be ready to go for it. That is my doctrine, and that will be the doctrine of the whole free people of the North before two years roll round.

"As for the end of the war, until the rebels are subdued, no man in the North thinks of it. If the Government are equal to the people, and I believe they are, there will be no bargaining, there will be no negotiation, there will be no truces with the rebels, except to bury the dead, until every man shall have laid down his arms, disbanded his organization, submitted himself to the Government, and sued for mercy. And, sir, if those who have the control of the Government are not fit for this task and have not the nerve and mind for it, the people will take care that there are others who are—although, sir, I have not a bit of fear of the present Administration or of the present Executive."

[1] Italics added.

4

Stevens's indignation about what the present generation regards with so much tolerance is understandable when one considers that many prominent Southerners, before being swept off their feet by the course of events, regarded the secession movement with almost equal abhorrence. Alexander H. Stephens, who was to become vice-president of the Confederate States, said at the Georgia Secession Convention: "When we and our posterity shall see our lovely South desolated by the demon of war, *which this act of yours will inevitably invite and call forth . . . who but this Convention* will be held responsible for it? and who but he who shall have given his vote for this unwise and ill-timed measure . . . *shall be held to strict account for this suicidal act by the present generation, and probably cursed and execrated by posterity for all coming time,* for the wide and desolating ruin that will inevitably follow this act you now propose to perpetrate? Pause, I entreat you, and consider for a moment what reasons you can give that will even satisfy yourselves in calmer moments—what reasons can you give to your fellow-sufferers in the calamity it will bring upon us. *What reasons can you give to the nations of the earth to justify it? . . . What right has the North assailed?* What interest of the South has been invaded? What justice has been denied? and what claim founded on justice and right has been withheld? . . . I challenge the answer . . . Now, for you to attempt to overthrow such a government as this . . . is the height of *madness, folly* and *wickedness,* to which I can neither lend my sanction nor my vote." [2]

Mrs. Robert E. Lee, wife of the man who was to become the Confederate commander in chief, wrote on February 9, 1861, to her friend Mrs. W. H. Stiles:

Has all love for and pride in the country died at the South, that they are willing to tear her in pieces and some even *exult* to see her glorious flag trailing in the dust? . . . What is the use of a government combined as ours is of so many parts, the Union of which forms its strength and power, if any *one part* has the right for any wrong, real or imaginary, of withdrawing its aid and throwing the whole into confusion as Carolina,

[2] Thomas V. Cooper, *American Politics,* p. 116. Italics in original.

who refuses all overtures for peace and imagines the world will admire her independence, whereas they laugh at her folly which is perfectly suicidal? . . . You know my feelings are all linked with the South and you will bear with me in the expression of my opinion, but while there are many Northern politicians who deserve no better fate than to be hung as high as Haman, believe me that those who have been foremost in this Revolution will deserve and meet with the reprobation of the world, either North or South, for having destroyed the most glorious Confederacy that ever existed.[3]

It is now known that the majority of the people of the South did not want separation from the Union. The late Professor James G. Randall, having carefully weighed the evidence, wrote: "There were evidences that Secession as the answer to Lincoln's election by no means commanded the preponderant support of the Southern people." [4] Lincoln said in his message of July 4, 1861: "It may be questioned whether there is to-day a majority of the legally qualified voters of any State, except, perhaps, South Carolina, in favor of disunion." Stephen A. Douglas, in his speech in Chicago, May 1, 1861, called secession an "enormous conspiracy." It was indeed a conspiracy of unscrupulous Southern politicians and the slaveholding class against the government of the United States and against their own people. Being in control of political power in all the Southern states and of all avenues of information, they were able temporarily to nullify "the wish of a vast majority of Americans North and South to preserve the Union." [5]

Only when we realize that it was in this light Stevens and others viewed secession can we comprehend the feeling of outrage and indignation that animated them.

[3] Sir Frederick Maurice, *Robert E. Lee, the Soldier,* p. 53. By special permission of Houghton Mifflin Co. Italics in original.

[4] From *Lincoln the President* by J. G. Randall, copyright 1945. Quoted by special permission of the publishers, Dodd, Mead & Company, vol. I, p. 217.

[5] *Ibid.,* vol. I, p. 209.

CHAPTER V

The Struggle Begins

Was Stevens merely "a thorn in Lincoln's side," as has been claimed by some? Those who have made that claim have shown little understanding of the situation. Great as were Lincoln's merits as a man and as a statesman, owing to his fear of immediate general emancipation—his belief that the two races could not live in freedom in the same country—he was ill-equipped to deal with the slavery issue, hence reluctant to grapple with it. Stevens, having no such misgivings, was for striking at the institution boldly and resolutely—too boldly and too resolutely perhaps considering border state and Northern sentiment. Here Lincoln's distrust of immediate emancipation proved valuable, acting as a brake to Stevens's relentless driving power. Thus the two men complemented and needed each other, and the country needed both. "The opposing qualities of each were potent upon the other," wrote McClure.[1] If Lincoln was to Stevens an indispensable brake, Stevens was to Lincoln an equally indispensable goad.

McClure, lawyer, journalist, politician, and one of Lincoln's most trusted advisers, has analyzed the relationship between the two men in these words:

I am quite sure that Stevens respected Lincoln much more than he would have respected any other man in the same position with Lincoln's conviction of duty. He could not but appreciate Lincoln's forbearance even with all of Stevens's irritating conflicts, and Lincoln profoundly

1 McClure, *op. cit.*, p. 256.

appreciated Stevens as one of his most valued and useful co-workers, and never cherished resentment even when Stevens indulged in his bitterest sallies of wit and sarcasm at Lincoln's tardiness. Strange as it may seem, these two great characters, ever in conflict and yet battling for the same great cause, *rendered invaluable service to each other, and unitedly rendered incalculable service in saving the Republic.* . . . Each in his great trust attained the highest possible measure of success, and the two men who more than all others blended the varied currents of their efforts and crystallized them in the unchangeable policy of the government were Abraham Lincoln and Thaddeus Stevens.[2]

2

On December 2, 1861, the first day of the regular session of the Thirty-seventh Congress, Stevens introduced, for enactment into law, a joint resolution containing the following proposals:

General emancipation with compensation for all loyal slaveholders.

The President to be requested to declare free, and to direct his generals to order freedom to, all slaves who shall leave their masters, or who shall aid in quelling the rebellion.

On the third day of the session something happened that gave meaning to the proposals. William S. Holman, Democrat from Indiana, had offered a resolution calling for reaffirmation of the Crittenden Resolution which gave assurance to the slaveholders that slavery would not be interfered with. In July of that same year the Crittenden Resolution had passed the House with but two dissenting votes. In the Senate, where only four had dissented, so confirmed an antislavery advocate as Senator Hale of New Hampshire had declared that the government had no more right to strike at slavery in the slave states than to interfere with serfdom in Russia. Yet now, when Stevens moved that Holman's resolution be tabled, his motion carried 71 to 65!

Refusal to reaffirm the Crittenden Resolution marked the division of the Republican party in Congress into Radicals and Conservatives. Twenty-six of the Conservatives voted with the Democrats against Stevens's motion. There was to be no love lost between the two factions. Referring to William P. Fessenden, one of the Conservatives

[2] *Ibid.*, pp. 262-263. Italics added.

in the Senate, Stevens was to write in a letter: "He has too much of the vile ingredient called conservatism, which is worse than secession."

The term "Radical" should not be misconstrued. Neither Stevens nor his followers were radicals in the accepted meaning of the term. They agreed with the Conservatives on nearly all political and economic questions of the day except on measures dealing with the slavery problem. When it was a question of raising the tariff or voting land grants to railroads Stevens was as ready as any Conservative to come to the aid of big business. On this he should be judged by the light of the prevailing ideas of his time, not of our time. Such sincere friends of labor as Wendell Phillips and Horace Greeley favored a high tariff, which they considered as necessary for the protection of labor as for the growth of industry. Nor can it be denied that without land grants to railroads the development of the country would have been greatly retarded. During his second term in Congress Stevens had opposed a Homestead Act, saying, "It would be a very unhappy condition in society if that country [the West] was to be settled entirely by paupers—by men who have no means," but so ardent a proponent of the measure as Horace Greeley was bitterly disappointed when he journeyed west and saw the rural slums the act had produced. And no other man in Congress championed the interests of the common people against the bankers, wealthy bondholders, and speculators with more ardor and persistency than Stevens.

3

On January 2, 1862, Stevens rose to speak on the resolution he had introduced the first day of the session.

"Let us not be deceived," he said. "Those who talk about peace in sixty days are shallow statesmen. . . . So long as the rebels are left the means to cultivate their fields through forced labor, you may expend the blood of tens of thousands of freemen and billions of money, year after year, without being any nearer the end. . . . Their domestic institutions give them great advantages over the free States in time of war. . . . Every able-bodied white man can be spared for the army. The aged and infirm can stay at home to oversee the slaves, and all their industrial pursuits be uninterrupted. Although the black man never lifts a weapon, he is really the mainstay of the war.

"Those who furnish the means of war, but who are the natural enemies of the slaveholders, must be made our allies. Universal emancipation must be proclaimed to all. . . . Oh, for six months' resurrection in the flesh of stern old Jackson! He would abolish slavery as the cause and the support of the insurrection; he would arm the free people of color, as he did at New Orleans; he would march into the heart of slavedom to put weapons into every freedman's hands.

"It may be asked why liberate the slaves of all instead of confining it to those belonging to rebels? I see great difficulty in executing such a law. Perjury, fraud, and falsehood, would screen half of the guilty. But I can see no good cause for the discrimination. *Our object should be not only to end this war now, but to prevent its recurrence.* All must admit that slavery is the cause of it. Without slavery we should this day be a united and happy people. So long as it exists we cannot have a solid Union. Patch up a compromise now and leave this germ of evil, it would soon again override the whole South, even if you freed three-fourths of the slaves. You would have expended countless treasures and untold lives in vain. The principles of our Republic are wholly incompatible with slavery. They cannot live together. While you are quelling this insurrection at such a fearful cost, remove the cause, that future generations may live in peace.

"But I would do no injustice to loyal men. I do not admit the rightful ownership of any human soul. But in deference to chronic error and prejudice, I would treat them as if such a thing were possible. Let Government pledge the faith of the nation to make compensation for the loss of loyal citizens. With such assurances every patriotic slaveholder ought to be satisfied. . . . Every Government allows private property to be taken for public use when the necessity is imperative. . . . The *real* patriots who are still loyal to the Union would, I am sure, willingly lay this sacrifice on the altar of their country. The rebels, and those who would not acquiesce, deserve not to be consulted.

"I deem manumission merciful, but admit it to be the most terrible weapon in our armory. Is that an argument against its use? Instruments of war are not selected on account of their harmlessness. You choose the cannon that has the longest range. You throw the shell that will kill the most men by its explosion. You grind to its sharpest edge the saber bayonet."

He reproached the administration for its lack of "that determined and invincible courage that was inspired in the Revolution by the grand idea of liberty, equality and the rights of man. . . . Our statesmen, unlike the men of the Revolution, do not seem to know how to touch the hearts of freemen and rouse them to battle. No declaration of the great objects of Government, no glorious sound of universal liberty has gone forth from the capital. . . . We have put a sword into one hand of our generals and shackles into the other. Freemen are not inspired by such mingled music. Let the people know that this Government is fighting not only to enforce a sacred compact, but to carry out to final perfection the principles of the Declaration of Independence, which its framers expected would long since have been fulfilled on this continent, and the blood of every freeman would boil with enthusiasm, and his nerves be strengthened in this holy warfare."

Granted that Stevens's proposal was premature; granted that the time was not yet ripe for its adoption—who can doubt that such language as his speeded the ripening? Congress, the people, the administration needed to be told these things, and he told them in language that made a deep and lasting impression. The fact that he advocated emancipation as a war measure—as a means of shortening the conflict—appealed to thousands upon whom a purely humanitarian appeal would have been wasted. Others were stirred as by a bugle call by the idealistic fervor of his speech. Letters rained in upon him. "You have made more hearts glad than are beating within the bounds of your congressional district, for I doubt not every true patriot throughout the North, as he rises from the reading of that speech, ejaculates from the Holy of Holies of his heart, 'God bless you, Thaddeus Stevens!' " wrote one. "All lovers of freedom have been made to rejoice in thy conduct," wrote a Quaker. The New York *Times* chided him for wasting the time of Congress with proposals which he knew would not be adopted. But he was not merely talking to the House, but to the nation. He was preparing the soil for the harvest of liberty.

4

The rejection of the reaffirmation of the Crittenden Resolution meant a break with the President's policy of noninterference with slavery. In the succeeding few months, by successive acts of Congress, army and navy personnel were forbidden to return fugitive slaves; slavery was abolished in the District of Columbia and excluded from the territories; finally, in July, 1862, the second Confiscation Act—a veritable emancipation act—was passed. The only one of these measures the President fully approved was the exclusion of slavery from the territories, which, strangely, was the one the unconstitutionality of which could not be doubted, the Supreme Court having pronounced against exclusion in the Dred Scott decision.

The question of constitutionality was to arise repeatedly during the war. Stevens defined his position unequivocally at the beginning of the conflict. On August 2, 1861, he said: "It is idle to tell me that the obligations of an instrument are binding on one party while they are repudiated by the other. Obligations to be binding in war must be mutual, equally acknowledged, and admitted by both parties. There is another principle just as universal:—when parties become belligerent the war between them abrogates all compacts, treaties and constitutions which may have existed between them."

The administration did not adopt this position until almost two years later. Thus while the Confederates, considering themselves an independent nation, waged war as against a foreign enemy, the government's hands were tied by the assumption that the rebels were entitled to the protection of the Constitution which they repudiated and scorned. Union commanders were delivering fugitive slaves to rebel slaveholders at a time when Confederate commanders were seizing slaves in Kentucky and carrying them off to work for the rebels.

Stevens's doctrine enabled him to dispense with the twistings, turnings, sophistries, and equivocations to which the administration and many of his Republican colleagues were compelled to resort in order to fit indispensable war measures into the framework of their legalistic conception of the Constitution. When Virginia seceded, several of her western counties formed a separate government. They decided to apply for admission to the Union under the name of West Virginia, but found themselves confronted with the difficulty that under the Constitution a state could not be divided without the consent of its legislature. So the leader of the loyalists in the western part of the state, Francis H. Pierpont, moved to Alexandria, and under the protection of Northern guns an election was held in about eleven *townships* out of the one hundred and forty-two *counties* in the state. Those elected called themselves the duly constituted government of the State of Virginia and granted the necessary consent for the formation of the new state! They even sent representatives to Congress, about whom Stevens was to say: "We know that members have been elected to the House by only twenty votes and these cast under the guns of a fort. To say that these gentlemen represent any district is mockery."[3] Congressmen who appeared to have forgotten the scriptural warning that "the letter killeth, but the spirit giveth life" seriously argued that this pseudolegal hocus-pocus met the requirements of the Constitution. Stevens scorned such sophistry. "It is but mockery," he said, "to tell me that the Legislature of Virginia has ever consented to the division. We may admit West Virginia as a new State, not by virtue of any provision of the Constitution, but under the absolute power which the laws of war give us. I shall vote for this bill upon that theory, and upon that alone; for I will not stultify myself by supposing that we have any warrant in the Constitution for this proceeding."

[3] *Globe,* Dec. 2, 1861.

CHAPTER VI

Congressional Assault upon Slavery

We have seen that on the first day of the regular session of the Thirty-seventh Congress Stevens had proposed that "the President be requested to declare free, and to direct his generals to order freedom to, all slaves who shall leave their masters or who shall aid in quelling the rebellion." This implied nonenforcement of the Fugitive Slave Law.

The question of the enforcement of that law—one of the most drastic and objectionable the slaveholders had managed to wring from a reluctant North—was a moot question from the beginning of the war. In May, 1861, a little over a month after the fall of Fort Sumter, Major General Benjamin F. Butler occupied Fort Monroe in Virginia. The second day after his arrival three Negroes had presented themselves and had related that their master, Colonel Mallory of the Confederate Army, had given orders that they be sent to North Carolina to help construct Confederate fortifications. Butler needed laborers, and told an officer: "These men are contraband of war. Put them to work." His remark became widely known and caught the popular fancy. Henceforth fugitive slaves were to be known as "contrabands."

Eventually over nine hundred fugitive slaves—men, women, and children—sought and found refuge in Butler's camp. The general wrote to Secretary of War Cameron for instructions. On August 8, 1861, he received a long, rambling, ambiguous reply. The opening sentence, part of which was underscored for emphasis, could, however, not be misconstrued. It read: "It is the desire of the President that *all existing rights in all the States be fully respected and maintained.*" After reading the letter Butler commented: "This is too ridiculous to be laughed at." [1]

Other Union generals received similar instructions. Since three-fourths were proslavery Democrats they had no difficulty interpreting them in the interest of the slaveholders. Some drove fugitive slaves from their lines, others received them but permitted rebel slaveholders to come and claim them. General McCook was so accommodating that he received praise from a Confederate newspaper. General Henry W. Halleck issued an order that read in part: "We will prove to them [the Confederates] that we came to restore not to violate the Constitution and laws. . . . No fugitive slave will, therefore, be admitted within our lines or camps, except when especially ordered by the General commanding." The fact that a fugitive had rendered valuable service to the Union Army made no difference. Senator James W. Grimes of Iowa shocked his colleagues in the Senate with his account of what happened to two fugitive slaves in Missouri belonging to a Confederate lieutenant colonel. They had brought information concerning Confederate bridge burners, who as a result were arrested. Yet when the owner's agent came to claim them they were turned over to him. One broke away and was killed by a rifle bullet fired by a federal soldier.

2

The day after Stevens had presented his resolution, his friend Owen Lovejoy introduced a bill making it a penal offense for any officer or private of the army or navy to capture, return, or aid in capturing or returning, fugitive slaves. We can take it for granted that Stevens was no stranger to that bill. A week later the Commoner introduced a resolution requesting the President to direct General Halleck to withdraw his order concerning fugitive slaves. It was, however, not until February 28, 1862, that the Committee on Military Affairs reported out a bill, in the form of an Article of War, forbidding all persons in the military or naval forces of the United States to return

[1] C. Edward Lester, *Life and Public Services of Charles Sumner,* p. 358.

fugitive slaves on pain of court-martial and dismissal from the army. While the bill did not emancipate the fugitives, nobody doubted that it was the intention of its sponsors to see to it that they were never returned to slavery. Pearce of Maryland said during the debate in the Senate: "It is an invitation to all such people to resort to the lines of the army as a harbor of refuge, a place of asylum, a spot where they can be safe from the operation of the undoubted legal rights of the owner. . . . It is not an act of emancipation in its terms; but as far as it can operate, and does operate, it leads directly to that result." When an amendment was offered in the Senate that slaves belonging to border state slaveholders should be excepted, it was defeated by a vote of thirty to seven.

Had the President been in favor of the policy the bill represented he could have put it into effect by executive order long before the matter came up in Congress. His failure to do so is sufficient proof that he did not favor the measure. Did he consider it his duty, war or no war, to enforce the Fugitive Slave Law? Did he fear it would antagonize border state slaveholders? Or was it that he saw in the measure another step toward the form of emancipation the effect of which he had always dreaded? He did not veto the bill, but after it became law fugitives continued to be driven from the Union lines, or if given temporary asylum, were surrendered to owners who came to claim them. The Committee on the Conduct of the War made an investigation, and on April 10, 1862, General Daniel Sickles testified that the President had never officially communicated the new Article of War to the army. As late as June, 1862, Colonel D. R. Anthony of the Second Kansas Volunteers was placed under arrest for having issued an order forbidding his subordinates to return fugitive slaves. It has been estimated that before the President adopted Stevens's "law of war" policy, over twenty thousand fugitive slaves were either driven back or turned over to the rebels—many times the number that had been returned to loyal slaveholders since the foundation of the republic. One can only speculate on how great the exodus from the plantations might have been had a more realistic policy been followed.

Failure to enforce the Article of War had an unfortunate effect on relations between the President and Congress. On July 5, 1862, Stevens decided to speak out. "There are many things in the conduct of this war of which I cannot approve," he said on the floor of Congress. "I cannot approve of putting generals who sympathize with the slaveholders at the head of our armies, or of putting our generals under express orders to pursue and return fugitive slaves belonging to traitors."

William Kellogg of Illinois interrupted, saying: "I would inquire of the gentleman from Pennsylvania, when he makes these charges against the conduct of the war, whether he applies them to the President and Secretary of War, or merely to the generals in the field?"

Stevens replied: "I intend they should apply where they belong. I am no sycophant, no parasite. What I think, I say. These acts have been perpetrated without rebuke. Let the world determine where the responsibility rests."

He apparently did more than merely protest. In a letter written by Lincoln to Cuthbert Bullitt of New Orleans, July 28, 1862, appears the following significant statement: "The truth is, that what is done and omitted about slaves is done and omitted on the same military necessity. It is a military necessity to have men and money; and we cannot get either, in sufficient numbers or amounts, if we keep from or drive from our lives slaves coming to them."

One is forced to conclude that the chairman of the Ways and Means Committee had given the President privately to understand that if the will of Congress in this matter continued to be disregarded, the President would find it difficult to obtain credits for the army.

Eventually Lincoln realized that the war could be greatly shortened by encouraging the slaves to leave the plantations rather than discouraging them from doing so. Reverend John Eaton, assistant commissioner of freedmen, has given the following account of what Lincoln told him in August, 1864, during an interview at the White House:

He referred to the really astonishing extent to which the colored people were informed in regard to the progress of the war, and remarked that he wished the "grapevine telegraph" could be utilized to call upon the Negroes of the interior peacefully to leave the plantations and seek the protection of our armies. This as a war-time measure he considered legitimate. Apart from the numbers it would add to our military forces, he explained the effect such an exodus would have upon the industry of the South. The Confederate soldiers were sustained by provisions raised by Negro labor; withdraw that labor, and the young men in the Southern army would soon be obliged to go home to "raise hog and hominy," and thus promote the collapse of the Confederacy.[2]

What is this but a paraphrase of what Stevens had been saying since the beginning of the conflict?

3

Since the commencement of hostilities Stevens had urged the abolition of slavery in the District of Columbia. He was pleased when a bill to that effect was adopted in the Senate and lost no time introducing it in the House. A Democrat proposed an amendment providing that "the Act shall not go into operation unless the qualified citizens of the District of Columbia shall, by a majority of votes polled, approve and ratify the same?" Stevens caustically remarked: "It is somewhere provided that the wicked shall be damned. I would suggest to my colleague that he propose a proviso to that: 'providing they consent thereto.'" The amendment was lost and Stevens moved the previous question. The bill passed by a vote of 92 to 38.

The President believed the measure should not have been adopted without the consent of Maryland, and that qualified citizens of the District should have been given an opportunity to vote on the matter. He was, however, mollified by the fact that provision had been made to give reasonable compensation to the slaveholders and that $100,000 had been appropriated to colonize the freedmen. So on April 16, 1862, the bill became law, and slavery was banished forever from the nation's capital.

In June of that year Congress abolished slavery in the territories. Although the measure was clearly a violation of the Supreme Court's decision, the President fully approved. On matters of constitutionality he was inclined to be opportunistic. He once told Chase: "The rebels are violating the Constitution to destroy the Union, I will violate the Constitution, if necessary to save the Union, and I suspect, Chase, that our Constitution is going to have a rough time of it before we get done with this row." [3] Stevens was more consistent.

[2] From *Grant, Lincoln and the Freedmen* by John Eaton. Quoted by special permission of the publishers, Longmans, Green & Co., Inc., p. 173.
[3] Donn Piatt, *Memories of Men Who Saved the Union,* p. 109.

He did not believe the Constitution was being violated when such measures were taken. In his speech of January 22, 1862, he said that in the event of "an armed rebellion too powerful to be quelled by peaceful means, or by any rules provided for the regulation of the land and naval forces, the Constitution itself grants the President and Congress a supplemental power, which it was impossible to define, because it must go on increasing and varying according to the increasing and varying necessities of the nation."

The bill became law on June 19, 1862, settling forever the question of slavery in the territories.

On July 16, Stevens, by moving the previous question, rushed through the House in record time a Senate bill which Senator Saulsbury of Delaware characterized as "a wholesale scheme of emancipation." The bill authorized the President to receive into the service of the United States for the purpose of "any war service for which they may be found competent, persons of African descent"; and provided that "when any man or boy of African descent shall render any such service . . . he, his mother, and his wife and children, shall for ever thereafter be free, any law, usage, or custom whatsoever, to the contrary notwithstanding." Slaves belonging to slaveholders in the loyal border states were, however, excluded from the measure.

4

By far the most important measure passed by the Thirty-seventh Congress was the second Confiscation Act. Lincoln's scholarly biographer Professor Randall has written: "The second confiscation act . . . of July, 1862, which preceded Lincoln's proclamation, *went further than that edict*. . . . It declared all slaves of persons adhering to the 'rebellion' to be forever free. *The law was not qualified by the hundred day warning or escape clause, or by the very considerable territorial exceptions of the President's decree*. It was one of the several antislavery acts of Congress that antedated the proclamation." [4]

In one form or another the bill had been before Congress for many months. Its passage at this juncture appears to have been provoked partly by resentment at the nonenforcement of the Article of War

[4] From *Lincoln the Liberal Statesman* by J. G. Randall, copyright 1947. Quoted by special permission of the publishers, Dodd, Mead & Company, p. 27. Italics added.

voted in March of that year, partly by dissatisfaction with the President's annulment of an order by Major General David Hunter, commander of the Department of the South, freeing the slaves in that department. The section dealing with confiscation of property other than slaves had, according to James G. Blaine, been provoked by the sequestration of Union property by the Confederacy. This appears probable, especially where landed property was concerned. The part concerning confiscation of real estate, having been modified to avoid a presidential veto, was never again able to command a majority in both houses.

The act freed "all slaves of persons who shall hereafter be engaged in rebellion against the Government of the United States"; all slaves "escaping from such persons and taking refuge within the lines of the army, and all slaves captured from such persons, or deserted by them and coming under the control of the Government of the United States, and all slaves of such persons found or being within any place occupied by rebel forces and afterwards by the forces of the United States." In practice the act meant that the slaves would be freed *as fast as the army could free them.* If it did not free all slaves in the rebel states it was in deference to the President's well-known opinion that such a measure would be unconstitutional.

The part dealing with the seizure of property other than slaves made it incumbent upon the President, in order "to insure the speedy termination of the present rebellion," to seize the estate and property, money, stocks, credits, and effects of certain classes of persons responsible for the revolt. It was the seizure of real estate beyond the natural life of the offender to which the President principally objected as unconstitutional. Blaine remarks, however, that as far as the freeing of slaves was concerned, "he [Lincoln] felt he could deal with that subject without the co-operation of Congress." [5] That he felt that way there can be no doubt, but considering his conviction that to free the slaves when there appeared to be no hope of colonizing them abroad was to do them and the country a disservice, it was well that Stevens and his followers were determined not to leave the matter entirely in his hands.

Lincoln decided to veto the bill and prepared a veto message. When congressional leaders learned about this their indignation was

[5] *Twenty Years of Congress,* vol. I, p. 377.

profound. Since, however, doubt existed that a veto could be overridden, an explanatory joint resolution was passed meeting the President's objections. Lincoln then signed the bill, which became law on July 17, 1862, when Congress adjourned not to meet again until December.

5

To no man was the modification of the provision concerning the confiscation of real estate a greater disappointment than to Stevens. He had not favored that provision because it was retaliatory, but had regarded it as a means "to insure the speedy termination of the present rebellion" and to shatter the power of the South's landed aristocracy. It was not his intention that it should be used to the injury of the common people of the South. The opposite is true. On January 22, 1864, when trying to obtain the repeal of the explanatory joint resolution which had virtually annulled the provision, he said: "Such confiscation of course would spare the property of those who took no part in the war, and of the common soldiers, who were compelled by the laws of their States to enter the army." On May 2 of that year he said: "In enforcing the rights of conquest the innocent should be spared; even those actually bearing arms against us who were compelled by the laws of their government to enter their armies should also be spared; but the property of the morally and politically guilty should be taken for public use."

What "public use" did he have in mind? In his speech of May 2 he said: "I inferred that under the laws of war the conqueror has the right to seize the property, real and personal, of the enemy and appropriate it to the payment of the expenses and damages of the war, and make provision for our wounded soldiers, and for the families of the slain." This, however, was only a part of his program. No sooner had the war ended than he again advocated confiscation of real estate, this time letting the cat out of the bag: part of the confiscated land was to be used to give each adult male freedman a homestead of forty acres. From a statement made by his disciple George W. Julian we learn, however, that he and his followers had not only this but something else in mind that might well have resulted in the speedy termination of the war and have at the same time settled the vexing problem of reconstruction. In 1886 Julian wrote:

Congress was obliged to make the modification required as the only means of securing the important advantages of other features of the measure; but the action of the President was inexpressibly provoking to a large majority of Congress. It was bitterly denounced as an anti-Republican discrimination between real and personal property when the nation was struggling for its life against a rebellious aristocracy founded on the monopoly of land and the ownership of negroes. The President was charged with thus prolonging the war and aggravating its cost by paralyzing one of the most potent means of putting down the rebellion, and purposely leaving the owners of large estates in full possession of their lands at the end of the struggle. He was arraigned as the deliberate betrayer of the freedmen and poor whites, who had been friendly to the Union, while the confiscation of life-estates as a war measure could prove of no practical value to the government or disadvantage to the enemy.[6]

It is obvious, therefore, that the Radicals considered the confiscation of landed property of certain classes of rebels "one of the most potent means of ending the rebellion" and that this was in some way connected with "freedmen and poor whites, who had been friendly to the Union." One can only conclude that at this juncture Stevens was in favor of dividing a portion of the confiscated land not only among freedmen, but also among landless poor whites. "The property thus taken," Stevens said in his speech of January 22, 1864, "is not confiscated under the Constitution after conviction of treason, but is held by virtue of the laws of war. No individual crime need to be proved against the owners. The fact of being a belligerent enemy carries the forfeiture with it. Here was the error of the President when he vetoed the confiscation bill passed by Congress." [7]

It does not appear unreasonable to believe that if the news had spread through the South that the invaders meant to become the benefactors not only of the slaves, but of a large portion of the South's white population—that, in other words, they were waging war not against the South but against the oppressors of the South—Confederate resistance might have collapsed. The poor whites, who did most of the fighting, were by no means as eager to die for the

[6] Rice, *op. cit.*, pp. 57-58.
[7] *Globe,* Jan. 22, 1864.

preservation of slavery as professional Southerners would have us believe. As early as April 16, 1862, the Confederacy found itself obliged to resort to conscription of all white men between the ages of 18 and 35. Secretary of War George W. Randolph wrote concerning the law to Jefferson Davis: "The plan of voluntary enlistment having failed to preserve the organization, and to recruit the strength of our armies at a time when the safety of the country required both to be effected, a resort to draft or conscription was the only alternative." [8] On October 30, 1863, Robert E. Lee wrote to Secretary of War James A. Seddon: "Early in the war, it was found that stringent measures alone would keep the army together." [9]

To have offered such men homesteads carved out of the property of the slaveholders might indeed have brought the conflict to an early close and have created a bond between the North and the South such as had never before existed.

[8] *Offic. Rec.*, vol. 128, p. 43.
[9] *Ibid.*, vol. 49, p. 806.

CHAPTER VII

The Truth about the Emancipation Proclamation

Lincoln merits the title of Great Emancipator posterity has conferred upon him. He merits it for his unshakable determination to preserve the Union when Garrison, Phillips, Greeley, and other antislavery leaders were in favor of not opposing secession. He merits it for his decision not to evacuate Fort Sumter against the advice of so confirmed an antislavery advocate as Secretary Chase. All this, however, does not alter the fact that reliable evidence shows him to have issued the proclamation not because he considered it desirable from the military or social viewpoints, but from fear of what an exasperated Congress might do when it reassembled in December, 1862. Nor does it alter the fact that although he himself had serious doubts concerning the postwar validity of the proclamation, he continued to exert every possible effort to get the border states to adopt gradual emancipation. Yet he must have known that had his advice been followed, ratification of a constitutional amendment abolishing slavery throughout the republic would have been impossible and the freedom of the slaves would have been dependent upon a court decision. Only when he finally realized that his efforts could not succeed did he declare himself in favor of the amendment.

2

Was it mere coincidence that the President should have made a proposal to Congress for compensated gradual emancipation with federal aid on March 6, 1862—four days before the Article of War forbidding the military to return fugitive slaves was adopted by that body? It will be recalled that Senator Pearce of Maryland had said of that measure: "It is not an act of emancipation in its terms; but so far as it can operate, and does operate, it leads directly to that result." It does not, therefore, appear unreasonable to believe that the President made the proposal in order to arrest, if possible, the congressional drive toward general emancipation the measure portended, and which was to gain momentum during the succeeding months. He proposed the passage of a joint resolution to the effect that the United States would give pecuniary aid to any state that adopted gradual emancipation, "to compensate it for inconvenience, public or private." "In my judgment," he wrote, "gradual and not sudden emancipation is better for all."

Stevens was impatient with Lincoln's proposal. "I have read it over," he said, "and confess I have not been able to see what makes one side so anxious to pass it, or the other so anxious to defeat it. I think it is about the most diluted milk-and-water-gruel proposition that was ever given to the American nation."

He considered general emancipation indispensable and believed the President's proposal only served to delay a measure that would shorten the conflict and save thousands of human lives. Most of all he objected to the following paragraph in the President's message: "Such a proposition on the part of the General Government sets up no claim of a right by the Federal authority to interfere with slavery within State limits—referring as it does the absolute control of the subject, in each case, to the State and the people immediately interested. It is proposed as a matter of perfectly free choice to them."

What was this but a reaffirmation, after a year of insurrection and war, of the President's pronouncement at his inaugural that the federal authority had no legal right to interfere with slavery in the slave states? Stevens repudiated that doctrine, as John Quincy Adams had repudiated it, and as Lincoln himself was to finish by doing. If there never was a time when the federal authority could interfere with slavery in the slave states, then the cause of the rebellion, and of possible future rebellions, could never be eradicated except with the consent of the rebels! What would hinder them from accepting the President's proposal as a matter of expediency and later restoring slavery? That Lincoln himself did not exclude that possibility is evident from the bill he offered to Congress on July 12, 1862, and from the elaboration of his compensated emancipation plan he presented to Congress in December of that year. Both contained a clause dealing with that contingency. The clause in the December document read:

> Any State having received bonds as aforesaid, and afterwards reintroducing or tolerating slavery therein, shall refund to the United States the bonds so received, or the value thereof, and all interest paid thereon.

Since in the existing situation emancipation by the slave states themselves could not by the furthest stretch of the imagination have been called "a matter of perfectly free choice," any supposedly voluntary agreement made with them on the matter must necessarily have been of doubtful value.

Stevens did not think such a policy solved anything. He felt that now that the slaveholders had plunged the country into war, the struggle must not cease until its cause had been completely eradicated. "The reunion of the States must be perfected, and so effected as to remove all causes of disturbance in the future; and to attain this end, it is necessary that the original cause should, if possible, be rooted out." These are Lincoln's words, spoken to a crowd gathered in front of the White House on January 31, 1865. It was the doctrine Stevens preached from the beginning of the war.

The President's proposal was, however, adopted by large majorities in both houses of Congress and approved by him on April 10, 1862. Not wishing to be counted on the side of the proslavery representatives, Stevens abstained from voting.

During the succeeding two months Stevens and the two senators from Massachusetts, Sumner and Wilson, importuned the President to issue an Emancipation Proclamation, but to no avail. Lincoln complained to Senator John B. Henderson of Missouri: "Stevens, Sumner and Wilson haunt me with their importunities for a Proclamation of Emancipation. Where I go and whatever way I turn, they are on my trail, and still in my heart, I have a deep conviction that the hour has not yet come." [1]

[1] Don C. Seitz, *Lincoln the Politician,* p. 333.

3

On July 12, 1862, the report of the conference committee concerning the second Confiscation Act was accepted by the Senate and the bill was now ready for the President's signature. What must have been the surprise of senators and representatives when on that very day Congress received from the President the draft of a bill, passage of which he recommended, embodying the compensated emancipation proposal, by action of the slave states themselves, he had made four months earlier. The bill specified that pecuniary aid would be given to any state that emancipated its slaves either gradually or immediately, that the aid was to be in the form of interest-bearing bonds, and that the bonds and all interest paid thereon were to be returned if a state "at any time afterwards by law reintroduce or tolerate slavery within its limits."

That the President should have presented the bill to Congress at this juncture is explicable by the fact that it was then his intention to veto the second Confiscation Act. It was therefore in the nature of a counterproposal. The chances that Stevens and his followers would lay aside the act for a renewal of the offer that had proved futile four months earlier were so slim that the President's move must be regarded as a well-nigh desperate attempt to halt the congressional drive toward general emancipation. The bill was referred to committee and never taken up. When one compares this with the vote of 89 to 31 the President's proposal had received in April of that year, one realizes the extent to which Stevens had succeeded in winning over his colleagues. It was no idle boast on his part when he told his constituents at a public meeting at Lancaster in the fall of that year: "In the last week [of the session], after a few remarks of mine, the vote was 84 to 42—84 agreeing with me, when a year ago not fifty could have been found." [2]

The bill was not the President's only attempt to take the rudder from the hands of Stevens and his followers and steer emancipation into what he considered a safer channel. That same day he sought and obtained an interview with the congressional representatives of the border states and addressed them in moving language, imploring

[2] *Liberator,* Sept. 19, 1862.

them to use every effort so their states would adopt compensated gradual emancipation with federal aid. "I do not speak of emancipation at once," he told them, "but of a decision at once to emancipate gradually. Room in South America for colonization can be obtained cheaply, and in abundance, and when numbers shall be large enough to be company and encouragement for one another, the freed people will not be so reluctant to go."

In his first message to Congress concerning the matter, the President had expressed the opinion that if the border states accepted his proposal, it would deprive the rebel states of the hope that they would ever join them. "This," he had said, "substantially ends the Rebellion." He now repeated: "In my opinion, if you had voted for the resolution in the gradual emancipation Message of last March, the war would now be substantially ended."

No one can read Lincoln's address to the representatives of the border states without profound sympathy for the speaker and an equally profound conviction of the benevolence of his intentions. He believed it to be a task imposed upon him by Providence to restore the Union, but experienced agony of soul at the thought that restoration might prove a curse to the South and to the Negro if general emancipation without colonization was its concomitant.

4

Lincoln had by no means abandoned the hope that the border states might yet adopt compensated gradual emancipation with federal aid, nor the hope that the rebel states might then fall into line and offer to make peace on that basis. He was, therefore, opposed to the second Confiscation Act not only for the reasons he had mentioned in his veto message and to which Congress had given satisfaction in the explanatory joint resolution, but also and especially for a reason he had preferred not to mention: that the act interfered with a solution of the problem he considered far more desirable. He has sometimes been accused of being vacillating. The fact is, however, that when he believed he was right he would stick to his purpose with amazing persistency. His was not the clumsy unyielding stubbornness of his successor Johnson. He would yield, but in such a manner that the advantage usually remained with him.

He had made two attempts to sidetrack the second Confiscation Act—by sending a bill to Congress embodying his compensated gradual emancipation proposal and recommending its adoption, and by making a moving appeal to the representatives of the border states. He must have felt none too sanguine about the success of either of these moves, for since the first of July he had been preparing a third move he meant to make if the two others failed. It was nothing less than a preliminary Emancipation Proclamation serving notice on the rebel states that if they did not lay down their arms by January 1, 1863, he would issue a final proclamation declaring their slaves free. What did this mean? Had Stevens triumphed? Had Lincoln decided to yield? Only apparently so. *The move was obviously intended for the purpose of rendering the second Confiscation Act inoperative for the remainder of that year, since the issuing of the preliminary proclamation would fully justify nonenforcement of the act until January, 1863.* Thus the *status quo* on slavery would be maintained for over five months, during which time, the President hoped, first the border states and then the rebel states might realize the wisdom of accepting his gradual emancipation proposal. It was a shrewd move that gave some promise of success. With two such swords of Damocles hanging over them as enforcement of the second Confiscation Act and a final Emancipation Proclamation there was reason to believe that the slave states might weaken, although it is hardly likely that, had they done so, they would have regarded it as "a matter of perfectly free choice."

5

On July 13, 1862, while on his way in a carriage to the funeral of an infant child of Secretary Edwin M. Stanton, in the company of Secretaries William Seward and Gideon Welles and the wife of Seward's son Frederick, the President told them about his intention. Welles wrote in his *Diary:*

> It was a new departure for the President, for until this time, in all our previous intercourse whenever this question of emancipation or mitigation of slavery had been in any way alluded to, he had been prompt and emphatic in denouncing any interference by the general government with the subject. . . . He dwelt earnestly on the gravity, importance and deli-

cacy of the movement, said he had given it much thought and had about come to the conclusion that it was a military necessity absolutely essential for the salvation of the Union, that we must free the slaves or be ourselves subdued.[3]

Lincoln was a man who liked to keep his own counsel. This may possibly explain why he gave his companions a reason for his proposed action that conflicted with everything he had hitherto been saying about the matter. Only nine days before, on July 4, 1862, Charles Sumner had called on him and had pleaded with him to issue the proclamation on that day, so as to make the day "more sacred and historic." The President had replied: "I would do it if I were not afraid that half the officers would fling down their arms and four more States would rise." [4] Obviously this statement cannot be reconciled with the one he made to Seward and Welles. Neither the one nor the other represented his real thought.

It must have been in the hope that his efforts with Congress or with the representatives of the border states might still bear fruit that he delayed communicating his intention to his entire cabinet. It was not until July 22, 1862, that the famous reading of the first draft of the preliminary proclamation took place. Seward suggested that the measure be postponed until a victory had been won, since otherwise "It may be viewed as the last measure of an exhausted Government, a cry for help; the Government stretching forth its hands to Ethiopia, instead of Ethiopia stretching forth her hands to the Government." [5] Since Seward was opposed to large-scale immediate emancipation even more than Lincoln, he made the proposal undoubtedly in the hope that if victory came it would be sufficiently decisive to enable the President to refrain from committing himself. The readiness with which Lincoln accepted the proposal should dispel any lingering belief that military necessity had decided him to make the move. As James C. Welling, editor of the *National Intelligencer,* shrewdly remarked: "If military necessity were held to domi-

[3] Welles, *Diary,* vol. I, pp. 70-71. On February 6, 1864, Lincoln made a similar statement to the artist Francis B. Carpenter, saying: "It had got to be midsummer, 1862. Things had gone from bad to worse, until I had felt that we had reached the end of our rope on the plan of operations we had been pursuing; that we had played our last card, and must change our tactics or lose the game. I now determined upon the adoption of the emancipation policy."

[4] Edward L. Pierce, *Memoirs and Letters of Charles Sumner,* vol. IV, p. 83.

[5] F. B. Carpenter, *Six Months at the White House,* pp. 20-22.

nate the situation . . . the proclamation could never have come more appropriately than when the military need was greatest." [6]

When Seward made the proposal the thought that prompted him must have also flashed through the President's mind. Why not wait? Congress did not reconvene until December. He would maintain the *status quo* by not enforcing the second Confiscation Act. If a decisive victory came he would be able to keep Stevens and his followers in check and persist in nonenforcement, while at the same time striving to secure the adoption of gradual emancipation by the slave states, rebel as well as loyal. If the victory did not come or was indecisive, he would still have plenty of time to issue the preliminary proclamation before the meeting of Congress.

6

The prevailing thesis that Lincoln was now anxiously awaiting a victory to issue the preliminary proclamation is contradicted by the evidence. Why that evidence has been ignored is difficult to understand. There was nothing dishonorable about the course Lincoln had decided to adopt. It was in strict harmony with his convictions. He was playing his cards shrewdly and was justified in playing them as he did as long as any hope remained that his own plan of emancipation might prevail. Whether under the circumstances that plan was realistic is another story, but there can be no question of the sincerity of his intentions.

On August 14, 1862, the interview took place between the President and the colored delegation he had summoned to the White House in the hope of obtaining their co-operation for the colonizing of freedmen on the Panamanian isthmus. In the course of the interview the President said: "There is an uneasiness on the part of our people, harsh as it may seem, for you free colored people to remain with us." It requires considerable credulity to believe that the man who said this was anxiously awaiting an opportunity to present the country with several million more free colored people.

After the President had decided to follow Seward's advice he returned to his former thesis that to issue an Emancipation Proclamation meant to court disaster. This should not surprise us. No man,

[6] Rice, *op. cit.*, p. 530.

however truthful, can practice statecraft without occasionally resorting to subterfuge. Lincoln could hardly have told believers in immediate emancipation that he was waiting for a victory sufficiently decisive so he would *not* have to issue the document.

On August 19, 1862, Horace Greeley, in an open letter in the New York *Tribune*—reprinted in the weekly *Tribune* which had a large nationwide circulation—appealed to the President to issue an Emancipation Proclamation. What is more, he took Lincoln severely to task for the nonenforcement of the Confiscation Act. The President, he said, was ignoring a law of Congress out of "mistaken deference for rebel slavery." He was bowing to the influence of "certain fossil politicians hailing from the Border States" and was humoring army officers who "evinced far more solicitude to uphold slavery than to put down the rebellion." Wendell Phillips, too, rushed to the attack and wrote in the New York *Independent:* "The confiscation law and all the action of Congress in that direction, are as yet nullities, because the President omits to put them into force." Lincoln replied to Greeley on August 22, 1862, with the famous letter in which he said: "What I do about slavery and the colored race, I do because I believe it helps to save the Union, and what I forbear, I forbear because I do not believe it would help to save the Union." This sounded too much like Stephen Douglas's saying that he did not care whether slavery was "voted up or down" to satisfy the editor, all the more so as the President remained discreetly reticent concerning the nonenforcement of the Confiscation Act. He renewed his attack.

John P. Usher, assistant secretary of the interior, who at the beginning of the new year was to succeed Caleb B. Smith as head of that department, has written:

> Mr. Greeley was evidently dissatisfied with the explanation of Mr. Lincoln, and the *Tribune* teemed with complaints and criticisms of his administration, which very much annoyed him; so much so that he requested Mr. Greeley to come to Washington and make known in person his complaints, to the end that they might be obviated if possible. The managing editor of the *Tribune* came. Mr. Lincoln said:
>
> "You complain of me. What have I done or omitted to do which has provoked the hostility of the *Tribune?*"
>
> The reply was: "You should issue a proclamation abolishing slavery."

Mr. Lincoln answered: "Suppose I do that. There are 20,000 of our muskets on the shoulders of Kentuckians, who are bravely fighting our battles. Every one of them will be thrown down or carried over to the rebels." [7]

It is hardly necessary to point out that this is a direct contradiction of what the President had told Seward and Welles. Had he been merely waiting for a victory so he could issue the document what reason would he have had to make use of an unconvincing subterfuge when the simple truth would have almost certainly conciliated the editor?

Early in September Cassius M. Clay of Kentucky, back from his mission to Russia, called at the White House and pleaded with the President to issue an Emancipation Proclamation. Clay, too, was a believer in immediate general emancipation and could not be told the truth, so the President replied: "There is much in what you say which has had my serious thought, but we have as much as we can now carry, and I fear if the proclamation of freedom should be issued, Kentucky would go out to the South." [8]

On September 13, 1862, a delegation of clergymen from Chicago called and pleaded with the President that he issue the proclamation. He gave the following reason for his reluctance to do so: "I do not want to issue a document that the whole world will see must be necessarily inoperative, like the Pope's Bull against the comet!" Having evidently decided to remain consistent in his inconsistency he added a little later: "There are 50,000 bayonets in the Union army from the Border States. It would be a serious business if, in consequence of a proclamation such as you desire, they would go over to the rebels." Then he bethought himself. Lee was marching through Maryland. A battle was impending. What if it turned out to be indecisive? When Congress met Stevens would rise in the House, arraign the administration for ignoring a law of Congress, demand strict enforcement, and perhaps put through other measures even more drastic. So the President added: "Do not misunderstand me because I have mentioned these objections. They indicate the difficulties that have thus far prevented my action in some such way

[7] *Ibid.*, pp. 87-88.
[8] *Ibid.*, pp. 302-304.

as you desire. I have not decided against a proclamation of liberty to the slaves, but hold the matter under advisement."

Postmaster General Montgomery Blair was one of the President's most trusted advisers. After Lincoln's death he wrote to Gideon Welles, secretary of the navy, concerning the proclamation:

> On the Emancipation Proclamation . . . it was due to Lincoln himself that I hesitated. I had urged him previously to make the proclamation and a letter of mine will be found among his papers arguing the point, he had scarcely a week before ridiculed the idea of such a proclamation . . . and I had to support him against Chase and therefore [was] taken aback by his somersault at first, and so hesitated, but after sleeping on it I came to my former position.[9]

Chase, like Blair, had become convinced that the President had given up all intention of issuing the proclamation. On September 10, 1862, he wrote in his *Diary* that Lincoln "has yielded so much to the Border State and negrophobic counsels that he now finds it difficult to arrest his own descent to the most fatal concessions." On September 12—ten days before the appearance of the preliminary proclamation—he wrote: "He has clearly separated himself from the great body of the party that elected him, distrusts those who represent its spirit, and waits—for what?"

It is evident from the above that not only important outsiders like Greeley and Clay were allowed to depart with the impression that the President had no intention of issuing the proclamation, but that since the cabinet meeting of July 22 he had sedulously cultivated that same impression among members of his cabinet. Why should he have done so? Only one plausible explanation suggests itself: *he wished to prepare them for the nonappearance of the proclamation if the victory proved decisive.* To believe otherwise is to believe that in the midst of a serious crisis he amused himself by mystifying and confusing members of his official family.

[9] William E. Smith, *The Francis Blair Family in Politics,* vol. II, p. 186. Quoted by special permission of The Macmillan Company. The "somersault" referred to was the issuing of the preliminary proclamation on September 22, 1862, nine days after the President had "ridiculed" such a move by comparing it with the "Pope's Bull against the comet."

7

On September 17, 1862, the battle took place at Antietam. Lee's march through Maryland was halted, but McClellan's victory was inconclusive. The Confederate commander retreated in good order. His army remained intact and was destined to win important victories. Five days later, on September 22, 1862, Lincoln issued the famous preliminary Emancipation Proclamation. Secretary Chase tells us about it in his *Diary*. He quotes Lincoln as saying:

> The action of the army against the rebels has not been quite what I should have best liked. But they have been driven out of Maryland, and Pennsylvania is no longer in danger of invasion. When the rebel army was at Frederick, I determined, as soon as it should be driven out of Maryland, to issue a Proclamation of Emancipation such as I thought most likely to be useful. I said nothing to any one; but I made the promise to myself, and [hesitating a little]—to my Maker. The rebel army is now driven out, and I am going to fulfill that promise. I have got you together to hear what I have written down. I do not wish your advice about the main matter for that I have determined myself.[10]

There exists, however, a diary entry made by James C. Welling, editor of the *National Intelligencer,* concerning a statement made to him by Edward Stanly, military governor of North Carolina, to whom Lincoln gave an entirely different version about what prompted him to issue the proclamation. Since Welling and Stanly are reliable witnesses and since, as we have seen, Lincoln was in the habit of contradicting himself, it is the historian's duty to give both versions and to try to ascertain the truth in the matter.

Stanly had been a congressman from North Carolina. He was an avowed Unionist but was opposed to any interference with slavery. He had accepted the military governorship of his state at great personal sacrifice and only after Lincoln had given him the assurance that he had no intention of interfering with slavery. When the preliminary Emancipation Proclamation appeared he thought Lincoln had played him false. So he hastened to Washington with the intention of handing in his resignation. He had several interviews with Lincoln and decided to remain at his post. Having made that deci-

[10] *Diary,* vol. II, pp. 87-88.

sion he went to the office of the *National Intelligencer* and talked to Welling, who made the following entry in his diary:

September 27th.—Had a call at the *Intelligencer* office from the Honorable Edward Stanly, Military Governor of North Carolina. In a long and interesting conversation Mr. Stanly related to me the substance of several interviews which he had had with the President respecting the Proclamation of Freedom. Mr. Stanly said that the President had stated to him that the proclamation had become a civil necessity to prevent the Radicals from openly embarrassing the government in the conduct of the war. The President expressed the belief that, without the proclamation for which they had been clamoring, the Radicals would take the extreme step in Congress of withholding supplies for carrying on the war—leaving the whole land in anarchy. Mr. Lincoln said that he had prayed to the Almighty to save him from this necessity, adopting the very language of our Saviour, "If it be possible, let this cup pass from me," but the prayer had not been answered.[11]

The extreme reticence of Lincoln's biographers and Civil War historians in general concerning this and other contradictory statements made by Lincoln during this trying period makes it evident that they have found them embarrassing. They ill accord with the image of Lincoln they appear to have been determined to present to the public. To the author of this volume they make Lincoln more, not less, sympathetic, since they make him appear more human. He was not all-wise, he made mistakes, he often contradicted himself. Notwithstanding all this he went steadfastly toward his goal—the preservation of the Union. Emancipation and all else—even truth sometimes—were subordinated to this. He wished to preserve the Union without having to resort to general emancipation if at all possible because he feared the postwar consequences of that form of emancipation to the country and to the Negro. It does not appear unlikely that his persistence in this prolonged the war. Stevens and many others thought so, and they may have been right. Lincoln finally was to acknowledge that far from having the serious consequences he had so often predicted, the Emancipation Proclamation had the opposite effect.[12] Yet we shall see that after he issued the final document he continued trying to get the border states to adopt gradual emancipation. Had he succeeded it would have made the

[11] Rice, *op. cit.*, pp. 532-533.
[12] See Lincoln's letter to James C. Conkling, Aug. 26, 1863.

ratification of the Thirteenth Amendment abolishing slavery impossible and have led to serious complications.

8

Lincoln's statement to Stanly harmonizes with what we know concerning his dislike of general emancipation. It likewise harmonizes with his words and actions both before and after he issued the proclamation. The statement he made at the cabinet meeting does not. In corroboration of the version he gave to Stanly there can be cited his statement in his letter to Cuthbert Bullitt, July 28, 1862, in which he also expressed fear of congressional displeasure unless a change of policy is adopted by the administration. He wrote: "It is a military necessity to have men and money; and we cannot get either in sufficient numbers or amounts if we keep from or drive from our lines slaves coming to them."

Welling, who as editor of the *National Intelligencer,* an old and influential publication, had considerable inside information, and whose relations with members of Lincoln's cabinet were, as Allen Thorndike Rice assures us, "intimate and often confidential," was of the opinion that what Lincoln told Stanly accurately reflected his state of mind. He has written: "The proximate and procuring cause of the proclamation, as I conceive, is not far to seek. It was issued primarily and chiefly as a political necessity, and took on the character of a military necessity only because the President had been brought to believe that if he did not keep the Radical portion of his party at his back he could not long be sure of keeping an army at the front." [13]

Congressman George W. Julian, who although one of those whom Lincoln's young secretary Hay called "Jacobins," was on the best of terms with the President, was of the same opinion. He wrote: "Mr. Lincoln feared that enlistments would cease, and that Congress would even refuse the necessary supplies to carry on the war, if he declined any longer to place it on a clearly defined antislavery basis." [14] Lincoln's friend and partner William H. Herndon must

[13] Rice, *op. cit.,* pp. 530-531.
[14] *Ibid.,* p. 62.

have received information of a similar nature, for he wrote: "When he freed the slaves there was not heart in it." [15]

That unless McClellan won a decisive victory he would have to do something to placate the Radicals or there would be the devil to pay as soon as Congress met must have become obvious to Lincoln on September 17, 1862, the day the battle took place. While the guns were booming at Antietam, Stevens was speaking at Lancaster and what he said must have sounded ominous to the President. The Commoner made it plain that as soon as Congress reassembled he meant to strike where Lincoln was most anxious for Congress not to interfere—at slavery in the border states. Here is what he said:

"I have protested against the present policy, not only to the people, but to the face of the President and his Cabinet, and on the floor of Congress; . . . told them that they were exercising too much lenity at the request of border statesmen—not one of whom, in my judgment, has loyalty in his heart. I have accused the prime minister [Seward] to his face of having gone back from the faith he taught us, and instead of arming every man, black or white, who could fight for the Union, withholding a well-meaning President from doing so. . . . I have told these things to the President and Cabinet, and they replied—'It may come to this'. *'Come to this!'* when 200,000 men have melted away, and $2,000,000,000 spent! *'Come to this!'* when another half million lives have been lost, and a billion dollars more laid upon you in taxation. *I cannot and will not stand this.*" He then told his constituents that if they returned him to Congress he would introduce a bill providing *"that every man be armed, black and white, who can aid in crushing the rebellion; that every inch of rebel soil be taken and sold to pay the debt of this war."* [16]

What did this mean?

It meant that Stevens intended to introduce a bill requiring the administration to draft into the armed forces not only white men but black men, *including all able-bodied slaves in the border states.* On June 16 of that year he had managed to have a bill adopted authorizing the President to employ persons of African descent in the armed forces and providing that "when any man or boy of African descent shall render any such service . . . he, his mother, and his wife and

[15] *Life of Lincoln* (edition annotated by Paul Angle), p. 483.

[16] *Liberator,* Sept. 19, 1862. Italics in original.

children, shall for ever thereafter be free, any law, usage, or custom whatsoever to the contrary notwithstanding." The bill had excluded slaves belonging to border state slaveholders, now the exclusion was to end. To draft able-bodied slaves in the border states, or even to permit them to enlist, meant the end of slavery in those states. Now Lincoln had pinned his hopes on the border states helping him to solve the slavery problem in the only way he considered practical—by the adoption of compensated gradual emancipation with federal aid. More than that! He believed that if they did so the war would be practically ended. If Stevens succeeded in getting his bill adopted all hope of reaching that solution would have disappeared. For if the President threatened to veto the bill, the powerful chairman of the Ways and Means Committee might answer with the threat of holding up appropriations for the army. Now that McClellan's victory had proved indecisive there appeared to be only one way to head off Stevens—to issue a preliminary Emancipation Proclamation.

9

None of the calamities the President had predicted might happen if he issued an Emancipation Proclamation put in an appearance. Kentucky did *not* "go out to the South." Twenty thousand soldiers from that state did *not* "throw down their muskets." Half the officers did *not* "fling down their arms." Fifty thousand soldiers from the border states did *not* "go over to the rebels." The President's predictions—some of which were sufficiently publicized—added to assurances given by border state slaveholders led the Confederates to believe, however, that if they took advantage of the opportunity some of these things might come to pass. They promptly invaded Kentucky. But on October 12, 1862, the Confederate commander Baxton Bragg ruefully reported to Richmond: "The campaign here was predicated on the belief and the most positive assurances that the people of Kentucky would rise in mass and assert their independence. No people ever had so favorable an opportunity, but I am distressed to add there was little or no disposition to avail of it." [17] In the fall elections, when Lincoln's own state went over to

[17] *Offic. Rec.*, 1 ser., vol. XVI, pt. 1, p. 1088.

the opposition, Kentucky and other loyal border states sent an almost solid delegation of Unionists to Congress.

Stevens had always claimed that the President's anxiety concerning Kentucky and other loyal border states was exaggerated. As early as December 16, 1861, he said on the floor of Congress: "I do not understand where the President gets the facts in this respect. I believe he has been misled. I believe he is laboring under a hallucination of mind upon the subject as fatal as that of Samson under the manipulation of Delilah." The fact that in the Kentucky state elections of August, 1861, three-fourths of those elected to the legislature were Unionists makes his skepticism understandable. Lincoln appears to have used the border state argument to delay issuing the proclamation in the hope that the slaveholders of those states would have the wisdom and the patriotism to adopt the solution he so greatly favored.

On December 1, 1862, he again presented to Congress—and in doing so to the slave states, rebel as well as loyal—his compensated gradual emancipation plan. It evoked no response from the slave states and was coldly received by Congress. On January 1 of the new year, he issued the final proclamation. After the document had made its appearance, Adam Gurowski wrote in his *Diary:* "The patriots of both Houses, as the exponents of the noble and loftiest aspirations of the American people, whipped in—and this literally, not figuratively—whipped Mr. Lincoln into the glory of having issued the Emancipation Proclamation. The laws promulgated by this dying Congress initiated the Emancipation—generated the Proclamation of the 22d of September, and of January 1st. History will not allow one to wear borrowed plumage." [18]

Robert Mallory of Kentucky, in a speech in the House on February 24, 1863, charged that the President had yielded to pressure from Stevens. The Commoner did not reply, and no supporter of the President ventured to contradict the charge. Mallory said in part:

"Soon after the War broke out, the gentleman from Pennsylvania and his great allies Horace Greeley and Wendell Phillips, and all his little allies in the House, began their pressure on the President and the Republican Party. In vain the President from time to time

[18] *Diary,* vol. II, pp. 99-100.

besought his friends, and those who had not been his friends, to relieve him from this pressure.

"The gentleman from Pennsylvania and his allies persevered. They demanded of the President his proclamation of emancipation. He refused. Again they demanded it; he refused again, but more faintly and exhibited himself in his letter to his 'dear friend Greeley' in the most pitiable and humiliating attitude in which an American President was ever exhibited to the American people— But the gentleman from Pennsylvania still pressed him and educated him and the Republicans.

"The Committee of Divines from Chicago, armed with authority from the other but not the better world, was brought to aid in the pressure; but apparently in vain. Sir, do you remember the reply of the President to that committee? It was conclusive, unanswerable. The reasons given for refusing to proclaim the freedom of slaves in the rebel states are perfectly irrefutable. 'I have not the power to do it,' said the President, 'and if I had, the proclamation would be impotent; it would be like the Pope uttering his Bull against the comet.'

"We then supposed the matter had been settled. But scarcely had this confidence entered the great conservative heart of the nation, when feeble or false, or both, or yielding to the teachings of the gentleman from Pennsylvania, he suddenly without notice, issued his celebrated Emancipation Proclamation."

The Kentucky representative was seriously mistaken in believing that in issuing the final proclamation Lincoln had given up the struggle and had adopted Stevens's program. As has already been remarked the President had a way of yielding so the advantage remained with him.

CHAPTER VIII

Lincoln Outmaneuvers Stevens

The Emancipation Proclamation, notwithstanding its limitations, was well worth the struggle Stevens and his followers had made to obtain it. True that it turned some proslavery Democrats against the government, but they had been lukewarm supporters anyway. True that some Southern loyalists now rallied to the support of the Confederacy, but their opposition to it had been entirely passive. All this was overbalanced by the wave of enthusiasm that swept through the ranks of the government's most active supporters. The proclamation—notwithstanding its pedestrian language, so entirely unlike Lincoln's noblest utterances and betraying his lack of enthusiasm—did for the war for the Union what the Declaration of Independence had done for the War of the Revolution, what the slogan "Liberty, Equality, Fraternity" did for the French Republic in its struggle against the aristocracy of all Europe.

Not to be overlooked was its effect upon the slaves. The policy hitherto pursued by the administration—against which Congress had vainly legislated and Stevens had vehemently protested—had discouraged Negroes from leaving the plantations. It took some time to overcome the distrust this had engendered. Eventually, however, the grapevine telegraph managed to convince the slaves that that policy had changed, and throughout the South Negroes began to desert in droves. The effect of this upon the economy of the South and its ability to continue the struggle should not be underestimated.

The proclamation, moreover, gained for the North the sympathy of the people of Great Britain and France. That sympathy was sorely needed. In September, 1862, Lord Palmerston, British prime minister, had sounded Lord Russell, minister of foreign affairs, regarding the advisability of combined intervention by Great Britain and France. Lord Russell had replied: "I agree with you that the time is come for offering mediation to the United States Government, with a view to recognition of the Confederates. I agree further, that, in case of failure, we ought ourselves to recognize the Southern States as an independent State." [1] When the proclamation made its appearance, British workingmen, although suffering bitterly from unemployment as a result of the war, became enthusiastic supporters of the North. British abolitionists, whose attitude had been one of comparative indifference, sprang into action. They organized meetings in support of the North throughout England and Scotland and distributed hundreds of thousands of pieces of literature. The specter of foreign intervention receded as a result of the proclamation.

2

When the enthusiasm had somewhat subsided doubt crept in. Thoughtful people began to wonder about the postwar validity of the proclamation. True that John Quincy Adams had been firmly convinced that either the President or Congress could abolish slavery in time of war or insurrection, but what if the Supreme Court thought otherwise? A court responsible for the Dred Scott decision might easily do so. Indeed, no sooner had the September proclamation been issued, than Benjamin R. Curtis, former associate justice of the Supreme Court, famous for his dissenting opinion in the Dred Scott case, published a pamphlet entitled *Executive Power*, in which he argued that the President had overstepped the authority conferred upon him by the Constitution. If such was the opinion of a dissenter in the Dred Scott case, what could be expected of the majority of his former associates?

Representatives from the border states were practically unanimous in the belief that the document was unconstitutional. They had long ago warned that no matter what measures might be taken during the war, when peace had been restored the Southern states

[1] Walpole, *Life of Lord Russell*, vol. II, p. 349.

would restore slavery and at the same time settle the problem of what to do with the free Negro by enslaving all such Negroes resident in the South. Senator Willard Saulsbury of Delaware, among others, had expressed that opinion on the floor of the Senate, saying: "In 1870, let the war terminate as it may, whether you conquer the seceded States or not, if local governments are preserved in this country there will be more slaves in the United States than there were in 1860. . . . I presume that local governments will be preserved. If they are, if the people have the right to make their own laws and to govern themselves, they will not only re-enslave every person that you attempt to set free, but they will re-enslave the whole race." [2]

Most Northern Democrats were likewise convinced that the Emancipation Proclamation was unconstitutional. In 1863 the Ohio Democratic Convention declared the document to be in violation of the Constitution, hence void. If with them the wish was father to the thought, this was hardly true of Republicans such as Charles Sumner in the Senate and Isaac N. Arnold in the House, both of whom had grave doubts regarding the constitutionality of the proclamation and submitted proposals which, they believed, might validate the slaves' freedom, but which Congress did not adopt. The historian George Bancroft had similar misgivings and wrote to General Robert C. Schenck: "I feel unwilling to rely on the President's Proclamation for the termination of slavery. Could not Congress enact that henceforward every one born in our common country should be free?" [3]

The President himself realized that a decision of the Supreme Court might render the proclamation null and void. What is even more significant, on two occasions he expressed doubt of its postwar validity. When on December 8, 1863, he outlined his Reconstruction plan in his message to Congress, he included a loyalty oath by which the oath taker bound himself to support all acts of Congress and presidential proclamations having reference to slavery "so long and so far as not modified or declared void by the Supreme Court." On January 31, 1865, addressing a crowd gathered before the White House, he said: "A question might be raised whether the proclamation was legally valid. It might be added, that it only

[2] *Globe,* May 2, 1862.
[3] *Bancroft MSS,* Massachusetts Historical Society, Nov. 18, 1863.

aided those who came within our lines, and that it was inoperative as to those who did not give themselves up; and that it would have no effect upon the children of the slaves born hereafter; in fact it would be urged that it did not meet the evil." Alexander H. Stephens, vice-president of the Confederacy, has written that in February, 1865, at the Hampton Roads Conference, "His [Lincoln's] own opinion was that as the Proclamation was a *war measure,* and would have effect only from its being an exercise of the war power, as soon as the war ceased, it would be inoperative for the future. . . . So far as he was concerned, he should leave it to the Courts to decide." [4]

3

One is forced to conclude that while the proclamation was useful as a war measure, its value as an emancipating medium was questionable and that the President was fully aware of this. It became evident that a constitutional amendment alone could guarantee freedom to the slaves. Prudence, if nothing else, counseled, therefore, that immediate steps be taken to clear the way for the adoption and ratification of the amendment. It is obvious that an amendment abolishing slavery throughout the republic could not be adopted and ratified if slavery continued to exist in the loyal border states, *or if those states adopted gradual emancipation over a long term of years.* One would have expected that after issuing the proclamation the President would have given all possible encouragement to those in the loyal border states who wished to bring their states into line with that document by getting them to adopt immediate emancipation. The President did the exact opposite.

In Missouri the struggle between the "Immediatists" and the "Gradualists"—or as they were called in that state, the "Charcoals" and the "Claybanks"—was particularly bitter. The former, feeling they were entitled to the President's support since they were preparing the ground for the adoption of a measure which alone could guarantee fulfillment of the promise given in the proclamation, sent a delegation to Washington headed by James Taussig of St. Louis to solicit his aid. To their disappointment and chagrin Taussig reported on May 10, 1863:

[4] Stephens, *War between the States,* vol. II, p. 611.

The President said that the Union men in Missouri who are in favor of *gradual emancipation* represented his views better than those who are in favor of *immediate emancipation.* In explanation of his views on the subject, the President said that in his speeches he had frequently used as an illustration, the case of a man who had an excrescence on the back of his neck, the removal of which, in one operation, would result in the death of the patient, while "tinkering off by degrees" would preserve life. . . . *The President announced clearly that, as far as he was at present advised, the Radicals of Missouri had no right to consider themselves the exponents of his views on the subject of emancipation in that State.* (Italics in original.)

Faithful to that pronouncement, the President threw all the immense prestige of his great office into the scale against those in Missouri and Maryland who wished to bring their states into line with the proclamation by having them adopt immediate emancipation.

How is this to be explained?

If, as the President said, he feared immediate emancipation in the loyal border states might have an effect comparable to that of too drastic an operation, resulting in the death of the patient, then, obviously, he must have had identical or even greater misgivings regarding its effect upon the rebel states. When he issued the proclamation he could, therefore, hardly have intended to bring about that form of emancipation in those states. As he was to explain to the Vice-President of the Confederacy, it was a war measure which, "as soon as the war ceased . . . would be inoperative for the future." Had it been truly his intention to accomplish what the proclamation purported to accomplish, then he would immediately have set to work bringing the loyal border states into line with that document. Assuredly he would not have followed a policy that risked making the proclamation a dead letter.

By the light of all this, the President's action in continuing to urge compensated gradual emancipation upon the loyal border states throughout the greater part of the year 1863 appears logical only if he still harbored the conviction that once those states adopted that form of emancipation, the rebel states would offer to make peace on that basis. If he no longer harbored that conviction then his action was not only illogical, but indefensible, since adoption by the border states of gradual emancipation over a term of years would have made ratification of a constitutional amendment abolishing slavery throughout the republic impossible, and emancipation in the rebel states would then have been entirely dependent upon a court decision. What that decision was likely to be was foreshadowed by the opinion of former Associate Justice Benjamin R. Curtis. If then, as we are forced to believe, the President still cherished the hope of making compensated gradual emancipation prevail in *all* the slave states, then we are likewise forced to believe that he cherished the hope of being able to retract the Emancipation Proclamation. This explains why that proclamation was drawn up in such a manner that it did not free a single slave *de facto*. Not only the border states and Tennessee, but such parts of Virginia and Louisiana as were occupied by Union troops had been carefully excepted. The document was valid only where it could not be enforced.

We thus arrive at the inevitable conclusion that the proclamation was, rightly speaking, not an Emancipation Proclamation at all. It was an adroit political maneuver intended to stop Stevens from freeing the slaves in the border states by enabling the men to enlist in the armed forces, a measure which would have made the rapid manumission of their mothers, wives, and children a certainty, and have put an end to the President's hope of making gradual emancipation prevail.

4

Alexander K. McClure has written: "Only once during Lincoln's administration can I recall Stevens' positive and enthusiastic commendation of Lincoln, and that was when he issued the Proclamation in 1862. He then believed in Lincoln, and expected a rapid advance in every line of aggression against slavery and rebellion, but soon new causes of dissent rose between them." [5]

When the final Emancipation Proclamation appeared, Stevens, who had hailed the preliminary proclamation with joy, realized that he had been outmaneuvered. It will be recalled that in December, 1861, he had proposed that slavery be abolished throughout the republic, but that all loyal slaveholders—those in the rebel states as well as those in the border states—receive a reasonable compensa-

[5] *Op. cit.*, pp. 261-262.

tion. He had expected the final Emancipation Proclamation to embody this or a similar proposal and thus pave the way for a constitutional amendment. When he read the document he immediately realized that the final Emancipation Proclamation *constituted a serious threat to the cause of emancipation.*

He realized that the President was counting on the border states succumbing to the pressure and adopting his thirty-seven-year gradual emancipation plan, and was furthermore gambling on the possibility of the rebel states then offering to do the same. But what if his first hope were realized and his second hope were not? A constitutional amendment would then have become impossible and the war might end with nothing but the Emancipation Proclamation standing between the Southern Negro and the continuance of slavery.

Granting, however, that both hopes were fulfilled and the proclamation were retracted, would not the situation be even more hazardous? The President's gradual emancipation plan contained the provision that "Any State having received bonds as aforesaid, and afterwards introducing or tolerating slavery therein, shall refund to the United States the bonds so received, or the value thereof, and all interest paid thereon"—an unconditional recognition of the right of any state to restore slavery whenever it chose. The President's plan having been adopted under duress, was there no danger of it being repudiated by the slave states shortly after the coming of peace? Could the nation afford to take that risk? Stevens did not believe it could.

Thus it happened that what Lincoln ardently desired, Stevens profoundly feared. Who was right? The laws affecting the Negro passed by the former Confederate States under presidential Reconstruction, and the general attitude of defiance exhibited by those states, make it appear well-nigh a certainty that if in 1863 the President's hopes had been fulfilled, the slave states would later have repudiated the plan as having been forced upon them. Realizing that the first step toward the adoption of a constitutional amendment was the destruction of slavery in the border states, Stevens set to work, grimly and resolutely, to accomplish that purpose.

CHAPTER IX

Stevens Strikes Back

From the beginning of the war Stevens had worked unceasingly for the employment of Negroes as soldiers. His primary purpose was to strengthen the armed forces and thereby shorten the conflict, but he also realized that if a hundred thousand or more Negroes fought valiantly for the restoration of the Union, slavery was less likely to survive the war. For that reason he wanted them employed not as the Confederates employed them—to do the drudgery of the army camps—but as soldiers at the front.

On July 5, 1862, the matter came up for discussion in the House. Robert Mallory of Kentucky said: "I believe that the slaves of the Southern rebels should be used as our army advances. I believe that they should be taken and used for all the manual services of the camp, and to work upon fortifications and everything of the sort." Stevens remarked: "I suppose they would be kept employed till after peace is made, and then sent to their masters unhurt, under the fugitive slave law. In the meantime I am for putting them in the front rank of this battle. I would raise a hundred thousand of them to-morrow, and have them drilled." He shrewdly appealed to the self-interest of the white population: "I would put the slaves where they could fight their former masters. If men are to be shot in this war, let it not be our cousins, relatives and friends. Let it be the slaves of those traitors who have caused the war. . . . The flower of our people are moulding in the swamps of Virginia because we will not employ those who ought to be fighting this battle. . . . And

I am to stand here and be told that it will not do to let black men shoot and be shot instead of white men! ["Hear! Hear!" from the gallery.] I no longer agree that this administration is pursuing a wise policy. Its policy should be to free the slaves, enlist and drill them, and set them to shooting their masters if they do not submit."

On July 17, 1862, the bill authorizing the President to employ, for military purposes, persons of African descent not the property of loyal slaveholders, became law. The second Confiscation Act likewise contained a clause to that effect. The President favored such employment, provided it was restricted as Mallory and other representatives from the border states wished to restrict it. In his veto message of the second Confiscation Act, which he had prepared but not used, he wrote: "I think it is proper for our military commanders to employ, as laborers, as many persons of African descent as can be used to advantage." He was not in favor of employing them as soldiers. Chase has written in his *Diary* that when the matter came up for discussion at the cabinet meeting of July 21, 1862, "the President expressed himself as averse to the arming of Negroes." The reason for his opposition was twofold. He did not believe public opinion would countenance such employment and he agreed with Mallory that the Negro would not be of much value as a combatant. Mallory had said in reply to Stevens's demand that Negroes be employed as soldiers: "One shot of a cannon would disperse thirty thousand of them"; and on September 13, 1862, Lincoln, in reply to a plea of the Chicago delegation of clergymen, had remarked: "If we were to arm them, I fear in a few weeks the arms would be in the hands of the rebels." It was an astonishing remark in view of the record of colored soldiers during the Revolutionary War and the enthusiastic praise bestowed upon a colored regiment by Jackson after the Battle of New Orleans.

When colored troops had proved their valor before Nashville, in the capture of Fort Fisher and in several other engagements, the President acknowledged that he had been mistaken. "So far as tested, it is difficult to say that they are not as good soldiers as any," he said on December 8, 1863, in a message to Congress. But soon a new anxiety came to plague him. About half of the nearly 200,000 colored men enlisted in the armed forces were from the South. What if after the war they returned there and demanded civil rights? If refused, might they not organize themselves into guerrilla bands and make war on the white inhabitants? This was the fear the President expressed shortly before his death to General Butler, and which in March, 1864, may well have prompted him to suggest to Michael Hahn, governor of the reconstructed State of Louisiana, that Negroes who had served in the Union Army be granted the right of suffrage.

2

When the Thirty-seventh Congress—which wrought so nobly for the abolition of slavery in the United States and has been rewarded with abuse—assembled for its third and last session on December 1, 1862, the President's popularity with the majority of his party in Congress was greater than it had been for a long time. He was generously praised for having issued the preliminary Emancipation Proclamation. But when a week later the President's message arrived, containing his thirty-seven-year compensated gradual emancipation plan, there was a raising of eyebrows. Had the President changed his mind? Did he mean to persist in his former policy? But the final proclamation came as promised, and amidst the general rejoicing many failed to consider that the postwar value of the proclamation was exceedingly doubtful and that if the border states succumbed to the pressure of the document and adopted the President's thirty-seven-year plan, emancipation in the rebel states might be gravely compromised. When the possibility of this dawned upon the Radicals they consoled themselves with the thought that the President would now leave nothing undone to bring the border states into line with the proclamation, so as to clear the way for a constitutional amendment. When he did the exact opposite, their disillusionment was profound. Sentiment veered abruptly, and in and out of Congress condemnation of him among opponents of slavery took on a new bitterness. "To such an extent did this condemnation reach," Congressman Albert G. Riddle of Ohio has written, "that, at the end of the Thirty-Seventh Congress [March, 1863], there were in the House but two men, capable of being heard, who openly and everywhere defended him—Mr. Arnold of Illinois, and Mr. Riddle of Ohio." [1]

[1] *Recollections,* p. 218 n.

Stevens apparently doubted the President's intentions, for he decided to go ahead with his plan of freeing the slaves in the border states by enlisting able-bodied males in the army, confident that the liberation of their mothers, wives, and children would inevitably follow and slavery in those states would cease to exist. The President had satisfied the demand for the employment of Negroes as soldiers with the following clause in the final proclamation: "And I further declare and make known that such persons, of suitable condition, will be received into the armed service of the United States, to garrison forts, positions, stations, and other places and to man vessels of all sorts in said service." The law of July 17, 1862, dealing with the enlistment of Negroes in the armed services, forbade the enlistment of slaves belonging to loyal slaveholders. Stevens felt that if the President was genuinely converted to the necessity of general emancipation he would welcome a measure that would bring the border states into line with the proclamation and avert the danger of that document becoming a hollow mockery.

He concluded that if slaves in the border states were offered the boon of freedom, they would be anxious to enlist and it would not be necessary to draft them. So, on January 12, 1863, less than two weeks after the appearance of the final Emancipation Proclamation, he introduced a bill consisting of two sections. The first section provided that the President was "authorized and *required* . . . to proceed *immediately* to raise, equip and organize one hundred and fifty thousand soldiers, persons of color or free African descent . . . into infantry, artillery and cavalry." The second section provided that "slaves as well as freemen may be enlisted and mustered into service, *and such persons shall never again be slaves, but the United States shall pay for each of them as belong to persons who have not been disloyal during this rebellion."* [2]

No sooner had the Commoner presented the bill than the administration bestirred itself. The Military Affairs Committee of the House was apparently prevailed upon to oblige, for it unaccountably delayed its report on the measure. On January 20, 1863, while the bill was still in committee, the War Department issued a general order for the enlistment of troops to Governor John A. Andrew of Massachusetts, containing this significant clause: "Such volunteers to be

[2] Italics added.

enlisted for three years, unless sooner discharged, *and may include persons of African descent organized into separate corps."* It was generally known that Andrew was heartily in favor of the employment of Negroes as soldiers and would make good use of the order, but if the President was under the impression that Stevens's main object was to hasten the organization of the Negro contingent and he would now withdraw the bill, he was mistaken. Formation of a Negro army did not dispel the danger of adoption by the border states of the President's thirty-seven-year plan. Stevens believed an immediate effort must be made to strike at slavery in those states. Impatient with the delay of the Military Affairs Committee in reporting his bill, he resorted to the unusual procedure of presenting the measure directly to the House. Notwithstanding frantic efforts of Democrats and administration supporters to stop him, he secured its assignment for consideration without awaiting the report of the committee.

3

Stevens must have known that in view of the concessions the President had made regarding an Emancipation Proclamation and the employment of Negroes as soldiers, there was little hope that his bill would pass. If it did pass it would be amended in such a manner as to be of little value. This was not the first time, however, that he had introduced a bill knowing it was doomed to defeat. The New York *Times* had chided him once for wasting the time of Congress with measures which he must have known would not be adopted. He knew exactly what he was doing. Human inertia did not yield to a single blow. One must strike again and again.

Border state representatives and their Northern allies were quick to perceive that adoption of the bill would sound the death knell of slavery. The Emancipation Proclamation had not greatly alarmed them, since they felt convinced that the Supreme Court would pronounce it unconstitutional. Stevens's bill, however, did not confer a doubtful *de jure* freedom upon the slaves. It did not merely apply where it could not be enforced. It meant *de facto* destruction of slavery in the border states, clearing the way for the adoption and ratification of a constitutional amendment abolishing slavery throughout the republic. Debate raged for over a week, frequently interrupted by roll calls and motions to adjourn. When it became evident that the measure could not be killed outright, amendments were offered. This tactic succeeded. The mandatory feature was eliminated and an amendment adopted specifying that "slaves of loyal citizens in the States exempt by the President's proclamation of January, 1863, shall not be received into the armed service of the United States." If even then Stevens did not withdraw the bill it must have been because he realized how greatly the country needed education on the subject and wanted the debate to continue.

Charles A. Wickliffe of Kentucky ridiculed the idea of "Sambo" serving as a soldier, and perhaps even as an officer giving orders to white men. Adoption of the bill, even in its amended form, would, he argued, prove conclusively that the war was being fought to free the slaves. He declared vehemently that he and others were ready to lay down their lives to save the Union or the hard-won liberties of their countrymen, but not for the freedom of an alien race. On February 2, 1863, Stevens made the closing speech, saying in part:

"The distinguished gentleman from Kentucky and his allies from Ohio have talked of 'Sambo's' commanding white men. Sir, the bill contains no such provisions. They are to be employed only as soldiers or non-commissioned officers. I do not expect to live to see the day when, in this Christian land, merit shall counterbalance the crime of color. True, we propose to give them an equal chance to meet death on the battle-field. But even then their great achievements, if equal to those of Dessalines, would give them no hope of honor. The only place where they can find equality is in the grave. There all God's children are equal.

"The gentleman from Kentucky objects to their employment lest it should lead to the freedom of the blacks. He says that he fights *only* for the freedom of his own white race. That patriotism which is wholly absorbed by one's own country is narrow and selfish. That philanthropy which embraces only one's own race, and leaves the other numerous races of mankind to bondage and to misery, is cruel and detestable. But we are not fighting for the freedom of the slaves; we are fighting for the life of the nation; and if in the heat of such a strife the chains of the bondman are melted off, I shall thank God all the more."

The amended bill was adopted by the House. In the Senate the Military Affairs Committee recommended that "it do not pass, because the authority intended to be given by it, was already sufficiently granted in the . . . act approved July 17, 1862." As the bill in its amended form was fully as restrictive as that act, it appears probable that Stevens himself requested that the recommendation be made.

The discussion had not wasted the time of Congress. It prepared the ground for the successful assault Stevens made a year later, which broke the back of slavery in the border states and cleared the way for the constitutional amendment. In the meantime he had the satisfaction of seeing the Negro army grow into a formidable force. After adjournment of Congress in March, 1863, he had gone to Lancaster, but in early June journeyed to Washington to inquire about the progress made in recruiting the Negro contingent. He had an interview with Lincoln, and wrote to his friend Simon Stevens: "I learned from the President (who professes still great friendship for Genl. Fremont) that he was about to offer the Genl. command of the negro army, which he hoped would soon be 100,000."

CHAPTER X

Confederate Vengeance

Following his inquiry at Washington concerning the growth of the Negro army, Stevens returned to Lancaster and soon after went to inspect the Caledonia Iron Works. War needs iron. At about this time he wrote to a friend that the works "were now (for the first time) in profitable operation." They were not to remain so for long.

On June 16, 1863, he was in the factory office conferring with the manager, John Sweeney, when a breathless man entered with the news that rebel cavalry was advancing from the direction of Mont Alto. Sweeney advised Stevens to leave. He might be recognized and taken prisoner. The Commoner consented reluctantly and departed in a carriage in the direction of Shippensburg.

Jacob Hoke has written in his volume *The Great Invasion:* "On Tuesday, June 16 . . . a marauding party visited these works, and upon condition that they should be spared, all the horses and mules belonging to the premises were delivered to them." Stevens estimated the loss at from seven to eight thousand dollars. This, however, was only a beginning.

On June 25, General Jubal A. Early, in command of a division of Lee's army, took possession of the Caledonia Iron Works. He made camp, and that day and the next the works were systematically looted. Hoke has written:

> Hon. John Sweeney, Mr. Stevens' business manager, had an interview with General Early, as he sat upon his horse that day, and endeavored to dissuade him from executing his threat to destroy the works. He told

him that so far as Mr. Stevens was concerned, he would be better off if his works had been destroyed ten years before, but for the sake of the many poor people who were dependent upon them for support, and would be thrown out of employment if they were destroyed, he should spare them. To this appeal General Early replied, "That is not the way Yankees do business. They do not go on unless they make money. Then Mr. Stevens is an enemy of the South. He is in favor of confiscating their property and arming the negroes. His property must be destroyed." General Early then specially detailed Colonel French to apply the torch, and the whole was soon a mass of smoldering ruins.

Early, in his *Autobiographical Sketch,* gives the following account of the matter: "I caused the iron works of Mr. Thaddeus Stevens near Greenwood, consisting of a furnace, a forge, a rolling mill—with a saw mill and store house attached,—to be burned by my pioneer party. . . . A quantity of provisions found in store at the furnace was appropriated to the use of my command, but the houses and private property of the employees were not molested."

This last was only partly true. Stevens wrote to a friend that the rebels "broke in the windows of the dwelling houses where the workmen lived. They could not have done the job much cleaner. . . . They finally expressed regret that they were not so fortunate as to meet the owner, who seems to be very popular with the chivalry. I know not what the poor families will do. I must provide for their present relief."

2

General Early has confessed that the destruction of Stevens's ironworks was prompted by vengeance: "Finding in my way the works of Mr. Stevens, who—as a member of the Federal Congress—had been advocating the most vindictive measures of confiscation and devastation, I determined to destroy them." He appears particularly anxious to exonerate his superiors: "Neither General Lee, nor General Ewell knew I would encounter the works."

That Early acted on his own responsibility appears probable. Destruction of private property during the invasion was contrary to the policy adopted by General Lee. Previous to the invasion he had written to Jefferson Davis that "we should neglect no honorable means of dividing and weakening our enemies," and had suggested that the best method of doing so was "to give all the encouragement we can . . . to the rising peace party in the North." He hoped to be able to accomplish this by gaining the good will of the civil population during the invasion and had issued an order that "no private property shall be injured or destroyed by any person belonging to or connected with the army." Destruction of a factory—even one belonging to Thaddeus Stevens—and thus depriving a considerable number of people of their means of livelihood was hardly in keeping with that order and with the end he had in view. On June 27, the day after the destruction of the Caledonia Iron Works, he issued an order in which he said:

There have been instances of forgetfulness on the part of some that they have in keeping the yet unsullied reputation of the army, and that the duties exacted of us by civilization and Christianity are not less obligatory in the country of the enemy than in our own. . . . Such proceedings not only disgrace the perpetrators and all connected with them, but are subversive to the discipline and efficiency of the army and obstructive to the ends of our present movements.

He warned that "we cannot take vengeance for the wrong our people have suffered without . . . offending against Him to whom vengeance belongeth." [1]

It is interesting to compare Lee's order of June 27, 1863, with the one he issued to Early on June 11, 1864, when the latter again invaded Union territory and it no longer appeared expedient to conciliate the civil population. This time the Confederate commander exhibited no further concern about "civilization and Christianity" or about "offendng against Him to whom vengeance belongeth," but wrote: "In your further operations you must of course be guided by the circumstances by which you are surrounded and the information you may be able to collect, and must not consider yourself committed to any particular line of conduct, but be governed by your judgment." [2] When giving these instructions Lee chose to ignore the reputation Early and his command had managed to acquire not only in Union, but in Confederate territory, and about which the Richmond *Enquirer*, in its issue of October 6, 1864, was to write: "They were in the habit of robbing friend and foe alike. They have been

1 *Offic. Rec.*, vol. 45, pp. 880, 912, 942-943.
2 *Ibid.*, vol. 71, p. 596.

known to strip Virginia women of all they had—widows whose sons were in our army—and then to burn their houses."

While Lee cannot be held responsible for the burning of the Caledonia Iron Works, he bears a heavy responsibility for the burning of Chambersburg in July, 1864.

3

Stevens estimated his loss at ninety thousand dollars. Except for his concern about the workmen and their families, it troubled him but little. Sweeney was undoubtedly right when he said that it would have been an advantage to the owner if they had been destroyed ten years earlier. On July 11, 1863, the Commoner wrote to Simon Stevens, giving him an account of the losses and added:

> But all this gives me no concern, although it was just about the savings of my life—not the earnings. The rest has been lavished in the payment of other people's debts and otherwise. I have, I think, enough to pay my debts. As for my personal wants nature will soon take care of them.
>
> We must all expect to suffer by this wicked war. I have not felt a moment's trouble over my share of it. If, finally, the government shall be re-established over our whole territory, and not a vestige of slavery left, I shall deem it a cheap purchase.
>
> I hope to be able with my remaining strength, to sustain myself, until that strength and my temporal events shall cease altogether.

Simon, without his friend's knowledge, opened up a subscription to reimburse Stevens. It is indicative of the country's feelings toward the Commoner that $100,000 was subscribed. Stevens, however, declined with thanks. He was touched by the offer, he said, but hoped to be able to pull through without troubling his friends. The money was applied to the relief of the Lancaster County poor.

In January, 1864, he reported a bill from the Ways and Means Committee to reimburse loyalists in Pennsylvania for the loss they had suffered. Democrats offered amendments calling for indemnification of people in the border states whose loyalty was questionable. To obtain Democratic support for his bill Stevens accepted the amendments. There was an amusing incident when Boutwell of Massachusetts called the entire proceeding "outrageous." Stevens shook his fist at him playfully and said: "You rascal! If you had allowed me to have my rights, I should not have been obliged to make a corrupt bargain."

The bill failed to pass, but Stevens's facetious remark has been interpreted as meaning that he had his own losses in mind. When in 1867 he introduced a bill a section of which called for reimbursement of loyalists whose property had been taken or destroyed, he expressly made it known that he himself would accept no indemnification.

CHAPTER XI

Stevens Outmaneuvers Lincoln

Professor William Ernest Smith, biographer of the Blair family, informs us that Postmaster General Montgomery Blair was "the natural recipient" of Lincoln's confidence.[1] He and his brother, Major General Francis Blair, Jr., agreed with the President that notwithstanding the Emancipation Proclamation, efforts should be made to make compensated gradual emancipation prevail. They likewise agreed with him that the two races could not live together in freedom and equality in the same country: "You think freedom and equality possible for the masses of blacks and whites in the same community; we think all history proves the contrary," Montgomery wrote in June, 1864, to William Lloyd Garrison.[2]

On October 3, 1863, shortly before the congressional election, Montgomery went to Rockville, Maryland, and delivered a speech that "fell upon the ears of the country like a thunderbolt." [3] He assailed the emancipationists in Congress in vituperative fashion. They were, he said, "equally despotic in their tendencies" as "the slavocrats of the South." He repeated the old amalgamation canard Southerners and Copperheads had been using against Republicans in general, claiming that the Radicals were seeking "to make a caste of another color by amalgamating the black element with the free white labor of our land, and would make the manumission of the

1 *Op. cit.*, vol. II, p. 243.
2 *Liberator*, June 21, 1864.
3 Smith, *op. cit.*, vol. II, p. 240.

slaves the means of infusing their blood into our whole system by blending with it *amalgamation, equality and fraternity.*" [4]

That a cabinet officer could have made such an attack upon the majority wing of the President's own party during a congressional campaign without being instantly dismissed is conceivable only on the supposition that it was made with his chief's knowledge and consent. That the President should have given his consent is inconceivable except on the assumption that he was seeking a political realignment which was to include the War Democrats and exclude Stevens and his followers.

Considering the situation in Congress such a move on the part of the President is understandable. Radical Republicans were now convinced that the postwar value of the Emancipation Proclamation was exceedingly doubtful. In view of this the President's continued support of those in the border states who favored gradual emancipation appeared to them as a deliberate attempt to subvert his own proclamation by preventing the adoption and ratification of a constitutional amendment. The fall election in 1863 became a veritable struggle between the President and the majority wing of his party. Governor Curtin of Pennsylvania wrote that Blair's speech had cost the Republicans twenty thousand votes in Pennsylvania alone.[5] In Missouri General Francis Blair, Jr., toward whose campaign Missouri slaveholders were said to have contributed $50,000, had the support of the administration. He defeated Samuel Knox, an advocate of immediate emancipation, by 153 votes and was known to be the President's choice for speaker of the House. In Maryland advocates of immediate emancipation defeated those whom Montgomery Blair had sought to aid with his Rockville speech, in four out of the five congressional districts. Little wonder that faced with such a situation the President should have believed the time had come for a political realignment.

2

On November 2, 1863, Lincoln wrote to Montgomery concerning Francis Blair, Jr.:

[4] *Address of Montgomery Blair,* Rockville, Montgomery County, Maryland.
[5] Smith, *op. cit.,* vol. II, p. 241.

My wish then is compounded of what I believe will be best for the country, and it is that he will come here, put his military commission in my hands, take his seat, go into caucus with our friends, abide by the nominations, help elect the nominees, and thus aid to organize a house of representatives, which will really support the government in the war. If the result shall be election of himself as speaker, let him serve in that position. If not let him retake his commission and return to the army for the country.

Who were the "friends" with whom Francis was to go into caucus? Assuredly not Stevens and his followers. As for the Conservative Republicans, the President well knew that by themselves they could not possibly have organized the House so it would support his gradual emancipation policy. There was at that time some dissatisfaction among the Radicals with Stevens's leadership. Representatives from the Western states believed him to be neglectful of the interests of their part of the country. The chief malcontent was Elihu B. Washburne of Illinois, whose project of connecting the Illinois River with Lake Michigan by means of a canal Stevens had treated cavalierly. But if the President had expected support from that quarter would he have allowed Montgomery to make a speech certain to make them forget minor differences and rally behind Stevens? It is difficult not to arrive at the conclusion that the President counted on support from a combination of Conservatives and Democrats. The fact that Democratic newspapers had given unprecedented publicity to Montgomery's speech, which "appeared to them to come from official quarters," [6] had undoubtedly led him to believe that such support would be forthcoming. Northern Democrats, however, had other plans. They expected, as soon as peace was restored, to obtain the undivided support of the South, and were shaping their policy with that end in view.

When in December, 1863, the Thirty-eighth Congress assembled, the Republicans, as might have been expected after Montgomery's speech, lined up solidly behind Stevens. Francis Blair, Jr., who did not lack political acumen and must have realized that wresting control of the House from Stevens was a hopeless undertaking, did not put in an appearance until January—long after the House had been organized. Schuyler Colfax, Stevens's choice for speaker, was easily

[6] *Ibid.*, vol. II, pp. 240-241.

elected after having been nominated by Washburne, the chief malcontent. Stevens remained chairman of the powerful Ways and Means Committee, dictated most committee appointments, and his friend Edward McPherson having been defeated for re-election, had him appointed chief clerk. James Brooks of New York, commenting on Stevens's dictatorship in the House, remarked: "The Gentleman is sure of the Clerk, sure of all other officers of the House and sure of the Committee on Elections, to whom all credentials of those seeking seats will be referred." [7]

Thus the President's attempt to wrest control of the House from Stevens came to naught. At the time the attempt was made the principal issue between the President and the Commoner was whether immediate or gradual emancipation should prevail in the border states. Stevens was entirely willing to compensate loyal slaveholders, but was not willing to jeopardize emancipation in the Southern states by having the border states adopt gradual emancipation and make ratification of a constitutional amendment abolishing slavery impossible. It is significant that Francis Preston Blair, Sr., the President's oldest and wisest adviser, who although a former slaveholder had counseled against the evacuation of Fort Sumter, agreed with Stevens on this. When Montgomery had tried to explain his Rockville speech by saying that all he had tried to do was "to stop depraved characters from forcing their revolutionary theories of State suicide and immediate abolition on the Republican party, which had repudiated them in 1860," his father, who well knew that 1860 and 1863 were worlds apart, sternly replied: "The true conservative policy is to make *short shrift of slavery* in the Border States and get it out of the way." [8]

3

After reading the report of Montgomery's Rockville speech, Stevens had written to Secretary Chase:

I have read with more sorrow than surprise the vile speech made by the P.M. Genl. It is much more infamous than any speech made by a Copperhead orator. I know of no rebel sympathizer who has charged such disgusting principles and designs on the republican party as this apostate.

[7] *Globe,* Dec. 7, 1863.
[8] Smith, *op. cit.,* vol. II, p. 253.

It has and will do us more harm at the election than all the efforts of the Opposition. If these are the principles of the Administration no earnest Anti-Slavery man will wish it to be sustained. If such men are to be retained in Mr. Lincoln's Cabinet, it is time we were consulting about his successor.

The President himself had evidently reached the conclusion that he had gone too far, and decided to hold out the olive branch to Stevens and his followers. In his message of December 8, 1863, he gave them this pledge: "While I remain in my present position, I shall not attempt to retract or to modify the Emancipation Proclamation, nor shall I return to slavery any person who is free by the terms of that proclamation, or by any acts of Congress."

Stevens was not convinced. Of what value was the President's pledge not to return any person to slavery so long as he followed a policy that might enable others to do so? The following month he said on the floor of the House: "Something more must be done than to declare all men free in the rebel States. . . . Even if you were to liberate every slave now and to readmit them [the rebel States] into the Union as free States, the moment they had acquired that standing they would re-establish slavery and enslave every man of color within their limits. You can prevent this only by amending the Constitution of the United States, prohibiting slavery throughout the Republic." [9]

Convinced that no aid could be expected from the administration in bringing the loyal border states into line with the proclamation, he decided to make another attempt to free the slaves in those states by enlisting them in the army. In March, 1863, a conscription law, known as the Enrolment Act, had been adopted. On February 10, 1864, the Commoner introduced an amendment to that act providing that all able-bodied male persons of African descent, free or slave, between the ages of twenty and forty-five, were to be subject to draft. When a slave belonging to a loyal master was drafted, the latter was to receive three hundred dollars and the slave was to be "forever free." The amendment was adopted by both Houses after having been referred to a conference committee. Such changes as were made did not diminish its efficacy. In its final reading the measure provided that when a slave belonging to a loyal master was drafted, the bounty of one hundred dollars was payable to the owner.

[9] *Globe,* Jan. 22, 1864.

If the slave volunteered, a commission appointed by the Secretary of War was to decide on the compensation, which, however, was not to exceed three hundred dollars for any slave. In either case the enlisted man was to be "forever free," not by the authority of the master, but of the federal government.

After the adoption of Stevens's amendment to the Enrolment Act, February 24, 1864, the President appears to have given up all hope that compensated gradual emancipation might yet prevail. On April 4, 1864, he wrote wistfully to A. G. Hodges about his "earnest and successive appeals to the Border States to favor compensated emancipation." Two months later, in his reply to the committee that came to notify him of his renomination for the presidency, he for the first time expressed himself in favor of a constitutional amendment.

4

It has been said that "Whom the gods would destroy they first make mad." After the passage of Stevens's amendment to the Enrolment Act it should have been obvious even to the dullest that slavery was doomed. Had the slaveholders of the border states immediately after its adoption offered to free *all* their slaves provided compensation was paid, there can be no doubt that their offer would have been enthusiastically accepted. Nor was compensation the only advantage they would have derived from such a move. Thousands of slaves who joined the army in order to gain their freedom would have remained on the plantations. Far from making so sensible and so patriotic a move, the slaveholders resorted to threats to keep their slaves from enlisting. Men were told that if they enlisted their wives and children would be made to suffer. The carrying out of such threats may well have been exceptional, yet well-authenticated cases of brutal mistreatment of wives and children of enlisted men came to the ears of Congress. This, together with the stubborn opposition of border state slaveholders to emancipation of any kind, resulted in the freeing of the mothers, wives, and children of all enlisted slaves without compensation to any owner. Thus long before the ratification of the Thirteenth Amendment slavery in the border states had virtually ceased to exist.

CHAPTER XII

End of the Struggle for Emancipation

Isaac N. Arnold relates in his *Life of Lincoln* that a Pennsylvanian on a visit to Washington asked Stevens to introduce him to "a member of Congress who was friendly to Mr. Lincoln's renomination." Stevens took him to Arnold and said: "Here is a man who wants to find a Lincoln member of Congress. You are the only one I know and I have come over to introduce my friend to you." Alexander K. McClure, in his *Lincoln and Men of War Times,* says: "I distinctly remember his [Lincoln's] reference to the fact that of all the Republican members of the House he could name but one in whose personal and political friendship he could absolutely confide. That one man was Isaac N. Arnold of Illinois." Congressman John B. Alley of Massachusetts wrote: "Many of the most distinguished men of the country, who were in daily intercourse with him [Lincoln], thought but little of his capacity as a statesman. And while entirely true, it is hardly to be believed, that those who knew him best had so little confidence in his judgment and ability to administer the government that very few of the members of the Senate and of the House were in favor of his renomination for the presidency in 1864." [1]

It was therefore a surprise to many when on May 2, 1864, Stevens said on the floor of the House: "I believe now among the people there is entire unanimity. Every man believes Mr. Lincoln to be an honest and patriotic man. So far as I have observed they look to him

[1] Rice, *op. cit.,* pp. 573-574.

to end this rebellion and extirpate slavery. I do not believe he is in any danger of becoming unpopular through his own acts; nor do I believe that even the constant boast by the gentleman from Missouri [Francis P. Blair, Jr.] and his kindred that they are the especial friends and organs of the President can sink him. If that cannot, certainly nothing can. I admit that the organization of the Cabinet is not satisfactory to the country. But the people make proper allowance for the difficulties of his situation; they understand how he has probably been deceived, in common with the Republican party, by the apostasy of men who had his and the party's confidence."

After this no one could have seriously doubted that Lincoln was Stevens's candidate for renomination at the forthcoming Republican National Convention. From one as politically wise as he nothing else could have been expected. He must have realized that no matter what "the most distinguished men of the country" thought of Lincoln, he was strong with the common people. He was, in Motley's phrase, "the great American Demos," with its virtues and its faults, its lofty aspirations and its narrow prejudices, its pioneering spirit and its innate conservatism. He was the link between Radicals and conservatives, Republicans and War Democrats. He was, as Professor Allan Nevins has aptly said, "the grand harmonizer of the North." [2]

Stevens must, moreover, have realized that, at bottom, he and his followers had little to complain about. "What was called Republican policy, 1861 to 1865, in the congressional sense was not Lincoln's policy, though Lincoln was a Republican President," Professor Randall has written.[3] It was the policy Stevens had advocated from the beginning of the war. Lincoln had frequently opposed that policy, but had almost invariably finished by championing it. For more than a year after the outbreak of hostilities he had been opposed to any interference with slavery, considering such interference unconstitutional, but he finished by writing to A. G. Hodges, April 4, 1864: "I felt that measures otherwise unconstitutional, might become lawful, by becoming indispensable to the preservation of the Constitution, through the preservation of the nation." He had winked at the practice of his generals in driving fugitive slaves from the Union

[2] Nevins, *The Statesmanship of the Civil War,* p. 66.

[3] From *Mid-Stream* by J. G. Randall, copyright 1952. Quoted by special permission of the publishers, Dodd, Mead & Company, pp. 111-112.

lines, but he finished by saying in August, 1864, to John Eaton, assistant commissioner of freedmen, that "he wished the 'grapevine telegraph' could be utilized to call upon the Negroes of the interior peacefully to leave the plantations and seek the protection of our armies." He had resisted the demand for an Emancipation Proclamation and the employment of Negroes as soldiers, but he finished by writing to James C. Conkling, August 26, 1863, that "some of the commanders of our armies in the field, who have given us our most important victories, believe the Emancipation policy and the use of colored troops constituted the heaviest blows yet dealt the rebellion." He had sought to thwart adoption and ratification of a constitutional amendment abolishing slavery by continuing to urge the border states to adopt gradual emancipation, but he finished by being so anxious for its ratification that, according to Charles A. Dana, assistant secretary of war, he authorized the offer of $20,000 (or patronage to that amount) to a Democratic congressman, to secure his vote for a bill admitting Nevada to statehood, so the requisite number of ratifications might not be wanting.[4]

So consistently had Lincoln followed in Stevens's footsteps that one might easily be deceived into thinking that the difference in their policies was merely one of timing. The evidence, however, proves conclusively that their differences were the result of two fundamentally different viewpoints. Lincoln believed that the Union could best be saved by having the federal government interfere with slavery as little as possible; Stevens believed it could best be saved by vigorously attacking and destroying the institution. Lincoln believed that the Negro was unassimilable, a stranger in a strange land, and must eventually emigrate or be deported; Stevens believed that he was an integral part of the American nation and that national policy must be shaped accordingly. Stevens advocated his antislavery measures from conviction; Lincoln adopted them from necessity. The delay in their application, occasioned by Lincoln's resistance, may well have been salutary, but it should be considered that when Stevens advocated the measures he undoubtedly took the President's resistance into account, as he took into account the time required to mold public opinion for their acceptance. That Lincoln should have championed them when he believed the situation required it, even though

[4] Dana, *Recollections of the Civil War,* pp. 175-178.

himself not fully convinced, is proof of his adaptability and his suppleness as a statesman. "I claim not to have controlled events, but confess plainly that events have controlled me," he wrote in his letter to Hodges.

If it was influence and power Stevens wanted he assuredly had no reason for opposing Lincoln's renomination. Professor Randall, who is highly critical of Stevens, acknowledges the extent of his influence when he writes: "People came to look to him as more of a spokesman of the party than Lincoln." [5] He informs us that when the Union Leagues had "congressmen pledged to 'abide by the Administration caucus for Speaker of the House of Representatives,' " it had nothing to do "with the President and his policy," but "in reality the pledge to vote according to the 'caucus' meant, being interpreted, to follow the dictates of Thaddeus Stevens." [6] Nor is it without significance that those who failed to follow those "dictates" were usually retired by their constituents.

How hazardous it was to cross Stevens was experienced by Francis Blair, Jr., who took his seat in the House in January, 1864. In 1862 he had advocated "confiscating the property of all rebels and emancipating their slaves by law, and compensating the loyal owners whenever it is necessary to free them to secure the present safety or future peace of the country" [7]—precisely what Stevens advocated. Since then, however, he had made a complete about-face. After he had launched an attack upon the Radicals in general and Secretary Chase in particular, Stevens introduced a resolution questioning his right to occupy a seat in Congress and hold a military commission at the same time. The man who had been the President's choice for speaker of the House was promptly expelled and his seat given to Samuel Knox, advocate of immediate emancipation in Missouri. Not satisfied with this, the House passed a resolution favoring the revocation of Blair's army commission.

2

Shortly before the Republican National Convention—which for reasons of political strategy was called the National Union Conven-

[5] Randall, *Mid-Stream,* p. 100.
[6] *Ibid.,* pp. 280-281.
[7] Smith, *op. cit.,* vol. II, p. 216.

tion—met in Baltimore, there was a conference at the White House between the President, Stevens, and Cameron concerning who should occupy second place on the ticket. Stevens's choice was Hannibal Hamlin. Lincoln's first choice had been General Ben Butler. He had sent Cameron to ask him if he would accept the nomination. Butler had replied laughingly he would only on condition that the President "give me bond with sureties, in the full sum of his four years' salary, that he will die or resign within three months after his inauguration." [8] Lincoln, worried about the outcome of the election, then decided on Andrew Johnson of Tennessee, a War Democrat, who, he believed, would attract Democratic support. Johnson was a North Carolina "poor white" who had migrated to Tennessee as a young man, and by dint of ambition, perseverance, combativeness, and a ready flow of speech had become a man of importance in his adopted state. He had served five terms in the House, had been elected governor, and in 1857 was sent to the United States Senate. In March, 1862, Lincoln had appointed him military governor of Tennessee. The historian James Ford Rhodes has written that "A severe scrutiny of Johnson's personal character would have prevented his nomination." [9] Stevens was apparently of the same opinion, for he told Lincoln that Johnson was a "rank demagogue" and a "damned scoundrel." [10] The President, however, stuck to his choice.

Before the opening of the convention, the Pennsylvania delegation held a caucus. The question of whom to support for second place on the ticket was put to a vote. McClure, a delegate at large, voted for Johnson. Stevens turned to him and said: "Can't you find a candidate for Vice-President in the United States, without going down to one of these damned rebel provinces to pick one up?" [11] Nevertheless, in obedience to the caucus, he allowed his vote to be recorded for Johnson at the convention.

Lincoln was renominated on the first ballot, almost unanimously, but the convention made it abundantly clear that it did not approve of a policy that jeopardized fulfillment of the promise made in the Emancipation Proclamation. It declared itself in favor of the adoption of a constitutional amendment abolishing slavery throughout

[8] Rice, *op. cit.*, pp. 157-159; McClure, *Lincoln and Men of War Times*, pp. 440-443.
[9] Rhodes, *History of the United States and the Compromise of 1850*, vol. IV, p. 470.
[10] C. E. Hamlin, *Life and Times of Hannibal Hamlin*, p. 472.
[11] McClure, *op. cit.*, p. 260.

the republic and passed a resolution which made it unmistakably clear that it desired a reorganization of the cabinet with Blair eliminated. When on June 9, 1864, the committee appointed by the convention to inform the President of his renomination waited upon him, he said concerning the constitutional amendment: "I will say now . . . that I approve the declaration in favor of so amending the Constitution as to prohibit slavery throughout the nation. . . . I now perceive its importance and embrace it."

That his conversion was of recent date is evident from the wording of the statement.

3

After adjournment of Congress Stevens returned to Lancaster. His townsmen greeted him with acclaim. The Union League band serenaded him and he made a speech to the crowd. There were many Quakers, Mennonites, Dunkers, Amish among his constituents who objected to the Enrolment Act. He defended the act, saying it would oblige Copperheads to fight for the preservation of the Union, but expressed regret at having been unable to obtain the exemption of those who had religious scruples.

The summer was a trying one for the North, especially for Pennsylvania. The Confederates again invaded the state and burned Chambersburg. Grant seemed to be getting nowhere and his losses were appalling. He has explained this by saying that "Richmond was fortified and intrenched so perfectly that one man inside to defend was more than equal to five outside besieging or assaulting." [12] Gold soared to a new high, public morale plunged to a new low. Many Conservative Republicans—including the new chairman of the Republican National Committee, Henry J. Raymond—favored peace at any price. "Mr. Raymond thinks commissioners should be immediately sent to Richmond offering to treat for peace on the basis of Union," Thurlow Weed wrote to Secretary Seward. That very day Raymond had sent a letter to Lincoln advising such a course.[13] The fact that its adoption would have involved retraction of the Emancipation Proclamation, which Lincoln had promised not to retract, he apparently did not consider an insurmountable obstacle.

[12] *Personal Memoirs,* vol. II, pp. 141-142.
[13] Nicolay and Hay, *Abraham Lincoln,* vol. IX, pp. 218-219, 250.

Stevens was aware of the sentiments of those who had the President's ear—Raymond, whom Lincoln was wont to call "my Lieutenant-General in politics"; Montgomery Blair, still a member of the cabinet notwithstanding the expressed wish of the National Convention that he be dismissed. Stevens knew that Lincoln feared general emancipation almost as much as he hated slavery. Might he not succumb to the pressure? He came to the conclusion that the situation demanded some concrete demonstration on the President's part that he meant to abide by the will of the party, and left for Washington to demand Blair's dismissal.

We know little about the interview except that it took place sometime in August, 1864, and that Cameron was present. Stevens is reported to have said: "In order that we may be able in our State to go to work with a good will I want you to make us one promise, that you will reorganize your cabinet and leave Montgomery Blair out of it." There followed a discussion that lasted over two hours. Lincoln is said to have paced the floor agitatedly and to have finally declared that while he wanted to be re-elected, he did not want it at the price of being a puppet in other men's hands. Stevens returned to Lancaster and announced that he would be unable to support the President.[14] He undoubtedly made the announcement to add to the pressure already exercised by others. He did not join those who set up Frémont as a rival candidate, nor those who wanted Lincoln to withdraw so another might be nominated in his place. He confidently waited for Lincoln to yield, and Lincoln did yield. Assured that if he accepted Blair's resignation Frémont would withdraw from the race, he agreed. He had no sooner done so than Stevens threw himself with enthusiasm into the campaign. His speech in Philadelphia, October 4, 1864, was characteristic. He rejected all thought of peace on the basis of Union only:

"Shall we agree for the sake of a disgraceful and precarious peace to re-enslave four million human beings? Shall we aid to rivet the chains on a whole race of God's children that we may purchase the boon of a temporary peace from triumphant traitors? If we are men we will resist it to the death. If we are Christians we will sooner suffer martyrdom. Let us consent to no peace merely on the simple con-

[14] *Lancaster Intelligencer,* Aug. 18, 1864; Carl Sandburg, *Abraham Lincoln: The War Years,* vol. III, p. 206.

dition of the maintenance of the Union. That would be a weak betrayal of noble men who fought our battles."

He paid his respects to the Blairs and the Raymonds in these words:

"Men who make such suggestions in the Cabinet or out, can be naught else than miserable cowards and traitors. Men who aspire to march at the head of a nation or to be foremost in the party of progress, have no right to tremble or despair when danger threatens."

He praised Lincoln for having rejected their counsels:

"Well may every honest man, well may every man who loves God and loves liberty, exclaim, 'Thank God for Abraham Lincoln!' Wiser and firmer than his official or officious admirers, he has saved the nation from disgrace; he has rescued liberty from destruction."

But he made no apology for having criticized the President:

"I would not bestow indiscriminate praise upon every act of the President. Whoever heaps fulsome eulogy on those in power is a parasite and a sycophant and not an honest counselor. . . . An honest critic who points out the errors of his friends may be believed when he speaks of their virtues. He who denies any errors to his idol makes him more than human and is entitled to no credit." [15]

4

Following his re-election, Lincoln, in his message to Congress of December 5, 1864, for the first time recommended adoption of a constitutional amendment abolishing slavery. An attempt to have the amendment adopted had been made in the House as early as December, 1863, by James M. Ashley of Ohio. In January, 1864, a resolution to the same effect was introduced in the Senate by John B. Henderson of Missouri. It was amended by the Judiciary Committee and adopted by the requisite two-thirds majority on April 8, 1864. William Windom of Minnesota offered an identical resolution in the House, which, however, failed to obtain the necessary two-thirds vote. It was just as well. Stevens's amendment to the Enrolment Act had been adopted only a few months earlier and time was needed for it to do its work. On January 6, 1865, Ashley moved re-

[15] *Union League Gazette,* Oct. 4, 1864.

consideration of the resolution, and supporters of slavery in the House prepared for a final desperate stand.

Not only representatives from the border states, but Democrats from New York, Ohio, Indiana, New Jersey, and Wisconsin entered the lists in defense of slavery. On January 11, George H. Pendleton of Ohio, minority leader, took the floor and made an impassioned speech. Addressing himself particularly to Stevens, whom he appeared to regard as principally responsible for the disaster that had befallen the South's cherished institution, he paid tribute to the Commoner's "sledge-hammer power of logic," but said: "Let him be careful lest when the passions of these times be passed away and the historian shall go back to discover where was the original infraction of the Constitution, he may find that sin lies at the door of others than the people now in arms."

On January 13, Stevens rose to reply. He spoke of his lifelong effort to mold public opinion so it would oppose the spread of the institution, of his early years in Congress, when he had denounced slavery "in language which possibly now, on looking at it, I might deem intemperate, but which I then deemed necessary to rouse the public attention and cast odium upon the worst institution on earth." Never, however, had he or those associated with him advised that the Constitution be disregarded and slavery be interfered with in the slave states. "I challenge the scrutiny of my respected colleague on the Committee of Ways and Means, or any other gentleman, through all the records and utterances of this House, to find one single motion or one single word which claimed on our part to touch slavery in the States where it existed. We admitted that it was there, protected by that instrument. We claimed that in the Territories we had full power over it and in the District of Columbia; and I, with those who acted with me, could not hesitate as to what our duty required in excluding it from the free soil of the country and confining it to the spots it already polluted. . . . I claimed the right then as I claim it now, to denounce it everywhere, even in foreign lands, so that if such language could anywhere affect public opinion it might do so."

Pendleton having spoken of his constant efforts to defend the South and its institutions against attacks by his Republican colleagues, the Commoner said in his peroration: "I will be willing to take my chance, when we all molder in the dust. He may have his epitaph written, if it be truly written, 'Here rests the ablest and most pertinacious defender of slavery and opponent of liberty,' and I will be satisfied if my epitaph shall be written thus: 'Here lies one who never rose to any eminence, and who only courted the low ambition to have it said that he had striven to ameliorate the condition of the poor, the lowly, the downtrodden of every race and language and color.' "

The peroration, in which the Commoner idealized himself somewhat, but which contained a fair amount of truth, was greeted with applause by the House and the galleries.

Agreement had been reached that debate should close on January 31, at three o'clock in the afternoon, when the roll was to be called. From early morning of the appointed day the public gallery was crowded. As the hour approached the reserved gallery filled. Senators, cabinet ministers, and spectators mingled with representatives on the floor. Outside a crowd had gathered. In newspaper offices throughout the North presses waited for the click of the telegraph instruments.

There was a hitch in the proceedings. Ashley, in charge of the resolution, had allowed himself to be persuaded to extend the time of debate. The extension was short, but men were too wrought up to view the matter calmly. An angry crowd gathered around the congressman from Ohio. Conspicuous among them was the bewigged Commoner, who with wagging finger read Ashley a lecture. "Stevens' face looked fire, while Ashley's was as red as a fresh cut of beef," the New York *Herald* reported. Finally the matter was settled. The clerk began calling the roll. Ayes of border state representatives and of Northern Democrats were greeted with applause. The result was announced—119 ayes, 56 nays. The resolution had carried! "When the announcement was made," Blaine has written, "the Speaker became powerless to preserve order. The members upon the Republican side sprang upon their seats cheering, shouting, and waving hands and canes, while the spectators upon the floor and in the galleries joined heartily in the demonstration." Outside there was cheering. Batteries fired a salute. The House adjourned in honor of the occasion.

5

President Lincoln held that since the rebel states lacked the constitutional right to leave the Union, therefore, *as states,* they had never left it, but were merely "out of proper relation with the Union." When their governments had been put in order by the executive, they would again be entitled to all their constitutional rights, hence to participation in the ratification of the Thirteenth Amendment.

Stevens rejected that reasoning. On May 2, 1864, he said: "The law forbids a man to rob or murder, and yet robbery and murder exist *de facto* but not *de jure*. . . . If the naked facts palpable to every eye, attested by every day's hostile legislation both in Washington and Richmond, are to prevail, then the rebellious States are no more in the Union, *in fact,* than the loyal States are in the confederacy."

In his speech of January 22, 1864, he had thus defined his stand: "Having committed treason, renounced their allegiance to the Union, discarded the Constitution and laws, organized a distinct and hostile government, and by force of arms having risen from a condition of insurgents to the position of an independent Power *de facto,* and having been acknowledged as a belligerent, both by foreign nations and our own Government, the Constitution and laws of the Union are abrogated as far as they are concerned, and that as between the two belligerents, they are under the laws of war and the laws of nations alone, and that whichever Power conquers may treat the vanquished as conquered provinces, and may impose upon them such conditions and laws as it may deem best."

He cited court decisions, including a decision of the Supreme Court, in support of his claim, and said: "Being subsisting States, capable of corporate action, they have *as States* changed their allegiance from the United States to the confederate States. . . . All the inhabitants of such hostile corporations have forfeited all rights under the Constitution which they have renounced. . . . It is indeed true that the United States may give them those rights if it choose, but they cannot claim them."

Had Stevens's viewpoint prevailed, Reconstruction would have been vastly simplified. At the conclusion of hostilities the former Confederate States would have been put under territorial government until the situation had been sufficiently stabilized to permit their readmission as states without injustice to the loyal portion of the South's population and to the North. Since the South had claimed that it had left the Union *de jure* as well as *de facto,* it could hardly have objected to Stevens's claim that it had done so *de facto* and should be treated accordingly. As territories the Southern states would not have been permitted to participate in the ratification of the Thirteenth and Fourteenth Amendments, but the necessity of forcing immediate Negro suffrage upon them would not have arisen.

President Lincoln, however, believed that even if only 10 per cent of the qualified voters in a rebel state managed, under the protection of Northern bayonets, to organize a state government loyal to the Union, the state should be recognized as repossessed of all its rights under the Constitution. It was his opinion that unless three-fourths of all the states that had constituted the United States before the war ratified the Thirteenth Amendment, its constitutionality would be questionable. Why it should have been less so if states reconstructed in the manner he proposed were allowed to participate, is not clear. The Democratic leader Pendleton remarked during the debate on the amendment: "If these States are to vote in their present condition it would be a broad farce if it were not a wicked fraud," and for once Stevens agreed with him.

Eight reconstructed states were allowed to participate, and on December 15, 1865, Secretary Seward announced that ratification had been completed. Congress had the last word and refused to recognize Johnson's "reorganized States" as states of the Union. This, however, was not considered as invalidating the Thirteenth Amendment.

CHAPTER XIII

Beginning of Reconstruction

To win a peace is often more difficult than to win a war. President Lincoln loved justice and mercy. He knew, moreover, how to obtain results by reasonable compromise. "On all questions of expediency," Blaine has written, "the President maintained not only the right but the frequent necessity of change. 'Principle alone,' said he, 'must be inflexible.' "[1] There can be no doubt that had he lived, he would have arrived at an understanding with Stevens and with Congress which would have resulted in a Reconstruction program that would not have left festering wounds. The program he himself proposed had serious drawbacks, which he undoubtedly would have corrected, if he had not decided to abandon it altogether. That he was considering its abandonment is evident from his last speech. Referring to his Reconstruction plan he said: "As to sustaining it, my promise is out, as before stated. But as bad promises are better broken than kept, I shall treat this as a bad promise and break it, whenever I shall be convinced that keeping it is adverse to the public interest; but I have not yet been so convinced."

The first step toward Reconstruction was taken by the President in August, 1862, with the appointment of General George F. Shepley as military governor of Louisiana. The General received permission to order an election for members of Congress in that part of the state over which Union authority extended—about one-third of the whole. The election was to take place in December, and toward the end of

[1] *Op. cit.*, vol. II, p. 50.

November the President wrote to Shepley to refrain from sending "a parcel of Northern men here as representatives, elected . . . at the point of Northern bayonets," which would be "disgraceful and outrageous." He said that representatives from Louisiana were not particularly needed in Washington, but that it might be useful to ascertain if respectable Southerners would be willing to swear allegiance to the Constitution and become members of Congress and if other respectable Southerners would be willing to vote for them. The election was held and 7,760 votes were cast. Two Southern men, Michael Hahn and Benjamin F. Flanders, were elected, and were seated by the House on February 9, 1863.

Encouraged by the success of his first move, the President, in his message of December 8, 1863, presented a reconstruction plan to Congress. It was not offered for that body's consideration, but as a *fait accompli*. The President told Congress that the people of the rebellious states who wished to re-establish a state government in accordance with his plan, "are assured in advance that it will not be rejected here." He apparently was of the opinion that Reconstruction was entirely an executive function. The preponderance of opinion among authorities is that he was mistaken. Professor John W. Burgess has written: "The question as to how the population in the rebellious district shall be civilly organized anew, is one for the legislative department of the central Government exclusively. . . . These things are matters in which the President, as the executive power, cannot interfere. As participant in legislation, however, he may, at his own discretion, use his powers of recommendation and veto." [2]

The only concession to the legislative power the President made in his message was that "whether members sent to Congress from any State shall be admitted to seats, constitutionally rests exclusively with the respective Houses, and not to any extent with the Executive." Later he also conceded that "the two Houses of Congress . . . have complete power to exclude from counting all electoral votes deemed by them to be illegal." If Congress had the right to refuse to seat representatives from states reconstructed by the President and to count the electoral votes of such states, then it is obvious that a form of Reconstruction Congress did not approve could not restore the

[2] *Op. cit.*, p. 6.

Southern states to full membership in the Union. Much annoyance and misunderstanding would have been averted had the President consulted congressional leaders before giving a promise which without their co-operation he would be unable to fulfill.

2

"An attempt to guarantee a revised State Government, constructed in whole or in part from the very element against whose hostility and violence it is to be protected, is simply absurd," the President said in his message. He prescribed a loyalty oath those wishing to obtain a full pardon, with restoration of rights of property, except as to slaves, would be required to take. They must swear loyalty to the Constitution and to the Union and to abide by all laws of Congress and all proclamations of the President, having reference to slavery, adopted or issued during the war, "so long and so far as not modified or declared void by the Supreme Court." Certain classes of persons were excepted: all who had held civil or diplomatic office in the Confederacy; all who had left seats in Congress or judicial offices; all who had resigned commissions in the army or navy to aid the rebellion; all military officers above the rank of colonel in the army and lieutenant in the navy; all who had treated colored persons in the service of the United States or white persons in charge of such "otherwise than lawfully as prisoners of war."

When a number of qualified voters "no less than one-tenth in number of the votes cast" at the presidential election of 1860, had taken the oath and had "re-established a State Government which shall be Republican, and in no wise contravening said oath, such shall be recognized as the true Government of the State."

Such, in brief, was the President's Reconstruction program. It did not meet with a friendly reception. The Democrats, as usual, shouted "unconstitutional!" As for the majority of the Republicans, they believed it to be the business of Congress to decide on what terms the rebel states should be restored to full partnership in the Union, and the terms proposed by the President did not meet with their approval. It appeared to them that a state government able to rely on the support of only 10 per cent of the qualified voters was hardly "republican," as that term is understood in a democracy. Such a government could maintain itself only with the support of Union troops. The moment that support was withdrawn it would fall. "Upon this point," Professor Burgess has written, "Mr. Lincoln's reasoning was crude and erroneous, and when applied was destined to result in mischievous error." [3]

What the President was really proposing was a continuance of military government, assisted by a small minority of Southern loyalists, some genuine, others mere opportunists. It is undoubtedly true that had an honest referendum on secession been taken in the Southern states, not more than one or two of those states would have voted for disunion. But two and a half years of war and Confederate propaganda had made a difference. During the war and for several years thereafter no government could have been organized in any of the rebel states, with the possible exception of Tennessee, that would be truly loyal and yet have the support of the majority of the voting population. Nor was it safe to rely on a loyalty oath as a guarantee of loyalty. To believe that men put into office by the planter class, which had always ruled the South, would observe the spirit as well as the letter of a federal order or of a constitutional amendment abolishing slavery, was to deceive oneself. It seems strange that Lincoln, usually so prudent and deliberate, should have been in such a hurry to restore the rebel states to participation in the federal government. It was like being in a hurry to have a member of your household who has just made an attempt on your life come and live with you again. Surely it would have been wiser to have administered the rebel states as territories until passions had cooled, and the situation had been stabilized.

3

Stevens's objections to the President's Reconstruction plan went far deeper than those of his colleagues. The famous Italian statesman Count Cavour has said that "statesmanship is the ability to foresee." Stevens foresaw that as soon as the war was over and thousands of Confederate officers and soldiers had returned home, Southern leaders would urge the Southern people to take the loyalty oath so state governments could again be entirely in Southern hands. *He realized*

[3] *Ibid.*, p. 13.

that the Republican party was a minority party. It had come into power as a result of a schism in the Democratic party. The Northern wing of that party—as its National Convention in Chicago in 1864 conclusively proved—was dominated by the Copperheads. As soon as the war was over, the Northern and Southern wings would be quickly reunited. More than that! While before the war the South had been divided into two or more political camps, it was practically certain that with the coming of peace it would give its undivided support to the party that had hindered rather than aided the government in suppressing the rebellion. Nor was this all. Before the war only three-fifths of the slaves had been included in the enumeration for representation in the House and the Electoral College. When the slaves were free all would be counted, yet none would be permitted to vote. The former Confederate states would therefore have a considerably larger representation in the House and the Electoral College than before the rebellion. *As a consequence of all this, at the first presidential election after the war, a combination of Copperheads and former rebels, would, with the assistance of four million nonvoting Negroes, gain control of the government they had sought to destroy.*

No one who has studied the returns of the presidential election of 1868 can fail to agree that Stevens was right when on May 2, 1864, he warned his colleagues in the House: "Where does such doctrine lead you to? It leads you into subjection to traitors and their Northern allies." William Ernest Smith, Professor of History in Miami University, having analyzed the election returns, wrote: "There was reason for objecting to the return of the Democracy to early control of the government. No Northerner who had fought for the Union could have been expected to turn the government over to Copperheads and ex-rebels. Thousands of them were not only untrustworthy, but dangerous to the new Union." [4] Victors are not in the habit of surrendering to the vanquished. To believe that scarcely four years after the war those who had saved the Union would have allowed its government to be turned over to those who had sought to destroy the Union is to exhibit scant knowledge of human nature. Had presidential Reconstruction been allowed to take its course, the

[4] *Op. cit.*, vol. II, p. 380.

result might have been an uprising in the North that would have shaken the very foundations of the republic.

In justice to Lincoln it should be said that his plan was experimental. It was subject to change, and, as he hinted in his last speech, subject to abandonment if he became convinced "that keeping it is adverse to the public interest." There exists, moreover, evidence that he would not have been in favor of rewarding secession by giving the South increased representation in the House and the Electoral College—in other words, that he would have favored adoption of the Fourteenth Amendment. Hugh McCulloch, who became comptroller of the currency in April, 1863, and in March, 1865, was appointed by Lincoln secretary of the treasury, has testified: "From some of his incidental expressions, and from his well-known opinions upon the subject of suffrage and the States to regulate it, my conclusion is that he would have let that question remain as it stood before the war; with, however, such amendments to the Constitution as would have prevented any but those who were permitted to vote in Federal elections from being included in the enumeration for representatives in Congress, thus inducing the recent slave States, for the purpose of increasing their Congressional influence and power, to give the ballot to black men as well as white." [5]

The fact that McCulloch was an ultraconservative Republican adds weight to his testimony. Blaine has said of him that "he was hostile to the creed of the Abolitionists, was conservative in all his modes of thought, and wished the United States restored quite regardless of the fate of the Negro." [6] That Lincoln would have been in favor of the Fourteenth Amendment is, moreover, in keeping with his high sense of justice. To permit four million nonvoting Negroes to figure in the basis of representation in the House and the Electoral College was unjust both to the North and to the Negro. Since Negroes then constituted two-fifths of the South's population, it would have meant that three votes cast in the former rebel states would have been equivalent to five in the loyal states as far as representation in the House and the Electoral College was concerned. One will search the pages of history in vain for an example of victors ever having consented to such an arrangement with the vanquished. Nor was this

[5] Rice, *op. cit.*, p. 422.
[6] *Op. cit.*, vol. II, p. 59.

all. Two-fifths of the representatives from the South, supposedly representing the colored people of that region, would be helping to defeat any measure favorable to the Negro.

4

Stevens had voted against the seating of representatives from Louisiana in February, 1863. When in December of that year the Thirty-eighth Congress convened, he resolved to oppose with all possible vigor the seating of any representative from a reconstructed state. No sooner had the clerk finished reading the credentials than Stevens moved that the names "of the persons claiming to be representatives of the so-called State of Louisiana" be stricken from the roll of the House. Since the House was not yet organized the motion was out of order, and the clerk so ruled. Stevens explained that he had merely wished to go on record as being opposed to "the appearance of the names of these gentlemen on the rolls of the House." Feeling sure of the Committee on Privileges and Elections he had little anxiety concerning the outcome.

He was opposed to the restoration of any Southern state to full membership in the Union until fundamental changes had been wrought in the South's economy and social structure. "The whole fabric of Southern society *must* be changed and it never can be done if this opportunity is lost," he was to say.[7] He believed that in the interest of national unity and of the people of the South, white and colored, the landed aristocracy must be driven from power. They had shown themselves devoid of social conscience and had ruled the South without regard for the well-being of the great majority of its people, blind even to their own best interests, deaf to the pleadings of the great men of the South—Washington, Jefferson, Patrick Henry, John Randolph, Henry Clay, and many others—for the gradual abolition of slavery. They had finally maneuvered the South into a disastrous civil war. If permitted to retain power they would again misrule the South, and in order to justify themselves before their own people would distort responsibility for the war and foster distrust and sectionalism. The source of their power was ownership of the

[7] New York *Herald,* Sept. 8, 1865.

land. To destroy that power the land must be taken from them. With that purpose in view, Stevens now introduced a resolution calling for the repeal of the joint explanatory resolution adopted in July, 1862, which rendered valueless the clause in the second Confiscation Act dealing with the confiscation of real estate. On January 22, 1864, he rose to deliver a carefully prepared address in defense of the clause Lincoln had considered unconstitutional.

He presented arguments, backed by quotations from numerous authorities and by court decisions, to the effect that "when an insurrection becomes sufficiently formidable to entitle the party to belligerent rights, it places the contending Powers on precisely the same footing as foreign nations at war with each other. For all the consequences of war, of combat, and of conquest they are foreign nations." The Constitution therefore had, he claimed, no bearing upon the matter. Confiscation would take place under the law of war and of nations. He made it plain that only the landed property of the planter class would be confiscated, not the holdings of small Southern farmers. He believed such confiscation not only necessary as a measure of state, but eminently just. In his speech of May 2 of that year he elaborated upon this, saying: "A band of men sufficiently formidable to become an acknowledged belligerent, have robbed the Treasury of the nation, seized the public property, occupied our forts and arsenals, severed in twain the best and most prosperous nation that ever existed, slaughtered two hundred thousand of our citizens, caused a debt of $2,000,000,000, and obstinately maintain a cruel warfare. If we are not justified in exacting the extreme demands of war, then I can hardly conceive a case where it would be applicable."

He rejected the President's Reconstruction plan insofar as it meant reinstating the rebel states to immediate membership in the Union: "When the doctrine that the *quality* and not the number of voters is to decide the right to govern, then we have no longer a Republic, but the worst form of despotism. The saints are the salt of the earth but the 'salt of the earth' do not carry elections and make governors and presidents. Within the State of South Carolina a rebel's vote weighs just as much as a loyal voter's. We may conquer rebels and hold them in subjection, and legislate for them as a conquered people; but it is a mere mockery to say that, according to any principle of popular government yet established, a tithe of the resident inhabitants of an organized State can change its form and carry on government because they are more holy than the others."

He pointed out that the President's way of dealing with the problem proved that, at bottom, he agreed with the contention that the rebel states were no longer states of the Union but conquered provinces: "I am glad to find that the President after careful examination, has come to the same conclusion. In details we may not agree, but his plan of reconstruction assumes the same general grounds. *It proposes to treat rebel territory as a conqueror alone could treat it. His plan is wholly outside and unknown to the Constitution. But it is within the legitimate province of the laws of war.*"

In July, 1862, even Francis Preston Blair, Jr., had favored confiscation of the land of the planters. Since then, however, opinions had changed. Property interests in the North were afraid of the measure. It would, they believed, create a dangerous precedent. Yet Stevens's influence was sufficiently great to secure the adoption of his resolution by the House, but it suffered shipwreck in the Senate where the Committee on the Judiciary asked "to be discharged from its further consideration" and secured agreement.

5

It has been claimed that Lincoln would have been opposed to confiscation of the land of the planters even if he had not had constitutional scruples. There exists, however, evidence to the effect that early in 1864 he overcame those scruples and was willing to sign a bill "striking at the fee of rebel landholders."

Stevens's resolution, which would have restored the original meaning of the clause in the second Confiscation Act concerning confiscation of landed property, had died in committee in the Senate on February 17, 1864. A short time later Congressman George W. Julian of Indiana presented a bill passage of which would have had the same effect as adoption of the resolution. On March 18, 1864, he made a lengthy speech in defense of the measure, during which he said: "Congress must repeal the joint resolution of last year [*sic*] which protects the fee of rebel landholders. *The President, as I am well advised, now stands ready to join in such action.*" [8]

[8] Italics added. The "joint resolution" Julian referred to had been adopted in July, 1862.

Since this information was bound to affect the vote on the measure, it is inconceivable that the President should not have promptly issued a denial had Julian been misinformed. No refutation of Julian's statement came from the White House, nor did any of the border state representatives who opposed the measure deny it either then or later, although they certainly must have hastened to inform themselves concerning its accuracy. In 1886, in an article forming part of a collection entitled *Reminiscences of Abraham Lincoln by Distinguished Men of His Time,* edited by Allen Thorndike Rice, editor of the *North American Review,* Julian gave the following details:

> Having heard of this change, I called to see him [Lincoln] on the 2d of July, 1864, and asked him if I might say to the people that what I had learned on this subject was true, assuring him that I would make a far better fight for our cause if he would permit me to do so. He replied that when he prepared the veto of our law on the subject two years before he had not examined the matter thoroughly, but that on further reflection, and on reading Solicitor Whiting's law argument, he had changed his view, and would now sign a bill striking at the fee of rebel land-holders, if we would send it to him. I was much gratified by this statement, which was of great service to the cause in the canvass; but, unfortunately, constitutional scruples respecting such legislation had gained ground, and although both houses of Congress at different times endorsed the measure, it never became a law, owing to unavoidable differences between the President and Congress on the question of reconstruction.

The great majority of the contributors to the collection were men who had been active in national politics during Lincoln's administration. Two had been members of his cabinet. One had been speaker of the House at the time of Julian's visit to the White House. Another had been assistant secretary of war. It is inconceivable that had Julian misrepresented Lincoln on so vital a matter, one of them, or some other personality close to Lincoln, would not have publicly taken issue with him. To the best of my knowledge the statement has remained unchallenged to this day.

It will be said that Julian's statement is contradicted by the fact that in February, 1865, Lincoln proposed to his cabinet that a peace offer be made to the South which was to include payment of $400,000,000 to reimburse the slaveholders for the loss of their slaves. The contradiction is more apparent than real. It should be considered that Congress had twice rejected proposals to restore the original meaning of the clause in the second Confiscation Act concerning the confiscation of real estate. If the land was to remain in the hands of the planters, the most practical way of helping the people of the South, white as well as colored, was to provide the former slaveholders with working capital.

6

The President's Reconstruction plan produced two mutually antagonistic results. On the one hand loyalists in Louisiana and Arkansas decided to set up free state governments in accordance with the plan; on the other, Congress set out to formulate a plan of its own and refused to seat congressional representatives elected in accordance with the President's plan. The congressional plan of Reconstruction, in charge of Henry W. Davis of Maryland in the House, and Benjamin F. Wade of Ohio in the Senate, became known as the Wade-Davis plan. Its principal differences with the presidential plan were as follows: It made it unmistakably clear that Reconstruction was a congressional, not an executive function; reconstruction could begin in a state only when all armed resistance in the state had ceased and the *majority* of the duly qualified voters had taken the loyalty oath; all Confederate debts had to be repudiated and the abolition of slavery recognized in the state constitution; slavery was abolished in all rebel territory.

The plan was adopted by Congress, but was vetoed by the President by means of a "pocket veto." In a state paper he issued he said that he did not wish to be "inflexibly committed to any plan of restoration," which is further proof that he was not inflexibly committed to his own plan. He was "unprepared," he wrote, "to declare that the Free State Constitutions and Governments already adopted and installed in Arkansas and Louisiana, shall be set aside and held for naught," or "to declare a constitutional competency in Congress to abolish slavery in States."

Incensed by the President's action Wade and Davis issued a violent manifesto. Considering that a presidential election was impending it was a political blunder besides being in bad taste. Radicals no less than Conservatives disapproved. Its only practical result was that Davis failed to be renominated for Congress.

The failure of the Wade-Davis plan to become law was no great loss. Had it been put into effect its results would not have differed materially from those of the presidential plan. It required a postwar demonstration of what a continuance of planter rule in the South would mean to the country, to the freedmen, and to Southern loyalists to make Congress and the people of the North realize that sterner measures were required if the sacrifices of the war were not to have been in vain. Stevens had abstained from voting on the plan. He wrote a letter to Davis condemning Lincoln's way of disposing of the measure, but there is reason to believe that he was not displeased with its failure to become law.

Reconstruction was not an issue during the presidential campaign of 1864. On April 11, 1865, the war being practically over, Lincoln delivered a speech in defense of his Reconstruction plan, making it clear, however, that under certain circumstances he would not hesitate to withdraw it.

PART FOUR

THE STRUGGLE WITH JOHNSON

CHAPTER I

The New President

Lincoln's successor, Andrew Johnson, was fifty-seven, of medium height, compactly built, with black hair turning gray, and a swarthy complexion. Carl Schurz describes his face as "sullen . . . betokening a strong will inspired by bitter feelings . . . with no genial sunlight in it." Unlike his predecessor he was, in the matter of dress, "particular to the point of fastidiousness," usually wearing a broadcloth coat, a silk vest, a stiff collar, a stock cravat, and well-cut trousers. He was born in Raleigh, North Carolina, in 1808, of poor white parents and had never gone to school, but at fifteen had taught himself to read a little. At fourteen he had been apprenticed to a tailor. He had taken French leave before his apprenticeship was completed, but had managed to acquire mastery of the trade. He was eighteen when the family migrated to Greeneville, Tennessee, where a year later he opened a tailor shop and married a girl of some education, who improved his reading and taught him how to write.

In North Carolina, as in all the slave states, poor whites were looked down upon even by many of the slaves, and Johnson had early developed "an underdog and a plebeian complex." [1] He had no love for the Negro, but unlike most of his fellow victims of the slave system realized that it was mainly responsible for the degradation of those who had to earn a living by the labor of their hands. He was too shrewd to raise his voice against the institution, but this did not prevent him from nursing resentment against its bene-

[1] From *Andrew Johnson, Plebeian and Patriot* by Robert W. Winston, copyright 1928. Quoted by special permission of the publishers, Henry Holt & Company, p. xv.

...iaries, to whom he later often was to refer as "the inflated and heartless landed aristocracy." He became a Democrat, went into politics, and at twenty-two was elected mayor of Greeneville. Then followed election to the legislature—to Congress, where he served ten years in the House—to governor of Tennessee. When war broke out he represented his state in the Senate. For one of his humble origin and lack of education such a rise would have been remarkable anywhere. It was especially so in a slave state, where poor men were seldom elected to any office of consequence. While this was less true in Tennessee than in the older slave states, it is obvious that Johnson must have possessed characteristics that brought about his political preferment, which, however, is not necessarily indicative of merit.

He has received much praise for his loyalty to the Union, but it should be considered that Tennessee, like Virginia, had been plunged into secession by a veritable *coup d'état*. When in the winter of 1860-61 the question of union or disunion was put squarely before the people, 91,813 voted for union, 24,749 for disunion. Notwithstanding this the legislature ratified the Secession Ordinances subject to another popular vote. With the consent of state officials the state was occupied by Confederate troops. Under the threat of Confederate bayonets secession was approved by a vote of about two to one. There was only one slaveholder to every twenty-seven nonslaveholders in the state. In the mountainous eastern part, where Johnson lived, what few slaves there were, were household servants. Johnson himself owned eight. When the Confederacy tried to conscript the men of that region thousands fled to Kentucky and enlisted in the Union army. Under these circumstances Johnson obviously found himself between Scylla and Charybdis, and it did not require an exceptional amount of moral courage on his part to remain loyal.

One of Johnson's admiring biographers concedes that when he was a member of the House his speeches were "pedantic, personal and sophomoric." [2] He was, however, an effective rough-and-ready stump speaker. In October, 1864, when war governor of Tennessee and Lincoln's running mate on the National Union ticket, he made a speech that sounded as if he had become a disciple of Stevens. Assailing the slave barons, whom he considered responsible for plunging

[2] *Ibid.*, p. 56.

Tennessee into rebellion, he said that "if their immense plantations were divided up and parceled out amongst a number of free, industrious and honest farmers, it would give more good citizens to the Commonwealth, increase the wages of our mechanics, enrich the markets of our city, enliven the arteries of trade, improve society, and conduce to the greatness and glory of the State."

Although Johnson was then considered in sympathy with the Radicals and appeared even to have adopted Stevens's confiscation policy, the Commoner did not trust him. It will be recalled that he had told Lincoln he considered Johnson a "rank demagogue" and a "damned scoundrel." That Johnson had no fixed principles and would veer from one extreme to another whenever he found it expedient is undeniable. Except for singing his own praises there was nothing about which he held forth with greater gusto than the Homestead Law. He was one of the early advocates of that measure and would wax eloquent when describing the happiness and independence of a man living with his family on his own homestead in one of the territories. "He becomes better qualified to discharge the duties of a freeman," he said on one occasion on the floor of Congress. "He is, in fact, the representative of his own homestead, and . . . comes to the ballot box and votes without fear of the restraint of some landlord. After the hurry and bustle of election day are over . . . he and his wife and children sit down at the same table together to enjoy the sweet product of their own hands, with hearts thankful to God for having cast their lots in this country where the land is made free under the protecting and fostering care of a beneficent government."

No one knew better than Johnson what would become of his idyl once slavery invaded the territories. He must have read the report of the Congressional committee on what happened in Kansas. The report told how ruffians hired by the slaveholders invaded the territory from Missouri on Election Day. It told how they intimidated election officials, cast their ballots, and "threatened to shoot any Free State man who should come up to vote." It told about the "bombarding" and sacking of the town of Lawrence; about the burning of cabins, the driving off of horses and cattle, the tarring and feathering, jailing and killing of free state homesteaders. "All the provisions of the Constitution of the United States securing persons and property, are utterly disregarded," said the report. "The officers of the law, instead of protecting the people, were in some instances engaged in these outrages, and in no instance did we learn that any man was arrested, indicted or punished for any of these crimes." [3] Johnson must have known all this. Yet, when in February, 1860, Jefferson Davis offered his resolution in the Senate maintaining that slavery followed the flag into the territories, who but Andrew Johnson, champion of the homesteader, made a speech in its support! It need, therefore, not surprise us that from advocating a veritable massacre of those responsible for the rebellion, Johnson, within a few weeks, should have become metamorphosed into their principal champion when he became convinced that by doing so he might advance his political fortunes.

During the bitter quarrel between Johnson and Stevens, the latter used occasionally to refer to the former as "that drunken tailor at the other end of the avenue." It should be said, however, that Johnson's reputation for overindulgence in strong drink is based mainly on the spectacle he made of himself when sworn in as vice-president in the Senate chamber. Disgraceful as was that occurrence, there were extenuating circumstances. He had been ill, and having fortified himself with a few drinks at the Senate bar, his physical condition may well have been responsible for the liquor mounting to his head. *In vino veritas.* The impromptu speech he made on that occasion so typifies him that a few lines are worth quoting: "I'm a-goin' for to tell you—here to-day; yes, I'm a-goin' for to tell you all, that I'm a plebeian! I glory in it; I'm a plebeian! The people—yes, the people of the United States have made me what I am; and I'm a-goin' for to tell you here to-day—yes, to-day, in this place—that the people are everything." [4]

When, after Lincoln's death, he was sworn in at the Kirkwood House in the presence of members of the cabinet and of senators who had remained in Washington after adjournment of Congress, he delivered a three-minute speech in which he made no mention of Lincoln, but in which *I, me, my,* and *mine* appear more than a score of times. "Toil and an honest advocacy of the great principles of free government, have been my lot," he declared. "The duties have been

[3] *Report of Congressional Committee,* July 1, 1856.

[4] Whitney, in his *Life of Lincoln,* quotes a passage from the speech as it appeared in the *Year Book.*

mine—the consequences are God's." Senator Hale was to comment: "Johnson seemed willing to share the glory of his achievements with the Creator, but utterly forgot that Mr. Lincoln had any share of credit in the suppression of the Rebellion."

2

Incredible as it may seem, there were those who believed that the country would benefit by the change from Lincoln to Johnson. They had come to the conclusion that Lincoln's Reconstruction plan did not take sufficiently into account that leniency toward the oppressor might spell cruelty toward the oppressed. They did not believe that those who had shed torrents of blood so slavery might not be endangered could be trusted with sole responsibility of deciding what should or should not be the Negro's rights as a freeman. They thought that before the rebel states were restored to full partnership in the Union, some measure or measures should be taken to guarantee to the Negro a few essential human rights. Considering that nearly two hundred thousand Negroes had served in the Union army and navy during the war, this was not only humane, but might be said to have been owing to them. To have left them entirely at the mercy of a white population many of whom believed that the Negro had no rights a white man need respect, without even the protection formerly given them by those who owned them, would indeed have been cruel and unjust.

They had, moreover, reached the conclusion that Stevens's warning about the danger of victory being turned into defeat at the first presidential election after the war should not be taken lightly. Granting that many Republican politicians and officeholders may have been more concerned about their own political fortunes than about the country, yet the fact remains that the presence in the South of four million nonvoting Negroes could not be permitted to be turned into account by former Confederates and Copperheads to gain control of a government they had attempted to destroy. Those who believe that Lincoln would have failed to realize all this and would not have either changed or abandoned his Reconstruction plan to meet changed circumstances do him a great injustice. If one thing more than any other was characteristic of Lincoln's statesmanship it was its flexibility. *He seldom stuck to what he originally proposed.* Almost every important proposal made by him during the war was either subject to change or to abandonment if circumstances required it. His Reconstruction plan was no more final and irrevocable than was his decision not to interfere with slavery in the slave states, or his policy of allowing his generals to drive fugitive slaves from the Union lines, or his gradual emancipation plan, or his plan to colonize Negroes abroad or in Texas, or his decision to have the army employ Negroes only as laborers, or his attempt to thwart the adoption and ratification of a constitutional amendment abolishing slavery by having the border states adopt compensated gradual emancipation over a long term of years. None of these had proved final and irrevocable, and it is as unreasonable to claim that Lincoln's Reconstruction plan of December, 1863, was his last word on the subject as it would be to claim that his statement of March, 1861, in which he gave the slave states the assurance that he had neither the "lawful right" nor the "inclination" to interfere with slavery in those states was his last word on *that* subject, or his statement of July, 1862, that Negroes should be employed by the army only as laborers was his last word on *that* subject. Had he died before he had reversed himself on either or both these matters, we may be sure that such a claim would have been made.

Had Lincoln lived to witness the attitude of the South shortly after the conclusion of hostilities, we may take it for granted that he would no more have remained faithful to his original plan of Reconstruction than Congress remained faithful to the Wade-Davis plan. If he was willing to have the Southern states ruled by 10 per cent of the voting population rather than see them fall into the hands of men he considered unfit to govern in a republic, what reason is there to believe that he would have run the risk of having the federal government fall into such hands? Moreover, while it is generally assumed that the plan of Reconstruction championed by Johnson and rejected by Congress was Lincoln's plan, *the fact is that it was not Lincoln's plan at all, but the first congressional plan, known as the Wade-Davis plan.* John Sherman of Ohio pointed this out in a speech in the United States Senate, February 26, 1866. Said Sherman: "In carrying out his plans of reconstruction he adopted all the main features of the only bill passed by Congress—the Wade-Davis bill. I have the bill before me, but I have not the time to go into details. My colleague [Fessenden], who remembers the features of that bill, will know that the general plan adopted by President Johnson is the only plan that was ever adopted by Congress." We shall see that since that plan was adopted the situation had changed so radically that the Wade-Davis plan, no less than Lincoln's plan, had become obsolete. Lincoln, particularly sensitive to social changes, would have grasped this at once. He would, moreover, have realized that while during the war there might have been some justification for the President to act independently of Congress in a matter of that kind, in time of peace that justification no longer existed. He would have co-operated with Congress in devising a plan to fit the changed situation. Johnson refused all co-operation.

Stevens was not one of those who harbored the strange delusion that the passing of a Lincoln and the accession to power of a Johnson could be of any possible value to the country or to the party. Whatever his and Lincoln's differences had been in intervals between the adoption of important measures, *in the end they had nearly always agreed.* Many of the Commoner's followers, however, did harbor that delusion. It is in the nature of radicals to be impatient. They failed to understand Lincoln's careful, experimental mode of procedure and were deceived by Johnson's spurious radicalism. Even they, however, felt concerned about the new President's emphasis on punishing the rebels and feared that such a policy might provoke a reaction that would hinder the adoption of indispensable measures of state.

CHAPTER II

Johnson's Metamorphosis

When on March 2, 1861, news reached Washington of the firing by the Confederates on the *Star of the West* and their seizure of arsenals, docks, forts, and navy yards, Andrew Johnson exclaimed in the Senate: "Were I President of the United States, I would do as Thomas Jefferson did in 1806, with Aaron Burr. I would have them arrested, and if convicted within the meaning and scope of the Constitution, *by the Eternal God I would execute them!*"

He maintained that attitude throughout the war—as senator, as military governor of Tennessee, as vice-president. After the fall of Richmond, on April 3, 1865, less than two weeks before Lincoln's death, he said at a public meeting in Washington: "My notion is that treason must be made odious, and traitors must be punished and impoverished, their social power broken, that they must be made to feel the penalty of their crime. . . . Hence I say this: 'the halter to intelligent influential traitors.' But to the honest boy, the deluded man who has been deceived into the rebel ranks, I would extend leniency; I would say, return to your allegiance, renew your support of the Government, and become a good citizen; but the leaders I would hang."

On May 3 a delegation from Pennsylvania, headed by Cameron and accompanied by Stevens, called at the White House and was told: "To the unconscious, deceived, conscripted—in short to the great mass of the misled—I would say mercy, clemency, reconciliation, and the restoration of their Government. To those who have deceived—to the conscious, influential traitor, who attempted to destroy the life of the nation—I would say, on you be inflicted the severest penalties of your crime."

He had in the meantime had an interview with Ben Wade, who was to succeed him as presiding officer in the Senate, and had asked the Ohio senator what he would do if he were in his place. Wade replied: "I should either force into exile or hang about ten or twelve of the worst of those fellows: perhaps by way of full measure, I should make it thirteen, just a baker's dozen." "But how," said Johnson, "are you going to pick out so small a number and show them to be guiltier than the rest?" "It won't do to hang a very large number," Wade replied, and added that everybody would agree Jefferson Davis, Toombs, Benjamin, Slidell, Mason, and Howell Cobb were the most guilty. "If we did no more than drive these half-dozen out of the country we should accomplish a great deal." Johnson appeared displeased and expressed surprise that the Senator should be willing to let "the traitors escape so easily." He said he had expected the heartiest support from Wade in a policy which "as he outlined it seemed in *thoroughness* to rival that of Strafford." [1]

2

Toward the end of April Johnson told an Indiana delegation that in his opinion the rebel states were still members of the Union and that it was a constitutional obligation "to secure each of these States in the possession and enjoyment of a republican form of government." As a first step toward this he recognized on May 9, 1865, the phantom state government of Francis H. Pierpont as the rightful government of Virginia. By what process of reasoning he considered this a restoration of a "republican form of government" in Virginia defies analysis. Lincoln had required the support of a minimum of 10 per cent of the voters before a reconstructed state government was worthy of recognition—a sufficiently doubtful claim of popular support for a "republican form of government." The Pierpont government had been put into office by only a fraction of that minimum. "All the archives, property and effects of the Pierpont government

[1] Blaine, *op. cit.*, vol. II, p. 14.

were taken [from Alexandria] to Richmond in an ambulance," Stevens later informed his colleagues in Congress.

On May 10 Johnson, together with members of his cabinet, called on Secretary Seward, who had not yet recovered from the murderous attack made upon him by one of Booth's accomplices. The meeting was productive of momentous results. On May 29 he issued an Amnesty Proclamation for the benefit of those who had not yet availed themselves of the two Amnesty Proclamations issued by his predecessor. On that same day he issued a Proclamation of Reorganization for North Carolina and appointed William S. Holden provisional governor of that state.

Johnson's Amnesty Proclamation excepted more classes of persons than Lincoln's. Among those excepted were "all persons . . . the estimated value of whose taxable property is over twenty thousand dollars," for, as he was to explain to a Virginia delegation that came to protest, "it is the wealthy men of the South who dragooned the people into Secession." While Johnson was thus apparently more severe than his predecessor, in reality he was less so. Neither of Lincoln's two Amnesty Proclamations made provision for the pardon of those who had been excepted; Johnson's contained the proviso "That special application may be made to the President for pardon by any person belonging to the excepted class." It, moreover, held out the promise that "such clemency would be liberally extended." It is not to be supposed that Lincoln would not ultimately have extended pardon to many of the excepted, but he was too sensible to have done so at a time when it could only serve to permit notorious rebels to be elected to the new state governments and to Congress.

By the middle of July, 1865, three months after Lincoln's death, every rebel state, with the sole exception of Texas, had been reconstructed. Pardons rained down upon the South like manna from heaven. Within less than nine months more than fourteen thousand were granted.

3

What was responsible for Johnson's sudden change of heart? The change coincided with the arrival in Washington of numerous Southern personalities, women as well as men, who sought and obtained interviews with the President. The women were daughters, wives, or mothers of prominent secessionists. Alarmed by the reports of Johnson's threats against "conscious influential traitors" they had come to plead with the President. The men were for the most part Whig loyalists who had been opposed to secession and had co-operated reluctantly if at all with the Confederate government. There were among them men of culture, intelligence, and great personal charm. Many had always been in favor of gradual emancipation, but had found themselves in a hopeless minority. They, too, came to plead for clemency, not only for the sake of relatives and friends, but as a quieting measure. Their offers of co-operation with the administration were entirely sincere.

That Johnson should have given the visitors from the South a sympathetic hearing is to his credit. But in drawing conclusions from the interviews he displayed an amazing lack of judgment and grasp of reality. It apparently never occurred to him that for all their good intentions the visitors were giving him an entirely false impression of the situation the government would have to deal with. The men for whom the Southern women came to plead were not repentant but defiant. They considered that the South had had a right to secede and that Lincoln was to blame for having failed to recognize this. If one pointed out to them that the people of the South had not been consulted, or consulted under circumstances that made an honest expression of opinion impossible, the argument left them cold. The South had always been ruled in the interest of the slaveholding minority, and since that minority had been in favor of secession they considered themselves justified. As for the loyal Whigs, they were no more representative of Southern slaveholders in general than Lincoln would have been representative of them.

Blaine has suggested that Johnson was blinded by his vanity and egotism. "It was," he wrote, "with a sense of exaltation that Johnson beheld as applicants for his consideration and suppliants for his mercy many of those in the South who had never recognized him as a social equal. A mind of true loftiness would not have been swayed by such a change of relative positions, but it was inevitable that a mind of Johnson's type, which if not ignoble was certainly not noble, should yield to its flattering and seductive influence. In the present attitude of the leading men of the South towards him, he saw the one triumph which sweetened his life, the one requisite which had been needed to complete his happiness. In securing the good opinion of his native South, he would attain the goal of his highest ambition, he would conquer the haughty enemy who during all the years of his public career had been able to fix upon him the badge of social inferiority." [2]

One of Johnson's biographers informs us that when military governor of Tennessee he had shown himself particularly susceptible to feminine charm. "If there was one thing more irresistible to the Governor than another it was a pretty woman," he has written.[3] When a pretty secessionist came to solicit a favor it had been invariably granted. It may well be, therefore, that some of the Southern women, who not unlikely had only a short time before referred to him as "that vulgar renegade," or "that drunken Tennessee tailor," played a leading part in Johnson's conversion.

It was, however, after his visit to Seward that Johnson's changed attitude began to take shape. There had in the past been little sympathy between the two men, and it had been generally believed that Seward would not remain in the cabinet. The visit changed all this. The wily old Secretary, who himself had nothing more to hope from the Republican party, had apparently dropped a few artful hints that had given definite orientation to Johnson's wavering state of mind. It is not difficult to surmise their nature.

Now that the war was over it appeared more than doubtful that the Republicans would care to nominate Johnson as their standard-bearer in 1868. If he wanted a second term he must look elsewhere. Northern Democrats had been denouncing Lincoln's Reconstruction plan and the first congressional plan—the Wade-Davis plan—as unconstitutional. When, however, it dawned upon them that both plans were favorable to the fulfillment of their political ambitions, their attitude had changed. Most conservative Republicans had favored the Wade-Davis plan and many Radicals had voted for it in 1864. Moreover, it appears that Lincoln himself, shortly after he issued his state paper rejecting the plan, had changed his mind about it. Sumner has testified: "I had an interview with the late President Lincoln immediately after the publication of that paper, and it was the subject of very minute and protracted conversations,

[2] *Op. cit.*, vol. II, p. 70.
[3] Winston, *op. cit.*, p. 246.

in the course of which, after discussing it in detail, he expressed his regret that he had not accepted the bill." [4]

There is, therefore, good reason to believe that Seward advised Johnson to make the Wade-Davis plan his own. In doing so he would be executing a plan adopted by Congress,[5] and would be able to count on the support of Northern Democrats, the solid South, and many Conservative Republicans. With such support he could be certain of nomination and election on the National Union ticket in 1868.

Seward failed to take into account Southern intransigence, Johnson's inaptitude, and Stevens's genius for politics.

[4] *Globe,* Appendix, Feb. 26, 1866.

[5] We have seen that on February 26, 1866, John Sherman pointed this out in a speech on the Senate floor. A study of the Lincoln and the Wade-Davis plans makes it obvious that it was the latter plan Johnson adopted.

CHAPTER III

Consequences of Johnson's Metamorphosis

That Lincoln should have been deceived regarding the South's probable attitude at the conclusion of hostilities is understandable. Radicals like Ben Wade and Henry Winter Davis had been equally deceived, as were the great majority of Stevens's followers. The Wade-Davis Reconstruction plan adopted by Congress offered no more safeguards against an early capture of the federal government by a Copperhead–ex-rebel combination and no more protection for the freedmen than Lincoln's plan. In 1864 Stevens appears to have been the only one to have realized the danger. His warning that reintegration of the rebel states into the Union without proper safeguards meant "subjection to traitors and their Northern allies" had fallen upon deaf ears. The reason for this undoubtedly was that those elected during the war to Congress and to state offices in states or parts of states reconstructed by Lincoln were without exception loyalists. They were so entirely out of sympathy with the men who had maneuvered the South into the disastrous adventure that one could easily have believed their election heralded a complete revulsion of feeling in the South. Had not Alexander H. Stephens, before allowing himself to be persuaded or intimidated into becoming vice-president of the Confederacy, said at the Georgia Secession Convention that those responsible for secession would be *"held to strict account for their suicidal act by the present generation, and probably*

cursed and execrated by posterity for all coming time"? [1] His prophecy appeared to be coming true.

Johnson had no such excuse. Before he issued his Reorganization Proclamation for North Carolina he had had a conference with a committee from that state, headed by B. F. Moore. He had read the document to them, undoubtedly believing they would be highly gratified. He was wrong. They objected to the appointment of a provisional governor, saying it was the business of the legislature to call a convention to revise the state constitution. As for the demands made by Johnson—repudiation of the secession ordinances, abolition of slavery forever, ratification of the Thirteenth Amendment, repudiation of the Confederate debts, state and national—they considered them unwarranted interference with state rights. The only demand he could constitutionally make, they told him, was a declaration by the proper state authorities that North Carolina had laid down its arms. When he replied that he could not recognize the existing legislature and appointed William S. Holden provisional governor, they withdrew, saying they could have nothing more to do with the proceedings.[2] When Holden, a loyalist, presented himself at the election as candidate for the office he had provisionally occupied, he was defeated.

Mississippi, the second state reconstructed by Johnson, defeated his appointee for provisional governor at the election, put a former Confederate general in his place and refused to ratify the Thirteenth Amendment. South Carolina chose a former Confederate senator for governor and objected to the repudiation of the Confederate debts. Georgia demurred against ratification of the amendment and repudiation of the debts, and a stern warning was needed to bring her into line. Alabama defeated Johnson's provisional governor at the election. The Louisiana Legislature denounced—and was with difficulty persuaded not to repudiate—the new state constitution Lincoln had lauded in his last speech. What was the reason for this intransigence, so unlike the spirit that had prevailed when Lincoln had busied himself with Reconstruction?

Confederate officers and soldiers, embittered and angry, had returned home. Unfortunately their anger was not, as Stephens had

[1] Thomas V. Cooper, *American Politics*, p. 116. Italics in original.
[2] J. G. Hamilton, *Reconstruction in North Carolina*, p. 106.

prophesied, directed against the authors of their woes—the Southern politicos and landed aristocracy—but against the North. The gray Confederate uniform, no matter how worn and stained, was a mark of distinction. It was now considered an honor to belong to one of the "excepted" classes in Lincoln's or Johnson's Amnesty Proclamations, and since obtaining a pardon was a mere formality, the "excepted" had a distinct advantage in the nominating conventions and the elections. Thus, men whom Lincoln had regarded as dangerous to the future peace and unity of the republic were nominated and elected. In the states reconstructed by Lincoln during the war those seeking political office had made a boast of their loyalty. Now loyalists were considered traitors to the Southern cause, were ostracized, hounded, and persecuted. Many were forced to seek refuge in the North. The newly elected state officials were bitter, vindictive men, proud of having been rebels, anxious to assert themselves and to demonstrate to the North that emancipation or no emancipation they would do with the Negro as they pleased.

What appeared especially ominous to loyalists in the North was the practically unanimous support Johnson was receiving from Northern newspapers that during the war had assailed Congress and the administration with equal virulence. The foremost Copperhead organ, the New York *World,* which had once referred to Johnson as "this insolent drunken brute," could now hardly find terms strong enough to praise his "enlightened leadership." When the newly elected Southern legislatures set to work on laws concerning the Negro, and the South elected representatives to Congress, the North took one look at the laws and at the representatives and became convinced that unless stern measures were taken, not only would slavery have a rebirth, but, as Stevens had warned, a combination of Copperheads and "whitewashed rebels" might soon be in control of the government in Washington.

2

Lincoln's friend and counselor Francis Preston Blair, Sr., was wise to the ways of the slaveholders. On November 14, 1864, he had written to Andrew Johnson suggesting that "a portion of Texas on the Rio Grande" be set apart "for such a refuge for the freedmen of the South to go to, as they might seek under the protection of the United States. . . . I really believe," he wrote, "that unless the blacks have some region of refuge when the power of State Legislation resumes its sway; if as a body the Africans remain in the South, the Egyptian taskmasters will still make it a house of bondage. And the apprehension of this will make the President's plan of reconstruction very difficult, with the present feeling dominating in the North." [3]

The "apprehension" proved to have been fully justified. Before Congress assembled in December, 1865, "the power of State Legislation" had resumed its sway in the South and promptly set to work making it "still a house of bondage." Had Lincoln's friend found himself in Mississippi after the adoption in November, 1865, of the bill regulating the conduct of freedmen, free Negroes, and mulattoes, and had he tried to aid any of the unfortunates to find a refuge from the "Egyptian taskmasters," he would have found himself in the clutches of the law. One part of the bill provided that "if any person shall attempt to persuade or entice any freedman, free negro, or mulatto . . . without the limits of the State, such person, on conviction, shall be fined not less than fifty dollars and not more than five hundred dollars and the costs, and if said fine and costs shall not be immediately paid, the court shall sentence said convict to not exceeding six months imprisonment in the county jail." Another part of the bill provided that if a person "shall give or sell to any deserting freedman, free Negro or mulatto, any food, raiment, or other thing, he shall . . . upon conviction, be fined not less than twenty-five dollars and not more than two hundred dollars and the costs; and if said fine be not immediately paid, the court shall sentence said convict to not exceeding two months imprisonment in the county jail and he shall moreover be liable to the party injured in damages."

One cannot help wondering what the South's landed aristocracy would have thought of Lincoln had he lived out his second term and seriously set to work colonizing the freedmen in Texas or abroad. His unpopularity with the planter class might have surpassed the unpopularity of those responsible for the Fifteenth Amendment, for one is inclined to believe that had the planters been given the

[3] Smith, *op. cit.*, vol. II, p. 338.

choice between granting the freedmen the elective franchise and seeing them depart they would have preferred the former.

3

Working conditions must have been little short of intolerable if laws such as those cited were considered necessary to keep starving men and women at work. Since unemployed freedmen, free Negroes, and mulattoes were subject to arrest, and when arrested were either hired out by the sheriff or forced to work for the county without pay, colored persons were obliged to accept employment on the employers' own terms. Few of those employed ever saw any money. The majority were in debt to the employer for food and their few rags of clothing. If a Negro quit his employment before the expiration of the work contract, any civil officer was required to, and any person could, arrest him and return him to the employer. Once arrested he became practically a bondman for life, for he had forfeited his wages until the time of quitting, and these together with the reward for his capture and the cost of transporting him were charged against him, a debt he could seldom repay.

As in slavery days, Negro parents had no assurance whatever that they would be allowed to keep their children. The Mississippi law—in imitation of which the Black Codes of other reconstructed states were fashioned, with a few sadistic provisions thrown in—provided that if the court held the parents could not take care of their children "properly," they should be apprenticed, preferably to the former owner—the boys until they were twenty-one, the girls until they were eighteen. Since the parents barely received enough to feed themselves, "proper" care of the children was seldom possible. Thus the former slaveholders were assured of a plentiful supply of unpaid youthful labor.

Members of the Mississippi Legislature deserve some credit for scorning to ratify a constitutional amendment they had no intention of obeying. Those of other reconstructed states were not so scrupulous and some of the laws affecting the Negro passed by them bear unmistakable evidence of vindictiveness and spite. What possible justification could there have been for the law adopted by Florida and several other Southern states obliging the colored people to pay for the education of their children entirely out of their own resources?

Border state representatives had said repeatedly during the war that if the slaves were emancipated, not only would they be reenslaved under state law as soon as peace had come, but free Negroes living in the South would likewise be enslaved. Their prophecy appeared to be coming true. The slaves had not been elevated to the status of free Negroes, the free Negroes were reduced to the status of slaves. It has been said that if the planter oligarchy—which although impoverished was again in the saddle everywhere in the South—had deliberately undertaken to provoke the North it could not have done so more effectively. The Chicago *Tribune,* in its issue of December 1, 1865, exclaimed: "The men of the North will convert Mississippi into a frog-pond before they allow such laws to disgrace one foot of our soil." Such warnings, however, did not deter other reconstructed states from following Mississippi's example.

4

On July 2, 1862, Congress had adopted what became known as the "Ironclad Oath," making it incumbent upon anyone elected to that body to be able to swear that he had "never willingly borne arms against the United States," and had "voluntarily given no aid, countenance, counsel, or encouragement to persons engaged in armed hostility to the National Government." The difficulty was that a man able to take the oath could, after the war, not have been elected to office in any of the former rebel states except Tennessee. It smacked, however, of deliberate provocation to elect to Congress the former vice-president of the Confederacy, Alexander H. Stephens—who only four months before had been released from Fort Warren, where he had been awaiting trial for treason, six former members of the Confederate cabinet, four Confederate generals, and five Confederate colonels! Even Johnson thought this was going too far. When he heard that Stephens was being considered by the Georgia legislature as a fit candidate for United States senator he wired the military governor of the district: "It would be exceedingly impolitic for Mr. Stephens's name to be used in connection with the senatorial election. . . . He stands charged with treason, and no disposition had been made in the case." Neither the legislature nor Stephens heeded the protest.

John Minor Botts, a Virginian who had represented that state in Congress from 1839 to 1843 and again from 1847 to 1849, in testimony before the Joint Committee, expressed the conviction that Johnson's metamorphosis was in a large measure responsible for the changed attitude of the leading secessionists: "When Mr. Lincoln was assassinated, and Mr. Johnson took his place, they felt exceedingly apprehensive for the security of their property, as well as the security of their lives; and a more humble, unpretending set of gentlemen I never saw than they were at that time. But from the time that Mr. Johnson commenced his indiscriminate system of pardoning all who made application, and from the impositions which, I have no doubt, were practiced on Mr. Johnson in pardoning the worst class of secessionists among the first, they became bold, insolent and defiant. . . . I think the spirit of disloyalty and disaffection has gone increasing day by day, and hour by hour, until among the leaders generally there is as much disaffection and disloyalty as there was at any time during the war. This is the conclusion to which my mind has been brought by the licentiousness of the press, and by communications which are made to me from all parts of the state, either verbally or by letter, from the most prominent and reliable Union sources."[4]

Out of forty-four other persons who gave testimony before the Committee regarding this matter, no less than forty-two confirmed Botts's statement that Johnson's "special pardons and leniency to these leading rebels had had a very bad effect upon them and had caused them—humbled and meek at the close of the war—to assume again all their former hauteur and insolence towards the North."[5]

[4] *Testimony,* Part II, pp. 120-121, 123.

[5] From *The Journal of the Joint Committee of Fifteen on Reconstruction* by Benj. B. Kendrick, copyright 1914. Quoted by special permission of the publishers, Columbia University Press, p. 286. *Testimony,* Part IV, pp. 175-176.

CHAPTER IV

Was Stevens Vindictive?

Stevens was in Lancaster when on the morning of April 22 Lincoln's black-draped funeral train passed the town on its way to Philadelphia. He had not joined the crowd at the railway station, but stood, a brooding solitary figure, on the hillside above the cut through which the train was passing. He was now seventy-three and in poor health. Less than three and a half years of life remained to him. During three of these he was to be not only the leader of the House and of the party in power, but of the nation, with influence far surpassing that of the President.

He met the new President face to face when on May 3 he accompanied the Pennsylvania delegation, headed by Cameron, on its good-will visit to Washington. Johnson, who had not yet moved into the White House, received them in a room in the Treasury Building. Cameron made a short address, Johnson replied at greater length, but was noncommittal on Reconstruction.

A week later Stevens was in Philadelphia on business connected with his law practice when, picking up a newspaper, he read that the President had recognized the phantom Pierpont government as the rightful government of Virginia. It was an ill omen. He wrote to Charles Sumner: "I see the President is precipitating things. Virginia is reorganized! I fear before Congress meets he will have so bedeviled matters as to render them incurable."

Back in Lancaster he brooded about the matter and on May 16 decided to write to Johnson. "Reconstruction," he wrote, "is a very delicate question. The last Congress (and I expect the present) looked upon it as a question for the Legislative power exclusively. . . . How the Executive can remodel the *States in the Union* is past my comprehension. I see how he can govern them through military governors until they are recognized. . . . My only object is to suggest the propriety of suspending further 'reconstruction' until the meeting of Congress. Better call an extra session than to allow many to think the Executive was approaching usurpation."

If Stevens was right and the "present Congress" like the last looked upon Reconstruction "as a question for the Legislative power exclusively," then Johnson's failure to reply to the letter of the most powerful congressional leader and his subsequent action of issuing the "Reorganization Proclamation" for North Carolina were a serious blunder. If Seward was responsible for giving him that advice then no President ever had a worse counselor. It was unfair to the South and to the country to proceed with a Reconstruction plan when there was no guaranty that congressional representatives of the reconstructed states would be admitted, or even that the entire proceeding would not be annulled. When Lincoln put his Reconstruction plan into execution he had no idea that it would be rejected by Congress. Indeed, he had reason to believe it would be approved, since representatives from Louisiana had previously been admitted. When he saw that Congress disapproved he had refrained from carrying the matter further. He had promised, moreover, that if he became convinced the plan was "adverse to the public interest" he would withdraw it. Even if there had been no other reason for its abandonment, would he not have considered it "adverse to the public interest" for the President to cling to a plan to which more than two-thirds of both Houses—the entire Republican party in Congress with the exception of four in the Senate and two in the House—proved to be opposed? The most characteristic feature of Lincoln's statesmanship was its flexibility; the most characteristic feature of Johnson's bungling was his obstinacy.

On June 3, a few days after Johnson had issued his proclamation reconstructing North Carolina, Stevens wrote to Sumner: "Is it possible to devise any plan to arrest the government in its ruinous course? . . . Could we collect bold men enough to lay the foundation of a party to take the helm of this government and keep it off the rocks?" On June 14, the day after Mississippi had been reconstructed, he wrote: "Is there no way to arrest the insane course of the President in 'Reconstruction'?" There apparently was not, for Reconstruction of Georgia, Alabama, and South Carolina followed in rapid succession. On July 6, Stevens again wrote to Johnson: "I am sure you will pardon me for speaking to you with a candor to which men in high place are seldom accustomed. Among all the leading Union men of the North with whom I had intercourse I do not find one who approves of your policy. They believe that 'Restoration' as announced by you will destroy our party (which is of little consequence) and will greatly injure the country. Can you not hold your hand and wait the action of Congress, and in the meantime govern them by military rulers? Profuse pardoning also will greatly embarrass Congress if they should wish to make the enemy pay the expense of war or part of it."

This letter, too, remained unanswered. Yet, on August 17, Stevens wrote a letter to Sumner that still manifested a conciliatory spirit: "I have written very plainly to the President urging delay. But I fear he will pursue his wrong course . . . usurping 'reconstruction.' I know not where you and I shall be. While we can hardly approve of all the acts of the government we must try to keep out of the ranks of the opposition. The danger is that so much success will reconcile the people to almost anything."

Stevens's fear was not unfounded. Lincoln's attempts at Reconstruction—made at a time when those elected in the reconstructed states to state offices and to Congress were almost without exception loyalists—had had the unfortunate effect of creating an entirely false impression of what the situation was likely to be at the conclusion of hostilities. In the early summer of 1865 it had not yet become apparent to what extent the situation had changed and the effects of Johnson's indiscriminate pardoning had not yet made themselves felt. There was, therefore, some reason to fear that the people of the North might not awaken to the danger until it was too late.

2

The charge of malevolence and vindictiveness has been made so persistently against Stevens that now when his plan for reconstructing the South is about to have our attention it seems pertinent to inquire if its conception was motivated by sentiments of that character. One must begin by saying that nothing in his past life gives reason to believe that he was vindictive by nature. What evidence we possess points to the contrary. It will be recalled that once when awarded damages for libel against an editor, whose property was ordered sold to satisfy the judgment, Stevens bought the property at sheriff's sale and returned it to the man who had wronged him. This is hardly the act of a vindictive man. There is an abundance of evidence that he was uncommonly charitable and throughout his career generously aided the poor and afflicted.

Carl Schurz has pointed out that Stevens was wont to hide his feelings behind a forbidding facial expression and a brusque manner. He often indulged in bitter and sarcastic speech, but as every psychologist knows this does not necessarily denote a harsh and unforgiving nature. What he said has, moreover, been often misrepresented, even by historians of note, by being quoted out of context. He never was guilty of saying he wished the South "to be laid waste and made a desert." When he used these words he was referring to statements made by Southern leaders that in order to subdue the South the North would have to resort to that sort of procedure. "War," he said, "is a grievous thing at best, and civil war more than any other; *but if they hold such language, and the means which they have suggested must be resorted to;* if their whole country *must* be laid waste and made a desert, in order to save this Union from destruction, so let it be." To say that this meant he wished the South to be "laid waste and made a desert" is like accusing Lincoln of having said at his second inaugural he wished the war to "continue until all the wealth piled by the bondman's two hundred and fifty years of unrequited toil shall be sunk, and until every drop of blood drawn with the lash shall be paid by another drawn with the sword." What Lincoln *did* say was, *"Yet if God wills that it* continue until all the wealth piled up by the bondman's two hundred and fifty years of unrequited toil shall be sunk, and until every drop of blood drawn with the lash shall be paid by another drawn with the sword, *as was said three thousand years ago, so, still it must be said that the judgments of the Lord are true and righteous altogether."* Leave out the words in italics and you have changed the entire meaning.

Stevens did not exaggerate when he said that the Southern leaders "hold such language." They had done so repeatedly and were to do so again. Jefferson Davis, during his conference with Colonel Jacquess and James R. Gilmore, was to say: "We are fighting for independence—and that or *extermination* we will have. . . . We will govern ourselves. We will do it if we have to see *every Southern plantation sacked, and every Southern city in flames.*" If stern and even ruthless measures finally had to be resorted to to save the Union, were not those to blame who in order to satisfy their pride or ambition, or to preserve the "way of life" of a small social class, declared themselves ready to sacrifice the South and all its people?

The present generation of Americans is free from rancor toward those responsible for the rebellion, but it should be considered that during the war and for several years thereafter loyalists regarded secessionists as traitors. In fairness to them we should consider how we ourselves feel toward those whom we believe to be guilty of treason. Robert Toombs of Georgia forecast the attitude of posterity toward secession when he cynically remarked: "When traitors become numerous enough, treason becomes respectable." If, however, we study the climate of opinion prevailing in Stevens's time, we shall see that he was not more but *less* inclined than the majority of his loyal contemporaries to demand the infliction of harsh punishment upon those responsible for what was then considered not a "war between the States," but a "slaveholders' rebellion."

3

The National Union Convention which in June, 1864, nominated Lincoln and Johnson for President and Vice-President, had for temporary chairman a Kentucky War Democrat, the Reverend Robert J. Breckinridge, a distinguished Episcopal clergyman. There is no reason to believe that the reverend gentleman was more vengeful by nature than most loyal Kentuckians, probably less so, yet we find him saying in his opening speech: "The fearful truth runs through the whole history of mankind that whatever else may be done to give stability to authority, whatever else may be done to give perpetuity to institutions, however wise, however glorious, practical and just may be the philosophy of it, it has been found that the only imperishable element of all institutions has been the blood of traitors. No government has ever been built upon imperishable foundations, which foundations were not laid in the blood of traitors."

This could only mean that Dr. Breckinridge believed the men responsible for the rebellion should be executed.

The convention, composed of Republicans and War Democrats, was probably as representative of loyalist sentiment as any body of men that could have been assembled. It greeted these remarks with loud applause. The first plank of the platform it adopted, and to which Lincoln took no exception when he accepted the nomination, read: "*Resolved,* That it is the highest duty of every American citizen to maintain, against all their enemies, the integrity of the Union and the permanent authority of the Constitution and laws of the United States . . . and in bringing to the punishment due to their crimes the rebels and traitors arrayed against it."

The ultraconservative Senator John Sherman of Ohio said on February 26, 1866, on the floor of the Senate: "If I had any power in arranging a plan [of Reconstruction] I would mark the line as broad and deep between the loyal people who stood at our side and the rebels who fought against us as between heaven and hell."

Governor Fairchild of Wisconsin, in his inaugural address of January 1, 1866, declared: "Not until Jefferson Davis shall have been tried, convicted, and hanged for treason, and the fact that treason is a crime which cannot be committed with impunity shall have thus been fully demonstrated, will the American people be content." [1]

So widespread and profound was the feeling against the leaders of the rebellion that a gentle old lady, the mother of Senator Doolittle of Wisconsin, one of the four administration Republicans in the Senate, wrote to her son: "Tell President Johnson to be sure to have Jeff Davis tried and executed." [2] Johnson would have been nothing loath. As late as August 3, 1868, he was to write to B. G. Truman: "I shall go to my grave with the firm belief that Davis, Cobb, Toombs and a few others of the arch-conspirators and traitors should

[1] *Globe,* Feb. 5, 1866. Cited by Representative Lawrence of Ohio.

[2] From *A History of the United States since the Civil War* by E. P. Oberholtzer, copyright 1917, The Macmillan Company, publishers. Quoted by special permission of Mrs. McBride Oberholtzer, vol. I, p. 19.

have been tried and hanged for treason. . . . If it was the last act of my life I'd hang Jeff Davis as an example." [3]

Loyalists in Tennessee, who had suffered merciless persecution during the war, were particularly bitter. The Legislature of Tennessee, a state reconstructed during Lincoln's administration, at its second session, October 2, 1865, to May 28, 1866, adopted a joint resolution demanding that Davis, Mason, Hunter, Toombs, Cobb, Benjamin, Slidell, and Lee be executed.[4]

Lincoln, who was not given to name-calling, referred to civil and military leaders of the secession movement as "traitors." The historian Benson J. Lossing, who participated in an interview with Lincoln concerning the *Trent* affair, informs us that speaking of the two Confederate envoys, Mason and Slidell, whom the overzealous captain of a Union man-of-war had taken from the British steamer *Trent,* the President said: "I fear the traitors will prove a white elephant." [5] In a letter to "Hon. Erastus Corning and Others," of Albany, New York, June 13, 1863, Lincoln names several prominent Confederate military leaders, including Robert E. Lee, and writes that "they were all within the power of the Government since the rebellion began, and were nearly as well known to be traitors then as now."

That Lincoln was far more interested in reconstructing than in punishing may be taken for granted, but his Reconstruction plan, like Stevens's, was unavoidably punitive. It "excepted" most of the prominent men in the South from his two Amnesty Proclamations, thus depriving them of civil rights and making much of their property subject to confiscation. We have seen, moreover, that he later changed his mind concerning the constitutionality of the confiscation of real estate and expressed himself willing to sign a bill to that effect if Congress chose to pass it. In September, 1863, he issued an order to the tax commissioners of that part of South Carolina occupied by Union troops to seize and sell 40,845 acres of land belonging to rebel owners.[6]

There probably was no measure the South considered more "vindictive" than the Emancipation Proclamation. Even before the war

[3] *Century Magazine,* 1913, vol. LXXXII, pp. 438-440.
[4] J. T. Moore and A. P. Foster, *Tennessee,* p. 531.
[5] Lossing, *Pictorial History of the Civil War,* vol. II, pp. 156-157.
[6] Grace Julian Clarke, *George W. Julian,* p. 256.

began, Alexander H. Stephens warned the Georgia Secession Convention of "the vindictive decree of universal emancipation, which may be reasonably expected to follow." [7]

Lincoln, like Stevens, was opposed to any bloody reprisals, but there is indisputable evidence that at the conclusion of hostilities he meant to exile the principal leaders of the rebellion. Testimony to that effect has been given by Frederick Seward, assistant secretary of state, who shortly before Lincoln's assassination became acting secretary while his father was incapacitated as a result of a fall from his carriage. It was he the President instructed to call a cabinet meeting on the morning of the fateful day, April 14, 1865. He tells us in his *Reminiscences* that a discussion arose at the meeting concerning what should be done with the leaders of the rebellion. Some of those present believed it would be unwise "to let the leaders in treason go entirely unpunished." Postmaster General Dennison turned to the President and said: "I suppose, Mr. President, you would not be sorry to have them escape out of the country."

"Well," said Mr. Lincoln slowly, "I should not be sorry to have them out of the country; but I should be following them up pretty close, to make sure of their going." [8] If this does not mean that he intended to send them into exile, what does it mean?

Others close to Lincoln went much further. Attorney General James Speed, brother of Lincoln's bosom friend Joshua Speed, whom in 1864 Lincoln had appointed to succeed Edward Bates, wrote on January 4, 1866, to President Johnson: "I think that it is the plain duty of the President to cause criminal prosecutions to be instituted before the proper civil tribunals and at all proper times against some of those who were mainly instrumental in inaugurating, and most conspicuous in conducting, the late hostilities. I should regard it as a direful calamity if many whom the sword has spared the law should spare also." [9]

John Hay, Lincoln's secretary and biographer, who rose to be secretary of state in the McKinley and Roosevelt cabinets, wrote as late as August 10, 1885, to John G. Nicolay, Lincoln's other secretary and biographer: "Gilder was evidently horrified at your saying that

[7] Cooper, *op. cit.*, p. 116.
[8] *Reminiscences*, pp. 254-255.
[9] *Globe*, Feb. 5, 1866. Cited by Lawrence of Ohio.

Lee ought to be shot: a simple truth of law and equity." Hay's biographer informs us that he "regarded Secessionists as plain rebels; in theory either criminals, scoundrels or madmen, deserving neither charity or quarter." [10]

Such was the climate of opinion at the time Stevens indulged in his invective. That he and others should have regarded secessionists as traitors need not surprise us. One of the South's greatest legal lights, William L. Yancey, former congressman from Alabama and author of the Alabama Platform demanding from Congress the positive protection of slavery in the territories, which became the creed of the entire South, expressed the following opinion at the famous presecession convention in Montgomery, Alabama, in 1858: "If I understand my distinguished colleague from Virginia [Mr. Pryor], the election of a Black Republican President would be an issue of disunion. I understand my learned colleague [Mr. Hilliard] to say that upon that issue he would be ready to dissolve the Union. . . . When I am asked to raise the flag of revolution against an election under the forms of laws and the Constitution, *I am asked to do an unconstitutional thing,* according to the Constitution as it now exists. *I am asked to put myself in a position of a rebel, of a traitor;* in a position where, if the government should succeed in putting down the revolution, *I and my friends can be arraigned before the Supreme Court of the United States, and there be sentenced to be hanged for violating the Constitution and laws of my country."* [Italics in original.]

Since it was Yancey who at the Democratic National Convention in Charleston in 1860 had led the delegates of the cotton states from the convention hall with the express purpose of creating a party split that would insure the election of Lincoln and furnish a pretext for secession, there can be no doubt that he and others were perfectly aware that their conduct would justly be regarded as treason. Toombs assuredly must have thought so when he made his cynical remark about treason being respectable when traitors were numerous enough.

Before we condemn Stevens for his passionate invective we should, therefore, consider that what to us is like a tale that is told, was to

[10] William Roscoe Thayer, *The Life of John Hay,* vol. II, p. 32; vol. I, p. 150.

him and others of his time an act of treason, the awful consequences of which stirred men to the depths of their souls. We should consider that language such as his, when uttered today against men we ourselves consider traitors, is applauded as the natural expression of righteous indignation.

4

Long before Lincoln had become convinced that a war cannot be fought "with elder-stalk squirts, charged with rose-water" and that "civilized belligerents do all in their power to help themselves and hurt the enemy" Stevens had reached that conclusion.[11] But this did not prevent him from being merciful to individuals. When during the war John W. Forney, secretary of the Senate, asked him to sign a petition for the release of a Confederate officer, he immediately complied. When Forney chaffed him about it he shrugged and said: "I saw you were going heavily into the pardoning business, so I thought I would take a hand in it myself." [12] When the war was over and the North vociferously demanded the hanging of Jefferson Davis and other rebel leaders, he was not swept off his feet by the hysteria. When Davis and Clement Clay, former senator from Alabama, were arrested and charged with complicity in the assassination of Lincoln, their friends and defense counsel turned to Stevens for aid. R. J. Haldeman, a friend of Clay, hastened to Lancaster to see him. Stevens told him he considered the charge of complicity absurd and offered to defend Clay.[13] Later he gave Haldeman a letter to Johnson asking that Clay be released. Johnson, who in matters of minor importance thought it expedient to humor him, complied with the request. George Shea of Davis's counsel called upon Stevens in Washington. The Commoner told him he had examined the alleged evidence and considered it "insufficient and incredible." "I know these men," he added. "They are no friends of mine, but they are gentlemen and incapable of assassination." [14]

That punitive measures advocated by Stevens were prompted by

[11] Lincoln's letters to Cuthbert Bullitt, July 28, 1862, and to James C. Conkling, Aug. 26, 1863.

[12] Forney, *Anecdotes of Public Men,* vol. I, p. 38.

[13] *Lancaster County Historical Papers,* No. 17, pp. 162-163.

[14] *Southern Historical Reports,* vol. I, p. 325.

reasons of state, not by animus toward individuals, becomes especially clear when we examine his stand against a bill introduced by Lawrence of Ohio at the beginning of the second session of the Thirty-ninth Congress. The bill called for the repeal of the statute of limitations in cases involving rebellion and treason against the national government, and for a change in the manner of trial of such cases. The conservative leader Bingham favored the bill, as did many other Conservatives. Stevens rose and said: "I do not believe that it becomes this nation, I do not believe it is safe for us to undertake to pass laws by which we can or may be able to punish men however guilty who could not be punished under the law existing when the crimes were committed. . . . I would rather let every man of them run unpunished forever than to make a law now by which they could be punished. I think our Government would be endangered in its future existence, in its sense of justice, in its character before the world by conduct of that kind, more than it would by enduring the evil.

"This professes to be a bill to make indefinite the prosecution of one of those offenses which of all others should be quieted by lapse of time. Although treason is as high a crime as can possibly be committed, yet there are generally so many engaged in the crime of treason and in rebellion that there must be some quieting law, and in my judgment there ought to be." [15]

To this Bingham, leader of the Conservatives, replied: "The gentlemen's hypothesis would operate as a general jail delivery. All the murderers, all the assassins, all the poisoners of our captured prisoners anywhere within the rebel States, are to go unwhipped of justice at the bar of our tribunals, because, forsooth, their crimes were not committed within a State of the Union and a judicial district in such State previously prescribed by law." [16]

Vindictiveness was not lacking during this period of American history. Most of it was in the South where, as we shall see, Southern loyalists and Negroes were mercilessly persecuted. Some of it was in the North, and but for the firm stand taken by Stevens and some others blood might well have been spilled. Stevens made no secret of the fact that his land confiscation plan was meant to punish as

[15] *Globe*, Dec. 11, 1866.
[16] *Ibid.*, Jan. 16, 1867.

well as to reconstruct, but he indignantly repudiated the implication that he was acting from motives of revenge. "When public tribunals, municipalities, nations pass sentence for crimes committed and decree confiscation for crimes unrepented," he said on the floor of Congress, "there is no question of malignity. When the judge sentences the convict he has no animosity. These acts have no faculty of cruelty in them. Cruelty does not belong in their vocabulary. The law has no feeling of malignity, no feeling of vengeance." [17]

Benedict de Spinoza, a philosopher famed for his elevated yet practical view concerning the individual's duty toward society, would have agreed with him. He has written: "In a well-ordered state where justice is administered every one is bound, if he would be accounted just, to demand penalties, not for the sake of vengeance, but in order to defend justice and his country's laws and to prevent the wicked from rejoicing in their wickedness." [18] If such is the duty of the ordinary citizen, how much more so is it the duty of the statesman?

Stevens believed the landed aristocracy of the South to be collectively guilty of treason in a cause which the dispassionate General Grant has characterized as "one of the worst for which a people ever fought, and one for which there was the least excuse." [19] He was not opposed to the President exercising his pardoning power on behalf of those who had not aided the rebellion of their own free will. As for the others, he believed their property—especially their landed property—should be confiscated, so their influence, which had proved a curse to the country and to the South, might be permanently shattered and the victims of their wrongdoing compensated. "Who can object?" he was to ask. "Is it not just? Look around and see the men with one leg, one arm, one eye, carried away by rebel bullets, or others wearing the weeds of mourning for those sacrificed by rebel perfidy and ask if too much is required. In ordinary transactions he who raises a false clamor or institutes an unfounded suit is required to pay the cost of his defeat. How much more should this well-recognized principle apply in such a case as this!" [20]

[17] *Ibid.*, Feb. 13, 1867.
[18] *A Theologico-Political Treatise*, pp. 105-106.
[19] *Memoirs*, vol. II, p. 489.
[20] New York *Herald* Supplement, Dec. 13, 1865.

CHAPTER V

Stevens's Confiscation Plan

Congressman George W. Julian said in the House on May 18, 1864: "This rebellion has frequently, and very justly, been styled a slave-holders' rebellion. It is likewise a landholders' rebellion, for the chief owners of slaves have been the chief owners of land. Probably three-fourths if not five-sixths of the land in the rebel States at the beginning of the war belonged to the slaveholders."

When in July, 1862, the second Confiscation Act was adopted by Congress, not only the Radicals, but most moderates and conservatives were in favor of confiscating the landed property of the leading rebels. Senator Sherman of Ohio, one of the most conservative Republicans in Congress, had said in the Senate on June 28 of that year: "Upon the question of confiscation, I have clear convictions that it is our right and our duty to seize the property of all the leading rebels, and apply it for the use of the Government in suppressing the rebellion. I therefore desire, by some practical proposition, to get the largest measure of confiscation which the majority of the Senate and of the House is willing to extend." We have seen that Lincoln, having overcome his constitutional scruples to the seizure of real estate, expressed his willingness to sign a bill "striking at the fee of rebel landholders." This, however, was in time of war. Even before the conflict was over a sufficient number of senators had changed their minds about the matter to accomplish the defeat of Stevens's proposal to repeal the "explanatory resolution" that prevented the second Confiscation Act from functioning as originally intended.

Stevens, however, felt that emancipation did not suffice to make the Southern states worthy members of the republic. As long as the land monopoly prevailed republican institutions could not flourish there. He believed the rebellion furnished a golden opportunity to put an end to the land monopoly which together with slavery was responsible for the wretched condition of the majority of the South's population.

2

In a speech delivered September 6, 1865, in Lancaster, the Commoner thus outlined his land confiscation plan:

There were approximately 6,000,000 white freemen in the South and some 465,000,000 acres of land. Some 70,000 former slaveholders owned over two hundred acres each. Their land and that owned by the Southern states themselves accounted for 394,000,000 acres. The remaining 71,000,000 acres belonged to farmers with holdings of less than two hundred acres. If the land of the 70,000 large planters were confiscated, nine-tenths of the Southern landholdings would remain untouched. Forty acres should be given to each adult male freedman, of whom there were about one million. This would leave 354,000,000 acres, which should be divided into farms of suitable size and sold. At an average price of ten dollars per acre it would yield $3,540,000,000, which should be applied as follows:

Three hundred million dollars should be invested in government bonds and the interest used to increase the pensions of Union soldiers and the families of the slain.

Two hundred million dollars should be appropriated to reimburse loyalists—Southerners as well as Northerners—whose property had been seized, destroyed, or damaged.

The balance of $3,040,000,000 should be applied toward the payment of the national debt.

"In reconstruction," Stevens explained, "no reform can be effected in the Southern States if [as claimed] they have never left the Union. But reformation *must* be effected; the foundation of their institutions, political, municipal and social, *must* be broken up and *relaid* or all our blood and treasure have been spent in vain. This can only be done by treating and holding them as a conquered people. . . . As conquered territory Congress would have full power to legislate for them; for the Territories are not under the Constitution except so far as the express power to govern them is given by Congress. They would be held in a territorial condition until they are fit to form State Constitutions, republican in fact, not in form only, and ask admission to the Union as new States."

He pointed out the social advantages of the measure:

"Heretofore Southern society has had more the features of aristocracy than democracy. The Southern States have been despotisms. It is impossible that any practical equality of rights can exist where a few thousand men monopolize the whole landed property. . . . How can republican institutions, free schools, free churches, free social intercourse exist in a mingled community of nabobs and serfs, of owners of twenty-thousand-acre manors, with lordly palaces, and the occupants of narrow huts inhabited by low white trash? If the South is ever to be made a safe republic let her land be cultivated by the toil of its owners, or the free labor of intelligent citizens. This must be done, even though it drive the nobility into exile. If they go, all the better. It is easier and more beneficial to exile seventy thousand proud, bloated and defiant rebels than to expatriate four million laborers, native to the soil and loyal to the Government." [1]

3

Stevens's speech did not receive a friendly reception, even from newspapers that usually supported him. Greeley's New York *Tribune,* which favored the immediate granting of political rights to the freedmen, commented: "We protest against any warfare against Southern property . . . because the wealthier class of Southerners, being more enlightened than the ignorant and vulgar, are less inimical to the blacks." [2] Since the "wealthier class" had profited by the labor of slaves, while the "ignorant and vulgar" had found it impossible to make a decent living in competition with slave labor, their difference in attitude is understandable. Frederick Douglass and others have charged that the planters and their minions in office deliberately fostered distrust and enmity between Negroes and poor whites for fear they might make common cause against them.

[1] New York *Herald* Supplement, Dec. 13, 1865.
[2] New York *Tribune,* Sept. 12, 1865.

If Stevens received little encouragement from the press of his own country, the American correspondent of the Paris *Le Temps* seemed to be in hearty agreement with him. He wrote to his paper: "A question is never settled until it is settled right. The real misfortune of the Negro race is in owning no land of its own. There cannot be real emancipation for men who do not possess at least a small portion of soil." [3]

The correspondent's name was Georges Clemenceau, the same who half a century later led France to victory against the combined might of Germany and Austria. He arrived in New York toward the end of September, 1865, and remained in the United States until April, 1870. He was to become well-acquainted with the Commoner and conceived a great admiration for him. There was an affinity of character between the two men. As a war leader Clemenceau reminds one of Stevens. It was the Commoner's misfortune, however, to be a leader not in a foreign, but a civil war. And when the war in the field was over there was still another, more bitter, war to fight to prevent the former rebels and their Northern allies from gaining control of the government they had sought to destroy. When finally that struggle, too, was ended, it was considered expedient to sacrifice the reputations of Stevens and some others on the altar of reconciliation and national unity. Had the Commoner, like Clemenceau, been able to exercise his extraordinary talent for leadership and his iron determination in a struggle with a foreign foe, his name would be one of the most honored in American history. Assuming, however, that he erred in his Reconstruction policy (and we shall see that the error was not his but his party's), it yet remains a melancholy comment on the ways of history in a democracy that one who erred in trying to benefit the lowly and the downtrodden should be so bitterly condemned, while all sorts of specious excuses are found for those who did not hesitate to unleash a bloody war in the interest of a slaveholding aristocracy.

Clemenceau did not join in the posthumous immolation of Stevens but retained his admiration for him until the end of his days. When an old man he told Wythe Williams, correspondent of the New York *Times:* "I was greatly interested in meeting Thaddeus Stevens, and liked him tremendously. He was tough and vigorous, and I thought

[3] Clemenceau, *op. cit.*, p. 40.

he was the ablest member of the Congress. I told him I couldn't fully agree with his attacks against President Andrew Johnson during the impeachment proceedings—not that what I thought made any impression. I was just a young cub in his estimation, but I guess he liked me because I argued with him so he didn't throw me out." [4]

4

The reception his confiscation proposal had received from the Republican press must have convinced Stevens that efforts in that direction were futile. The minutes of the Joint Committee on Reconstruction show that he never so much as mentioned the matter in the committee. It must have been from a sense of duty that he continued to advocate it in the House. When in March, 1867, he made a speech in defense of a bill embodying most of what he had proposed in his Lancaster speech, he prefaced it by saying: "No committee or party is responsible for this bill"—a frank confession that he had been unable to interest his colleagues.

On February 5, 1866, Stevens offered an amendment to the Freedmen's Bureau Bill proposing that the President be authorized to set aside from unoccupied lands in Florida, Mississippi, Alabama, Louisiana, and Arkansas, and from lands forfeited by the enemy, three million acres for the exclusive use of freedmen and loyal refugees, male or female. The land was to be divided into parcels not exceeding forty acres and rented to them for not over ten cents per acre a year. After a term of years they could acquire title for a sum not exceeding two dollars per acre. He pointed out that when the Czar of Russia freed 22,000,000 serfs "he compelled their masters to give them homesteads upon the very soil which they had tilled . . . not at a full price, but at a nominal price; 'for,' said he in his noble words, 'they have earned this, they have worked upon the land for ages, and they are entitled to it.' "

The proposal was defeated by a vote of 126 to 37. "That wrathful voice had lost its mastery, that severe satire its power, and that extended forefinger its omnipotence," commented the New York *Herald*.[5] This was wishful thinking, but the vote must have brought

[4] From *The Tiger of France* by Wythe Williams, copyright 1949. Quoted by special permission of the publishers, Duell, Sloan and Pearce, p. 49.

[5] New York *Herald*, Feb. 8, 1866.

home to Stevens how little his party cared for the welfare of the freedmen. That by this neglect it overlooked an excellent opportunity to create a following of small property owners in the South upon whose support it would be able to rely for generations to come, admits of no doubt.

5

Stevens's most ambitious effort to make his land distribution plan a reality was undertaken by him in March, 1867. He introduced a bill calling for immediate enforcement of the second Confiscation Act of July, 1862. All public lands in the former Confederate states were to be attached, as well as all land and other property *in excess of $5,000* belonging to former rebels. From the attached property, a homestead of forty acres and fifty dollars with which to build a dwelling was to be allotted to each adult male freedman and to each freed woman if she was the head of a family. Title to the homesteads was to be vested for a period of ten years in trustees appointed by the secretary of war, after which it was to be conveyed to the owners or their heirs.

A fine of $500,000,000 was to be levied and proportionately assessed against the remainder of the attached property. If the owner paid his assessment within ninety days, his property was to be released. If he failed to do so, it was to be converted into cash and the assessment deducted before restitution was made. In any case, however, a minimum of $5,000 worth of property was to be left to the owner, so that no one would have been beggared.

Of the fine collected $300,000,000 was to be invested in government bonds and the interest used to increase the pensions of incapacitated Union soldiers and the families of the slain. The remaining $200,000,000 was to be used to reimburse loyalists in the South as well as in the North whose property had been seized, destroyed, or damaged during the war.

On March 19, 1867, Stevens spoke in defense of the bill, saying: "I know there is a cry for the perfect immunity of the enemy. It is a dangerous and unwholesome doctrine. Inflict salutary punishments to prevent future civil wars and to punish the criminals. . . . I have never believed in bloody penalties. I have long since adopted the milder views of Montesquieu. But when I say that, it does not mean immunity to criminals. . . . This bill is very merciful towards a cruel, outlawed belligerent, who when their armies were dispersed, would gladly have compromised if their lives were spared. Those who will be affected by this bill will not exceed seventy thousand out of a population of six million whites. . . . The fine proposed would be but one-twentieth of their estates. Were ever such great malefactors so gently dealt with? It would be well if all their large estates could be subdivided and sold in small tracts. No people will ever be republican in spirit and practice where a few own immense manors and the masses are landless."

He pleaded for the adoption of at least that part of the bill that would give homesteads to the freedmen: "Whatever may be the fate of the rest of the bill, I must earnestly pray that this may not be defeated. Homesteads to them are far more valuable than the immediate right of suffrage. . . . The guardianship of the Freedmen's Bureau, that benevolent institution, cannot be expected long to protect them. . . . Make them independent of their old masters, so that they may not be compelled to work for them upon unfair terms. . . . Nothing is so likely to make a man a good citizen as to make him a freeholder."

Of the fund for the benefit of Union soldiers or their dependents he said:

"Three hundred million dollars put at interest at six per cent would just about double present pensions. Eight dollars a month to men unable to work is wholly inadequate. . . . Their present allowance is a mere mockery; it must be doubled out of some fund. Shall it be at the cost of loyal men, or of those who mangled and slew our soldiers? You talk of pity. Pity for whom? Your tears flow for pompous traitors; ours for maimed, halting, crippled patriots."

He spoke about losses suffered by Southern as well as Northern loyalists: "Southern loyalists who have suffered are everywhere to be seen. The valley of Virginia and the course of Sheridan's operations are full of them. The smoking ruins of Lawrence and Chambersburg, almost every county of Missouri and Maryland, and the frontier portions of Ohio are samples [of losses suffered by Northern loyalists]. . . . Neither can receive a dollar out of the Treasury of the United

States . . . neither has any chance of being remunerated except through congressional legislation. . . . I know not if $200,000,000 will pay them. Certainly it would be a great relief."

The speech, as nearly all his speeches, contained a fair proportion of sardonic humor. He quoted from a speech Johnson had made in the summer of 1864, when candidate for vice-president, reading with gusto: "Treason must be made odious, and traitors must be punished and impoverished; their great plantations must be seized and divided into small portions, and sold to honest, industrious men. . . . I have been most deeply pained at some things which have come under my observation. We get men in command, who, under the influence of flattery, fawning, and caressing, grant protection to the traitor, while the poor Union man stands out in the cold."

Having read this to his appreciative audience, he commented: "This is all the eloquent language of Andrew Johnson as 'he was.' . . . Andrew Johnson was the apostle whose preachings I followed. His doctrine pervades this whole bill. . . . While he was 'clothed in his right mind' he uttered the thoughts of a statesman; but Seward entered into him, and ever since they have both been running down steep places into the sea."

That the cause of justice would have been served and the sum total of human misery have been vastly reduced for generations to come had Stevens's bill, or a reasonable facsimile, been adopted, appears certain. Nearly half a century later, on September 27, 1914, the Atlanta *Constitution* published an article by J. F. Holleman who, as the editor informed his readers, "has made what was conceded to be the most searching analysis of the situation." Holleman wrote: "The South is in the grip of a cotton-growing oligarchy more powerful than the ante-bellum slave-owning oligarchy. Seventy per cent of the South's farm lands are under control of landlords, largely absentee. Ninety per cent of the South's agricultural activities are influenced by this oligarchy."

The *Manufacturers' Record,* an ultraconservative publication, in its issue of October 7, 1920, had the following to say concerning the condition of the Southern Negro after the return to power of the planter oligarchy following the rule of the carpetbaggers:

There became established an economic serfdom far worse, in many cases than personal slavery had ever been. Thousands upon thousands of

Negroes worked their entire lives without accumulating ten dollars worth of property. . . . They lived on butts and hominy, and they were thankful to Providence if they could secure enough old clothes and old shoes to keep them going. . . . Unless, therefore, the Nation as a whole is reconciled to the idea of maintaining in its midst some millions of serfs, and unless the South itself wants such a population, the time has come when the physical emancipation of the black must be followed by their economic emancipation, which would mean the emancipation also for the white people of the South.

Such was the situation in the South nearly half a century after the rule of the carpetbagger. Can it be truthfully said that it was an improvement on that regime? Are not legalized robbery and peonage greater evils than waste and corruption in office? The carpetbagger, honest or corrupt, was usually, if only from self-interest, on the side of the oppressed against the oppressor; the politician who succeeded him was the pliant tool of the oligarchy.

It should be noted that Stevens introduced his confiscation measure in March, 1867, when Congress adopted the Reconstruction Act conferring the elective franchise upon the freedmen. To him it was an indispensable part of Reconstruction without which neither the civil nor the political rights of the freedmen could be maintained. "Nothing will so multiply the productions of the South as to divide it into small farms. Nothing will make men so industrious and moral as to let them feel that they are above want and are the owners of the soil which they till," he pleaded. "It will also be of service to the white inhabitants. They will have constantly among them industrious laborers, anxious to work for fair wages. . . . They and their ancestors have toiled not for years, but for ages, without one farthing of recompense. They have earned for their masters this very land and much more." [6]

Was it unreasonable for him to believe that men who were freeholders and taxpayers could be relied upon to vote for candidates for office who would not endanger their holdings by dishonesty and waste? And if this part of his plan was rejected can he be blamed if the remainder turned out badly? "Those who pay no taxes, disposing of other people's money have every motive to be lavish and none to economize," John Stuart Mill has written.[7] The trouble with con-

[6] *Globe,* March 19, 1867.
[7] *Representative Government,* p. 176.

gressional Reconstruction was not that it went too far, but that it did not go far enough.

Stevens's critics have charged that he advocated confiscation in the hope of receiving indemnity for losses he had suffered during the war. The New York *World* went so far as to say that he was "mad with longing to get back from the Government at least twice the value of his iron mills destroyed by the rebels." The New York *Herald,* although by no means favoring his proposal, considered the charge absurd, pointing out that Stevens had "most positively refused to accept . . . one hundred thousand dollars which his political sympathizers and personal friends . . . recently made up for the property destroyed by the rebels." [8] The absurdity of the charge is further demonstrated by the fact that Stevens had an appraisal made of losses suffered by those living in southern Pennsylvania, and had written to the appraiser that losses suffered by himself were not to be included, "as no remuneration is claimed for it." The letter was published in the Lancaster *Intelligencer* of June 4, 1867.

[8] New York *Herald,* July 8, 1867.

CHAPTER VI

The Joint Committee on Reconstruction

The Thirty-ninth Congress—of which it has been said that it was second in importance only to the First Congress that organized the government under the Constitution—was to convene on December 4, 1865. Southern leaders looked forward to it with confidence. Patronage at the disposal of the Chief Executive had grown enormously during the war. Skillful use of it would, they believed, enable the President to make or break any member of Congress. Democrats and administration Republicans would vote to seat Southern representatives. The Republican party would be hopelessly split and the way opened for a Democratic triumph. It would not be long before the South would hold the balance of power with a larger representation in the House and the Electoral College than before the war. Such was the pleasant prospect Southern leaders believed they discerned on the political horizon.

In the North there was a feeling of uneasiness. The vast army of officeholders was singing the praises of Johnson's Reconstruction measures, but people were beginning to wonder if having won the war, the North was fated to lose the peace. Governor B. G. Humphrey of Mississippi, a former Confederate general who had had no difficulty defeating the loyalist Johnson had appointed provisional governor, had said in his message to the legislature: "Under the pressure of Federal bayonets, urged on by the misdirected sympathies of the world in behalf of the enslaved African, the people of Mississippi have abolished the institution of slavery." The Black Code adopted by that state and by South Carolina, and those in preparation in other Southern states, appeared a bold and decisive move toward the restoration of slavery. When the "pressure of Federal bayonets" had been removed, how long would it be before the institution was fully restored, in fact if not in name? Was there never to be an end to the struggle about slavery? Those whom the South had elected to Congress were not loyalists but rebels who had yielded to the "pressure of Federal bayonets." Would they not hinder and obstruct, keep the country in constant turmoil? Might they not with the aid of their Northern allies repudiate the national debt or force recognition of the Confederate debt? Might they not demand payment for the emancipated slaves? Manufacturers worried about the tariff, bankers about the National Banking Law, the South having been traditionally opposed to national banks. Overshadowing all this was a genuine concern about national security. At the outbreak of the war more than a third of the senators had been from the South—a sufficient number to prevent the country from making a treaty, expelling a senator no matter how disloyal, or impeaching a cabinet member were he as faithless as Secretary of War John B. Floyd in Buchanan's cabinet. Could such power be entrusted to men who only a few months before had borne arms against the government?

In this dilemma the people and their representatives instinctively turned toward the man who throughout the war had stood firm as a rock when others had faltered—the man whose program Lincoln at first had opposed but had finished by adopting.

2

Stevens arrived in Washington on November 23. After a short stay at a hotel he established himself in the house on South B Street, which the New York *Tribune* once described as "a small dilapidated brick house, in a not very pleasant-looking and certainly an infrequented street." After his arrival it was no longer "infrequented." There was a constant coming and going of members of Congress wishing to confer with him.

There was much speculation about the outcome of the struggle everyone felt to be impending. Business did not trust Johnson, but feared a struggle between President and Congress might unsettle the national economy. Stevens had sensed the prevailing indecision and on October 5, 1865, had written to Sumner: "I fear we are ruined, for I have little faith in Congress," and on the 25th of that same month: "The patronage is hard to fight against." [1] He now appeared to have regained his habitual self-assurance. On November 29 he had an interview with Johnson and told the President that unless he changed his policy the party would not support him.[2] Johnson, however, was not alarmed. He had faith in the power of patronage and in the ability of Seward to keep the Conservatives in line.

Realizing that the President had no intention of changing his course, Stevens took the necessary precautions. On the first of December he called a conference of twenty-five of his most devoted followers. He proposed a joint committee of both Houses to study the problem of Reconstruction. No representative from any of the rebel states was to be seated by either House until the committee had brought in its report and it had been acted upon. He felt confident that if the Republicans in the House presented a united front on the matter the Senate would agree to co-operate.[3]

The regular Republican caucus was held the following evening. That in the intervening time Stevens's disciples had made it their business to visit their colleagues and had managed to convince them of the wisdom of the Commoner's policy is evident from the rapidity with which Stevens's proposal was adopted. Senator Doolittle of Wisconsin, an administration Republican, has given the following description of the proceedings: "I simply say that within three minutes, by the clock, after the hour the assemblage was called, Thaddeus Stevens had moved his committee on resolutions and was withdrawing with his committee from the body to make his report, and within ten minutes, without any discussion, without any consideration whatever, it was by that cool tact and talent of his pressed through the body and declared to be unanimously adopted." [4]

That adoption should have been unanimous has been ascribed by some historians to sinister machinations on Stevens's part. There is an entire absence of evidence to support this. True that among the one hundred and twenty-four representatives present there were

[1] *Sumner MSS.*
[2] New York *Herald,* Dec. 11, 1865.
[3] New York *Herald,* Dec. 2 and 4, 1865; New York *Tribune,* Dec. 2 and 11, 1865.
[4] *Globe,* Dec. 12, 1865.

two—Henry J. Raymond, chairman of the executive committee of the Republican party, and his friend William A. Darling—who favored Johnson's Reconstruction policy, but from this it does not necessarily follow that they were opposed to an examination of the matter by a joint committee of Congress. Surely admission to participation in the national government of representatives from a region that for four years had waged relentless war upon that government was a weighty enough matter to merit careful study.

News of what had taken place in the caucus was brought to the President by Secretary Welles. Johnson remained confident. No one, he knew, could question the loyalty of the reconstructed government of Tennessee. When that state's representatives demanded admittance they would, he felt sure, find supporters on the Republican side of the House. The rampart Stevens had so carefully erected would be breached by the admission of the Tennesseeans. Once it was breached it would crumble, and all the Southern representatives would be admitted. Stevens and his Radicals would be "knocked in the head from the start," he assured Welles.[5]

If the President was optimistic his supporters appeared to have been less so. Their principal organ, the New York *World,* expressed itself in this fashion:

> They [the Republicans] did not wait till the opening of Congress to-day, to give the plan the honor of a decent burial under the clerk's table, but put the party bow-string around it, and pitched it at midnight out of the window of a partisan caucus. The resolution adopted unanimously by the Republican members in their caucus, shows with what promptitude Thaddeus Stevens strangled the infant "Restoration," stamped upon it with his brutal heel, and proclaimed his plan for keeping the Union disunited.[6]

This was a curious utterance. Thus far nothing except an inquiry had been proposed. The *World* must have been fully aware of the dangers lurking in the President's plan to have felt so sure that once it was examined it would be discarded.

[5] Welles, *Diary,* vol. II, p. 387.
[6] New York *World,* Dec. 4, 1865.

3

On Monday, December 4, 1865, when the clock in the assembly hall pointed to twelve, Edward McPherson, clerk of the last House of Representatives, called the House to order. McPherson, son of one of Stevens's oldest friends, was devoted to the Commoner, who, as will be recalled, had secured his appointment when he had failed to be re-elected to the House. He was even then collecting material for a biography of his friend and patron, an ambition he did not live to fulfill.

Stevens's seat was on the aisle, toward the front. A correspondent in the New York *Independent* has given the following description of him at this stage of his career:

> Thaddeus Stevens is just coming in from his committee room, and looks so feeble, the great old man, it makes me sad. His spirit is not abated, his sarcasm cuts as keenly as ever, his wit flashes as brightly, and his great intellect seems in no wise dimmed; yet the hand of Time lies heavy upon him. The will which never swerves, which always conquers and rules men, is powerless to resist the pressure of pain and the infirmity of age.
>
> His face in outline approaches the Indian type. The square perceptive brow, the deeply set eyes, the high cheek bones, the broad jaw and saturnine mouth are most marked. The face in repose is stern, but not savage. Thaddeus Stevens' inevitable sarcasm and wit seem purely intellectual gifts. The "sardonic smile" that we read so much about is a very human and kindly smile after all.[7]

On the Democratic side of the House sat James Brooks of New York, minority leader, able, polished, a trifle pedantic—a sort of minor Sumner who delighted in making a display of his knowledge of history and literature. He was to become the champion of a President he did not respect and of a program which during the war his party had denounced as unconstitutional. The galleries and even the corridors were crowded, for all felt certain that battle would be joined at the very first session.

The Clerk began calling the roll. When he reached the names of the Indiana representatives, Horace Maynard of Tennessee rose, waved his credentials, and shouted: "Mr. Clerk, I beg to say that in

[7] New York *Independent*, June 14, 1866.

calling the roll of members . . ." McPherson cut him short with the remark that the roll call must not be interrupted. When the last name had been called a motion was made that the House proceed with the election of a speaker. Maynard again protested, but was called to order by Stevens. Brooks rose and said that if Tennessee was not a state in the Union then the President was usurping his power and must be a foreigner. He should like the Clerk to explain why Tennessee and Virginia had been excluded. McPherson was about to offer an explanation, but Stevens stopped him with a wave of his hand and the remark: "It is not necessary. We know all." Brooks replied: "I should know but little if I had not the record of the resolution adopted by the Republican majority in the House, that Tennessee, Louisiana and Virginia were to be excluded, and excluded without debate. . . . If the gentleman from Pennsylvania would but inform me at what period he intends to press this resolution of which he is to be the organ, I would be happy to be informed by him." Stevens, conscious of his power, replied with sardonic good humor: "I have no objection to answering the gentleman. I propose to press it at the proper time." This provoked laughter and applause. Brooks remarked: "Talleyrand, the great diplomatist, said that language was given to man to conceal ideas; and we all know the gentleman's ingenuity in the use of language."

Stevens moved the previous question. Maynard again rose and pleaded: "I appeal to the gentleman from Pennsylvania to listen to me for a moment." He was silenced by Stevens with the words: "I cannot yield to any gentleman who does not belong to this body—who is an outsider." The Clerk hammered for order, and Stevens's motion having been seconded it was put and carried.

The House proceeded to elect a speaker. Colfax received 139 votes, Brooks 36. McPherson was to remain at his post, in which he had been and would continue to be of assistance to his friend.

Stevens harbored no animosity against Maynard and his colleagues from Tennessee. He did not doubt their loyalty and later was to move that they "be invited to occupy seats in the Hall of the House of Representatives" until a decision regarding their status had been reached. But a principle was at stake. To have made an exception for Tennessee would have confused the issue. Greeley's *Tribune* later was to sum up the situation in these words:

Such action would mean the abandonment of the guarantee policy of the Republican majority in Congress; and that principle once abandoned, the majority will hopelessly flounder about in the mazes of arbitrary theories and special pleadings. Then, without a fixed policy to guide them, they will unconsciously yield point after point, until Tennessee, with all her good and laudable qualities, will prove the Trojan horse carrying all rebeldom concealed in her belly.[8]

The incongruity of the President being a resident of a part of the country Congress did not recognize as a state in the Union did not trouble Stevens. He later was to explain: "While the President must be a citizen of the United States, he can live in a Territory or even the District of Columbia, which was never a State." [9]

4

Stevens waited until the routine business had been concluded before he rose to introduce the concurrent resolution that was to spell the doom of Johnson's and Seward's well-laid plans. Perfect silence reigned as the gaunt old man, holding a paper in his hand, read in a husky voice the resolution the party caucus had unanimously adopted. It called for the appointment of a joint committee of fifteen—nine from the House and six from the Senate—"who shall inquire into the condition of the States which formed the so-called confederate States of America, and report whether they or any of them are entitled to be represented in either House of Congress." Until the committee's report had been received and acted upon, neither House was to admit any representative from the "so-called confederate States." All matters relating to the representation of those states were to be referred to the committee without debate.

When he finished reading and had moved the adoption of the resolution there followed a parliamentary skirmish, which he brought to a close by obtaining suspension of the rules and moving the previous question. The resolution was adopted by a strict party vote, 133 to 36. Raymond and Darling voted for its adoption.

It was not until December 12 that the resolution was adopted by the Senate in a curtailed form. Senator Anthony of New Jersey pointed out that the part dealing with the admittance of Southern

[8] New York *Tribune,* Feb. 19, 1866.
[9] *Globe,* March 10, 1866.

representatives might be misconstrued. It might be interpreted as referring to their personal qualifications. If so construed the resolution would not be "concurrent" but "joint" and would require the President's signature. Stevens accepted the change with good grace, saying he would introduce a separate resolution covering the matter. Later in the session he presented such a resolution and it was adopted by both Houses.

The Senate chose the following to serve on the Joint Committee of Fifteen on Reconstruction: William P. Fessenden, James W. Grimes, Ira Harris, Jacob M. Howard, Reverdy Johnson, George H. Williams. The House chose: Thaddeus Stevens, Elihu B. Washburne, Justin S. Morrill, Henry Grider, John A. Bingham, Roscoe Conkling, George S. Boutwell, Henry T. Blow, Andrew J. Rogers. Fessenden, head of the Senate delegation, became chairman of the committee. Stevens, head of the House delegation, was to dominate committee meetings. There were three Democrats on the committee, one from the Senate, two from the House, which was not far out of line with Democratic strength in Congress. Henceforth Stevens's main activity was on the Joint Committee on Reconstruction. Some of the functions of the Committee on Ways and Means were turned over to other committees and a new committee—the Committee on Appropriations—was created of which Stevens became chairman.

The Commoner was now not merely the leader of the majority faction of the Republican party, but had practically the entire party behind him in his opposition to the administration's program and in support of an important part of his own Reconstruction plan. In the House only two Republicans—Raymond and Darling—were to vote with the Democrats on most Reconstruction measures. In the Senate four Republicans became consistent supporters of the administration. In both Houses antiadministration Republicans were in a position to override the President's veto and were to do so with monotonous regularity.

5

The ensuing struggle was not merely between the President and Congress. Nor did the Republicans wholly represent the forces of light heroically arrayed against the forces of darkness—loyalty against disloyalty. Most Northern Democrats were loyal men, but they were of the opinion that there were other ways of being disloyal than the one the South had chosen. They had no fondness for the South's landed aristocracy, but the North's industrial and financial aristocracy, to whom the Republican party was excessively partial, appeared to them nearly as great a menace to republican institutions. They were opposed to a high tariff, which the industrialists wanted, and to resumption of specie payments, which the financiers wanted. They saw no hope of driving the Republicans from power except with the aid of the South and were willing to take their chances with Southern disloyalty in order to gain that aid.

What is now called the Middle West, but was then known as the West, likewise had its grievances against the party in power. The West wanted internal improvements, especially canals that would connect its rivers with the Great Lakes, furnishing cheap transportation and access to Eastern markets. Railroad interests and Eastern farming interests opposed this, and the Republican party sided with them. So the West, too, was beginning to cast wistful glances toward the South, whence support might be obtained in exchange for favors.

There were crosscurrents. For example, manufacturers wanted a high tariff, but not resumption of specie payments, which they feared might mean a ruinous fall in prices. Farmers were inclined to agree with them. Others were opposed to a high tariff because of its effect upon the cost of living, but somewhat illogically also wanted cheap money, even more responsible for the rise in prices. Workingmen complained about the puritanical notions the Republican party was adopting. In New York it advocated closing the saloons on Sunday, and in Massachusetts it advocated closing them altogether. This not only angered the Irish, most of whom were Democrats, but also the Germans, most of whom were Republicans.

Stevens's preoccupation with Reconstruction often made him neglect other important issues. "It must be admitted that Mr. Stevens stands out as a man of only one idea," wrote Clemenceau, but added that "he put on blinders in order to see more clearly." [10] He did see clearly. The answer he evolved to the Reconstruction

[10] *Op. cit.*, p. 226.

problem was a sensible one. In fact it was the only sensible solution offered by any man. Unfortunately his party refused to follow him, and, strangely, it was its innate conservatism that was responsible for the rejection of a plan that would not have involved forcing Negro suffrage prematurely upon the South.

CHAPTER VII

Stevens's Reconstruction Plan

On December 5, 1865, Andrew Johnson sent his first message to Congress. There is a difference of opinion regarding its authorship, which some attribute to the historian Bancroft, others to Secretary Seward. The document was moderate in tone, but yielded nothing to those who believed Reconstruction primarily a congressional function. Reverdy Johnson, senator from Maryland, praised it extravagantly, at the same time maintaining that "the moment the insurrection was terminated there was no power whatever left in the Congress of the United States over those States; and I am glad to see, if I understand his Message, that in the view I have just expressed, I have the concurrence of the President of the United States." [1]

Shortly before the President's message was read in the House, Stevens put his cards on the table. He made known what measures he considered indispensable before the rebel states could with reasonable safety be readmitted to participation in the national government. Like Plato, who having described the ideal state in his *Republic,* compiled a book of *Laws* for the government of what he called his "second-best state," so Stevens may be said to have had an ideal and a second-best Reconstruction program. The former included his land confiscation plan, discussed in a previous chapter.

Granting the right of suffrage to the freedmen was not a part of Stevens's original plan. Blaine has written: "Mr. Stevens's obvious theory at that time was not to touch the question of suffrage by

[1] *Globe,* Dec. 13, 1865.

National interposition, but reach it more effectively perhaps by excluding the entire colored population from the basis of congressional representation, until by the action of the Southern States themselves the elective franchise should be conceded to the colored population." [2] Speaking in Lancaster before the opening of the Thirty-ninth Congress, Stevens had said: "I do not touch on the question of Negro suffrage. If in the Union, the States have long ago regulated that, and for the Central Government to interfere with it would be mischievous impertinence. If they are to be admitted as new States, they must form their own Constitution, and no enabling act could dictate its terms. . . . Congress, to be sure, has some sort of compulsory power by refusing the States admission until they shall have complied with its wishes over this subject." The New York *Tribune* had complained: "He seems not to care for the enfranchisement of the blacks." [3]

The *Tribune* was wrong. He cared very much. In 1837, when a member of the Constitutional Convention in Pennsylvania, he refused to sign the new state constitution because it deprived the colored people of the right of suffrage they had hitherto enjoyed. Shortly after the opening of the Thirty-ninth Congress we find him saying: "Demagogues of all parties, even some high in authority, gravely shout, 'This is a white man's government.' . . . Wherein does this differ from slavery except in degree? Does not this contradict all the distinctive principles of the Declaration of Independence? . . . Our fathers repudiated the whole doctrine of the legal superiority of families or races, and proclaimed the equality of men before the law. . . . This is not a 'white man's Government,' in the exclusive sense in which it is used. To say so is a political blasphemy, for it violates the fundamental principles of the gospel of liberty. This is a man's Government; the Government of all men alike." [4]

He believed Congress should set an example to the states, and in January, 1866, managed to get a bill adopted by the House (which, however, was sidetracked in the Senate) granting the colored people of the District of Columbia, the great majority of whom had been

[2] *Op. cit.*, vol. II, p. 129.
[3] New York *Tribune*, Sept. 11 and 12, 1866.
[4] *Globe*, Dec. 18, 1866.

free before the war, the right of suffrage. There can, however, be no doubt that at this time he wished to leave the matter of Negro suffrage entirely to the states. Indeed, when speaking in defense of the constitutional amendment basing representation in the House and the Electoral College on the number of voters in each state, he was to express the hope that the Southern states would not, in order to increase their representation, grant the immediate right of suffrage to the freedmen. He feared that accustomed as the Negroes were to taking orders from their former masters, they would vote as they were told.[5] "The infernal laws of slavery," he said, "have prevented them from acquiring an education, understanding the commonest laws of contract, or of managing the ordinary business of life." [6]

It is obvious that he did not believe the freedmen, just risen from slavery, any more fit for the immediate exercise of the right of suffrage than he considered the white people of the South fit for immediate participation in a government they had sought to destroy only a few months earlier. Realist that he was he undoubtedly also realized that the moment federal troops were withdrawn, even a constitutional amendment would be unable to protect the freedmen in the exercise of that right.

2

The Reconstruction measures Stevens considered indispensable he embodied in four joint resolutions, each proposing an amendment to the Constitution to be submitted to the states for ratification. The first forbade any state ever to assume or pay any part of the Confederate debt, state or federal. The second, dealing with taxation of exports, is of minor importance and need not be discussed. The third proposed that "representatives shall be appointed among the States which may be within the Union according to respective legal voters." The fourth nationalized equality before the law in these terms: "All national and State laws shall be equally applicable to every citizen, and no discrimination shall be made on account of race or color."

How accurately he appraised the requirements of the situation may be judged from the fact that in an amended (but far from im-

[5] *Globe,* Jan. 31, 1866.
[6] *Ibid.,* Dec. 18, 1865.

proved) form the three proposals became a part of the Fourteenth Amendment to the Constitution.

There was still another measure Stevens considered indispensable, the importance of which cannot be overestimated. Indeed, the success or failure of his original Reconstruction plan hinged upon that measure. The failure of the Republican party to accept his advice on this matter led directly to the granting of the elective franchise to the freedmen. In his speech in the House of December 18, 1865, in which he discussed his Reconstruction plan, he put this measure first, saying: "It is obvious that the first duty of Congress is to pass a law declaring the condition of these outside or defunct States, and providing civil governments for them. Since the conquest they have been governed by martial law. Military rule is necessarily despotic and ought not to exist longer than is absolutely necessary. As there are no symptoms that the people of these provinces will be prepared to participate in constitutional government for some years, I know of no arrangement so proper for them as territorial governments."

To believe that after having for four years stubbornly fought against the government the people of the South had within a few months changed their mental outlook so completely that they could be safely trusted with immediate participation in that government was to believe an absurdity. It will be objected that Lieutenant General Grant, in a report to the President, had stated that "the mass of thinking men in the South accept the present situation in good faith." Grant's report, however, was based on a flying visit to three of the Southern states, and his inquiry was secondary to a military mission he had to perform. He had left Washington on November 27, 1865, had passed through Virginia "without conversing or meeting with any of its citizens," had spent one day in North Carolina, one in South Carolina, and two in Georgia.

There was, however, another report, made at the request of the President by Major General Carl Schurz, which deserves greater consideration. Schurz had departed for the South in the early part of July, had remained there until the middle of autumn, had traveled extensively, had devoted all his time to the inquiry, and had talked with all classes of persons. He reported that "the rapid return to power and influence of so many of those who but recently were engaged in a bitter war against the Union had had one effect which was certainly not originally contemplated by the Government. Treason does, under existing circumstances, not appear odious in the South. . . . And secondly, there is as yet among the Southern people an utter absence of national feeling." Southerners, he wrote, were submitting because they could "do no better" and "because submission was the only means by which they could rid themselves of the Federal soldiers, and obtain once more control of their own affairs."

He painted a shocking picture of the Southern attitude toward the freedmen: "Some planters held back their former slaves on their plantations by brute force. Armed bands of white men patrol the county roads and drive back Negroes wandering about. Dead bodies of murdered Negroes were found on and near the highways and byways. Gruesome reports came from the hospitals—reports of colored men and women whose ears had been cut off, whose skulls had been broken by blows, whose bodies had been slashed by knives and lacerated by scourges. A number of such cases, I had occasion to examine myself. A veritable reign of terror prevailed in many parts of the South." He reached the conclusion that "although the freedman is no longer considered the property of the individual master, he is considered the slave of society, and all independent State legislation will share the tendency to make him such. The ordinances abolishing slavery, passed by the conventions under the pressure of circumstances, will not be looked upon as barring the establishment of a new form of servitude."

Schurz's report was fully corroborated by fifty out of sixty-four witnesses testifying before a subcommittee of the Joint Committee on Reconstruction. The witnesses—loyal Southerners, army officers, and employees of the Freedmen's Bureau—gave it as their opinion that the population of the Southern states was still under the influence of its wartime leaders, was still secessionist at heart, and had submitted only from necessity. They gave it as their opinion that in case of war between the United States and a foreign power, the leaders would not hesitate to take the side of the enemy if they believed such a course might enable the South to gain its independence.[7]

In the face of evidence such as this how could any prudent states-

[7] *Testimony,* Part IV, pp. 176-177.

man have failed to reach the conclusion that a probationary period under a territorial form of government was the only practical solution, and that to readmit the Southern states to immediate participation in the national government would be little short of madness? We shall, moreover, see that the adoption of such a measure was indispensable to the success of Stevens's original Reconstruction plan.

3

He discussed fully his proposal that representation in the House and in the Electoral College should be based on the number of legal voters in each state. He pointed out that before the war the rebel states had had seventy representatives in the House. Forty-six of these had represented the white population, nineteen had supposedly represented three-fifths of the slaves, and the remaining five the free Negroes. Now that slavery had been abolished, all the former slaves would be counted in the representation, giving the rebel states an additional thirteen representatives in the House and the Electoral College—a total of eighty-three. Thirty-seven of these would supposedly be representing the South's colored population, not one of whom would be permitted to vote. "With the basis [of representation] unchanged," he argued, "the eighty-three Southern members, with the Democrats that will in the best times be elected from the North, will always give them a majority in Congress and in the Electoral College. They will at the first election take possession of the White House and the Hall of Congress. I need not depict the ruin that would follow. Assumption of the rebel debt, or repudiation of the Federal debt would be sure to follow. The oppression of the freedmen; the reamendment of their State constitutions, and the re-establishment of slavery would be the inevitable result."

That these fears were not unfounded was brought out by testimony before the committee. A particularly reliable witness, Judge John C. Underwood, whom Lincoln had appointed federal judge of the District Court of Virginia, when asked what measures he believed would be adopted if a combination of Northern Democrats and former Confederates gained control of the federal government, replied: "They would attempt either to accomplish a repudiation of the National debt, or an acknowledgment of the Confederate debt, and compensation for their negroes. I think this would be their leading measures, their leading demands." [8]

Stevens pointed out that if his proposal of basing representation on the number of voters in each state were adopted, the Southern states, when readmitted to the Union, would be confronted with the following two alternatives, both favorable to the loyalists: "If they should grant the right of suffrage to persons of color, I think there would always be Union white men enough in the South, to divide representation, and thus continue Republican ascendancy. If they should refuse to thus alter their election laws it would reduce the representatives of the Slave States to about forty-six and render them powerless to do evil."

It will be objected that Stevens identified loyalty to the country with loyalty to the Republican party. He was not a strict party man. In 1868, when the Republicans contemplated a raid on the national Treasury in the interest of the bondholders, he went so far as to threaten to go over to the Democrats. But whatever the virtues of the Democratic party in our own day and in the days of Jackson, and whatever the shortcomings of the Republican party at that time (and they were many) it cannot be overlooked that the peace and security of the country depended upon the continuance in power of the Republicans for a number of years. The leading figures in the Democratic party were men who had obstructed the war effort in every conceivable manner. Their eagerness to collaborate with men whose loyalty to the Union was highly questionable made a speedy return of their party to power a danger no statesman could overlook.

Stevens solemnly warned that a constitutional amendment which would reduce Southern representation in the House and the Electoral College at a time when Southern leaders were gloating over the fact that emancipation would increase their power in the national government could not be ratified if the South were permitted to take part in the ratification: "It is plain that the amendment must be consummated before the defunct States are admitted to be capable of State action, *or it never can be.*"

In a later speech he put these questions to his colleagues: Did they or did they not wish the Constitution so amended that representation in the House and the Electoral College would be based

[8] *Ibid.*, Part II, p. 8.

on the number of voters in each state? Did they or did they not wish it so amended that all law, state and federal, shall operate equally on all? Did they or did they not wish it so amended as to prevent the assumption of the rebel debt or the repudiation of the national debt? "To you," he said, "who do not desire these reforms or any of them, I say frankly, it is of no importance by whom or when or how reconstruction is effected. For in three short years this whole Government will be in the hands of the late rebels and their Northern allies."

Assuming they were in favor of the proposals: "Will they with equal candor say whether they believe either of them could be adopted if the eleven confederate States were to be counted as States in making the requisite three-fourths? If those amendments are desirable, will not the gentlemen agree that even if we are not compelled to treat those States as out of the Union, yet that we are at liberty so to do by right of conquest? Surely the rebel States cannot gainsay it, as they have uniformly taken the same position." [9]

What he did not say was that unless that policy was adopted there would remain only one way by means of which the early capture of the federal government by the former Confederates and their Northern allies could be prevented: when the Southern states had refused to ratify what was to become the Fourteenth Amendment (as he felt certain they would), their state governments would have to be dissolved by the military; new elections would have to be held *with the freedmen participating;* and the amendment would have to be resubmitted to the newly elected state legislatures.

4

The question arises: Why did the Republican party not take Stevens's advice? Why did a party the great majority of whose representatives did not believe in Negro suffrage reject a plan that would have enabled it to accomplish all it wished to accomplish without the necessity of granting the elective franchise to the freedmen? Professor Burgess has given the answer: "The more moderate Republicans feared that the Southern communities would not feel obligated by a

[9] *Globe,* March 10, 1866.

Constitution amended in this manner." [10] This is fully corroborated by the following statement of James G. Blaine:

> The great majority of Republican leaders did not at all agree with the theory of Mr. Stevens. . . . The one signal proof of their dissent from the extreme doctrine was their absolute unwillingness to attempt an amendment to the Constitution by the ratification of three-fourths of the Loyal States only and their insisting that it must be three-fourths of all the States, North and South. Mr. Stevens deemed this a fatal step for the party, but . . . the party was governed by its own conservative instincts. They believed with Mr. Lincoln that the Stevens plan of amendment would always be questioned, and that in so grave a matter as a change in the organic law of the Nation, the process should be unquestionable—one that could stand every test and resist every assault.[11]

Lincoln indeed had said in his last speech, speaking of the method of ratification of the Thirteenth Amendment: "To meet this proposition, it has been argued that no more than three-fourths of those States which have not attempted secession are necessary to validly ratify the amendment. I do not commit myself against this, further than to say that such a ratification would be questionable, and sure to be persistently questioned, while a ratification by three-fourths of all the States would be unquestioned and unquestionable."

We have seen that Secretary McCulloch, who was in a position to know, has said that Lincoln favored a constitutional amendment preventing "any but those who were permitted to vote in Federal elections from being included in the enumeration for representation in Congress." The Southern legislatures would never of their own free will have voted to ratify a constitutional amendment to that effect. To get them to do so Lincoln would have had to use the severest pressure. One may well ask whether ratification obtained in such a manner would not have been more questionable than the method of ratification proposed by Stevens. Blaine and others knew, moreover, that Johnson, far from advising the Southern states to ratify the amendment would advise them not to do so. Thus, paradoxically, the plan the radical Stevens proposed would not have resulted in conferring the immediate right of suffrage upon the freedmen; when, however, the "conservative instinct" of the Repub-

[10] *Op. cit.*, p. 81.
[11] *Op. cit.*, vol. II, p. 140.

lican party triumphed over Stevens's "extreme doctrine," Negro suffrage became inevitable.

Alexander K. McClure appears to have been one of the few who realized what a golden opportunity was lost when Stevens's proposal failed to be adopted. He has written:

> His policy of reconstruction would have been a priceless blessing to the South, although at the time it would have been accepted as extremely vindictive. He would have held the rebellious States as provinces and governed them as Territories, to await the period when they might with safety be restored to the Union. Had that policy been adopted the desolation almost worse than war would have been averted in the Southern States. . . . Had they been held as provinces there would have been peace, their industries would have been speedily revived, mutual confidence between the North and the South would have rapidly strengthened, and in a very few years at the most they would have resumed their position in the galaxy of States; and universal negro suffrage would not have been in the cup of bitterness they had to drain. Stevens was bitterly denounced by many for his vindictive reconstruction policy; but stripped of its utterly impracticable and impossible confiscation and retributive features, it would have been the wisest policy for both North and South that could have been adopted.[12]

Professor Burgess has expressed a similar opinion. He has written: "The true theory on this point was that held by Mr. Stevens, viz. . . . to amend the Constitution by a three-fourths majority of these loyal 'States'; and then admit these reconstructed communities as new 'States' into the Union with its amended Constitution." And again: "It [Congress] ought to have created, as soon as armed resistance to the execution of the laws of the United States ceased, regular Territorial civil governments throughout the country which had been in insurrection, and then have admitted these Territories as 'States' whenever the conditions warranting the same should have been attained. The phantom of the 'indestructible State' had too strong an influence over the minds of all at that moment to admit of such a solution of the question." [13]

[12] *Lincoln and Men of War Times,* p. 267.
[13] *Op. cit.,* pp. 81, 111.

5

Johnson's Reconstruction plan did not remain without a defender on the Republican side of the House. On December 21, three days after Stevens had explained his Reconstruction plan, Henry J. Raymond rose to speak in defense of the President's policy. Why the party chairman should have taken a stand in opposition to practically the entire Republican representation in Congress is difficult to understand. It has been suggested that he was prompted by his hatred of his former employer Greeley, who was siding with Congress, or by his friendship for Seward, a close political associate. Whatever the reason, it did not take him long to discover that he was championing a policy so unpopular with his Republican colleagues that they found it difficult to listen to him with patience. During the first hour of his speech he was interrupted no less than half a hundred times. His time was extended, and a plea having been made that he be allowed to proceed without further interruption, he was able to finish his argument. When he had done so he must have known that he had signed his political death warrant.

On January 9, 1866, Voorhees, a Vallandigham type of Democrat, introduced a resolution calling for endorsement of the President's policy.[14] When it was put to a vote only two Republicans—Raymond and his friend Darling—voted in the affirmative. It was as decisive a vote of "no confidence" as an American President had ever received from the party that had elected him.

[14] Clement L. Vallandigham, member of Congress from Ohio from 1858 to 1863, and defeated for re-election in 1862, was a leading member of the faction of the Democratic party known as Peace-Democrats, commonly called Copperheads. He was supreme commander of the Sons of Liberty, a subversive organization for which he claimed 300,000 members. There exists evidence that during the war he plotted an armed uprising of his followers. (See article entitled "Civil War Subversives," by Rethania Meredith Smith, *Journal of the Illinois State Historical Society,* Autumn 1952.) On May 1, 1863, he made a subversive speech, was arrested, tried, and sentenced to imprisonment for the duration of hostilities. Lincoln commuted the sentence to banishment behind the Confederate lines. He re-entered Ohio by way of Canada and was not molested. During Reconstruction he became a staunch supporter of Johnson.

CHAPTER VIII

Breach between President and Congress

In his speech of December 18, 1865, the first he had made in the new Congress, Stevens restated his position regarding the status of the rebel states and affirmed the right of Congress to deal with the question of Reconstruction, saying: "It matters but little whether you call them States out of the Union, and now conquered territories, or assert that because the Constitution forbids them to do what they did do, that they are therefore dead as to all national and political action and will remain so until the Government shall breathe into them the breath of life anew and permit them to occupy their former position. In either case it is very plain that . . . dead States cannot restore their own existence 'as it was.' Whose special duty is it to do it? There is no difficulty in solving the question."

He quoted the fourth section of the fourth article of the Constitution, reading: "The United States shall guaranty to every State in this Union a republican form of government," and asked: "Who is the United States? Not the judiciary; not the President; but the sovereign power of the people, exercised through their representatives in Congress, with the concurrence of the Executive. It means the political Government—the concurrent action of both branches of Congress and the Executive. The separate action of each amounts to nothing, either in admitting new States or guarantying republican governments to lapsed and outlawed States. Whence springs the preposterous idea that either the President, or the Senate, or the

House of Representatives, acting separately, can determine the right of States to send members or Senators to the Congress of the Union?"

Thus, while claiming for Congress prime responsibility in deciding on what terms the rebel states were to be readmitted to participation in the national government, Stevens did not shut out the President. Johnson on the other hand made the same mistake Lincoln had made in assuming that the only responsibility Congress had in the matter was to decide whether or not senators and representatives elected by the rebel states were personally qualified—with this important difference: the supple Lincoln would not have persisted in maintaining so untenable a position, while the obstinate Johnson did. Johnson's principal biographer could not help remarking: "If the President had the right to require the States to abolish slavery as a condition to readmission to the Union, why had not Congress the right to impose other conditions? The reply of Lincoln and Johnson that that was their business and not Congress's is not convincing." [1]

One wonders if Johnson's biographer realized that with this admission he gave away his protagonist's entire case.

To make it easier for Johnson to recede from the position he had taken, Stevens pretended to believe that the President's message did not mean what it obviously did mean. He said: "After stating with great frankness in his able message his theory, which, however, is found to be impracticable, and which I believe very few now consider tenable, he refers the whole matter to the judgment of Congress. If Congress should fail firmly and wisely to discharge that high duty it is not the fault of the President. . . . It is time that Congress should assert its sovereignty, and assume something of the dignity of a Roman senate."

This Congress now proceeded to do.

2

The condition of the freedmen was little short of appalling. Governor Aiken of South Carolina, one of the largest slaveholders in the South, was quoted by Senator Doolittle of Wisconsin, an Administration Republican, as having stated "unequivocally" that

[1] Winston, *op. cit.*, p. 339.

"more than a million of blacks had perished—more than twenty-five per cent of the whole number." [2] The condition of loyal white refugees was almost as desperate. On March 3, 1865, Congress had established the Freedmen's Bureau to deal with the situation. The bureau had been authorized to issue food, clothing, fuel, medicines, and other necessities to freedmen and white refugees in need of assistance. It was furthermore authorized to take possession of lands belonging to the United States or abandoned by their owners and parcel them out to freedmen and loyal white refugees, not more than forty acres to each adult male. They were to be protected in the possession of the land for three years.

It was now decided to enlarge the function of the bureau. Its personnel was to be increased and placed under the protection of the military. The bureau was authorized to build asylums and schools for the freedmen and to intervene in civil and criminal cases affecting people of color when equality before the law was denied them. The bill was adopted by large majorities in both Houses. That its provisions were unusual cannot be denied, but so was the situation that had to be dealt with. On February 19, 1866, Johnson vetoed the measure as an invasion of state rights and took pains to question the right of Congress "to shut out, in time of peace, any State from the representation to which it was entitled by the Constitution."

Republican newspapers had with few exceptions not taken sides in the controversy between President and Congress; now, however, they were well-nigh unanimous in their criticism of the Executive. The New York *Tribune,* which had been trying to pour oil on the troubled waters, epitomized Republican sentiment in these words: "Mr. Johnson has made a grave mistake. He has relieved those who elected him of a great responsibility by taking it on his own shoulders. Hereafter, whatever wrongs may be inflicted upon or indignities suffered by the Southern blacks, will be charged to the President, who has left them naked to their enemies." [3]

[2] *Globe,* March 7, 1866.
[3] New York *Tribune,* Feb. 20, 1866.

3

Stevens struck back promptly and resolutely.

On February 17, 1866, he had moved in the Committee on Reconstruction that "until the next congressional election the State of Tennessee shall be entitled to eight representatives." [4] This was partly a peace offering to the President, partly recognition of the fact that among the rebel states Tennessee was in a class by itself. Thousands of men from that state had served in the Union Army, and the principal fault to be found with its reconstructed government was that its loyalty was too aggressive and demonstrative. Nevertheless Stevens's motion constituted a retreat from his former position.

The day after Johnson's veto message had been read in the House, Stevens came to the committee meeting with fire in his eye. He said that since in his message the President had questioned the right of Congress to decide on what terms the rebel states should be readmitted, it was the duty of Congress to reaffirm its authority. "The President," he was to say later, "is made to misconceive his duties, and to treat with too little respect the powers of Congress." He had as a consequence changed his mind regarding Tennessee and asked that the matter be postponed. He then introduced a concurrent resolution to the effect that "to close agitation which is likely to disturb the action of the Government . . . no senator or representative shall be admitted into either branch of Congress from any of said States until Congress shall have declared such State entitled to such representation." [5]

Stevens's resolution embodied that part of his earlier concurrent resolution the Senate had thought it advisable to eliminate. It was now adopted by substantial majorities in both Houses. An attempt to override the President's veto failed, however, by two votes in the Senate. It was an empty victory for Johnson since toward the end of the session the bill, with a few minor changes, was again adopted by both Houses and passed over the President's veto.

[4] Kendrick, *op. cit.,* p. 64.
[5] *Globe,* March 10, 1866; Kendrick, *op. cit.,* pp. 71-72.

4

It became evident that Johnson meant to veto every bill, regardless of merit, affecting the Southern states, unless Congress consented to bow to his will and admit the Southern representatives unconditionally. On March 18, 1866, the Civil Rights Bill was submitted to him for his signature. The bill conferred neither social nor political privileges upon the freedmen, but pronounced all persons born in the United States (except Indians, not taxed) to be citizens. All, irrespective of race, color, or previous condition of servitude, were to have the equal benefit of all laws and proceedings for the security of person and property and were to be subject to like punishments and penalties. The measure designated the officers whose duty it would be to prosecute offenders and fixed the penalties. On March 27, against the advice of all but two members of his cabinet, Johnson vetoed the bill.[6]

Influential Republican senators who had exerted every possible effort to patch up the quarrel now joined the antiadministration forces. Senator Sherman who had found excuses for the President's veto of the Freedmen's Bureau Bill, now said bluntly: "Johnson is insincere; he has deceived and misled his best friends. I know he has led many to believe he would agree to the Civil Rights Bill." Senator Trumbull, who had fathered the bill, said with obvious astonishment and disappointment: "I regret it [the veto] . . . because the just expectations raised when the bill was presented to the President before its introduction into the Senate have been disappointed. He never indicated to me or to any of his friends the least objection to any of the provisions of this bill."

Johnson's veto was overridden, but had far-reaching results. Southern politicians were now firmly convinced that they had the administration safely in their pockets. They became increasingly arrogant. Southern legislatures continued to pass laws that Johnson's military commanders pronounced as constituting a rebirth of slavery. Southern newspapers kept urging the President to make use of the army to bring Congress to heel and heaped abuse upon congressional leaders, especially upon Stevens.

[6] *Globe,* April 4, 1866.

CHAPTER IX

Personal Quarrel between Stevens and Johnson

The struggle between President and Congress, involving fundamental principles, was complicated by a personal quarrel between Stevens and Johnson. Stevens was not guiltless in the matter. He had always disliked and distrusted Johnson, even when the latter was popularly believed to belong to his camp. There are natures that mutually repel each other. The repulsion Stevens felt for Johnson was such that although at the beginning of the session he had made an attempt to show him some of the respect due if not to the man then to the office, he could not keep it up. Soon he was referring to him sarcastically as "the high authority at the other end of the avenue." Mrs. Jefferson Davis has related that once when she called on Johnson, Stevens came limping in and "threatened the President in such a manner as would have been inadmissible to one of the servants." [1]

On January 28, 1866, Johnson gave an interview to Senator Dixon of Connecticut, one of the four Administration Republicans in the upper House. He said propositions to amend the Constitution "were becoming as numerous as preambles and resolutions at town meetings." Such a procedure, he opined, tended to diminish the people's respect for that document. He did not believe any further amendment "at all necessary at the present time," but if Congress was determined to adopt one concerning the basis of representation then he suggested that it read "Representatives shall be appointed among

[1] Robert McElroy, *Jefferson Davis: The Unreal and the Real,* vol. II, p. 563.

the several States which may be included within the Union according to the number of qualified voters." [2]

Apparently then Johnson and Stevens were not far from being in agreement, but only apparently so. There were but two ways in which such an amendment could be ratified: the rebel states must not be permitted to take part in the ratification—must, therefore, be regarded as out of the Union—or the reconstructed state governments must be dissolved and new elections held with the Negroes participating. Johnson would not hear of the first method and was moving heaven and earth to get the Southern representatives readmitted to Congress so the second could not be employed. He was, therefore, merely speaking for political effect and was blowing hot and cold at the same time. This enraged Stevens. On January 31 he referred to Johnson's statement in these words:

"We are told that no amendment is necessary. I take this to be an authorized utterance of one at the other end of the avenue. This is the proclamation, the command of the President of the United States, made and put forth by authority in advance, and at a time when Congress was legislating on this very question; made in my judgment, in violation of the privileges of this House; made in such a way that centuries ago, had it been made to Parliament by a British king, it would have cost him his head. But, sir, we pass that by; we are tolerant of usurpation in this tolerant Government of ours."

He was too good a politician to have made such a statement had he not been convinced that nothing more could be expected from Johnson and that he must be combated as an enemy. Others, however, had not yet given up hope. Senator John Sherman was then still one of these and rebuked Stevens in this fashion: "I know him well—a man of great intellect, with a controlling will, and possessing the dangerous power of sarcasm, which he wields against friend and foe, cutting like a Damascus blade. In a recent debate he made use of an expression that would irritate any man, especially when coming from a leader in the House of Congress." [3]

Two months later Sherman was to denounce Johnson as "insincere" and as having "deceived and misled his best friends."

[2] Edward McPherson, *The Political History of the United States of America during the Period of Reconstruction,* p. 51.

[3] *Globe,* Feb. 26, 1866.

2

Washington's birthday, February 22, appeared to the administration a suitable occasion to strike back at its critics. Secretary Seward was to make a speech in defense of the President's policy in Cooper Union, New York. In Washington, Johnson himself was to hold forth in front of the White House. The weather was propitious. A huge crowd gathered. During the war a captain of the watch at the Capitol had been dismissed for suggesting that the national colors should not be hoisted on the building as was customary when Congress was in session, "because it hurt the people about here to look at it." [4] Patriots of that kidney were now supporters of Johnson. When he appeared on the White House portico with his retinue—among whom was a former mayor of Washington whom Lincoln had thought it advisable to imprison in a fortress during the war—a great cheer went up.

The reception he received was music to Johnson's ears. He drank in the cheering and the applause, forgetting that those who cheered him would, had they dared, have cheered every Confederate victory during the war—forgetting that they cheered him now because they believed that with his aid the former Confederates and their Northern allies might gain their most formidable victory at the next presidential election. Having satiated himself with the applause, he launched into his speech. He paid the usual tribute to Washington, then took up his favorite topic—the trials and tribulations of one Andrew Johnson, champion of the people. "I can lay my hand on my heart," he declaimed, "and say . . . I have never deserted the people, nor do I believe they will desert me. . . . Who has suffered more than I have? I ask the question. I shall not recount the wrongs and sufferings inflicted upon me. . . . I know some are jealous in view of the White House, and I say all that flummery has as little effect upon me as it had heretofore."

He ignored the real issue between him and Congress, which was whether he and he alone had the right to lay down the terms upon which the rebel states should be readmitted to participation in the national government. In the manner of Louis XIV, who said "I am

[4] *Globe,* July 10, 1862. Cited by Preston King.

the state!" he chose to regard the refusal of Congress to submit to his usurpation as rebellion against the government, saying: "The rebellion is put down by the strong arm of the Government . . . and before we fully get from the battle-field . . . we are now almost inaugurated into another rebellion. . . . I am opposed to the Davises, the Toombses, the Slidells, and the long list of such. But when I perceive men still opposed to the Union . . . I am still for the preservation of the Union."

A voice called for the names of three of those whom he accused. Johnson accommodated, saying: "The gentleman calls for three names. . . . Suppose I should name to you those whom I look upon as being opposed to the fundamental principles of the Government, and as now laboring to destroy them. I say Thaddeus Stevens of Pennsylvania; I say Charles Sumner of Massachusetts; I say Wendell Phillips of Massachusetts."

An obscure member of the House had said in a speech that the "presidential obstacle must be got out of the way." No one had regarded the ill-phrased remark as having any other meaning than that the President's resistance must be overcome. Such an interpretation was too prosaic to suit Johnson. According to him it meant nothing else than that his assassination was being planned. Figuratively baring his breast to the imaginary assassin he exclaimed melodramatically: "Does not the blood of Lincoln appease the vengeance and wrath of the opponents of the Government? Is their thirst still unslacked? Do they want more blood? . . . I am not afraid of assassins. . . . If my blood is to be shed because I vindicate the Union and the preservation of the Government in its original purity, so let it be." [5]

3

Johnson's speech pleased those whom it was intended to please. "To the South and the northern Copperheads the Washington Birthday speech gave great satisfaction," Johnson's biographer has written.[6] The supposedly nonpartisan New York *Herald* called it "bold, manly and outspoken"; Raymond's New York *Times* found it "strong, direct, manly." Thurlow Weed opined that "traitors will now seek

[5] McPherson, *op. cit.*, pp. 58-63.
[6] Winston, *op. cit.*, p. 345.

hiding places and the Government is safe." Seward "heartily approved the speech." But there were few thoughtful men who did not agree with the editor of the *Nation* that "the mere fact that the President of the United States should have shown such disregard for decency, is, of itself, a scandal and a disgrace." Secretary McCulloch was to write that the speech "hurt the President." [7]

Word went out that Stevens meant to reply to Johnson on March 10, and when that day he rose to speak there was not a vacant seat in the House or in the public and reserved galleries.

He began in a casual way, saying the speech he meant to deliver had originally been prepared as a reply to the gentleman from New York (Raymond). He had yielded the floor to a young member from West Virginia and had since not had the opportunity to deliver the remarks, which, he said, he did not consider important at any time. "I have dug up the old manuscript, which is consequently tame, as the most of it has been since said by myself or others; and not being willing to lose the paper, I have come here for the purpose of saying now what I had intended to say then."

Since everybody knew that the old curmudgeon had come there for quite a different purpose, his explanation provoked merriment. Stevens had in the meantime produced a disorderly looking manuscript and launched into the promised reply to Raymond, who had been so thoroughly refuted by Shellabarger of Ohio early in January that no further reply was necessary. All this while, like a skilled matador, he had been maneuvering for position. Judging that the opportune moment had arrived to prepare to deliver the deadly thrust, he remarked: "At this point, I desire to say a word which may seem egotistic. Since I made my first speech at the opening of Congress certain newspapers have been attempting to disturb the harmony which existed between the President and myself. In the most polite language and the most flattering epithets they have denounced me as the enemy of the President, and as having waged successful war against him. These journals have, perhaps unintentionally, done me too much honor. I will say, however, once for all, that instead of feeling personal enmity to the President, I feel great respect for him. . . . He stood too firmly for the Union, in the midst

[7] McCulloch, *Men and Measures,* p. 393.

of dangers and sacrifices, to allow me to doubt the purity of his wishes. While I can have no hostility to the President . . . I have very grave objections to the course he is pursuing."

There was a murmur of surprise. Pierce of Iowa, who undoubtedly had been coached by Stevens for the role he was to play, rose and said: "I desire to ask the gentleman whether there may not be some mistake here. When I remember most distinctly that the public press for the last few weeks has been repeating the name of a certain '*Thaddeus Stevens*' as having been used by the President in a certain speech at the White House, and when I hear a gentleman whom I suppose to be the *Thaddeus Stevens* referred to speak in such strong terms in favor of the President, I wish to know whether he is the same gentleman, or some other."

When the laughter had subsided, Stevens said with the utmost gravity: "Does the learned gentleman from Iowa suppose for a single moment that that speech to which he refers as having been made in front of the White House, was a fact? . . . Sir, that speech which has imposed upon the gentleman from Iowa and has made some impression upon the public mind, was one of the grandest hoaxes ever perpetrated, and has been more successful than the moon hoax, which I am told deceived many astute astronomers. I am glad to have the opportunity to exonerate the President from ever having made that speech. It is a part of the cunning of the Copperhead party, who have been persecuting our President since the 4th of March last. Taking advantage of an unfortunate incident which happened on that occasion, they have been constantly denouncing him as addicted to low and degrading vices. To prove the truth of what I say I send to the Clerk's desk to be read a specimen of this system of slander. It is an extract from the New York *World* of March 7, 1865."

The Clerk now read as follows:

The drunken and beastly Caligula, the most profligate of Roman emperors, raised his horse to the dignity of consul—an office that in former times had been filled by the greatest warriors and statesmen of the Republic, the Scipios and Catos, and by the mighty Julius himself.

The consulship was scarcely more disgraced by that scandalous transaction than is our Vice-Presidency by the late election of Andrew Johnson. That office has been adorned in better days by the talents and accomplishments of Adams and Jefferson, Clinton and Gerry, Calhoun and Van Buren. And now to see it filled by *this insolent, drunken brute, in comparison with whom even Caligula's horse was respectable,* for the poor animal did not abuse its own nature!

And to think that only one frail life stands between *this insolent, clownish drunkard* and the Presidency! May God bless and spare Abraham Lincoln!

Stevens allowed the full meaning of this to sink in. Then, shaking his head with feigned concern and disapproval, he said: "That was a serious slander. That party have been persecuting the President with such slanders as that ever since. . . . Now, when these slanderers can make the people believe that the President ever uttered that speech, then they have made their case. But we all know that he never did utter it. It is not possible, sir, and I am glad of this opportunity to relieve him of that odium. Now, sir, having shown that all this is fallacious, I hope they will permit me to occupy the same friendly position with the President as I did before."

The obliging Pierce now rose again and said with a gravity worthy of his mentor: "I am satisfied the House and the country will agree with me there was a mistake. . . . I have found history cannot always be depended upon, and but for this accidental occurrence that would have gone down in history as a fact. Probably, sir, the present and succeeding generations would not have discovered it had not this fact been opportunely developed."

Stevens gravely replied: "I know the gentleman is satisfied now it is all a hoax."

"Laughter," "Renewed laughter," and "Great laughter" are bracketed throughout the report of these proceedings in the *Congressional Globe*. Yet there must have been some in that hall who were painfully affected at seeing the President of the United States so mercilessly ridiculed, and perhaps even more by the realization that the country had a President who inspired so little respect.

CHAPTER X

The Fourteenth Amendment—First Try

What in the meantime were the activities of the redoubtable Joint Committee on Reconstruction—the "irresponsible central directory" as Johnson chose to call it?

The New York *World* once compared the committee with the Committee of Public Safety during the French Revolution. If we carry the comparison further then Stevens was assuredly its Robespierre. That practically every measure of importance the committee formulated and presented to Congress was initiated by him is proved by the record. But from this to conclude that his fellow members were men of mediocre ability is erroneous. The committee chairman, William Pitt Fessenden, senator from Maine, had been in the Senate since 1854, except for nine months he had served in Lincoln's cabinet as secretary of the treasury, a post he resigned voluntarily at the conclusion of Lincoln's first term. He had been resolutely opposed to slavery extension, and when secession threatened would hear of no compromise. Conservative by nature he rejected Stevens's plan of confiscating the landed property of the planter aristocracy and creating a large class of white and colored small property owners loyal to the Union. Realizing, however, that the Republican party was a minority party, and that unless drastic measures were taken the government stood in imminent danger of falling into the hands of those who had tried to destroy it, he declared himself in favor of keeping the Southern states under military government until they consented to confer civil and political rights upon their colored population.[1]

[1] Francis Fessenden, *Life of Fessenden,* vol. II, pp. 23-24.

That the leader of the conservatives in the Senate should have taken such a stand is proof of the seriousness of the crisis.

Two other members of the committee—John A. Bingham and Roscoe Conkling—were men of outstanding ability. Bingham, a conservative with whom Stevens often clashed, had been elected to Congress from Ohio in 1854. When in 1862 he temporarily lost his seat, Lincoln appointed him judge advocate in the army and later solicitor general of the court of claims. In the trial of Lincoln's assassins he served as special judge advocate. He was re-elected to the House in 1865 and was promptly recognized as one of the leading members in that body. Unlike Fessenden he favored the impeachment of Andrew Johnson and was a member of the Board of Managers in the prosecution of the President.

Conkling, representative from New York, was an admirer and protégé of Stevens, who was more than twice his age. Tall, broad-shouldered, blond-bearded, young, and handsome, with a Hyperion curl which he was in the habit of shaking across his forehead when he spoke, he was an impressive figure and an orator of great ability. In 1867 he was elected to the Senate and became a veritable political dictator of the Empire State. During Grant's administration the political patronage in the state was entirely in his hands, and when in 1873 Chief Justice Chase died the President offered to appoint him to the high office. He declined the honor and is reported to have said: "I would forever be gnawing at my chains." Conkling owed his place on the committee to Stevens, whose leadership he followed in most matters, but with whom he differed on questions of finance. In 1882 his plea before the Supreme Court as chief counsel for the Southern Pacific Railroad Company was largely responsible for the perversion of the first section of the Fourteenth Amendment—conceived by Stevens as a humanitarian measure for the protection of a downtrodden race—into the "Magna Charta of accumulated wealth and organized capital." [2]

The leader of the Democrats on the committee was Senator Reverdy Johnson of Maryland. Robert E. Lee has been characterized as a "virtuous upholder of the wrong." The same may be said of Reverdy Johnson. Upright and honorable in private life and a

[2] From *The Fourteenth Amendment* by C. W. Collins, copyright 1912. Quoted by special permission of the publishers, Little, Brown & Co., p. 138.

brilliant lawyer, he was in public life a consistent defender of slavery. His plea before the Supreme Court in the Dred Scott case is said to have greatly influenced the tribunal's questionable decision. Throughout the war his voice was heard in Congress in defense of slavery and in opposition to almost every measure Congress or the administration considered indispensable to victory. That he should have become a champion of Johnson's policies was to be expected. He was the author of the minority report presented by the three Democrats on the committee, of which no less a constitutional authority than Professor Burgess has written that it was "the veriest dry bones of legal reasoning, the veriest sophistry of juristic abstraction." [8]

2

In its report to the country the Joint Committee on Reconstruction was to state the problem with the solution of which it had been entrusted, in these words:

> The question before Congress is whether conquered enemies have the right, and shall be permitted at their own pleasure and on their own terms, to participate in making laws for their conquerors; whether conquered rebels may change their theatre of operations from the battlefield, where they were defeated and overthrown, to the halls of Congress, and through their representatives seize upon the Government which they fought to destroy; whether the national treasury, the army of the nation, its navy, its forts and arsenals, its whole civil administration, its credit, its pensioners, the widows and orphans of those who perished in the war, the public honor, peace and safety, shall all be turned over to the keeping of its recent enemies without delay, and without imposing such conditions as, in the opinion of Congress, the security of the country and its institutions may demand.

> In all these States, except Tennessee and perhaps Arkansas, the elections which were held for State officers and members of Congress had resulted, almost universally, in the defeat of candidates who had been true to the Union, and in the election of notorious and unpardoned rebels, men who could not take the prescribed oath of office, and who made no secret of their hostility to the Government and the people of the United States. . . . The southern press denounces and reviles southern men who adhered to the Union; and strives constantly and unscru-

[8] *Op. cit.*, p. 86.

pulously, by every means in its power, to keep alive the fire of hate and discord between the sections; calling upon the President to violate his oath of office, overturn the Government by force of arms, and drive the representatives from their seats in Congress.

No fair-minded historian can deny the truth of these charges. Indiscriminating and advantageous to the enemies of the Union as was Johnson's pardoning policy, the South refused to abide by it and elected to office whomever it pleased. Johnson had vainly protested against the election to the United States Senate of the former vice-president of the Confederacy, Alexander H. Stephens, one of numerous "unpardoned rebels" elected to office. Loyalists like Hahn and Flanders of Louisiana, who had co-operated with Lincoln, were defeated. Indeed, the unfortunate result of Lincoln's premature attempt at Reconstruction proved to be that loyal Southerners who had collaborated with him became marked men.

Particularly enlightening is the testimony before the committee of secessionists themselves. Stephens, who at one time had denounced secession in the severest terms, boldly declared that it was the constitutional right of a state to secede whenever it pleased and return to the Union whenever it felt like it, with all its rights unimpaired! [4] The utter inability of the government of the Confederate States of America to reconcile its state-rights doctrine with the necessities of national existence was probably as much responsible for the collapse of the Confederacy as military defeat. Yet these men had learned nothing. Their indignation at the unwillingness of the North to readmit them into the Union unconditionally appears to have been as genuine as it was fatuous. Confronted with this situation the committee reached the conclusion that to run the risk of the federal government falling into such hands was unthinkable and must be prevented at *any* cost. They were to say in their report:

> The instinct of self-preservation protests against it. The surrender by Grant to Lee, and by Sherman to Johnston, would have been disasters of less magnitude, for new armies could have been raised, new battles fought, and the Government saved. The anti-coercive policy which under pretext of avoiding bloodshed, allowed the rebellion to take form and gather force, would be surpassed in infamy by the matchless wickedness that would now surrender the halls of Congress to those so recently in

[4] *Testimony,* Part III, pp. 158-166.

rebellion, until proper precautions shall be taken to secure the national faith and the national safety.[5]

It should be noted that the report was not written by Stevens, but by the conservative Fessenden. Clemenceau was right when he wrote to his paper in Paris: "In spite of what is said, the North is not hostile to the South. The reverse is true. The South hates the North, and the latter wishes to guard against the effects of this hatred; that is all." [6]

3

On December 5, 1866, the second day of the session, Stevens had introduced in the House his proposed constitutional amendment basing representation in the House and the Electoral College on the number of legal voters in each state. It had been referred to the Judiciary Committee. Considering that committee dilatory in bringing in its report, he decided to go over their heads, and at the first meeting of the Joint Committee on Reconstruction, January 9, 1866, submitted his proposal to that committee. It is indicative of the respect in which he was held that the Judiciary Committee did not even venture to complain about the slight. His proposal read as follows:

> Representatives shall be apportioned among the several States, which may be included within the Union, according to the number of their respective legal voters; and for this purpose none shall be considered as legal voters who are not either natural born or naturalized citizens of the United States, of the age of twenty-one years.
>
> Congress shall provide for ascertaining the number of said voters. A true census of legal voters shall be taken at the same time with the regular census.

The proposal, which was self-regulating, compelled no state to confer the elective franchise upon the Negro. It merely aimed to establish the principle that "political representation did not belong to those who had no political existence." Several of Stevens's colleagues, especially Blaine, raised, however, objections to the wording of the measure. Many young men had heeded Greeley's advice "Go

[5] McPherson, *op. cit.*, pp. 84-90.
[6] *Op. cit.*, p. 85.

West, young man!" with the result that some of the Western states, especially California, had a disproportionately large number of voters in relation to their population. They would, it was believed, gain in representation at the expense of the Eastern states. Subsequent calculations were to show that with the exception of California none of the Western states would have been greatly benefited and none of the Eastern states seriously affected. The proposed amendment was, however, rewritten to read as follows:

> Representatives shall be apportioned among the several States which may be included within this Union according to their respective number, counting the whole number of persons in each State, excluding Indians not taxed.
>
> *Provided,* That whenever the elective franchise shall be denied or abridged in any State on account of race or color, all persons therein of such race or color shall be excluded from the basis of representation.

Stevens must have realized that in its new form the amendment would no longer be self-regulating, but accepted the change. Some of his followers, however, were displeased. It will be recalled that in his letter to Governor Hahn of Louisiana and in his last speech, Lincoln had advised reconstructed states to confer the elective franchise upon the "very intelligent" among the Negroes and "on those who serve our cause as soldiers." If the proposed amendment became a part of the Constitution, nothing would hinder the Southern states from following Lincoln's advice, but the incentive would be lacking since their representation would not be increased until they had extended the right of suffrage to their entire colored population.

Stevens did not find this a serious drawback. What Negroes would the former slaveholders have regarded as "very intelligent"? Assuredly not those whose intelligence told them that the reign of the planter aristocracy had been disastrous to the South, however great its advantages to the favored few. "They will give the suffrage to their menials, their house servants, those they can control, and elect whom they please to make our laws," Stevens was to say.[7] As for Lincoln's suggestion that the former slave states confer the elective franchise by preference upon Negroes who had served in the Union Army, it furnishes startling proof of the Emancipator's misconcep-

[7] *Globe,* Jan. 31, 1866.

tion of the probable attitude of the South at the conclusion of hostilities. By what miracle did he expect that the people of the South would change their mental outlook so completely as to be willing to reward their former slaves for having taken up arms against them?

It is interesting to note the absence of the word "male" as a qualification for being a voter in Stevens's original proposal as well as in the amended version. "Why make a crusade against women in the Constitution of the nation?" he was to say. "I do not think we ought to disfigure the Constitution with such a provision. . . . I certainly shall never vote to insert the word 'male' or the word 'white' in the national Constitution. Let these things be attended to by the States."

4

Stevens presented the joint resolution to the House on January 22. It was hotly debated. Andrew J. Rogers, Democrat from New Jersey, a member of the Joint Committee, made a speech in opposition to the proposed amendment. He was interrupted by William D. Kelley of Pennsylvania, who pointedly asked: "I want the gentleman to tell me, if he can, whether there is any reason that when our Government shall be reconstructed, one pardoned rebel of South Carolina who may not be able to read and write, and who may have fought for four years against the Government, shall, in political power, alike on the floor of Congress and in electing a President, outweigh three or five intelligent soldiers from New Jersey, who throughout the same four years fought for the Union." [8]

Needless to say he received an evasive reply.

Stevens's protégé Conkling made an able argument of which the following is a sample: "Shall one hundred and twenty-seven thousand white people in New York cast but one vote in the House, and have but one voice here, while the same number of white people in Mississippi have three votes and three voices? Shall the death of slavery add two fifths to the entire power which slavery had when slavery was living? Shall one white man have as much share in the Government as three other white men merely because he lives where blacks outnumber whites two to one? Shall this inequality exist, and

[8] *Globe*, Jan. 22, 1866.

exist only in favor of those who without cause drenched the land in blood and covered it with mourning?"

Stevens closed the debate with a speech on January 31. He made it unmistakably clear that the measure would not force any state to grant the elective franchise to its colored population: "I hold that the States have the right, and always have had it, to fix the elective franchise within their own States. And I hold that this does not take it from them. Ought it to take it from them? How many States would adopt such a proposition? . . . I venture to say you could not get five in this Union." [9]

He made no secret of the fact that he hoped the Southern states, in order to increase their representation, would *not* enfranchise the freedmen "at least for some years." "I want in the meantime that our Christian men shall go among the freedmen and teach them what their duties are as citizens—the philanthropists of the North, the honest Methodists, my friends the Hardshell Baptists, and all others; and then, four or five years hence, when the freedmen shall have been made free indeed, when they shall have become intelligent enough . . . I shall be glad to see them admitted here."

If the freedmen were enfranchised without previous preparation, he feared the former slaveholders would make use of them to increase their own representation, and then "not one beneficial act for the benefit of the freedmen or for the benefit of the country would ever be passed."

What he wanted for the freedmen immediately was equality before the law: "I had another proposition, which I hope may again be brought forward. It is this: *All national and State laws shall be equally applicable to every citizen, and no discrimination shall be made on account of race or color.* There is the genuine proposition; that is the one I love; that is the one which I hope, before we separate, we shall have educated ourselves up to the idea of adopting, and that we shall have educated our people to the point of ratifying."

5

The proposed constitutional amendment was adopted in the House by a vote of 120 to 46. Its passage was hailed with satisfaction by

[9] *Ibid.*

Republican editors, with the exception of a small minority who desired the immediate right of suffrage for the freedmen. Stevens was lauded for his leadership. The Chicago *Tribune,* which had often criticized him for neglect of Western interests, said the passage of the measure must be attributed to his "native shrewdness, boldness and power over the House; for the majority, divided but yesterday by a diversity of opinion, apparently puzzled, restive and at a loss whither to turn, seemed to yield to him as does a mettlesome charger to the hand of the practiced rider." [10]

Stevens's triumph was brief. When the measure reached the Senate it ran afoul of Charles Sumner.

Sumner's name is often linked with Stevens's. He was in the Senate what Stevens was in the House—the foremost champion of the Negro. But there was a vast difference between them. Lincoln said once that Sumner was his idea of a bishop. No one would have said this of the rough-hewn Stevens. Sumner's manner was polished and he was particular about his appearance; Stevens was brusque and did not care if his wig sat a little awry. Sumner was pontifical and prolix, Stevens simple and to the point. Sumner was an impractical idealist, Stevens a practical one. Sumner would ask himself if a thing was right; Stevens would stop to consider if it was right under existing circumstances. Sumner would go charging like a Don Quixote; Stevens favored careful strategy. Sumner would hear of no compromise; Stevens would take what he could get and try for more.

Believing that if ignorant white men *disloyal* to the Union were to be permitted to vote there was no valid reason why ignorant black men *loyal* to the Union should not be permitted to vote, Sumner thrust aside all objections to a constitutional amendment conferring the elective franchise upon the Negro. In this he proved himself unrealistic. The Negro did not possess that right in most of the Northern states. Connecticut had but recently rejected such a proposal by a plebiscite. Not until the people of the North became convinced that there was no other way of saving the government from falling into the hands of ex-rebels and their Copperhead allies would they be willing to adopt an amendment of that nature.

Stevens was aware of all this. "I would not for a moment," he was

[10] Chicago *Tribune,* Feb. 7, 1866.

to say, "inculcate the idea of surrendering a principle vital to justice. But if full justice could not be obtained at once I would not refuse to do what is possible. The commander of an army who should find his enemy intrenched on impregnable heights would act unwisely if he insisted on marching his troops full in the face of a destructive fire merely to show his courage. Would it not be better to flank the works and march round and round and besiege, and thus secure the surrender of the enemy, though it might cost time? The former course would show valor and folly; the latter moral and physical courage, as well as prudence and wisdom." [11]

While not favoring a constitutional amendment conferring the immediate right of suffrage upon the freedmen Stevens was more solicitous for their welfare than Sumner. He had already proposed a constitutional amendment granting them civil rights, which he considered a far more reliable guaranty than a mere law of Congress, and he continued to plead that homesteads be given them. In his reply to Sumner he was to say: "In my judgment, we shall not approach the measure of justice until we have given every adult freedman a homestead on the land where he was born and toiled and suffered. Forty acres of land and a hut would be more valuable to him than the immediate right to vote." [12]

Sumner's arraignment of the proposed constitutional amendment covered no less than twenty-three finely printed columns in the *Congressional Globe,* bristling with extravagant invective. The measure, he said, was a "disgusting tyranny." It was "nothing less than a mighty House of Ill Fame, which it is proposed to license constitutionally for a consideration." It was a "new sale of Indulgences on a larger scale than that of Fetzel." It was a " 'muscipular' abortion sent into the world by a 'parturient' mountain." It was a "wickedness on a larger scale than the crime against Kansas and the Fugitive Slave Law." It was a "new anathema marantha." It was "the very Koh-i-noor of blackness." It was a "political obscenity," a "disgusting ordure," a "loathsome stench," an "essential uncleanliness," an "abomination," a "paragon and masterpiece of ingratitude." As for those guilty of

[11] *Globe,* May 8, 1866.
[12] *Ibid.*

such a concoction, they reminded him of "Pontius Pilate, with Judas Iscariot upon his back." [18]

The influence of Sumner was sufficiently great to turn the tide against the amendment, which failed to obtain the requisite two-thirds vote in the Senate. The committee had to do its work over again.

[18] *Globe*, March 7, 1866.

CHAPTER XI

The Fourteenth Amendment—Second Try

More than three months had elapsed since Congress had assembled, and as far as Reconstruction was concerned nothing had been accomplished. The President's attempt at Reconstruction along the lines of the first congressional plan—the Wade-Davis plan—had been rejected. Stevens's proposal to place the rebel states under territorial government had fallen on deaf ears. The committee's attempt to change the basis of representation by means of a constitutional amendment had suffered shipwreck in the Senate. The country was becoming impatient. It was obvious that things could not remain in their present state, but the party in power did not appear to be able to make up its mind what to do about the matter. The editor of the *Nation* expressed his concern in the following language:

> The people are willing to keep the southern states out of the Union until certain conditions are complied with, but they want to know what those conditions are going to be. Congress has agreed upon none. The only thing Congress has agreed on is keeping the southern states out for the present, but this is simply the excavation for the foundation for the new building. The public is anxiously waiting to see the structure rise and is tired of hearing the builders wrangle over the style of architecture. More serious work than we have yet had must now begin. If it does not . . . we greatly fear that the coming fall will find the public thoroughly out of patience with Congress and quite ready to let the President and his friends have their own way.[1]

[1] *The Nation,* April 20, 1866.

The day after the appearance of this editorial Stevens presented a fairly comprehensive plan to the committee. It was, he said, not of his own framing, but acceptable to him.

The author of the plan was a former congressman from Indiana, Robert Dale Owen. He was the son of the famous British social reformer Robert Owen, originator of the abortive attempt to found an earthly paradise at New Harmony, Indiana. The son, now sixty-five, was a social reformer in his own right. He was responsible for the extension of property rights for married women and the provision for public schools in the revised Indiana constitution. He was the first man in the United States who publicly advocated birth control, had been active in the antislavery movement, and was now keenly interested in Reconstruction. That his attitude toward the South was conciliatory is evident from the following extract from a letter he wrote to the editor of the Washington *Chronicle:*

> The essential is that we approach this great subject in a fitting spirit. It avails nothing to talk about the enormity of secession and the condign punishment it merits. . . . If there be among our people a revengeful element, let us not ponder to it. If we impose conditions before we restore political rights to those who defying law and Constitution by force of arms, became public enemies, it ought to be in defense, not in requital.[2]

Owen had, as he expressed it, become "exercised" about the lack of progress in Reconstruction and had framed a proposal combining in a single constitutional amendment all three proposals made by Stevens in December with two of his own. With the manuscript in his pocket he had journeyed to Washington and had called on Stevens at the latter's house on South B Street.[3]

2

The Commoner gave the visitor a friendly reception. The latter produced his manuscript and read aloud what he had written. Stevens listened attentively and when Owen had finished asked him to read it again.

The proposed constitutional amendment consisted of five sections.

[2] *Globe,* May 24, 1866. Cited by Senator Stewart of Nevada.
[3] "Political Results from the Varioloid," *Atlantic Monthly,* June, 1875.

The first provided that there was to be no discrimination as to civil rights because of race or color. The second—Owen's own contribution—provided that on and after July 4, 1876, there was to be no discrimination because of race or color in the matter of political rights. The third provided that if prior to that date a state discriminated politically against any person because of race or color, then all persons of such race or color in the state would be excluded from enumeration in the basis of representation. The fourth forbade payment of Confederate debts, state or national, or remuneration for the loss of slaves. The fifth empowered Congress to adopt appropriate legislation to enforce these provisions.

After the second reading Owen asked Stevens if he had an hour to spare to discuss the proposal. The Commoner replied: "I have nothing half so important to do as to attend to this matter. Take your own time." The visitor explained why he considered it inadvisable to confer the immediate right of suffrage upon the freedmen: "The fact that the Negro is, for the present, unprepared wisely to use the right of suffrage, and, still more, incapable of legislating with prudence, is not less a fact because it has occurred through no fault of his. We must think and act for him as he is, and not as, but for life-long servitude, he would have been. We exclude minors from political rights, not because they are unworthy, but because for the time, they are incapable. . . . Consider if it be not for the freedmen's welfare and good name that he should be kept away from the duties and responsibilities of political life until he shall have been, in a measure, prepared to fulfill these with credit to himself and advantage to the public service."

Since, as we have seen, Stevens was himself opposed to granting the immediate right of suffrage to the freedmen, he did not need convincing. He considered ten years excessive, but as nothing would prevent the Southern states from granting the elective franchise to the Negro sooner if they were anxious to increase their representation in Congress, he merely remarked: "I hate to delay full justice so long."

Owen replied: "We shall have invested him, beyond repeal by law, with political rights, if it be prospectively only; and their former masters will feel that they have now to deal with men who, in a few years, will be able to control elections, make governors and congressmen, and confer office on whom they please."

Stevens picked up the manuscript, studied it, meditated, then said: "I'll be plain with you, Owen. We've had nothing before us that comes anywhere near being as good as this, or as complete. It would be likely to pass, too; that's the best of it. . . . I'll lay that amendment of yours before our committee to-morrow, if you say so; and I'll do my best to put it through."

It was decided, however, that Owen should call on Fessenden and other committee members and try to overcome their objections before Stevens took up the matter officially. He made the calls and in his account sums up the result in these words: "All the Republican members of the committee received the proposal more or less favorably. The Democrats held back."

3

Stevens offered the plan to the committee on April 21. Two days later it was adopted and ordered presented to the Senate and to the House. As Fessenden, the committee chairman, was in bed with the varioloid, it was decided, however, to wait a few days for his recovery, so he might participate in so important a decision. During those few days—in the period between April 23 and April 28—something happened that decided the committee to reverse itself. Stevens reported the matter to Owen as follows:

Our action on your amendment had, it seems got noised abroad. In the course of last week the members from New York, from Illinois, and from your State, too, Owen—from Indiana—held, each separately, a caucus to consider whether equality of suffrage, present or prospective, ought to form a part of the Republican programme for the coming canvas. They were afraid, so some of them told me, that if there was "a nigger in the wood-pile" at all, (that was the phrase), it would be used against them as an electioneering handle, and some of them—hang their cowardice!—might lose their elections. By inconsiderable majorities each of these caucuses decided that negro suffrage, in any shape, ought to be excluded from the platform; and they communicated these decisions to us. Our committee hadn't backbone enough to maintain its ground. Yesterday, the vote on your plan was reconsidered, your amendment was laid on the table.

After a while he added: *"Damn the varioloid! It changed the whole policy of the country."* [4]

That Fessenden's illness "changed the whole policy of the country" is questionable. Congress was determined that a constitutional amendment must be offered for ratification not only to the loyal, but also to the rebel states. Since the latter later refused to ratify a version leaving the matter of Negro suffrage entirely in their hands, what reason is there to believe that they would have ratified Owen's version?

4

Owen had, however, not labored in vain. In imitation of his model, the Fourteenth Amendment, as finally evolved by the committee, incorporated in a single measure of five sections all constitutional changes believed to be indispensable for the safety of the country and the preservation of the freedom of the Negro. The first section made civil rights of persons, irrespective of race or color, a national concern. As adopted by the House that section read:

No State shall make or enforce any law which shall abridge the privileges or immunities of citizens of the United States; nor shall any State deprive any person of life, liberty, or property without due process of law; nor deny to any person within its jurisdiction the equal protection of the laws.

The Senate believed it advisable to define citizenship and did so by adding the following:

All persons born or naturalized in the United States, and subject to the jurisdiction thereof, are citizens of the United States and of the State wherein they reside.

This served the further purpose of emphasizing the pre-eminence of national over state citizenship. As later interpreted by the Supreme Court this section, "humanitarian in origin and purpose . . . opened the door for organized capital to contest whatever laws of the State it considered disadvantageous." [5]

The second section, dealing with the basis of representation had, when first presented by Stevens, been self-regulating and simplicity

[4] *Ibid.*

[5] Collins, *op. cit.,* pp. 128-129.

itself. When in its revised form it was rejected by the Senate it still had the merit of simplicity and clarity. What was finally adopted by both Houses was the following mass of verbiage, destined never to be enforced:

Representatives shall be apportioned among the several States according to their respective numbers, counting the whole number of persons in each, excluding Indians not taxed. But when the right to vote at any election for the choice of electors for President and Vice-President of the United States, representatives in Congress, the executive and judicial officers of a State, or the members of the Legislature thereof, is denied to any of the male inhabitants of such State, being twenty-one years of age, and citizens of the United States, or in any way abridged, except for participation in rebellion, or other crime, the basis of representation therein shall be reduced in the proportion which the number of such male citizens shall bear to the whole number of male citizens twenty-one years of age in such State.

The third section—the only one that might be regarded as punitive, but which in view of the situation was a reasonable precautionary measure—read, in the House version:

Until the fourth day of July in the year 1870 all persons who voluntarily adhered to the late insurrection, giving it aid and comfort, shall be excluded from the right to vote for representatives in Congress and for President and Vice-President.

Let the reader ask himself whether if a rebellion of equal magnitude had taken place in his own time and had been suppressed by the government, he would have considered that government unduly severe in imposing such a restriction. The Senate, however, considered it too drastic. Believing that it penalized too many people and would be difficult to enforce, it substituted the following:

No person shall be a senator or representative in Congress or elector for President and Vice-President, or hold any office civil or military, under the United States or under any State, who, having previously taken an oath, as a member of Congress, or as an officer of the United States, or as a member of any State Legislature, or as an executive or judicial officer of any State, to support the Constitution of the United States, shall have engaged in insurrection or rebellion against the same, or given aid or comfort to the enemies thereof. But Congress may, by a vote of two-thirds of each House, remove such disability.

No white Southerner was therefore to be deprived, even for a limited time, of the right to vote, but the leaders of the rebellion were to be debarred from holding public office, unless the disability was removed by a two-thirds vote of Congress. It has been argued that a loyalty oath should have sufficed. Loyalist leaders, Democrats as well as Republicans, did not think so at that time. Had not Robert E. Lee—that paragon of honor and virtue whose sword is presented annually to the honor student at West Point—as late as March 30, 1861, accepted from Lincoln a commission as colonel in the United States Army? Had he not on that occasion solemnly sworn "allegiance to the United States of America"? Had he not sworn to "obey the orders of the President of the United States"? Yet had he not, less than a month later, on April 23, met in secret conclave with the conspirators of the Virginia secession convention and with the Vice-President of the Confederacy? Had he not on May 10—*thirteen days before the people of Virginia were to vote on secession*—taken command, under an order issued by the Confederate Secretary of War, L. P. Walker, of the Confederate troops occupying the state, so the result of the *viva-voce* referendum might be a foregone conclusion? [6] Had he not given as an excuse that his first duty was to his state? [7] Did he and other secessionist leaders, civil as well as military, not still believe this? And if believing this they had been disloyal once, might they not be so again if the opportunity offered in the form of a foreign invasion? Had they not tried to embroil their country with Great Britain and France in order to achieve their purpose? If it was wrong to debar them from holding office for having committed what was then considered treason, what is to be said of the South Carolina Constitution, which debarred citizens of that state from being elected to the legislature or to Congress for the crime of owning less than ten slaves?

The fourth section, as adopted by the House, forbade payment of Confederate debts, state or national, or remuneration for the loss of slaves. The Senate added to this that "the validity of the public debt

[6] Before the referendum took place Senator James Mason of Virginia publicly announced that anyone voting against secession would have to leave the state.

[7] General Edward D. Townsend, present at the interview between Lee and Scott, reported that Lee told General Scott "The property belonging to my children, all they possess, lies in Virginia. They will be ruined, if they do not go with their state. I cannot raise my hand against my children." Gamaliel Bradford, *Lee the American*, p. 30.

of the United States, authorized by law, including debts incurred for the payment of pensions and bounties for services in suppressing insurrection or rebellion, shall not be questioned."

The fifth section read: "The Congress shall have the power to enforce, by appropriate legislation, the provisions of this article."

Such then was the Fourteenth Amendment forged under the leadership of Stevens—the congressional plan on the basis of which, had the South willed it, Reconstruction could have been accomplished. It deprived no Southern white of the right to vote in either state or national elections. It gave the ballot to not a single Negro. It did not decree the execution, imprisonment, or exile of a single rebel leader, nor did it confiscate his land or any other property. It left the South master of its own affairs on condition that a small group of men, whose influence had proved fatal to the country and to the South, be not permitted to hold public office—that the presence of four million nonvoting Negroes be not used to give Southern whites undue power in the counsels of the nation—that colored citizens be allowed to enjoy equality before the law. It can be said without fear of contradiction that in all the world's history there can be found no comparable example of a legitimate government offering such terms to vanquished rebels who had tried to dismember the country. The historian James Ford Rhodes, for all his Southern bias, could not help losing patience with the perversity that rejected such a "magnanimous offer . . . marked by even-handed justice," which should have been taken advantage of "eagerly and at once." [8]

Perhaps it might have been but for the South's evil genius in the White House with whose help the vanquished hoped to be able to lord it over the victors.

5

The committee's version of the Fourteenth Amendment was presented to the House by Stevens on April 30, 1866, and on May 8 was defended by him in a speech in that body.

The Commoner again emphasized that the amendment should be submitted for ratification to the loyal states only: "I utterly repudiate and scorn the idea that any State not acting in the Union is to be

[8] *Op. cit.*, vol. V, pp. 602-610.

counted on the question of ratification. It is absurd to suppose that any more than three-fourths of the States that propose the amendment are required to make it valid; that States not here are to be counted as present."

There can be no question of the logic of his position. If the Southern states are to be blamed for refusing to ratify the amendment, the Republican party was almost equally to blame for giving them the opportunity to refuse.

The Commoner referred to the committee's original proposal—which as a result of Sumner's intervention had suffered shipwreck in the Senate—in these words: "It was slaughtered by a puerile and pedantic criticism, by a perversion of philological definition which, if when I taught school a lad who had studied Lindley Murray had assumed, I would have expelled him from the institution as unfit to waste education upon. . . . Let us again try and see whether we cannot devise some way to overcome the united forces of self-righteous Republicans and unrighteous copperheads."

What the committee was now proposing he believed to be "the best proposition that can be made effectual. . . . I shall not be driven by clamor or denunciation to throw away a great good because it is not perfect. I will take all I can get in the cause of humanity and leave it to be perfected by better men in better times."

He then took up the discussion of the proposed constitutional amendment section by section. He explained why he and his colleagues on the committee had decided to incorporate in the first section the principles of the Civil Rights Bill, passed over the President's veto: "A law is repealable by a majority. And I need hardly say that the first time the South with their copperhead allies obtain the command of Congress it will be repealed. The veto of the President and their votes on the bill are conclusive evidence of that. . . . This amendment once adopted cannot be annulled without two-thirds of Congress. That they will hardly get."

The second section concerning the basis of representation he considered inferior to the version the House had adopted earlier in the year, but which the Senate had rejected: "That article provided that if *one* of the injured race was excluded, the State should forfeit the right to have any of them represented. It would have hastened their full enfranchisement. This section allows the States to discriminate among the same class, and receive proportionate credit in the representation. This I dislike. But it is a step forward. The large stride which we proposed is dead; the murderers must answer to the suffering race. I would not have been the perpetrator."

Speaking of the third section—which in the version proposed by the committee but later amended by the Senate excluded until July 4, 1870, all persons who voluntarily took part in the Rebellion from the right to vote for representatives in Congress and for electors for president and vice-president—he said: "I know that there is a morbid sensibility, sometimes called mercy, which affects a few of all classes, from the priest to the clown, which has more sympathy for the murderer than for the victim. I hope I have a heart as capable of feeling for human woe as others. I have long since wished that capital punishment were abolished. But I never dreamed that all punishment could be dispensed with in human society. Anarchy, *treason,* and violence would reign triumphant. Here is the mildest of all punishments ever inflicted on traitors. I might not consent to the extreme severity pronounced upon them by a provisional governor of Tennessee—I mean the late lamented Andrew Johnson—but I would have increased the severity of this section. I would be glad to see it extended to 1876, and to include all State and municipal as well as national elections. In my judgment we do not sufficiently protect the loyal men of the rebel States from the vindictive persecutions of their victorious rebel neighbors. Still, I will move no amendment, nor vote for any, lest the whole fabric should tumble to pieces."

He finished with an appeal to those among his followers who desired the immediate enfranchisement of the freedmen: "To the friend of justice, the friend of the Union, of the perpetuity of liberty, and the final triumph of the rights of man and their extension to every human being, let me say, sacrifice as we have done your peculiar views, and instead of vainly insisting upon the instantaneous operation of all that is *right* accept what is *possible,* and 'all these things shall be added unto you.'"

6

There followed an animated discussion. On May 10 the conservative Bingham took the floor. He, too, spoke in favor of the proposed constitutional amendment, with the exception, however, of the third section which for a period of four years barred from participation in national elections all who had voluntarily aided the rebellion. He was, he said, not opposed to disfranchising such persons, but believed the provision would be difficult to enforce and might be regarded as a partisan measure designed to keep power in the hands of the Republicans. Since the Senate was to change this section entirely, the only significance of his argument is in the reply it received from Stevens.

Stevens spoke in a low, husky voice, but with extraordinary vigor. With his ravaged face, the smoldering fire in his deep-set eyes, his uplifted finger which at times he shook warningly at his listeners, he looked like an Old Testament prophet prognosticating the wrath of Jehovah. "Give us the third section or give us nothing," he said. "Do not balk us with the pretense of an amendment which throws the Union into the hands of the enemy before it becomes consolidated. Gentlemen say I speak of party. When party is necessary to sustain the Union, I say rally to your party and save the Union. I do not hesitate to say at once: that section is there to save or destroy the Union by the salvation or destruction of the Union party. Gentlemen tell us it is too strong—too strong for what? Too strong for their stomachs, but not for the people. It is too lenient for my hard heart. Not only to 1870, but to 18,070 every rebel who shed the blood of loyal men should be prevented from exercising any power in this Government. Gentlemen here have said you must not humble these people. Why not? Do not they deserve humiliation? If they do not, who does? What criminal, what felon deserves it more? They have not yet confessed their sins; and He who administers mercy and justice never forgives until the sinner confesses and humbles himself at his footstool. Why should we forgive any more than He? . . . For my part I am willing they shall come in when they are ready. Do not, I pray you, admit those who have slaughtered half a million of our countrymen until their clothes are dried, and until they are reclad. I do not wish to sit side by side with men whose garments smell of the blood of my kindred. Gentlemen seem to forget the scenes that were enacted here years ago. Many of you were not here. . . . Ah, sir, it is but six years ago when they were here, just before they went out to join the armies of Cataline, just before they left this Hall. Those of you who were here then will remember the scene in which every southern member, encouraged by their allies, came forth in one yelling body, because a speech for freedom was being made here; when weapons were drawn and Barksdale's bowie-knife gleamed before our eyes. Would you have these men back again so soon to reenact those scenes? Wait until I am gone, I pray you. I want not to go through it again. It will be but a short time for my colleague to wait. I hope he will not put us to the test."

Those who are of the opinion that Southern leaders should have been admitted to immediate participation in the national government should read the accounts of speeches made by some of them at this time, as reported in the Southern press. Former Governor Henry A. Wise of Virginia drew "prolonged cheers and applause" when he delivered himself of this sentiment at a public gathering at Alexandria, Virginia: "If I had triumphed I should have favored stripping them naked. Pardon! They might have appealed for pardon, but I would have seen them damned before I would have granted it. For myself, the boot being on the other leg, I take no oaths: I ask no pardon!" [9]

The proposed constitutional amendment, as reported by Stevens, was adopted in the House by a vote of 128 to 37. Bingham and even Raymond voted for its adoption.

On June 13 Stevens spoke again, recommending that the changes made in the House version of the amendment by the Senate be concurred in. He approved all the changes except the one made in the third section. That change, he feared, "may give the next Congress and President to the reconstructed rebels." He had hoped, he said, that Congress would take advantage of the opportunity the situation presented to have "so remodeled all our institutions as to have freed them from every vestige of human oppression, of inequality of rights, of the degradation of the poor, and the superior caste of the rich. In

[9] *Globe*, May 29, 1866. Cited by Ashley of Ohio.

short that no discrimination would be tolerated in this purified Republic but what arose from merit and conduct. This bright dream has vanished 'like the baseless fabric of a vision.' . . . Do you inquire why, holding these views and possessing some will of my own, I accept so imperfect a proposition? I answer, because I live among men and not among angels. . . . Mutual concession, therefore, is our only resort, or mutual hostilities."

CHAPTER XII

Stevens's Advice Rejected

Stevens had warned his colleagues in and out of season that if the Fourteenth Amendment was submitted for ratification to the rebel states, it would be defeated. Believing they could count on the administration for support, the Southern states were hardly likely to vote to have their representation in the national government reduced at a time when they had confidently expected to increase it substantially. Since the Republicans were, with few exceptions, convinced that in order to be valid the Fourteenth Amendment would have to be ratified by three-fourths of *all* the states, there would remain no other alternative than to dissolve the reconstructed state governments, confer the elective franchise upon the freedmen, hold new elections, and resubmit the amendment for ratification to the newly elected Southern legislatures. It was either that or accept Johnson's policy and at the next presidential election meekly hand over the federal government to those who had tried to destroy it.

How illogical the Republican theorem regarding ratification really was may be judged from the fact that when Congress later disbanded the Southern state governments it was as good as saying that it had never considered them valid. Had they been valid they could no more have been disbanded than the state governments of Pennsylvania or New York. But if they were not valid then their ratification was valueless. Why then bother to obtain it? They had ratified the Thirteenth Amendment, which meant that that amendment had never received a valid ratification from three-fourths of all the states, yet its validity was never questioned. Why then could the Fourteenth Amendment not have been ratified in the same manner?

2

When the Fourteenth Amendment was still under discussion in the Joint Committee on Reconstruction, Stevens had offered a bill to that body which he wished to have endorsed for presentation to Congress. He later decided to divide it into two separate measures. The first was entitled "A bill to provide for restoring the States lately in insurrection to their political rights." In its final reading it began with a preamble declaring that "whereas it is expedient that the States lately in insurrection should, at the earliest day consistent with the future peace and safety of the Union, be restored to full participation in all political rights," Congress had adopted the Fourteenth Amendment. It then recited the amendment, after which it made known that *"whenever the above Amendment shall have become part of the Constitution of the United States,* and any State lately in insurrection shall have ratified the same, and shall have modified its constitution and laws in conformity therewith, the Senators and Representatives from such State, if found duly elected and qualified, may, after having taken the required oaths of office, be admitted to Congress as such." [1]

It is to be noted that in its original version the bill read that if the proposal was accepted by the Southern states, they *"shall"* be admitted to Congress. The word *"may"* was substituted on motion by Fessenden. There can, therefore, be no doubt that at this juncture Stevens was willing for the Southern states to be readmitted as soon as the Fourteenth Amendment "shall have become part of the Constitution of the United States." In other words, the rebel states were to be presented with a *fait accompli.* When the amendment had been ratified by three-fourths of the loyal states, the Southern states could decide whether or not they wished to accept the amended Constitution. If they did not, they would become territories without representation either in Congress or the Electoral College until they changed their minds.

The second bill, entitled "A bill declaring certain persons ineli-

[1] Italics added.

gible to office under the Government of the United States," became, with some additions and modifications, the third section of the Fourteenth Amendment.

Both bills were approved by the committee and presented by Stevens to the House on April 30, 1866. Leaving the second bill out of the reckoning, the first came up for discussion on May 15, when the Fourteenth Amendment, recited in that bill, had already been adopted by the House. Since, however, the Senate had not yet been heard from and might decide to make some changes in the amendment, Stevens moved that consideration be postponed for two weeks —until May 29. When on the 29th the bill came before the House Stevens was ill in bed. A further ten-day postponement was voted. Finally, on June 14, when the Fourteenth Amendment had been adopted by both Houses, debate on the bill began and dragged on intermittedly until June 20. On that day Stevens rose and asked that the measure be put to a vote. A representative from Massachusetts moved that it be tabled. His motion carried.

Stevens ardently desired ratification of the Fourteenth Amendment. While far from satisfied with the change the Senate had made in the third section, he had advised his followers to accept it. The defeat of his bill confining ratification to the loyal states, would, he felt convinced, spell the defeat of the amendment. So, on July 20, a week before adjournment, he resolved to try again. He rose and said with uncommon solemnity: "I report, from the Joint Committee on Reconstruction, for consideration at the present time, a bill to provide for restoring to these States, lately in insurrection, their full political rights."

It was indeed a historic moment. Had he managed to get the bill adopted the history of the country might have been changed. He did what he could. Ill and barely able to stand he moved the adoption of the measure and asked that the bill be read. When the clerk had done so, he tried to shut off debate by moving the previous question. How often in the past had that move succeeded! This time it failed. The motion was lost by a vote of 42 to 51. Nearly half of those present had, however, abstained from voting. This gave him hope. He demanded tellers. The recount showed 41 *ayes* to 60 *noes*. He shrugged, and when a motion had been made to table the bill he voted with the majority.

3

In anticipation of defeat, which was not unexpected, Stevens had introduced House Bill No. 623, to fill in the vacuum that would be created by the defeat of his bill and the consequent defeat of the Fourteenth Amendment. It was a full-fledged Reconstruction bill providing as follows:

Existing Southern state governments were to be recognized for municipal purposes only, but no former rebel state was to be admitted to participation in the national government until it had adopted a state constitution giving equal rights to all its citizens and equal political rights to all male citizens twenty-one years old or older without distinction of race or color. Those who had held office, civil or military, under the Confederacy or had voluntarily aided the rebellion were not to be regarded as citizens. They could, however, be readmitted to citizenship on application after three years by taking a loyalty oath. "If there be any State that does not desire such organic law, let it remain in a state of pupilage until it shall have learned the elementary principles of justice and freedom," Stevens was to explain. In other words, no former rebel state was to be coerced into adopting Negro suffrage, but no such state would be readmitted to participation in the national government until it had done so.

On July 28, the last day of the session, he spoke in defense of the measure. There can be no doubt that he believed the speech to be his valedictory. He was mortally ill with what his earliest biographer has described as "dropsy of the heart and chest," and did not expect to live through the summer. He made a moving plea in behalf of justice for the Negro, saying in part:

"Notwithstanding surrounding discouragement, the exhortation, 'Be not weary in well-doing,' encourages me to make one more—perhaps an expiring—effort to do something which shall be useful to my fellow-men; something to elevate and enlighten the poor, the oppressed and the ignorant in this great crisis of human affairs. I do not feel that this august body, this grand council of a nation of freemen, has done anything worthy of its glorious opportunity, worthy of its duty to the immortal beings whose destinies for good or evil, for happiness or woe, it holds in its hands. . . . I beg it to be understood I do not claim a right to speak this reproachfully or complainingly; especially when I consider my own life, too much of which has been spent in idleness or frivolous amusement. . . . I cannot avoid feeling humbled, I cannot escape the pangs of self-condemnation.

"How precarious and worthless is that protection which depends wholly on the will of others, and leaves one's self defenseless! In a peaceful, well-governed republic, the only protection consists in the right to participate in the government. . . . They [the freedmen] must have the ballot or they will continue, virtually, to be slaves; they will be servants and tools of the rich. . . . A freeman deprived of human rights is the most degraded of human beings. . . . When this is done we shall have done but partial justice to the descendants of an oppressed race. . . . Why have we not given them homesteads? Their rebel masters owe it to them."

He was visibly moved when he said toward the close: "I have done in this matter what I deemed best for humanity. . . . I know it is easy to protect the interests of the rich and powerful; but it is a great labor to guard the rights of the poor and downtrodden; it is the eternal labor of Sisyphus forever to be renewed. I know how unprofitable is all such toil. But he who is in earnest does not heed such things. I know, too, what effect it has on personal popularity. But I will say that if there is anything for which I have entire indifference, perhaps I may say contempt, it is that public opinion which is founded on popular clamor.

"In this, perhaps my final action on this great question, upon a careful review, I can see nothing in my political course, especially in regard to human freedom, which I could wish to have expunged or changed. I believe that we must all account hereafter for deeds done in the body, and that political deeds will be among those accounts. I desire to take to the bar of that final settlement the record which I shall this day make on the great question of human rights. While I am sure it will not make atonement for half my errors, I hope it will be some palliation."

4

Secretary Seward forwarded the Fourteenth Amendment for ratification to all the states. When Governor William G. Brownlow of Tennessee received a copy, he immediately called a special meeting of the legislature. On July 20 he wired to the clerk of the Senate: "We have fought the battle and won it. We have ratified the constitutional amendment in the house—43 to 11, two of Johnson's tools not voting. Give my respects to the dead dog in the White House!"

A joint resolution was immediately offered in the House to the effect that "the State of Tennessee is hereby restored to her former, practical relations to the Union, and is again to be represented in Congress by senators and representatives duly elected and qualified upon their taking the oath of office required by existing laws." It was adopted by a vote of 125 to 12. The Senate concurred, but inserted in the preamble "said State Government can only be restored to its former political relations in the Union by the consent of the law-making power of the United States." The House did not object and the resolution was sent to the President for his signature.

Disagreeable as Johnson found it to sign a measure which asserted that only by the consent of Congress a rebel state could be readmitted to its former political relations in the Union, he could hardly veto a resolution that restored his own state to participation in the national government. In the message he forwarded with the document he commented: "My approval, however, is not to be construed as an acknowledgment of the right of Congress to pass laws preliminary to the admission of duly qualified representatives from any of the States." When this was read in the House it was greeted with derisive laughter; but the Democrats applauded and the Republicans looked annoyed when the author of the message (who was undoubtedly Seward) expressed his surprise that "while in the opinion of Congress the people of a State may be too disloyal to be entitled to representation, they may nevertheless have an equally potent voice with other States in amending the Constitution, upon which so essentially depends the stability, prosperity and very existence of the nation."

This, of course, was the manifest absurdity of the Republican position, against which Stevens had vainly protested. The Southern states had, *as states,* left the Union and had repudiated the Constitution. The fact that they had no constitutional right to do so did not do away with the fact that they had done so. To allow them to participate in deciding on what terms they should be readmitted was like allowing the accused to vote with the jury sitting in judgment over him. If they were allowed to *vote* with the jury they should also have been allowed to *deliberate* with the jury, which they were not. Johnson believed they should have been allowed to do *both,* Stevens believed they should have been allowed to do *neither.* Johnson's stand was at least consistent, which the Republican stand was not.

The Reconstruction muddle that followed was therefore the direct result of Republican inconsistency or ill-conceived strategy on the one hand, and Southern foolhardiness, encouraged by Johnson, on the other. Stevens was not responsible for either and did his utmost to counteract both. Yet history—more often the servant of politics than its mentor—has charged him with the responsibility. There can be no doubt that after Stevens's death Republican leaders, in order to exculpate themselves and their party, deliberately fostered the misrepresentation.

Stevens voted for the admission of Tennessee and in his speech on the last day of the session alluded to the matter in this fashion: "I know that two-thirds of the congressional districts [of Tennessee] will send us secessionists, which will greatly impair our two-third votes. But she has two or three men in her delegation who would have saved Sodom. In the Senate, at least, one man deserves the favor of Congress. Of the other I say nothing, as I know nothing, and I would do no injustice to one who has never done injury to me, or, as far as I know, to the country."

The man referred to was Johnson's son-in-law David T. Patterson, who had been elected to the Senate.

CHAPTER XIII

The People's Verdict

President Johnson was opposed to the Fourteenth Amendment, thereby adding another to the numerous inconsistencies in his political career. Had he not in January of that year, in an interview with Senator Dixon of Connecticut, declared himself in favor of a constitutional amendment apportioning representation among the several states "according to the number of qualified voters in each State"? Yet he was to wire to Governor Parsons of Alabama, who had telegraphed him that the rejection of the amendment by the Alabama Legislature might be reconsidered: "What possible good can be obtained by reconsidering the Constitutional Amendment? . . . There should be no faltering on the part of those who are honest in a determination to sustain the several co-ordinate Departments of the Government in accordance with its original design." [1] Since we know from Secretary McCulloch that Lincoln favored apportionment of representation in accordance with the number of qualified voters in each state, it is somewhat of an enigma upon what the claim is based that Johnson was merely attempting to carry out Lincoln's Reconstruction program. "Adopt new views if they are true views," Lincoln said once, and step by step adopted Stevens's program during the war. The new views Johnson adopted during Reconstruction had the blessing of Vallandigham, hardly a disciple of Lincoln.

The President's opposition to the Fourteenth Amendment pre-

[1] W. L. Fleming, *Documentary History of Reconstruction,* vol. I, p. 164.

cipitated a cabinet crisis. Several members of the old Lincoln cabinet had been restive for some time. Johnson's opposition to the amendment proved the last straw. The first to resign was Postmaster General William Dennison. Attorney General James Speed, brother of Joshua Speed, one of Lincoln's most intimate friends, followed a week later. A few days after that James Harlan, Secretary of the Interior, handed in his resignation. Former Vice-President Hannibal Hamlin, whom Johnson had appointed collector of customs at Boston, had already resigned. There is reason to believe that the cabinet members would have resigned sooner, but had hesitated doing so, knowing that their successors would be men who would use the enormous patronage at their disposal to promote Johnson's policy. Speed, after leaving the cabinet, denounced Johnson in no uncertain terms. "The loyal Congress of the United States," he said, "had refused to do his [Johnson's] commands; and whenever you have a Congress that does not resolutely and firmly refuse, as the present Congress has done, to merely act as the recording secretary of the tyrant at the White House, American liberty is gone forever." [2]

One who did not resign although relations between him and the President had been strained for some time, was Secretary Stanton. An eminent historian, careful in his judgments, has written that in holding on to his office he was "lacking in a proper sense of delicacy." [3] Others have been far more severe. It is no simple matter to judge a man's motives, especially those of a man like Stanton, who was a maze of contradictions. Granted that he loved power and was given to intrigue, he was nevertheless a patriot who had done invaluable service to his country. Johnson's postwar surrender to the enemies of the Union must have appeared to him little short of treasonable. Under these circumstances he might have believed it to be his duty to remain at his post.

Functionaries of lesser importance who did not resign were dismissed in large numbers. Lincoln's former secretary John Hay wrote in his diary: "It is hard for Seward to save Lincoln's friends from being pushed off their stools by hungry Copperheads; he defends them when he can." [4]

[2] Blaine, *op. cit.,* vol. II, p. 226.
[3] Burgess, *op. cit.,* p. 91.
[4] Thayer, *op. cit.,* vol. I, pp. 249-250.

2

Never before in the country's history had there been a congressional election comparable in importance to the one that took place in the autumn of 1866. Speculation about what would have happened had the outcome of this or that historical event been different is usually pointless. Yet, when during a congressional campaign popular interest far exceeds that usually aroused by a presidential canvass, it must be due to the fact that people have formed some alarming mental image of the possible consequences of a victory of the opposition. What was that image? There appear to have been two.

One possibility was that Johnson would obtain a majority in the House. If this happened there could be no doubt that the Southern representatives would be seated in the Senate as well as in the House. A sufficient number of conservative Republican senators might then desert to the administration to give the President a majority in both Houses. State laws already passed neutralizing the Thirteenth Amendment would then be sustained. The Freedmen's Bureau would be abolished, the Civil Rights law repealed. Union troops occupying the South would be withdrawn, leaving Southern loyalists and Negroes at the mercy of a hostile population. For all practical purposes slavery would be restored. Attempts would be made to recognize the Confederate debt and to compensate the slaveholders for the loss of their slaves. A feeling of frustration verging on despair would take possession of an increasing number of people in the North. If even victory on the battlefield could not free the country from domination by the Southern oligarchy, why not let the South go its own way? A powerful secession movement might spring up in the North.

Another possibility was that Johnson would not obtain a majority in the House, but that a sufficient number of representatives favorable to him would be elected who together with those Congress was refusing to seat would constitute a majority. If this happened what would prevent him from recognizing the combination as the true Congress? Was there no evidence that he and his advisers were considering such a move? Did not Frank Blair and others who contemptuously spoke of Congress as a "rump Congress" urge it upon him? Did not Johnson himself, when addressing a delegation that called upon him at the White House, refer to Congress as "a body called, or which assumes to be, the Congress of the United States, while, in fact, it is a Congress of only a part of the States, hanging, as it were, upon the verge of the government"? If he resorted to such a move would not Republican governors, senators, and representatives call the people to arms? Would not the administration meet force with force? Might not the President call upon the South for aid? Would not thousands of former Confederate officers and soldiers, thirsting for revenge, join his forces? Would not a civil war, more bloody, more ferocious than the one that had just ended be the result? Would that war not be fought in the North?

In the superior wisdom of hindsight we might scoff at such fears as exaggerated. Stevens did not believe they were. On July 20 he had risen in the House and had offered a resolution to the effect that when Congress adjourned to reconvene on December 1, it should do so subject to reconvocation prior to that date either by the President, or "by the joint call of the Presiding Officers of both Houses." "Suppose," he said, "there were a *coup d'état*. I am supposing what may well happen—what has happened in other countries and made it necessary for legislative bodies to declare themselves in session *en permanence*. Supposing anything of that kind should happen—I hope it may not, but I dread it—are we to have our hands tied, with nobody able to sound the alarm and call us together?"

The resolution did not pass, and the situation which might have tempted Johnson to attempt a *coup d'état* did not materialize. Notwithstanding serious grievances many had against the Republican party they realized that victory of that party was at that time essential to national welfare.

3

Things were happening in the South that were hardly favorable to "my policy," as Johnson was pleased to call his astonishing surrender to those whom a little while before he had threatened with wholesale execution. Before adjournment of Congress an estimated one thousand Negroes had been murdered in the South without any attempt having been made to punish the offenders. But what made a profound impression upon the people of the North were two wholesale massacres of Negroes, one not long before, the other immediately after adjournment.

The first occurred in Memphis, Tennessee, early in May, 1866. A drunken Negro soldier had wounded a policeman, whereupon a mob invaded the Negro quarter and massacred forty-six Negroes. The second took place on July 30, two days after adjournment of Congress, in New Orleans, and had an important bearing not only upon the election, but upon Reconstruction policy.

When Lincoln had reconstructed Louisiana, Southern Unionists had taken over. They elected Michael Hahn governor and held a Constitutional Convention. Having repudiated the Secession Ordinances and framed a new state constitution prohibiting slavery, the convention adjourned, but not before passing a resolution vesting the power in its presiding officer of reconvoking the convention if the constitution failed to be ratified by the people, or "for any other necessary reason."

It will be recalled that Lincoln had written a letter to Hahn recommending that the elective franchise be conferred upon the "very intelligent" among the Negroes and "especially upon those who have gallantly fought in our ranks." What may have prompted him to do so was that there was in New Orleans a class of Creole Negroes far superior in intelligence and education to the majority of whites in that state. There were among them businessmen, doctors, lawyers, architects, teachers, painters, musicians, inventors. One, Norbert Rillieux, had made an invaluable contribution to the sugar industry by his invention of the vacuum pan method of boiling sirup. His invention "laid the foundation for all modern industrial evaporation" and "revolutionized the manufacture and refining of sugar." In the Louisiana State Museum there is a commemorative plaque dedicated to him upon the solicitation of the International Society of Sugar Cane Technologists by "Corporations representing the Sugar Industry all over the world." [5]

To deny such men the right of suffrage while illiterate whites were permitted to vote was the height of absurdity. The Constitutional Convention had, however, not acted upon Lincoln's recommendation but passed it on to the legislature for consideration.

[5] "A Negro Scientist of Slavery Days," *The Scientific Monthly*, April, 1946.

When after Lincoln's death Johnson undertook his indiscriminate pardoning the legislature fell into the hands of rabid disunionists. The new state constitution, which Lincoln praised in his last speech, was termed by them in a resolution "a creature of fraud and violence and not in any sense the expression of the will of the people." [6] They then proceeded to adopt a Black Code that surpassed in viciousness any enacted in the former rebel states.

Louisiana Unionists as well as Negroes felt bitter about the matter and the former decided that "a necessary reason" existed for reconvoking the Constitutional Convention. Whether they meant to amend the constitution by conferring the elective franchise upon all colored people in the state or meant to follow Lincoln's advice is not known. That there should have been a considerable sentiment among law-abiding people in New Orleans for the extension of the suffrage to the better class of Negroes appears probable. For many years before the war the city had been in the grip of a corrupt and ruthless political machine. In its issue of May 6, 1860, the New Orleans *Delta* had declared: "For seven years the world knows that this city, in all its departments, judicial, Legislative and Executive, has been at the absolute disposal of the most godless, brutal, ignorant, and worthless ruffians the world has ever heard of since the day of the great Roman conspirator. . . . The electoral system is a farce and a fraud; the knife, the sling-shot, the brass knuckles determining who shall occupy and administer the offices of the municipality and the Commonwealth."

In 1862 General Butler had occupied the city and had given it the best administration it had known for years. When he had been recalled the city had still for a while been ruled by the military, but after the war the machine had taken over. In 1866, John F. Monroe—who had been mayor when Butler arrived and whom the General had imprisoned in a fortress—was again in the saddle. His chief of police was also chief of the Knights of the White Camelia, a "white supremacy" organization not unlike the Ku Klux Klan. Under these circumstances it is hardly surprising that many citizens should have reached the conclusion that reputable Negroes might be of assistance in helping to deliver the city from organized ruffianism. That the sentiment must have been widespread is evident from the dither into

[6] *Globe,* Feb. 12, 1867. Document cited by Shellabarger of Ohio.

which news of the reconvocation of the Constitutional Convention threw the city administration. Why otherwise should they have been so disturbed, since any amendment to the constitution the convention might have adopted would have had to be submitted for ratification to the voters, all of whom were white.

The Governor, a Unionist, favored reconvocation. The Lieutenant Governor and the Attorney General sided with the Mayor. Judicial proceedings were instituted to stop the gathering, but had not yet produced results when on July 30 the convention assembled in the Mechanics' Institute Building. A large force of police was on hand as well as a considerable crowd of raffish-looking adherents of the city authorities, but no attempt was made to hinder the delegates from assembling.

About an hour later an orderly procession of Negroes, demonstrating in favor of the extension of suffrage, came marching by. The crowd greeted them with jeers. Suddenly a shot rang out. The authorities were to claim that it was fired by a Negro, but no reliable proof exists. It had all the appearance of a prearranged signal, for police and onlookers immediately threw themselves upon the marchers, who appear to have been deliberately herded into the building where the convention was meeting. All but a few were inside when the police began firing at the windows, from one of which presently a white flag was hung. The policemen now rushed inside "with shouts and hurrahs for Jefferson Davis and Andrew Johnson" [7] and for half an hour or more those outside heard sounds of firing. When the firing ceased forty-eight Negroes lay dead and almost three times that number were wounded, many of them fatally. That the Negroes were unarmed is evident from the fact that only five policemen were slightly injured.

General Philip H. Sheridan, military commander of the department, officially reported that "the killing was in a manner so unnecessary and atrocious as to compel me to say it was murder." No action of any kind was taken against any member of the police force, but criminal proceedings were instituted against members of the convention on the theory that "whoever engaged in an unlawful proceeding from which death ensues to a human being, is guilty of murder." [8]

[7] *Ibid.*

[8] Blaine, *op. cit.*, vol. II, pp. 235-236.

The New Orleans massacre, and even more the failure of constituted authorities to proceed against the perpetrators, did much to convince Congress that to permit the Southern state governments to remain in disloyal hands meant not only to court national disaster, but was a crime against loyal Southerners and freedmen.

4

The congressional campaign of 1866 received its impetus from no less than four national conventions, two of which were soldiers' and sailors' conventions. The first to meet was the National Union Convention, organized by Johnson's supporters in both parties, which assembled on August 14 in the Wigwam in Philadelphia. Greeley claimed in the New York *Tribune* that it was "composed of ninety per cent rebels and copperheads." There was, however, a small contingent of Administration Republicans, headed by Henry J. Raymond and Senator Doolittle. They made up in activity what they lacked in numbers. Doolittle became permanent chairman, while Raymond not only made the keynote speech, but wrote the Convention's Declaration of Principles and its Address to the People.

Copperheads were out in force, but the two most notorious, Vallandigham of Ohio and Fernando Wood of New York, although well provided with credentials, were asked, for the good of the cause, to withdraw without making a protest, which they obligingly did. The prize exhibit were the Southern delegates, among whom was the former vice-president of the Confederacy, Alexander H. Stephens, and several former Confederate generals. James L. Orr of South Carolina, former speaker of the house, came walking down the aisle arm in arm with General Couch of Massachusetts, whereupon, we are told, "every eye was flooded with tears." This was a promotional blunder, and the Republicans made the most of it. The Convention promptly became known as the "Arm-in-Arm Convention." The delegates were pictured weeping and a Republican wit dubbed the Wigwam "Noah's Ark," into which "the animals entered two by two, the elephant and the kangaroo, of clean beasts and of beasts that are not clean, and of fowl and of everything that creepeth upon the earth."

It is sad to be obliged to report that General John A. Dix, temporary chairman of the convention, was soon to complain bitterly that the Democrats had broken faith and had appropriated the new party—that Raymond, the keynoter, was to fall out with Johnson and was to write: "We have tried hard to hold our original faith in his personal honesty, and to attribute his disastrous action to errors of judgment and infirmities of temper. The struggle has often been difficult, and we can maintain it no longer. We give it up," [9] and that Orr, the "arm-in-armer" eventually went over to the Radicals and was promptly dubbed a "scallawag" by his Southern colleagues.

On September 3 there met, again in Philadelphia, a convention of Southern loyalists. They invited Northern loyalists to send delegates and the response was quite satisfying. It was decided, however, that the latter should meet in a separate hall so the deliberations of the Southerners could be untrammeled. There was a constant interchange of speakers. James Speed of Kentucky, former attorney general in Lincoln's and in Johnson's cabinets, presided over the Southerners, who adopted a resolution condemning Johnson's policy. "After declaring that none but the loyal should govern the reconstructed South," said the resolution, "he has practiced upon the maxim that none but traitors shall rule." That the disloyal had regained power in the South was ascribed by them to Johnson's indiscriminate pardoning. While this undoubtedly had great influence upon the situation, the bitterness engendered by the war makes it appear doubtful if for some years to come Unionists could have been elected in the South unless the freedmen were given the right of suffrage or a considerable number of white Southerners were temporarily disfranchised. Stevens had a true understanding of the situation when he said: "I regret that the loyal men of these States cannot be brought in, but they cannot be brought in with a rebel constituency behind them. They would misrepresent their States. Therefore I cannot agree to let them in under the present state of affairs. Let us have probation; let us be sure something more than mere willingness to come in has been felt by them." [10]

Friends of the administration countered by calling a Soldiers' Convention in Cleveland on September 17. Few soldiers attended, but a number of the proslavery general officers who had got Lincoln into

[9] Augustus Maverick, *Henry J. Raymond and the New York Press*, p. 174.
[10] *Globe*, May 10, 1866.

trouble with Congress, by driving back fugitive slaves who sought refuge with the army or permitting rebel slaveholders or their agents to come into their camps and pick out slaves belonging to them, were present.

By far the most impressive of the conventions was the Soldiers' and Sailors' Convention in Pittsburgh on September 25 and 26. This time noncommissioned officers and soldiers turned out in force. Some twenty-five thousand took part in the proceedings. They had come from as far as California and Nevada, with which there was then no communication by rail. They passed stinging resolutions condemning the administration and pledging their support to Congress.

More than any Republican campaigner Johnson himself furthered the cause of Congress. In the spring of that year he had accepted an invitation to lay the cornerstone of a monument to be erected in Chicago for Stephen A. Douglas. The ceremony was to take place on September 6, and he decided to make use of the opportunity to "swing around the circle," speak in the principal cities and towns, enlighten the populace on "my policy," and castigate his opponents. He left Washington on August 28, in the company of Secretaries Welles and Randall (the new postmaster general), General Grant, Admiral Farragut, and half a hundred others. Seward was to join the party in New York.

I have given an account of the speaking tour in my volume *Two Friends of Man* and will not do so now. Suffice it to say that it was a disgraceful performance. Rhodes has called it an "indecent orgy" and has asserted as a positive fact that in Cleveland, where Johnson exclaimed, "Why not hang Thad Stevens and Wendell Phillips!" he was intoxicated. Johnson's principal biographer has denied this, but if the denial is accepted, then Johnson's behavior was even more to his discredit. In Cleveland, St. Louis, Indianapolis, and sundry other places he exchanged insults with the crowd. His well-wishers devoutly hoped that something would happen that would force him to quit. His enemies wished he would go on until election. Many, irrespective of party, felt a twinge of shame at presidential dignity being brought down to the level of a barroom brawl. The amazing thing is that he appears to have been blissfully oblivious to the impression he was making, although boys in the street were shouting: "I, me and mine!" and "I'll my-policy you!" He had done that sort of campaigning in the backwoods of Tennessee and had found it quite effective. He returned to Washington confident that the people would sustain him at the polls.

5

During all this time Stevens remained in his own congressional district, dividing his time between Lancaster and Bedford Springs, where he often went to take the water. His popularity was immense. He was the idol of the "boys in blue." At a soldiers' convention in Pittsburgh in June of that year a Pennsylvania delegate who had risen to speak prefaced his remarks by saying that he had the honor to represent the "home of Thaddeus Stevens." Instantly the entire convention rose to its feet and cheer after cheer went up for "Old Thad." [11] When Rufus P. Spalding of Ohio, a conservative Republican who often clashed with Stevens, was accused of being a "Johnsonite" and it appeared certain that the party would refuse to renominate him, he knew that only one thing could save him—a letter of endorsement from Stevens. He asked Stevens for such a letter and the Commoner sent it. He was renominated and elected and continued to oppose Stevens.

Thad did little campaigning. The doctor had forbidden him to do any public speaking during the recess, in fact to do anything but rest. He could not, however, remain altogether silent. On September 4 he made a speech in Bedford. There can be no doubt that he wished to prepare the country for the eventuality that when Congress reassembled Negro suffrage might have to be voted. He made it plain that he believed in it in principle, reminding his listeners that in 1838, when a member of the Constitutional Convention, he had refused to sign the new state constitution because it deprived the Negro of the right to vote. "The great issue to be met in this election is the question of negro rights," he said. "I shall not deny, but admit, that a fundamental principle of the Republican creed is that every being possessing an immortal soul is equal before the law. This doctrine of human equality may be unpopular with besotted ignorance. But, popular or unpopular, I shall stand by it until I am relieved of the unprofitable labors of earth. Being the foundation of

[11] *Stevens MSS.* S. Brisbin to Stevens, June 15, 1866.

our Republic I have full faith in its ultimate triumph. I may not live to see it. I may not be worthy of such happiness. If it is to be defeated and the hopes of man thus extinguished, I pray God that when it happens I may be insensible to human misery; that my senses may be locked in 'cold obstruction and in death.' "[12]

On September 23, at Lancaster, he spoke in a lighter vein. His physician, he said, had forbidden him to think, to speak, or to read until the next session of Congress so he might regain his strength. He had obeyed the first injunction religiously, had tried to obey the second until seduced by some friends to speak in Bedford, and the third almost literally. "It is true, I have amused myself with a little light frivolous reading. I have taken up the dailies and publications of that kind, and read things that would make no impression on my mind. For instance, there was a serial account from day to day of a very remarkable circus that traveled through the country, from Washington to Chicago and St. Louis, and Louisville back to Washington. I read that with some interest, expecting great wit from the celebrated character of its clowns. . . . They started out with a very respectable company. In order to attract attention they took with them, for instance, a celebrated general; they took with them an eminent naval officer, and they chained him to the rigging so that he could not get away, though he tried to do so once or twice.

"I am not following them all round. I shall not describe to you how sometimes they cut outside the circle and entered into street broils with common blackguards; how they fought at Cleveland and Indianapolis, and other points, I shall not tell you; for is it not all written in Colonel Forney's *Chronicle?*

"But, coming round, they told you, or one of them did, that he had been everything but one. He had been a tailor, I think he did not say drunken tailor; no, he had been a tailor. He had been a constable. He had been city alderman. He had been in the Legislature. God help that Legislature. He had been in Congress and now he was President. He had been everything but one—he had never been a hangman, and he asked leave to hang Thad Stevens."[13]

The speech was constantly interrupted by applause. When he came

[12] New York *Times,* Sept. 5, 1866.
[13] E. B. Callender, *Thaddeus Stevens,* pp. 58-61.

to the last part almost every sentence was received with roars of laughter.

In the fall elections of 1866 the Republicans swept everything before them. In New York the Republican majority was about double Lincoln's in 1864. Illinois went Republican by fifty-six thousand votes. Michigan and Iowa sent solid Republican delegations to Congress. Pennsylvania elected eighteen Republicans against six Democrats; Ohio sixteen against three. Indiana, a doubtful state, went Republican by fifteen thousand votes. New Jersey, traditionally Democratic, elected a majority of Republicans to the House. California and Oregon went Republican. Only three border states—Delaware, Kentucky, and Maryland—went Democratic; the Republicans carried Missouri and West Virginia. One hundred and forty-three Republicans were elected against forty-nine Democrats, giving the Republicans almost a three-fourths majority in the House.

CHAPTER XIV

The South Scorns the Proffered Hand

When in November, 1866, Stevens returned to Washington for the second session of the Thirty-ninth Congress, he was nearing his seventy-fifth birthday. Physically he was a ruin. On the journey to the capital he was overcome by weakness to such an extent that a bed had to be spread out for him on the floor of the coach. After a few days' rest he rallied, and when before the opening of the session the victorious Republicans held a banquet, he was able to attend. The chairman called on him to respond to the principal toast. As he rose to his feet the hall rang with cheers and applause. And well it might! He was the pilot who had saved the ship of state from foundering upon the rocks toward which its incompetent captain had sought to steer it. The people of the North had overwhelmingly endorsed his action.

We are told that the speech he made at the banquet was worth listening to. Few, however, were able to hear it. He had difficulty breathing and his voice did not carry far. When he made his first speech during the session the effort exhausted him so that on his return home he fainted in his study. It became increasingly difficult for him to climb the steps to the Capitol and arrangements were made for two husky young Negroes to carry him up in an armchair. One day when they were carrying him he said to them with sardonic humor: "Who will carry me boys when you are dead and gone?" It was not unusual with him to joke about his impending end. When Maynard of Tennessee expressed his regret on the floor of the House that Stevens "did not find it convenient to become one of the party on a recent occasion to spend the holidays in that part of the country," the Commoner replied: "Well, sir, I had made no preparations for a burial down there." [1] Yet it was upon this dying man that more than ever before the task devolved of steering the ship of state upon its hazardous journey.

During the early part of the session he was not only busy with legislative matters but was pursuing a personal ambition. In January, 1867, the Pennsylvania Legislature was to choose a senator. The previous summer John W. Forney, publisher of two influential newspapers and clerk of the Senate, had come out for him in a truly enthusiastic fashion. Stevens took the bait. Why he should have wanted the office is a psychological enigma. His influence in national affairs was infinitely greater than that of any senator. Had he realized his ambition that influence would not have increased but diminished. The rules of the Senate differed considerably from those of the House. With all his consummate parliamentary skill he could not have guided the course of legislation there as he did in the lower chamber. Most Republican newspapers, however, were of the opinion that he had a right to the office if he wanted it and supported his candidacy.

He was urged by his friends to come to Harrisburg and solicit support, but he felt disinclined to do so. He knew the Pennsylvania Legislature to be notoriously corrupt. The office would go to the highest bidder. His principal rival was the archcorruptionist Simon Cameron, and Stevens had neither the means nor the inclination to compete with him in that sort of electioneering. He wrote to one of his supporters: "To solicit votes for the office of Senator is repugnant to all my ideas of propriety. In that high office the Legislature ought to be left uninfluenced by solicitation *or any more substantial arguments.*" In the end he went anyway, but found the situation hopeless. Forney, who accompanied him on the journey, has related that Stevens said to one of those who had promised to support him but had apparently succumbed to "more substantial arguments": "You must be a bastard, for I knew your mother's husband and he was a gentleman and an honest man." [2]

[1] *Globe,* Jan. 5, 1867.
[2] *Anecdotes of Public Men,* vol. II, p. 181.

During the holiday recess Stevens had gone to Chambersburg to solicit the support of Alexander K. McClure. That able lawyer, journalist, and politician was amazed that a man in Stevens's position should want the office. "I appealed to him," he has written, "to dismiss the thought of being Senator; reminded him that any ordinary Congressman might reasonably be ambitious to reach the highest legislative tribunal of the nation, but for a man who was the recognized Commoner of the nation during the greatest period of its history, and who was undisputed and absolute leader, to accept a seat in the Senate, would be to give up the highest honors the nation can accord to any one, and descend to the position of a Senator, where he would be no greater than most of his fellows." [3]

2

As Stevens had predicted, the South rejected the Fourteenth Amendment in a peremptory fashion. By the first of the year only three Southern states had not yet been heard from and no one doubted what their verdict would be. In the end the record was as follows: the Florida, Mississippi, and Louisiana legislatures rejected the amendment unanimously; Virginia and South Carolina each gave it one vote, Georgia two, Arkansas three, and Texas five; Alabama gave it ten out of one hundred and six, and North Carolina eleven out of one hundred and forty-eight. Certainly there was no mistaking the attitude of the South toward congressional Reconstruction in its mildest form. The South acted in this matter exactly as it had toward Lincoln's proposal of compensated gradual emancipation with federal aid and was to be just as indignant about the consequences of its own intransigence.

During the debate on the measure Senator Dixon had summed up the South's probable attitude toward the amendment in these words: "It is hardly worth while to discuss the merits of measures which to be valid must be accepted by communities which are sure to reject them. . . . Does any one believe that the Southern States will accept the proposed constitutional amendment? Certainly they will decline it. They will say, 'Let us see what the next elections in the North develop. This Congress may recommend the Amendment; the next

[3] *Old Time Notes of Pennsylvania,* pp. 206-207.

Congress . . . may be of a different mind. It may repeal all that this Congress has enacted; we had better wait.' . . . The Amendment proposed is right enough, if the Joint Committee can get any southern State to accept it. But unless they do so it is only a shot in the air, which may be right and true, but will hit nowhere—unless it falls upon the heads of the gunners." [4]

This indeed was the crux of the matter. Postwar readjustment difficulties were beginning to make themselves felt in the North and were bound to grow worse. Many would ascribe them to the failure of Congress to settle the Reconstruction problem. Thus the presidential election in 1868 might result in a Democratic victory. If this happened the South's troubles would be over. The Southern states would be admitted to participation in the national government with increased, not decreased, representation. So Southern politicians were sitting pretty. The result of the fall elections had not discouraged them. They figured that all they had to do was wait.

It was not a bad calculation so far as it went, but it did not go far enough. It left an important factor out of the reckoning. *While the South could afford to wait, loyalists could not afford to wait.* Republican leaders had not been blinded by their recent victory. They knew that time was on the side of their opponents. If the Democrats won in 1868 and admitted the Southern states with an increased representation, it might well mean "perpetual ascendancy" of the Democratic party. That that party would henceforth receive the solid support of the South appeared certain, but this was not all. Now that the war was over the former slaveholders were again in the ascendancy in the border states and seemed determined to make common cause with the South. This meant that to a far greater extent than before the war the Democratic party would be dominated by the former slave states. Stevens's friend Glenni W. Scofield of Pennsylvania pointed out the political significance of this in a speech in the House. He said that owing to the presence of four and a half million nonvoting Negroes in the former slave states, eight million whites living in those states "would have thirty-two Representatives in the Senate, *and five more would give them a majority.* They would have ninety-seven members in the House, *and thirty more would give them a majority here.*" [5]

[4] *Globe*, May 2, 1866.

[5] *Globe*, Jan. 28, 1867.

No sensible man will deny that to have allowed such a situation to develop a few years after one of the bloodiest wars in history, of which slavery had been the cause, would have been inexcusable. For years to come the country would have been ruled by the representatives of a reactionary minority. The vanquished would have lorded it over the victors. The past would have triumphed over the present and over the future. Slavery, in a different but crueler form, would have been re-established. Something had to be done to prevent all this. It was not merely a question of saving the Republican party, but of saving the American ideal as expressed in the Declaration of Independence. That many of the saviors were unworthy is true, but so were many of those responsible for the American Revolution. Social forces use men both good and bad for ends that may be the one or the other.

3

Now that the Fourteenth Amendment had been rejected by the South what mode of procedure remained at the disposal of Congress? The fact is that when Congress rejected Stevens's thesis that the Southern states had forfeited their membership in the Union and that therefore their assistance was not needed for ratification, it had maneuvered itself into a position where it had only two alternatives: (1) It had to run the risk of having to turn over the federal government at an early date to those who had tried to destroy it; (2) it must resort to martial law, Negro suffrage, and temporary disfranchisement of those responsible for the rebellion to secure ratification. If there was still another method by means of which ratification could have been secured, Stevens's critics have kept it a well-guarded secret. He employed the only method left him. If responsibility has been thrown upon him the move is wholly political and has nothing to do with history.

That some of the responsibility devolves upon Lincoln is undeniable. It was he who had implanted in the public mind the idea of the indestructibility of statehood under any and all circumstances. In his last speech he had said that ratification of the Thirteenth Amendment in the manner Stevens proposed "would be questionable, and be persistently questioned." Constitutional authorities, of whom Professor Burgess is one, have denied this. Lincoln's responsibility, however, is a minor one. Had he lived there can be no doubt that he would have reversed himself as he had done on many previous occasions. Stevens must have felt convinced of this, for he never blamed Lincoln. On the contrary, in his speech on confiscation he said of him: "There is no danger that the highest praise that the most devoted friends could bestow on him would ever be reversed by posterity. So solid was the material of which his whole character was formed that the more it is rubbed the brighter it shines." [6]

It has been charged that Republicans in Congress welcomed rejection of the Fourteenth Amendment since it gave them an opportunity to confer the elective franchise upon the Negro. This was undoubtedly true of some, but not of the great majority. It was not true of Stevens. Giving Southern politicians credit for more acumen than they proved to possess, he had, in January, 1866, expressed the fear that Negro suffrage might merely result in increasing their power. In February, 1867, he was again to express that fear and tried to delay adoption of the measure. In March of the same year, in his speech on confiscation, he once more emphasized that a few acres of land would mean more to the freedmen than the immediate right to vote. Johnson was not altogether a tyro in politics, and he had Seward to advise him. If he had had any reason to believe that Stevens was anxious for the Fourteenth Amendment to be defeated so he might confer the elective franchise upon the freedmen, would he have advised the Southern states to reject it?

[6] *Globe,* March 19, 1867.

CHAPTER XV

Consequences of Southern Intractability

In a speech to his constituents in September, 1866, Stevens had said concerning Negro suffrage—then called "impartial" suffrage: "I am for it, first because it is right; second, because it protects our brethren there; third, because it prevents the States from going into the hands of rebels, giving them the President and Congress for the next forty years. When Congress meets, I will support it with all my might." [1]

This was a departure from his former stand on the matter. His conversion was, however, by no means as immediate and complete as one would infer from the above statement. When Congress met in December, 1866, he was still hesitating. This is evident from a Reconstruction bill for North Carolina he introduced on December 13. The measure called for impartial suffrage, but qualified it for both races. Only those able to read and write or owning real estate to the assessed value of one hundred dollars or more were to be permitted to vote and to be elected to office, but loyal men who had voted before would not be disfranchised. Certain categories of rebels were, however, to be excluded. The editor of the *Nation* said concerning the measure: "Mr. Stevens's bill would, a year ago, have looked horribly radical; but there is now little question that it is, supposing the [Fourteenth] Amendment to fail, the most sensible and conservative plan yet submitted to the public—and we may add that it, or something like it, is according to present appearances, pretty sure in

[1] Lancaster *Daily Evening Express,* Sept. 29, 1866.

the end to be adopted not for North Carolina only, but for all the States." [2]

Stevens's gradual conversion to immediate unrestricted suffrage for all loyal men irrespective of race or color, his hesitancy concerning the matter, and contradictory statements he made during this period, are strongly reminiscent of Lincoln's agony when he had to reach a decision on immediate general emancipation. Both men were forced by Southern intractability to resort to measures to which they would have preferred not to resort.

Stevens's decision to fight for unrestricted impartial suffrage was motivated primarily by the imperative necessity of keeping the federal government from falling, shortly after the war, into the hands of a political combination dominated by the former slave states. It was a necessity imperative from a national no less than a party viewpoint. Had he placed his superb talents of parliamentary leadership at the service of the Johnson-Seward Reconstruction program, that program might have triumphed, but its triumph might well have proved a greater disaster than the loss of the war. Military defeat would have meant Southern independence, but not domination of the entire country by an embittered, vengeful, and reactionary landed aristocracy. There may come a time when the country will realize that it owes almost as much to Stevens for his leadership in that struggle as it owes to Lincoln for his leadership during the war.

2

While the prevention of the formation of a political rock of Sisyphus that would have impeded the country's progress for generations to come was the prime reason for Stevens's decision, the plight of Southern loyalists and freedmen was likewise an important factor. Clemenceau wrote to his paper: "The whole region has become impossible as a dwelling place for those who believe in the Union. I have a friend among those ranks, a man who has lived many years in Louisiana, and made a fortune and a fine position for himself by his work. He has had to go into voluntary exile, because he was ostracised for his 'loyalist' feelings." [3]

[2] *The Nation,* Dec. 20, 1866.
[3] *Op. cit.,* p. 83.

Ostracism was but a minor annoyance compared with other outrages inflicted upon Unionists in the South. They were shot from ambush, assaulted, their houses or barns were burned, their windows broken, their cattle stolen, their fruit trees felled, their wells filled with manure, their children derided and often mistreated by former playmates. Complaints made to state or local authorities were coldly and often sneeringly received. Indeed, in some cases the authorities themselves were the guilty parties. Many, in fear of their lives, abandoned their property and sought refuge in the North. In Washington they besieged administrative offices and the halls of Congress imploring that something be done.

As for the freedmen, their suffering, according to John Eaton, general superintendent of freedmen, "in many cases must have far exceeded that which they had experienced in bondage." [4] Carl Schurz, in his report to the President, had written: "Wherever I go—the street, the shop, the house, the hotel, or the steamboat—I hear the people talk in such a way as to indicate that they are yet unable to conceive of the Negro as possessing any rights at all. . . . To kill a Negro they do not deem murder; to debauch a Negro woman, they do not think fornication; to take property from a Negro they do not consider robbery. The people boast that when they get freedmen's affairs in their own hands, to use their own expression, 'the niggers will catch hell.' "

There was every reason to believe they would "catch hell" to a far greater extent than they already did. The military commanders had forbidden the enforcement of some of the Black Codes the reconstructed legislatures had adopted. But the laws remained on the statute books to be enforced as soon as the military had departed. There was, for example, the bill known as "A bill providing for the punishment of vagrants," enacted by the legislature of Virginia. Major General A. H. Terry, military commander of the district, gave the following reasons for putting a stop to its enforcement: "In many counties of this State meetings of employers had been held and unjust and wrongful combinations have been entered into for the purpose of depressing the wages of the freedmen below the real value of their labor, far below the prices formerly paid to masters for labor

[4] *Op. cit.*, p. 207.

performed by their slaves. By reason of these combinations wages utterly inadequate to the support of themselves and their families have, in many places, become the usual and common wages of the freedmen."

Such things were of course not uncommon in the North, but the bill to which the General objected was peculiarly Southern. It provided that if a Negro refused to work for the wages offered him he was to be arrested as a "vagrant" and hired out "for a term not exceeding three months . . . for the best wages which can be procured, his wages to be applied to the support of himself and his family." If during the time of his enforced labor he ran away and was apprehended, he was returned to the custody of the employer, "who shall then have, *free of any further hire,* the services of such vagrant for one month in addition to the original terms of hiring, and that the employer shall then have power, if authorized by a justice of the peace, *to work such vagrant with ball and chain.*"

General Terry commented: "The ultimate effect of the statute will be to reduce the freedmen to a condition of servitude worse than that from which they have been emancipated, a condition which will be slavery in all but its name." [5]

In Florida another method was used. There the Thirteenth Amendment was circumvented by taking advantage of the clause "except as a punishment for crime whereof the party shall have been duly convicted." The legislature enacted a law providing that a person convicted of assault and battery may be sold into bondage for twenty years. A white man would jostle a Negro, seize him, and with the assistance of one or two of his friends take him to the nearest magistrate and accuse him of having assaulted him. His friends would confirm the accusation. Within fifteen minutes the Negro would be doomed to slavery for twenty years. Employees of the Freedmen's Bureau testified that they had witnessed six such convictions in a single afternoon. Hundreds of men were in this manner returned to slavery in that state.[6]

[5] *Globe,* March 10, 1866. Cited by Godlove S. Orth of Indiana.
[6] *Globe,* May 14, 1868. Cited by Stevens.

3

One will say that all this was but the result of an extraordinary situation produced by a disastrous war and the freeing of millions of slaves; that it would soon have corrected itself and did not justify congressional intervention. The fatuity of this argument is easily demonstrable.

In April, 1921, more than two generations after the war, Governor Hugh M. Dorsey of Georgia, a few weeks before the expiration of his second term of office, published a pamphlet entitled *The Negro in Georgia*. He writes: "In some counties the Negro is driven out as though he were a wild beast. In others he is being held as a slave. In others no Negroes remain. In only a few cases was there any prosecution of white men guilty of attacking Negroes. Acquittal or light fines are the usual result of trials." He gives one hundred and thirty-five case histories of Negroes who were lynched, wantonly slain, or horribly maltreated in his state during a period of two years and comments: "If conditions indicated by these charges should continue, both God and man would justly condemn Georgia more severely than men and God have condemned Belgium and Leopold for Congo atrocities." He further informs us that "in only two cases cited is the usual crime against white women involved." The Governor had been in office three years and eleven months. There can be no doubt of his desire to correct the situation. The publication of the pamphlet shows that he was not devoid of moral courage. One can only reach the conclusion that the disposition of the great majority of the people in his state at that time made it impossible for him to take any effective action.

William H. Skaggs of Alabama, in his work *The Southern Oligarchy,* published in 1924, makes it abundantly clear that conditions in other Southern states at that time differed little if at all from those described by the Governor of Georgia.

The Swedish novelist Frederika Bremer, who visited the United States in 1849, wrote in one of her letters: "That which the North testifies against the South I will not believe; but that which the South testifies against itself I am compelled to believe." [7] If such were con-

[7] *America of the Fifties: Letters,* p. 110.

ditions in the South in 1924, more than two generations after conclusion of armed hostilities, what must they have been shortly after the war? And if a well-disposed executive like Governor Dorsey had found it impossible so many years later to protect the colored people in his state, what could have been expected from the far from well-disposed public officials elected in the South under Johnsonian Reconstruction?

The *Nation, Harper's Weekly,* the *Atlantic Monthly,* the New York *Tribune* were filled with accounts of every variety of persecution of Unionists and Negroes in the South. The records of the Freedmen's Bureau tell the same story. Stevens, Sumner, and every other senator and representative known to be sympathetic, received innumerable letters from the South begging for relief. Is it any wonder that Stevens should have reached the conclusion that to allow this state of affairs to continue while the South awaited a victory of its friends in the North so it could have even a freer hand at persecution, would be a national disgrace? Since it was obvious that the military could not effectively protect Unionists and Negroes without the co-operation of the civil authorities, disloyal men must be driven from office and loyal men put in their places. Only impartial suffrage and the temporary disfranchisement of those responsible for the rebellion could accomplish this. True that 95 per cent of the freedmen were illiterate, but so were many of the poor whites. True that a risk was involved, but was there no risk involved in leaving one-third of the nation in disloyal hands? White loyalists and educated Negroes could do the governing, the freedmen could supply the votes. Yet Stevens hesitated, as the introduction of his North Carolina bill on December 13, 1866, which would have enfranchised only a small part of the Negro population of that state, plainly shows. But four days later something happened that convinced him of the necessity of stern and immediate action.

4

On December 17 came the news that the Supreme Court had handed down a decision in *Ex parte Milligan* refusing to support the policy of "arbitrary arrests," by declaring illegal a military trial of a civilian while the federal courts were "open and unobstructed." Whatever may be said in support of that decision, the fact remains that in the existing circumstances it meant turning over Southern Unionists and Negroes defenseless to the rage of their enemies. Bingham, leader of the Conservatives in the House, was to say: "Without a statute expressly authorizing it, no common law crime as such, is indictable in the courts of the United States. Therefore I say, for the burning of the property of a citizen, for the murder of a private citizen, for the robbery of a private citizen, or for any other crime whatever against the person or property of a private citizen, committed in any State of this Union, the party is not indictable now and never was indictable in any court of the United States." [8] If the military authorities could not prosecute people for such crimes against Unionists and Negroes, and if the civil authorities either would not or dared not do so, what protection did the loyal portion of the South's population have against the rage of the disloyal?

On December 19, two days after the court made its pronouncement, Stevens, in order to speed up proceedings, bypassed the Joint Committee on Reconstruction by means of a parliamentary maneuver and presented a Reconstruction bill to the House. The measure provided as follows:

Existing reconstructed state governments would be recognized for municipal purposes only. Conventions were to be held at a specified date to form state governments and frame new state constitutions, which must be submitted for ratification by the people. No constitution would be approved by Congress "which denies to any citizen any rights, privileges or immunities which are granted to any other citizen in the States. All laws shall be impartial, without regard to language, race or former condition." All male citizens above the age of twenty-one who had resided one year or more in the state, were entitled to vote and were eligible to office. Those who had held office, civil or military, under the Confederacy, or who had sworn allegiance to the Confederate government, had forfeited their citizenship and could neither vote nor were eligible to office. They could, however, five years after they had declared their intention to be reinvested with the rights of citizenship, become citizens by taking a prescribed oath of allegiance.

If anyone believes that in demanding the forfeiture of the rights

[8] *Globe*, Feb. 7, 1867.

of citizenship for a period of five years on the part of the principal supporters of the rebellion was a vengeful gesture. let him consider that a measure providing for the forfeiture of citizenship—not for five years but for all time—on the part of those guilty of merely advocating the overthrow of the government by force was but recently contemplated by Congress, and abandoned only because doubt existed concerning its constitutionality.

The fact is that in the matter of Negro suffrage in states where Negroes were numerous and for the most part illiterate, Stevens had acted with almost as much caution as had Lincoln in the matter of emancipation. He at first proposed that the matter be left entirely to the states, whom he wished to prod with the Fourteenth Amendment to educate the freedmen and eventually grant them the elective franchise. He had even expressed the hope that they would not be too hasty in granting them that right, as men unaccustomed to freedom were likely to take orders from their former masters in the matter of voting, which would not be productive of progressive legislation, either state or federal. When the legalism of conservative Republicans and the intransigence of Southern politicians had shipwrecked this statesmanlike proposal, he had, in his Reconstruction bill for North Carolina, proposed that the right of suffrage of whites as well as Negroes be restricted to those who could read and write or owned real estate assessed at one hundred dollars or more. The unwillingness or inability of Southern elected officials to protect Unionists and freedmen against persecution of the most atrocious character, combined with the decision of the Supreme Court depriving them of what protection they had been receiving from the military, finally decided him that the loyal people of the South must be furnished a means of self-defense—impartial suffrage. We shall see, however, that in the end he again hesitated and decided to be content with temporary military rule for the South, undoubtedly in the hope of being able to place the Southern states under territorial government, which he had advocated from the beginning of Reconstruction. Under that form of government the federal authorities would have been able to intervene whenever necessary to maintain order, public schools could have been established throughout the South, and Negro suffrage could have been introduced gradually. This, too, was frustrated by the desire of the Conservatives to be able to count on the electoral votes of the South in the presidential election the following year.

It is by this policy and by measures he advocated during the war—nearly all of which Lincoln finally adopted and praised after first having opposed them—that Stevens should be judged historically, not by a few intemperate remarks made in the heat of debate.

5

On January 3, 1867, immediately after the holiday recess, Stevens spoke in support of his bill.

"The late decision of the Supreme Court of the United States," he said, "has rendered immediate action by Congress upon the question of the establishment of governments in the rebel States absolutely indispensable. . . . That decision has taken away every protection in every one of these rebel States from every loyal man who resides there. That decision has unsheathed the dagger of the assassin, and places the knife of the rebel at the throat of every man who dares proclaim himself to be now, or to have been heretofore, a loyal Union man. . . . Unless Congress proceeds at once to adopt some means for their protection, I ask you and every man who loves liberty whether we will not be liable to the just censure of the world for our negligence or our cowardice or our want of ability to do so?

"There are several reasons for the passage of this bill. In the first place, it is just. . . . Have not loyal blacks quite as good a right to choose rulers and make laws as rebel whites? In the second place, it is a necessity in order to protect the loyal white men in the seceded States. The white Union men are in a great minority in each of those States. With them the blacks would act in a body; and it is believed that in each of said States, except one, the two united would form a majority, control the States and protect themselves. Now they are victims of daily murder. They must suffer constant persecution or be exiled.

"Another good reason is, it would insure the ascendancy of the Union party. Do you avow the party purpose? exclaims some horror stricken demagogue. I do. For I believe, on my conscience, that on the continued ascendancy of that party depends the safety of this great nation. If impartial suffrage is excluded in the rebel States then every one of them is sure to send a solid rebel representation to Congress, and cast a solid rebel electoral vote. They, with their kindred Copperheads of the North, would always elect the President and control Congress. While slavery sat upon her defiant throne, and insulted and intimidated the trembling North, the South frequently divided on questions of policy between Whigs and Democrats, and gave victory alternately to the two sections. Now, you must divide them between loyalists, without regard to color, and disloyalists, or you will be perpetual vassals of the free-trade, irritated, revengeful South.

"In monarchical Governments, where the sovereign power rests with the Crown, the king would have fixed the condition of the conquered provinces. . . . In this country the whole sovereignty rests with the people and is exercised through their Representatives in Congress assembled. . . . Though the President is Commander-in-Chief, Congress is his commander; and, God willing, he shall obey. He and his minions shall learn that this is not a Government of kings and satraps, but a Government of the people, and that Congress is the people."

6

Bingham, leader of the Conservatives in the House, replied to Stevens on January 16.

At the beginning of the session, Spalding of Ohio had introduced a resolution, undoubtedly inspired by Bingham, requesting the Joint Committee on Reconstruction to consider the advisability of issuing a statement to the effect that if the Southern states ratified the Fourteenth Amendment their representatives would be seated. Bingham now argued that adoption of that resolution was the proper action at this time.

It is true that Congress had never explicitly stated that ratification of the amendment by the Southern states would be followed by the seating of their representatives. Its action in regard to Tennessee was, however, indicative of its intention, and the Report of the Joint Committee on Reconstruction plainly implied that such action would be forthcoming. If the House refused to adopt the Spalding resolution it was mainly due to its conviction that it would serve no purpose except to delay matters. Southern politicians would have regarded it as a sign of weakness and would have become increasingly arrogant and obstinate.

Bingham made a statement during his speech that undoubtedly influenced Stevens's future policy. He said that if the Southern states for the second time rejected the opportunity of ratifying the amendment, he would be in favor of a declaration by Congress that ratification by three-fourths of the loyal states sufficed to make the amendment a part of the Constitution. He even went so far as to say that if the Supreme Court attempted to intervene he would be in favor of action by Congress to abolish the court! If this statement by their leader was an indication that Conservatives were willing to accept so essential a part of Stevens's original program as ratification of the amendment without participation of the Southern states, then there was every reason for him to believe that eventually they might be willing to adopt the second part of that program—placing those states under territorial government. This would not have been the first time that something he advocated more than a year earlier was adopted by Congress.

Bingham did not succeed in getting the House to adopt Spalding's resolution, but he did succeed in having Stevens's bill referred to the Joint Committee on Reconstruction, where such differences arose about the matter that it was permanently shelved.

CHAPTER XVI

Military Reconstruction

The historian James Ford Rhodes has remarked: "Despite the irritation caused by the rejection of the Amendment by the Southern States, such were the differences which cropped out when details of any measure were considered that no reconstruction would have been proposed had it not been for the able and despotic leadership of Stevens." [1]

He never wearied. When it became evident that his most recent proposal would be shelved, he immediately set to work preparing another. This time he decided to confine himself to something nearly all Republicans could agree on: the protection of Southern Unionists and freedmen. The South must be placed under the rule of the military until order had been fully restored. His friend Shellabarger was to justify his proposal in this fashion: "Every work on international law contemplates, recognizes and provides for two states of war, namely: one in which it is flagrant, and the other in which it is *cessante,* in the technical language of the books. The latter condition of things . . . is now upon the country, in which a rebellion is simply crushed by war, by the arms of the Republic, but is still sufficiently strong to overthrow and defy the courts in nearly half the territories of the Republic. That is state of war *cessante;* that is a state of things contemplated by our Constitution, and thank God, the wise men who framed the Constitution provided for the case." [2]

[1] *Op. cit.,* vol. VI, pp. 14-15.
[2] *Globe,* Feb. 8, 1867.

It would be doing Stevens an injustice, however, to believe that this was all he had in mind when he proposed military rule for the South. In his speech of December 18, 1865, he had said: "Military rule is necessarily despotic and ought not to exist longer than absolutely necessary." He had proposed that it be succeeded by territorial government: "I know of no arrangement so proper for them as territorial government. . . . In Territories Congress fixes the qualifications of electors; and I know of no better place nor better occasion for the conquered rebels and the conqueror to practice justice to all men." In what manner was justice to be practiced? By conferring the right of suffrage upon the freedmen. But not immediately. Once the vexing problem of the Fourteenth Amendment had been settled by recognition of the principle that ratification by three-fourths of the loyal states sufficed, the elective franchise could be conferred upon the freedmen when they were ready to assume that responsibility. It will be remembered that in his speech of January 31, 1866, he had said: "I do not therefore want to grant them this privilege for some years. I want, in the meantime, that our Christian men shall go among the freedmen and teach them what their duties are as citizens . . . and then, four or five years hence, when the freedmen shall have been made free indeed, when they shall have become intelligent enough, and there are sufficient loyal men there to control the representation from those States, I shall be glad to see them admitted here."

There can be no doubt that encouraged by the apparent willingness of the Conservatives to accept his claim that ratification of the Fourteenth Amendment by three-fourths of the loyal states sufficed (Bingham was not the only Conservative to make that declaration) Stevens now meant to return to his original plan of placing the Southern states under territorial government and introducing Negro suffrage only after the freedmen had been schooled for "four or five years" in the duties of citizenship. Preliminary to this he might have wished to introduce impartial suffrage such as he had provided in his Reconstruction plan for North Carolina, which would have permitted those to vote, irrespective of race or color, who could read and write or owned a small amount of landed property. We shall see that he still feared immediate suffrage for all the freedmen would merely result in increased representation for the former slaveholders.

2

This time Stevens did not bring his bill before the House until it had been thoroughly discussed in committee. Of the twelve Republicans in that body, the majority of whom were Conservatives, all but one had endorsed the measure. The exception was probably Bingham, who later reconsidered and voted for the bill. Southern intractability and vindictive persecution of loyalists and freedmen had united almost the entire loyal North behind Stevens.

The bill Stevens presented to the House on February 6, 1867, was sufficiently drastic. It was, as Garfield was to phrase it, "written with a steel pen made out of a bayonet." It provided that the former Confederate states (except Tennessee) be divided into five military districts under the authority of the national government. Virginia was to constitute the first district; North and South Carolina the second; Georgia, Alabama, and Florida the third; Mississippi and Arkansas the fourth; Louisiana and Texas the fifth. Not the President, but the General of the Army (Grant) was to assign an army officer, of no less rank than a brigadier general, to the command of each district and was to detail sufficient military forces to each. The commanders might, if they chose, employ civil tribunals for the enforcement of the laws, but if they considered them ineffective could appoint military commissions. No sentence was to be executed until approved by the commanding officer of the district. United States courts and judges were forbidden to issue writs of *habeas corpus* against the proceedings and judgments of the commissions.

The bill was ordered printed, and on February 7 Stevens made a speech in its support. It was short and to the point. "This is a bill," he said, "for the purpose of putting under governments ten States now without governments. Those States have no governments which are known to the Constitution or laws of the United States of America. . . . For two years the loyal people of those ten States have endured all the horrors of the worst anarchy in any country. Persecution, exile, murder have been the order of the day within all these Territories so far as loyal men were concerned, whether white or black, and more especially if they happened to be black. We have seen their best men, those who stood by the flag of the Union, driven from their homes and compelled to live on the cold charity of a cold North. . . . I am for making one more effort to protect these loyal men, without regard to color. . . . If we fail to do it, and do it effectually, we should be responsible to the civilized world for the grossest neglect of duty that ever a great nation was guilty of towards humanity."

His reference to the Southern states as "Territories" left no doubt of his intentions and did not escape the attention of his conservative colleagues.

He succinctly stated the provisions of the bill and said: "In brief that is the whole bill. It does not need much examination." He informed the House that "after the bill had been discussed through to-day and this evening, I shall feel myself justified . . . to ask the House at one o'clock to-morrow to sustain the previous question."

But the House would not have it so. Debate lasted until February 13.

Among those who took the floor was Bingham. He assailed Stevens's "dogma, that these insurrectionary States are a foreign and conquered country," but affirmed that Congress had the power to legislate for them "without their consent and against their consent." He quibbled about the preamble, which referred to the Southern states as "so-called States," but declared, "The general purpose of this bill has my hearty approval." [3] A Democrat remarked: "He quarrels with the shadow and embraces the substance."

Garfield took the floor and said that if the Southern states had ratified the Fourteenth Amendment, "I should have felt bound to let them in on the same terms prescribed for Tennessee. I have also been in favor of waiting, to give them full time to deliberate and act. They have deliberated; they have acted. The last of the sinful ten has, with contempt and scorn, flung back into our teeth the magnanimous offer of a generous nation. It is now our turn to act. They would not co-operate with us in rebuilding what they destroyed. We must remove the rubbish and build from the bottom." [4]

Boutwell, a member of the committee, said: "You might as well expect to build a fire in the depths of the ocean as expect to reconstruct loyal civil governments in the South until you have broken

[3] *Ibid.*, Feb. 7, 1867.
[4] *Ibid.*, Feb. 8, 1867.

down the rebel despotism which everywhere holds sway in that vast region of country." [5]

3

Conservative Republicans had been averse to forcing Negro suffrage upon the South as a means of securing ratification of the Fourteenth Amendment. Impartial suffrage in the South must inevitably lead to impartial suffrage in the North, and Congress was fully aware that the North was opposed to the enfranchisement of the Negro. In five of the six New England states Negroes were permitted to vote, the exception being Connecticut. In New York a Negro became a voter only after having resided in the state for three years and having been the owner for at least one year of an unencumbered freehold valued at two hundred and fifty dollars or more. All the rest of the North was a Sahara in the matter of Negro suffrage. What is more, in 1865 voters in Connecticut, Wisconsin, and Minnesota had by large majorities rejected the proposal to give the Negro the vote, and in 1867 voters in Ohio were to do the same. Under these circumstances the reluctance of the Republican party to resort to the measure is understandable, and it may well be that this situation contributed to the rejection of the Fourteenth Amendment by the former rebel states. Southern politicians had every reason to believe that the Republican majority in Congress would not dare to resort to a measure so unpopular in the North.

However, as time progressed and Republicans sized up the situation, they became increasingly alarmed about the probable result of the presidential election in 1868. Even if the Fourteenth Amendment became a part of the Constitution in the manner Stevens proposed, the outlook for Republican victory in 1868 would be far from promising. The Democratic candidate would be certain of receiving the solid electoral vote of the South, and in all probability of most, if not all, the border states. If as a result of this political realignment the Democrats won the election, the constitutionality of the Fourteenth Amendment, ratified by three-fourths of the loyal states only, would be sure to be called into question. If that move succeeded the representation of the former slave states would be

[5] *Ibid.*, Feb. 9, 1867.

substantially increased. Perpetual ascendancy of a Democratic party dominated by the Southern oligarchy loomed menacingly on the horizon. One has but to study the election figures of 1868 to realize that the fear was not unfounded.

That Stevens had come to realize the danger of the South—and more than likely also the border states—voting as a solid phalanx for the Democratic candidate at the next presidential election, we know. This may well have been the principal reason why he had decided to abandon for the present all idea of Reconstruction and to return to his original plan of placing the former states under territorial government. We find him now repeatedly insisting that the Fourteenth Amendment did not suffice for the readmission of the former rebel states. But if the Conservatives did not share his fear that to enfranchise the freedmen immediately would merely mean to increase the representation of the former slaveholders, he did not share their fear that to place the Southern states under territorial government might enable them to wait in that status until the Democrats gained control of the national government and admitted them with a greatly increased representation. He felt that if an intensive campaign of education were immediately begun among the freedmen, they could be enfranchised long before such an eventuality occurred. If in addition to this, as proposed by him, homesteads were given to the freedmen, it would be to their interest to be careful whom they elected to office.

The conservatives, however, appear to have made up their minds from the beginning of the second session of the Thirty-ninth Congress not to take any chances but to enfranchise the freedmen as quickly as possible. When the radical Stevens was still hesitating, wondering what course to follow—as evidenced by his Reconstruction plan for North Carolina—the conservative Blaine had already fully made up his mind. "I was the first member of the House," he was to say, "who spoke in the Committee of the Whole on the President's message at the opening of the session. I then stated that I believed the true interpretation of the elections of 1866 was that, in addition to the proposed constitutional amendment, universal, or at least impartial suffrage should be the basis of representation." [6] And when the radical Stevens was desperately striving to have his last

[6] *Ibid.*, Feb. 12, 1867.

proposal adopted as a police bill, nothing more, leaving the way open for the Fortieth Congress to place the South under territorial government, Bingham, leader of the Conservatives in the House, was to say: "When we enfranchise, as I trust we shall, *and as I propose to do*, all the emancipated citizens of those States, will not loyal men be in the majority, and can you not trust the majority?" [7]

So, on February 12, Blaine offered the following amendment to Stevens's police bill:

When the Fourteenth Amendment had become a part of the Constitution *after ratification by three-fourths of the loyal states only*, any former rebel state wishing the abolition of military rule and desiring its representatives to be seated in Congress could attain those ends by complying with the following: It must give its assent to the amended Constitution; it must frame a state constitution providing for the impartial enjoyment of the elective franchise "by all male citizens of the United States twenty-one years old or upward without regard to race, color, or previous condition of servitude, except such as may be disfranchised for participating in the late rebellion"; it must submit the constitution for ratification by a popular vote and must present it to Congress for examination and approval.

Blaine's amendment apparently left it to the Southern states themselves to decide whether or not they preferred Negro suffrage to a continuance of military rule, but only apparently so. With military rule prevailing it would be a simple matter for loyalists, freedmen, and carpetbaggers to bring about political changes. Blaine's concession to Stevens that the Fourteenth Amendment was to become a part of the Constitution after ratification by three-fourths of the loyal states only was therefore meaningless, yet he emphasized it, saying in his speech in support of his proposal: "It especially declares that three-fourths of the States now represented in Congress have the power to adopt the constitutional amendment, and it does not even by implication give them to understand that their assent or ratification is necessary to its becoming a part of the Constitution."

Stevens was not mollified by this meaningless concession to his policy. In his imperious fashion he beat down Blaine's amendment,

[7] *Ibid.*, Feb. 13, 1867. Italics added.

as he had done with six previous amendments, without even permitting it to come to a vote. On February 13, after making a short closing speech, he put the previous question, and his bill passed by a vote of 109 to 55. He turned toward the presiding officer and said with obvious satisfaction: "I wish to inquire, Mr. Speaker, if it is in order for me to say that we endorse the language of good old Laertes, that Heaven rules as yet and there are gods above."

4

Stevens's satisfaction was premature. Republican strategists in the Senate belonging to the conservative wing of the party agreed with Blaine. The Thirty-ninth Congress was to come to an end on March 4, to be immediately succeeded by the Fortieth, it having been considered inexpedient to leave an interval during which Johnson might do additional mischief. That Congress, elected during the upsurge of popular feeling against Johnson, was certain to be more radical than its predecessor and might well go along with Stevens's plan of placing the former rebel states under territorial government. The Conservatives in the Senate decided to block this move. Blaine's amendment was taken up, rewritten by the conservative leader John Sherman, and attached as a separate section to Stevens's police bill, in which only one important change was made—the President instead of the General of the Army was entrusted with the task of appointing the district commanders. This change, while perhaps necessary from a constitutional viewpoint, was to impair considerably the effectiveness of the bill. Whenever a general proved himself zealous in carrying out the will of Congress, he would be removed by the President and one favoring "my policy" would be put in his place.

The changes made in Blaine's amendment were likewise slight, and what had been a police bill was returned to the House on February 18 a full-fledged Reconstruction bill. Stevens, seeing his hopes for a sensible solution of the Reconstruction muddle again frustrated, expressed his disappointment in no uncertain terms. He moved that the amendments of the Senate be not concurred in and that the House ask for a conference committee. Taking the floor in opposition to the amendments, he said:

"The House a few days ago sent to the Senate a bill to protect loyal men in the southern States. That bill proposed but one single object, the protection of the loyal men of the South from the anarchy and oppression that exist and the murders which are every day perpetrated upon loyal men, without distinction of color. It did not attempt the difficult question of reconstructing these States by establishing civil governments over them. The House thought it wise to leave that question until a Congress which is to come in could have a long time to consider the whole question. The bill which we passed had not in it one single phrase or word which looked to anything but a police regulation for the benefit of these States."

He left no doubt that he did not believe men just released from slavery could be trusted to do anything except follow the orders of their former masters in the matter of voting: "I know there is an impatience to bring in these chivalric gentlemen lest they should not be here in time to vote for the next President of the United States, and therefore gentlemen postpone [?] the regular mode of bringing up that question, and put it on a police bill in order that it may be carried through so as to give them the opportunity to be here at the time they desire. Sir, while I am in favor of allowing them to come in as soon as they are fairly entitled, I do not profess to be very impatient to embrace them. I am not very anxious to see their votes cast along with others to control the next election of President and Vice-President; therefore it is that my impatience is not so great as that of others."

It is problematical whether he really feared that a substantial number of freedmen would vote for the candidates of their former masters, or whether for the sake of the freedmen he did not wish to put them to the trial of having a responsibility thrust upon them which they might be unable to fulfill with credit to themselves. In his struggle against the Conservatives to arrive at a sensible mode of Reconstruction, he was—like Lincoln in his struggle against him and other Radicals to make gradual emancipation prevail—sometimes contradicting himself. Only the previous month (January 3, 1867) he had said: "The white Union men are in a great minority in each of those States. With them the blacks would act in a body; and it is believed that in each of said States, except one, the two united would form a majority, control the States and protect themselves." Yet now he expressed fear of the majority and appeared to be convinced that unless thousands of former rebels were temporarily disfranchised the "chivalric gentlemen" would return to Congress and the Electoral College. Garfield, one of those who rose to reply, understood perfectly. He knew that placing the former rebel states under territorial government had been Stevens's favorite policy from the beginning and that he was trying to gain time in the hope that the Fortieth Congress would give him what he wanted. He turned to him during his speech and said: "The distinguished gentleman from Pennsylvania said one thing which I wish to call attention to. He complained the Senate had forced upon us a question of reconstruction we did not want to touch. I fear the gentleman does not want to touch the question of reconstruction. I do, and I believe the American people want to touch reconstruction." [8]

Stevens was exceedingly skillful in making use of the opposition when he found it to his interest to do so. This time, as on several other occasions, he managed to get his motion adopted with the aid of the Democrats. The Senate, after first refusing a conference, thought better of it and agreed to compromise. The bill was therefore further amended. One provision forbade those excluded from the privilege of holding public office by the proposed Fourteenth Amendment from serving as delegates to the constitutional conventions or voting for members of those bodies. Another specified that until representatives from a rebel state had been admitted to Congress, any government that state might have would be deemed provisional only "and in all respects subject to the authority of the United States, which might at any time abolish, modify, control or supersede the same."

The measure was submitted to the President on February 20, and on March 2, 1867, was adopted over his veto. On the twenty-third of that month a Supplementary Reconstruction Act was passed. It instructed the commanders of the military districts to hold a registration of qualified voters before September, 1867, and gave detailed instructions regarding steps to be taken if the people of a rebel state wished to be readmitted to participation in the national government.

Stevens had little to do with the fashioning of the first Supplementary Reconstruction Act, but four days before its adoption he

[8] *Globe,* Feb. 18, 1867.

made his speech on confiscation during which he especially pleaded that a homestead of forty acres and a small sum of money with which to build a dwelling be given to every adult male freedman and to every freed woman, the head of a family: "Whatever may be the fate of the rest of the bill I must earnestly pray that this may not be defeated. . . . Homesteads to them are far more valuable than the immediate right of suffrage, though both are their due." Why is it that history has shown so little sympathy for that proposal but has fixed our attention on a few intemperate utterances by the man who made it? Is it nothing to plead for the weak and the downtrodden? Is the Sermon on the Mount worthy of less attention than the time when the Nazarene lost his temper with the money-changers in the temple?

It was soon found that the Supplementary Act did not suffice. When the military commanders would ask the President for an interpretation of something not altogether clear, they usually received explanations not in accord with the intent of Congress. On July 19, therefore, another Supplementary Act was passed clarifying that intent. Later it was found that the provision requiring the majority of the *registered* voters to vote in the affirmative before a constitutional convention could be held, resulted in many white voters remaining away from the polls and intimidating others to do the same. So, on March 11, 1868, a third Supplementary Act was passed providing that the majority of votes *cast* sufficed in the matter.

5

Stevens cannot be held responsible for forcing Negro suffrage prematurely upon the South. No Republican leader had tried harder to arrive at a more sensible solution. On January 7, 1867, the Chief Justice of Louisiana, W. B. Hyman, wrote to Thomas D. Eliot, representative from Massachusetts: "Most of the persons with whom I have conversed would to-day join in any movement to rid themselves of the Government of the United States, provided there was a fair prospect of success." [9] To reintegrate such a region—a third of the country—into the nation's political organization without endangering the country's safety would have puzzled the greatest statesman of

[9] *Globe,* Feb. 13, 1867. Cited by Representative Van Horn of New York.

any age. The method proposed by Stevens from the beginning of Reconstruction was just and sensible. It was the South's contumacy, aided and abetted by Johnson, that was responsible for the measures finally adopted.

Stevens did not live to see the result of Negro suffrage in the South. Had he lived to see it there can be no doubt that he would have intervened. It is but fair to ask, however, whether it was Negro suffrage that was responsible for the alleged spoliation of the South by the carpetbaggers. An examination of the facts makes it appear that something else was responsible—*that the fault did not lie with the Negro but with the governing classes of the South.*

The newly enfranchised, perplexed and bewildered, were in need of advice and leadership. The Negroes of South Carolina, in the majority in that state, sent a committee to Washington to seek the advice of Stevens and Sumner. The statement of Francis L. Cardoza, onetime secretary of state of South Carolina, made several years before his death, that "both Mr. Sumner and Mr. Stevens advised the committee to tender leadership to native whites of the former master class of conservative views," [10] must be taken with reservations. Stevens had repeatedly expressed fear that leadership of the freedmen might fall into such hands. But there were men of the master class in the South whom he might well have advised them to consult and even to accept as leaders. John H. Reagan of Texas might serve as an example. He had been postmaster general in the Confederate cabinet and toward the end of the war secretary of the treasury. Arrested and imprisoned in Fort Warren after the collapse of the Confederacy, he addressed an open letter to the people of Texas appealing to them to grant Negroes equality before the law and to "fix an intellectual, moral, and if thought necessary, a property test for the admission of all persons to the exercise of the elective franchise, without reference to race or color." [11] One cannot help but notice the affinity between this and Stevens's North Carolina Reconstruction bill. There were such men in every Southern state, and some of them attempted to take the leadership of the newly enfranchised, who received them with open arms. A few persevered, but the majority became discouraged and withdrew when realizing

[10] *Journal of Negro History,* vol. V, pp. 110-111; vol. VI, pp. 24-47.
[11] *Globe,* Appendix, Feb. 14, 1866. Cited by Senator Henderson.

what was in store for them if they persisted. A couple of examples must suffice:

The Confederate General James Longstreet, of whom the Union commander Joseph Hooker has said: "The strength of the rebel army rests upon the broad shoulders of Longstreet. He is the brain of Lee and Stonewall Jackson was his right arm," [12] had after the war gone into the insurance business in New Orleans. "Affairs," he has written, "were more than prosperous until I was asked an opinion upon the political crisis in 1867." His opinion and that of several other former Confederate generals had been solicited by the editor of a New Orleans paper. On January 3, 1867, Longstreet replied:

> The serious difficulty arises from want of wisdom so important for the great work in hand. Still, I will be happy to work in any harness that promises relief to our discomfited people and harmony to the Nation, whether bearing the mantle of Mr. Davis or Mr. Sumner.
>
> It is fair to assume that the strongest laws are those established by the sword. The ideas that divided political parties before the war—upon the rights of the states—were thoroughly discussed by our wisest statesmen, and eventually appealed to the arbitrament of the sword. The decision was in favor of the North, so that her construction becomes the law, and should be so accepted.

The result of this letter is told by him as follows:

> The afternoon of the day upon which my letter was published [?] the paper that had called for advice published a column of editorial calling me "traitor," deserter of my friends, and accusing me of "joining the enemy," but did not publish a line of the letter upon which it based these charges. Other papers of the Democracy took up the garbled representation of this journal and spread it broadcast, not even giving the letter upon which they based their evil attacks upon me. . . .
>
> The day after the announcement old comrades passed me on the streets without speaking. Business began to grow dull. General Hood (the only one of my old comrades who occasionally visited me) thought that he could save the insurance business, and in a few weeks I found myself at leisure.
>
> Two years after that period, on March 4, 1869, General Grant was inaugurated President of the United States, and in the bigness of his generous heart called me to Washington. Before I found opportunity to

[12] Thayer, *op. cit.*, vol. I, p. 141.

see him he sent my name to the Senate for confirmation as surveyor of customs at New Orleans.[13]

In Mississippi Colonel James Lusk, "an influential representative of the Southern aristocracy of ante-bellum days" decided to take over the leadership of the freedmen in his part of the state. They received him enthusiastically, but he soon found it expedient to beat a retreat. When one of the Negroes called upon him and begged him not to abandon them, he received this reply: "You must remember that a man's first duty is to his family. My daughters are the pride of my home. I cannot afford to have them suffer humiliating consequences of the social ostracism to which they may be subjected if I remain in the Republican party. I must yield to the inevitable and surrender my convictions upon the altar of my family's good,—the outgrowth of conditions which I am powerless to prevent and cannot control. . . . If I could see my way clear to pursue a different course it would be done; but my decision is based upon careful and thoughtful consideration and must stand." [14]

6

Johnston, Beauregard, Harden, Hood, Wade Hampton, urged co-operation with Congress, as did ex-governors Magrath and Aiken of South Carolina and Joseph E. Brown of Georgia, but theirs were voices crying in the wilderness. Here and there an attempt was made to make contact with the newly enfranchised, who were pleased and flattered by such approaches, but the attempts were sporadic and of short duration. Oberholtzer has written:

Better it would have been, said the New Orleans *Picayune,* if the Southern people had enfranchised the negroes immediately after the surrender, so that they might have been attached in gratitude to the Southern side instead of to the Radicals, who were now to reap the fruits of their policy. They were working "for us in the fields; why should they not do so at the polls?" If the negroes were properly directed, said General Beauregard, the South could defeat its adversaries "with their own weapons." They were Southern born and they could be made to "side with the whites." United States Senator-elect Burnett of Texas ad-

[13] James Longstreet, *From Manassas to Appomattox,* pp. 636-638.
[14] John R. Lynch, *The Facts of Reconstruction,* pp. 106-107.

dressed a letter to the people of that State. "Teach these ill-informed and lately inducted politicians that their best interests are identical with ours," he said, "that they are Southerners by birth, by residence, in person, in property and in territorial prosperity." In Alabama the conservatives went so far as to ask the negroes to sit in a convention beside the whites, to the end that "Alabama should rule Alabama." The mothers who had given them birth had been nursed by the whites; they had played in infancy and childhood with the whites.[15]

Whether the Negroes would have benefited by co-operation with the Conservatives may well be doubted; certain it is, however, that had the policy been consistently followed no carpetbagger could have made much headway. James L. Orr of South Carolina, who had been speaker of the federal House of Representatives, member of the Confederate Senate during the war, and in 1865 was elected governor of the state under presidential Reconstruction, said: "Suppose one hundred of the most intelligent white citizens of each county had gone, in good faith, and with frank sincerity, into the Republican organization, can it be doubted that their intelligence and moral strength would have secured honest nominees?" [16]

According to Blaine, "moral strength" was precisely what was lacking among the South's governing classes. He wrote:

One of the most remarkable features was the complete control which the white men from the North, entire strangers to the negro, to his habits and his prejudices, so readily obtained over him. The late slavemasters did not adapt themselves to the new situation. They gave way to repining and regretting, to sulking and to anger, to resentment and revenge. . . . The lack of moral courage among the physically brave men of the South has already been indicated and illustrated. It was something of this same defect that held back the slavemasters from the condescension, as they expressed it, of establishing any relation whatever with the negro in his new condition of freedom.[17]

The Negro scholar Alrutheus A. Taylor has written:

The mistakes of the reconstruction were due in a measure to the native whites of the higher class. Approaching the task of reconstruction, the Negroes, acting upon the advice of their friends in the North, invited the better class of Southerners to assume the leadership in politics; but being

[15] *Op. cit.*, vol. II, pp. 11-21.
[16] A. A. Taylor, *The Negro in South Carolina During Reconstruction*, p. 197.
[17] *Op. cit.*, vol. II, p. 305.

too haughty to associate politically with their ex-slaves, and hoping to defeat the reconstructionists immediately, the aristocratic group lost this opportunity to the Northern adventurers who organized the Negroes against them.[18]

The contribution of the former slaveholders to Reconstruction was the Ku Klux Klan and similar organizations. One cannot sow the wind and expect to reap halcyon weather. The Union Leagues responded by arming the Negroes for self-defense. Benjamin Hill of Georgia was to exclaim: "The Ku Klux business is the worst that ever afflicted the South. Every day that we let it continue we cut our own throats. . . . It is a curse upon our land, a blight following slavery and the greatest blunder our people ever committed." [19]

Robert E. Lee counseled co-operation on the one hand and on the other secretly sponsored the Ku Klux Klan, which owes its name "Invisible Empire" to his statement—made to the committee which on behalf of the first national convention of Klansmen in Nashville, in May, 1867, came to tender him the leadership of the organization—that his support must remain "invisible." General Nathan B. Forrest was chosen "Grand Wizard" of the Invisible Empire after Lee had assured a committee that "he is the only man I know who could lead so large a body of men successfully. You may present to him my compliments and ask him if he will accept the leadership."

Claude G. Bowers, in *The Tragic Era,* hailed in the South as a masterful defense of its stand on Reconstruction, acknowledges that "General Forrest had been placed at the head of the Ku Klux Klan with the sanction of Lee, who strongly urged that the organization be kept a purely 'protective organization' " (p. 310). If Lee really believed that under the leadership of General Forrest the Klan would remain "purely protective," then *naïveté* should be included in the catalogue of his alleged virtues.

When the Klan had covered itself with infamy and measures were being taken to suppress it, Lee assured General John B. Gordon, Assistant "Grand Wizard" of the Invisible Empire, who had been with him at Appomattox, "that he did not believe his brave soldiers would stoop to such deeds as they were accused of as Ku Klux." [20]

[18] *Op. cit.,* p. 310.

[19] Skaggs, *op. cit.,* p. 323.

[20] Detailed and precise information concerning Lee's relationship with the Klan can be found in a volume entitled *Authentic History of the Ku Klux Klan, 1865-1877,*

Apparently, however, he believed *Union* soldiers capable of anything. In a letter to his wife, November 22, 1861, he wrote that Union soldiers had "foully polluted" Arlington, a charge without the slightest foundation in fact. In a letter to his daughter, December 8, 1861, he wrote: "I am afraid Cousin Julia will not be able to defend her home if attacked by the vandals, for they have little respect for anybody. . . . I fear, too, the Yankees will bear off their pretty daughters." [21] Yet such is the power of propaganda that a Northern poet refers to the man capable of such meanness as "the demigod that was Lee"! [22]

The nature of the organization Lee secretly sponsored may be judged from the following: Several citizens of North Carolina were indicted in the federal court as members of the Ku Klux Klan. They must have been men of standing in the organization, for no less a personage than Reverdy Johnson was retained as associate counsel by the defense. He had been a sympathizer with the Confederacy throughout the war and had voted against the Fourteenth Amendment and the Reconstruction acts. But when he heard the testimony of a number of witnesses and the confessions of some of the accused, he denounced them and their organization in these words: "I have listened with unmixed horror to some of the testimony that has been brought before you. The outrages proved are shocking to humanity; they admit of neither excuse nor justification; they violate every obligation which law and nature impose upon men; they show that the parties engaged were brutes, insensible to the obligations of humanity and religion." [23]

7

How much of what has appeared in print concerning the extravagance and dishonesty of the carpetbaggers is true, is a moot question. Eminent scholars have been deceived by the propaganda. In the Fifty-first Congress St. George Tucker made a speech in which he presented a table purporting to show the debts of the Southern states at the end of Reconstruction. The table was copied by H. Herbert in *Why the*

pp. 80-81, 203-204, privately printed by Susan Lawrence Davis, daughter of the "Cyclop" of the Alabama Klan during Reconstruction, and an ardent admirer of Lee.

21 R. E. Lee, *Recollections and Letters of General Robert E. Lee*, pp. 56-57.

22 Robert P. Tristram Coffin, in his poem *Mother of Presidents, Orators, Pride.*

23 Skaggs, *op. cit.*, p. 323.

Solid South; by Dr. J. L. M. Curry, Southern statesman and educator, in *Southern States of the American Union;* by Dr. E. Benjamin Andrews, onetime superintendent of schools in Chicago and at the time of his death chancellor of the University of Nebraska, in *History of the United States during the Last Quarter of a Century.* The horrendous example in the table was Mississippi, whose debt at the end of Reconstruction was given as $20,000,000. This was colossal indeed, considering that the highest computation of the state's debt before the carpetbaggers took over was $653,480.

When Dr. Andrews's work first appeared in 1895, Albert Ames, the last Reconstruction governor of Mississippi, was still living. He happened to read the book and wrote to Dr. Andrews that his authorities had led him into making "a $19,500,000 error in a $20,000,000 statement." Dr. Andrews sent for the official reports and found to his discomfiture that Ames was right. The debt of Mississippi at the end of Reconstruction was $520,138. He handsomely apologized, and having lost faith in the accuracy of the entire table, dropped it from succeeding editions of his book.[24]

James Ford Rhodes, too, has at times been made to look rather foolish. He wrote concerning the violent overthrow of Ames's administration in 1876: "Whilst regretting some of the means employed, all lovers of good government must rejoice at the redemption of Mississippi." [25] Yet during his two years as governor Ames had reduced the state debt by over $300,000, while at the same time lowering the tax rate from seven to four mills! "Lovers of good government" had little reason for rejoicing about the overthrow of Ames's administration, since the new state treasurer, William L. Hemingway, celebrated the return of the oligarchy to power by defaulting for $315,612, a circumstance Rhodes has failed to note.[26] Hemingway was not the only genteel advocate of "good government," as understood by the oligarchy, who indulged in such practices. In 1866, just before Reconstruction in Mississippi, the state treasurer had defaulted for $61,962, and shortly after Reconstruction the state treasurers of Alabama, Tennessee, and Louisiana defaulted for $212,000, $374,364, and $795,535 respectively.

[24] James Wilford Garner, *Reconstruction in Mississippi,* pp. 320-321.
[25] *Op. cit.,* vol. VII, p. 141.
[26] Lynch, *op. cit.,* pp. 87-90.

The fact that the former slaveholding class did not want Reconstruction to succeed and deliberately ruined the credit of the new governments has been demonstrated with documentary evidence by W. E. Burghardt Du Bois, professor of sociology in Atlanta University, in his work *Black Reconstruction in the South.* He has likewise demonstrated with irrefragable evidence that men of that class themselves often corrupted those governments and participated in the thefts. The reason there were so few prosecutions after the overthrow of the Reconstruction governments was because too many of the best families in the South would have been compromised had the facts been brought to light. In the end it was the North who paid the piper, since by far the greater part of the money spent or stolen was borrowed there and the South repudiated some $150,000,000 of Reconstruction debts.

Not Negro suffrage, but the attitude of the South's governing classes toward Negro suffrage paved the way for the carpetbagger

CHAPTER XVII
Impeachment

Toward the end of June, 1867, a correspondent of the New York *Herald* arrived in Lancaster, by then a thriving little city of some twenty thousand inhabitants. He had come with the intention of interviewing Stevens, and, if possible, getting some intimation of his plans for the extra session of Congress that was to take place the following month. It having occurred to him that Lancaster boasted a historical relic in the form of an ex-President, he engaged a citizen of the town in the following conversation on the matter:

"Ex-President Buchanan lives near this place, does he not?"

"Well, yes. He lives 'bout a mile and a half out of here."

"Is he at home at the present time?"

"I don't know whether he is at home or not. I suppose he is."

"Is his health good nowadays?"

"I don't know anything about his health."

"You do not appear to know a great deal concerning so distinguished a fellow citizen."

"Distinguished! Well, we know that such a man as Poppy Buchanan lives away out yonder, but that's about all we do know, and that's all anybody cares about knowing."

"Well, you know Mr. Stevens, I suppose?"

"Mr. Stevens—who's Mr. Stevens?"

"Why, Thad Stevens, the member of Congress, to be sure."

"Oh, you mean Old Thad! Well, I guess I do. Everybody knows him. But we call him Old Thad here."

"You seem to think more here of Old Thad, as you call him, than you do of the ex-President."

"More of him? Well, I should say we did. We're Democrats, here, in the city; but then we know Poppy Buchanan is played out and don't amount to anything. But as to Old Thad, while we mayn't like his politics, we know he is alive." [1]

Notwithstanding his failing health Old Thad was very much alive indeed. Not only the United States, but all the world knew about him. His name appeared in European newspapers more than that of any other American. Europeans regarded him as a Cromwell who had reduced the President to a figurehead and might decide to depose him at any time. President Johnson was fully aware of Stevens's influence and would have welcomed a reconciliation. He saw danger threatening. In December, 1866, and again the following January, Ashley of Ohio had introduced a resolution calling for his impeachment. The second resolution had been referred to the Judiciary Committee, which immediately set to work collecting evidence and taking testimony. Johnson felt uneasy and toward the end of February invited Stevens to come and dine with him. He received this reply:

Washington, February 27, 1867.

His Excellency Andrew Johnson,

Mr. Thaddeus Stevens acknowledges the receipt of the President's invitation to dinner on Sunday next at 6 o'clock and regrets that indisposition will prevent his attendance.[2]

2

The correspondent of the *Herald* informs us that "about the doors [of Stevens's office and dwelling], at almost any hour of the day, may be observed some half a dozen or more politicians, some local and some visitors from a distance, anxious for an interview." He himself had no difficulty in gaining admittance, and the two men sat down together for a friendly chat.

Secretary Welles has opined that the questions the correspondent asked had been prepared for him by the wily old Radical. Nearly everything the old man did, he noted in his *Diary,* was "premedi-

[1] New York *Herald,* July 8, 1867.
[2] Letter in possession of the author.

tated, dramatic and for effect." [3] Certain it is that the answers to the questions were meant to influence the political situation. The principal topic discussed was the proposed impeachment of Johnson. Stevens said: "If the people agree with me in the desire to put a man in the executive position who will faithfully see the laws of the United States executed, at all times and under all circumstances, and who will not usurp the powers and obstruct the action of the national Congress, then we should at once impeach and remove Andrew Johnson. . . . The action of the Judiciary Committee has been simply fussy, unnecessary and absurd. There was no occasion to take any testimony whatever on the subject of impeachment. The documents and the facts were evidence enough. They should not have called a witness, but have reported that Congress had quite sufficient ground for the impeachment, *if they desired to take that political step,* in the encroachments and usurpations of the President, which were a matter, not of oral testimony, but of official record." [4]

This obviously meant that he considered impeachment a remedy for political as well as indictable offenses. In other words, that the President could be impeached not only for the commission of a crime, but for differing so radically with Congress regarding the necessity or constitutionality of measures adopted by that body as to affect seriously his usefulness as an executive. That a President, without being demonstrably unfaithful to his oath of office, can thwart the will of Congress and of the people if he feels inclined to do so, admits of no doubt. The people of the North were overwhelmingly in favor of the Fourteenth Amendment, yet Johnson bore a heavy responsibility for its rejection by the South. They were in favor of effective protection for Southern loyalists and freedmen, yet Johnson, claiming it was unconstitutional for the federal government to interfere with law enforcement in states, had failed to provide such protection. What is more, after the adoption of the Reconstruction acts he had done everything in his power to destroy their effectiveness. The first Reconstruction Act provided that military commanders could make use of local law enforcement agencies if they chose, but if they found these ineffective could appoint military commissions to deal with the matter. In Louisiana the machinery of law enforcement had proved

[3] Welles, *op. cit.,* vol. III, pp. 130-131.
[4] New York *Herald,* July 8, 1867. Italics added.

so ineffective in the New Orleans massacre that General Sheridan, commander of the district, felt justified in ignoring it. Johnson removed him and put General Hancock in his place. General Grant has charged that the change was responsible for the disorders that took place in Louisiana during the presidential elections in 1868, when some two thousand were killed or wounded.[5]

It may be justly argued that the existing situation was intolerable. Professor Woodburn has written: "If Johnson had stolen a chicken . . . he could have been impeached and removed. But to throw himself athwart the national will and to circumvent important political ends upon which the nation is determined, while yet keeping within the limits of the criminal law,—in such a case there is operative no method of impeachment, or recall, within the sovereign power of the people." [6] There was no remedy. To say that the framers of the Constitution intended impeachment as a remedy for political as well as criminal offenses is to say that they had intended to establish a parliamentary, not a presidential form of government. A president who could be removed for disagreeing, however decisively, with a congressional majority would be in exactly the same position as a British prime minister.

Stevens agreed with Lincoln that the Constitution existed for the preservation of the country, not the country for the preservation of the Constitution. He believed, moreover, that owing to the intransigence of Southern politicians and the encouragement given them by Johnson, the war was not yet over, but had merely entered the phase defined by international law as a state of war *cessante*. Under these circumstances he believed Unionists had a right to remove a president who was scheming to turn the federal government over to former rebels and Copperheads—enemies of the Union. He was, however, too good a politician not to realize that unless Johnson committed some overt act that rendered him liable to impeachment under an orthodox interpretation of the Constitution, few of his colleagues in Congress would be willing to take that step. So he told his interlocutor that while he considered it incumbent upon him, as a representative of the people, "to propose the removal of the obstacle," he had no hope the move would succeed. On July 19, at the extra session

[5] Blaine, *op. cit.*, vol. II, p. 299.
[6] *Op. cit.*, p. 492.

of Congress, he was to say: "I have taken some pains to look into the position of the House and of the Senate, and am quite sure that there is power enough, first, to prevent the voting of the impeachment here; and secondly, if impeachment were voted, to prevent conviction elsewhere."

3

On March 2, 1867, when the Reconstruction Act was adopted over the President's veto, Congress also adopted the Tenure of Office Bill. From the beginning of his quarrel with Congress, Johnson appears to have been convinced that his best weapon was his control of patronage and his ability to remove from office protégés of those who opposed "my policy." It proved to be a double-edged sword. It failed to rally any additional support, but consolidated opposition against him. His persistence in the policy can be explained only on the supposition that he hoped to get the Democratic nomination for president and was constructing a political machine with that purpose in view. The dismissals were, however, wrecking the Republican political organization, hence the Tenure of Office Bill.

As adopted by the Senate, where it originated, the act provided that, *with the exception of members of the cabinet,* a civil servant holding an office appointment which was subject to approval by the Senate could not be removed until his successor had been appointed and the appointment had been approved by that body. When the Senate was not in session and sufficient evidence existed justifying suspension of a civil officer, the President had the right to suspend him and make a temporary appointment. Within twenty days after the Senate had reassembled, the President was to report the case and submit the evidence. If the Senate concurred, the officer was to be removed and his successor appointed "with the advice and consent of the Senate." If it failed to concur he was to resume his functions forthwith. Anyone making or accepting an appointment in violation of the act was guilty of a "high misdemeanor" punishable by a fine not exceeding ten thousand dollars or imprisonment not exceeding five years.

In the course of the debate a senator asked why members of the cabinet should be excepted. The answer was made that the personal and confidential relations between the President and cabinet members made this necessary. The House, however, was of a different opinion and after a conference a substitute was adopted providing that members of the cabinet "shall hold their offices, respectively, *for and during the term of the President by whom they may have been appointed,* and for one month thereafter, subject to removal by and with the advice and consent of the Senate."

When Jackson had inaugurated the spoils system, Webster had declared: "I cannot but think those who in 1789 denied the power [of the President to remove civil servants from office without the Senate's consent] had the best of the argument. . . . I believe it to be within the just power of Congress to reverse the decision of 1789." But it had not been reversed and had never again been seriously questioned until the adoption of the Tenure of Office Bill. Shortly after Grant took office, a Congress composed virtually of the same men who had adopted the bill restored the President's former right in the matter. The bill must, therefore, be regarded as an emergency measure.

4

"If the people do not entertain sufficient respect for their chief Magistrate to uphold him in his course, he ought to resign," Johnson said on one occasion to his secretary.[7] In the fall of 1866 the people had clearly demonstrated that they did not respect him and had no intention of upholding his course. But he did not resign and continued to obstruct the work of the representatives of the people in every conceivable manner. The result was increased opposition in the South and increased determination on the part of Congress to overcome it.

There were Southerners who realized this and who considered it a misfortune that the South had listened to Johnson. The former Confederate General Ethelbert Barksdale wrote in his paper, the Jackson (Mississippi) *Clarion:*

The ill-judged, though well-meant, plan of Mr. Johnson, to reorganize the excluded States without authority of Congress, produced a quarrel between the executive and legislative departments, which resulted in giving to the latter the perfectly overshadowing and irresistable control it now has. It reduced the former to the dimensions of a dwarf, and it

[7] Frank Moore, *Life and Speeches of Andrew Johnson,* p. 120.

increased the latter to the proportions of a giant. . . . Unfortunately for the South, she permitted herself to be drawn into this struggle and to become a partisan of the Executive. And she has by this ill-advised step contributed nothing towards his support, but has thrown obstacles in the way of a settlement of her difficulties.[8]

One of the results of Johnson's change of front was, as we have seen, his quarrel with Secretary of War Stanton. Since Johnson did not resign, although out of harmony with Congress and with those who had elected him, Stanton felt justified in holding on to his post. After the adoption of the Tenure of Office Bill he was in effect as much an employee of Congress as of the President and may well have felt that his duty to the former was greater than to the latter. He ceased to attend cabinet meetings, and he and Johnson were not on speaking terms.

Finally, on August 5, 1867, Johnson sent the Secretary the following curt note: "Public considerations of a high character constrain me to say that your resignation as Secretary of War will be accepted." He received this reply: "I have the honor to say that patriotic considerations of a high character, which alone have induced me to continue at the head of the Department, constrain me not to resign the office of Secretary of War before the next meeting of Congress." Johnson thereupon suspended him and appointed Grant secretary of war *ad interim*. Stanton surrendered the office to Grant, but did not resign, confident that the Senate would sustain him.

5

In September Stevens's illness took a turn for the worse. His life was despaired of and rumors flew about Washington that he had died. But with that marvelous recuperative power of his he rallied, and on November 13 set out for Washington. He was no longer able to attend to his voluminous correspondence himself and hired a secretary, which, considering the illegibility of his handwriting, must have been a boon to his friends and admirers.

Conferring the immediate right of suffrage upon Southern Negroes had not been without repercussions in the North. In the fall elections of 1867, the Republicans lost New York and New Jersey to the Demo-

[8] Cited by the New York *Herald,* July 8, 1867.

crats, and the legislatures of both states even wished to annul their ratification of the Fourteenth Amendment. That Stevens doubted the wisdom of the Reconstruction acts as finally adopted is evident from his interview with the correspondent of the New York *Herald,* July 8, 1867, during which he said: "I would give every adult freedman who was the head of a family a small holding, say of forty or fifty acres, out of the lands of their former masters . . . so that if he could not find other labor he could occupy himself and support his family by working his own farm at home. I think this would be productive of good to the whole country and to all classes of men—to the former masters as well as to the former slaves. The freedmen would then be an independent yeomanry, feeling their own freedom and manhood and self-reliance, *which would be better for them than the ballot.*"

It is evident from this that the Reconstruction acts were something he was obliged to accept, not what he really wanted. He would have gladly traded the immediate right of suffrage for homesteads for the Negro. But now that Southern Negroes had been given that right, he was determined that it should be extended to the colored people of the North. Undaunted by what had happened in New York and New Jersey he set to work preparing a Fifteenth Amendment to the Constitution that would make impartial suffrage a national institution. He did not, however, live to see his proposal become reality.

Toward the end of November, 1867, the Judiciary Committee of the House brought in its report concerning the impeachment of Johnson. The committee's majority resolution calling for the President's impeachment was, however, defeated by a vote of 108 to 57. Stevens voted for it on principle, but did not expect it to pass. On December 12 Johnson sent a message to the Senate giving his reasons for the suspension of Stanton. On January 13, 1868, the Senate notified him that "having considered the evidence and reasons given by the President for the suspension of Edwin M. Stanton from the office of Secretary of War, the Senate does not concur in such suspension." Copies of the resolution were forwarded to Stanton, to Grant, and to Adjutant General Lorenzo Thomas.

No sooner had Grant received a copy of the document than he left the office of the secretary of war, locked the door, and gave the key to the Adjutant General. Stanton immediately took possession. There now followed an angry interchange of letters between Johnson and Grant. Johnson accused the General of having broken faith with him. He claimed that Grant had accepted the office with the understanding that he would not relinquish it to Stanton, so the constitutionality of the Tenure of Office Act might be tested in the courts. Grant denied having made such a promise. It was obviously a misunderstanding, but Johnson, in his blundering way, managed to make an irreconcilable enemy out of the General.

The correspondence between Johnson and Grant became public, and Stevens seized upon it as the overt act he had been waiting for. He felt so certain that the President had made himself liable to impeachment that on February 10 he demanded that all evidence concerning Johnson in the hands of the Judiciary Committee be turned over to his committee. The demand was complied with, and the New York *Times* commented that this "looks a good deal like business. Thad Stevens's eyes are sharper in his old age than those of the chairman of the Judiciary Committee, and if he can't find some startling offense hidden somewhere between the covers of thirteen hundred pages, it will be strange indeed." [9] On February 13 Stevens proposed in the committee that the President be impeached, but the proposal was rejected. Johnson, as was his wont, came to his aid. On February 21 he dismissed Stanton in violation of the Tenure of Office Act and appointed Adjutant General Lorenzo Thomas secretary of war ad interim.

6

That Johnson had for a long time harbored the intention of testing the constitutionality of the Tenure of Office Act is evident from his correspondence with Grant. Yet there may have been another reason that prompted him to throw down the gauntlet to Congress. Clemenceau, who then as well as later proved himself a keen political analyst, wrote to his paper:

The Executive Committee of the Democratic Party was in session in Washington at the time, busy making preparations for the convention which will choose the presidential candidate of the Democratic party. The most influential Democrats were to select the city in which the

[9] New York *Times,* Feb. 12, 1868.

convention should be held and to send out a call to the whole Democratic party. It may be that Johnson intended to force himself definitely on the Democrats as their future candidate. A bold defiance of Congress might accomplish this.[10]

The young Frenchman was convinced that the President had laid himself open to impeachment and that he would probably be convicted. The case, however, was sufficiently complicated. That Johnson believed Stanton to be covered by the Tenure of Office Act and that the claim made at his trial that the act did not apply to the Secretary was an afterthought, is firmly established. Had he believed the act did not cover Stanton would he not have dismissed him in August, 1867, instead of merely suspending him? If he had not believed the act applied to Stanton would he have asked the General to aid him in testing its constitutionality by refusing to surrender the office if the Senate failed to concur? How could this have served as a test case if the act did not apply to Stanton? As late as February 10, 1868, when he wrote his famous letter to Grant he obviously still believed that Stanton was covered by the act and that Grant had perfidiously frustrated his plan to test its constitutionality.

On the basis of this evidence one is forced to conclude that Johnson had conspired to stop execution of a law of Congress, and that when the conspiracy had failed he had wantonly violated the law by dismissing Stanton. The claim that he had done so in order to test the law's constitutionality did not excuse him. As Bingham was to say in his argument before the Senate: "I ask you, senators, how long men would deliberate upon the question whether a private citizen, arraigned at the bar of one of your tribunals of justice for criminal violation of law, should be permitted to interpose a plea in justification of his criminal act that his only purpose was to interpret the Constitution and laws for himself, that he violated the law in the exercise of his prerogative to test its validity hereafter, at such day as might suit his own convenience in the courts of justice." [11] Professor Burgess has written that "such a power in the hands of the President would give him a double veto upon all the acts of Congress, a veto when acting as a part of the legislature in the enactment

[10] *Op. cit.*, p. 152.
[11] *Ibid.*, vol. II, pp. 467-468.

of the law, and then a purely executive veto which could be overcome only by an adverse judicial decision." [12]

There can therefore be no doubt that Johnson's claim that the Tenure of Office Act did not apply to Stanton was an afterthought. His counselors must have told him that he had not a leg to stand on and must make another claim. What was the basis for his claim that the act did not cover Stanton? It was based on the proviso that members of the cabinet "shall hold their offices, respectively, for and during the term of the President by whom they were appointed, and for one month thereafter." Since Stanton had not been appointed by Johnson, but by Lincoln, Johnson's counsel were to claim at the trial that the act did not apply to the Secretary of War. The impeachment managers appointed by the House were to claim that Johnson was serving out Lincoln's term. From this, they said, it logically followed that Stanton had a right to retain his office until one month after the expiration of Lincoln's term, unless the Senate concurred in his suspension. *The fact that the Senate had not concurred made it obvious that when it adopted the act, its intention had been what Johnson himself believed it to be when he tried to conspire with Grant for its nonexecution.*

One must therefore conclude that Johnson had knowingly violated a law of Congress and had made himself liable to impeachment, but one misses the real significance of the case unless one keeps in mind that it was not for the violation of the Tenure of Office Act that Congress was to impeach him. *He was impeached for one thing and tried for another.* He was tried for the commission of a trifling illegality because it was impossible under the Constitution to impeach him for his serious political offenses. Stevens's disciple George W. Julian was to admit this unequivocally when he said: "Does any one believe that if he had faithfully performed the duties of his high office up to the 21st of February last, the thought of impeachment would have occurred for the attempted removal of the Secretary of War, or for any of the particular acts now charged against him? Sir, it is only when these acts are interpreted in the light of his past course of lawlessness that his real character and guilt are made to appear. . . . Not alone the relatively trifling offenses now charged, but the

[12] *Op. cit.*, pp. 182-183.

deeply-rooted conviction of his previous guilt has at last brought Congress and the people to their feet in demanding his removal."[13]

7

When on February 21, 1868, the President informed the Senate of the dismissal of Stanton and the appointment of Adjutant General Lorenzo Thomas as secretary of war ad interim, that body reacted promptly. A resolution was passed informing him "that under the Constitution and laws of the United States, the President has no authority to remove the Secretary of War and to designate any other to that office *ad interim.*" Several senators rushed to the War Department to bring pressure to bear upon Stanton not to give up the office. Sumner, not usually laconic, sent him a message consisting of a single word—"Stick!" There followed a tragicomic controversy between him and the Adjutant General which resulted in Stanton remaining in office until the end of the trial.

In the House John Covode of Pennsylvania offered a resolution that "Andrew Johnson, President of the United States, be impeached of high crimes and misdemeanors." There was something awesome about the words. A feeling of solemnity pervaded the House. By a strict party vote the resolution was referred to Stevens's committee, which was to report on the morrow.

The telegraph flashed the news throughout the country. People from nearby cities and towns flocked to Washington to witness the historic scene. The fact that the day was Washington's birthday was almost forgotten, except by a few Democrats who were to attempt to hold up proceedings in the House by motions that Washington's Farewell Address be read. Congress was to meet at twelve o'clock. From early morning a large crowd stood at the doors of the Capitol waiting to be admitted. Long before noon all available space in the galleries and on the floor was occupied. The Capitol police was pressed into service to help the sergeant at arms preserve order.

The Reconstruction Committee had been meeting since 10:30. At 1:45 the rumor spread that the committee was about to report. The Senate had adjourned so its members might witness the scene, and senators and representatives now came pouring from cloakrooms

[13] *Globe,* Appendix, March 2, 1868.

and offices. At exactly two o'clock the door behind the Speaker's desk opened and Stevens, leaning on a hickory cane, entered, followed by members of his committee.

Rhodes and others have remarked that if Stevens had been in good health the proceedings might well have turned out differently.[14] When the impeachment proceedings began he stood on the brink of the grave. Clemenceau, who often had the opportunity to observe him from the press gallery, has written: "He used to sink down on his seat, and except for the fiery blaze of his eyes, deep set under his high bald forehead, one might sometimes have fancied that he had fainted or died. . . . Once in a while he rose, the members gathered round him, and he spoke for a few minutes in a voice not always heard even by the stenographers, never by the galleries." [15]

For this, the last great battle of his political career, he must have summoned all his reserve strength. The New York *Times* informs us that "Mr. Stevens took his place looking better than usual." Speaker Colfax warned first the galleries, then those on the floor that there must be no demonstration either of approbation or disapprobation. Then he nodded to Stevens who rose and said: "I am directed by the Committee on Reconstruction to present to the House a report with an accompanying resolution which I ask the Clerk to read."

The clerk read the short report, then the solemn words: *"Resolved,* That Andrew Johnson, President of the United States, be impeached of high crimes and misdemeanors in office."

8

The floodgates of oratory now were opened. Everybody wanted to participate in the historic occasion. James Brooks of New York, minority leader, made a speech in which appeared this significant statement: "And if the Democrats do not succeed in re-electing Andrew Johnson to the presidency, they will make his name immortal as one of the most illustrious of the defenders of liberty."

At half-past four on Monday, February 24, Stevens took the floor to make the closing argument. He had been resting in an adjoining committee room while speaker followed speaker. He now entered

[14] Rhodes, *op. cit.,* vol. VI, p. 135; Current, *op. cit.,* p. 294.
[15] *Op. cit.,* p. 227.

leaning on the arm of a colleague, amidst what *Harper's Weekly* has termed a "death-like silence." Slowly he made his way to a position close to the speaker's desk. His eyes roamed for a moment over the crowd, then he produced his manuscript and began to read in a voice that was surprisingly firm.

"The charge," he said, "against the official character of the Chief Executive, if falsely made, is a cruel wrong. If, on the other hand, the usurpations and misdemeanors charged against him are true, he is guilty of as atrocious attempts to usurp the liberty . . . of this nation as were ever perpetrated by the most detestable tyrant. Let us, therefore, discuss these questions in no partisan spirit, but with legal accuracy and impartial justice. The people desire no victim and they will endure no usurper.

"Andrew Johnson is charged with attempting to usurp the powers of other branches of the Government; with attempting to obstruct and resist the execution of the law, with misprision of bribery, with the open violation of the laws which declare his acts misdemeanors, and with removing from office the Secretary of War without the advice of the Senate."

With his customary frankness he did not deny that the most serious charges were political, but claimed they were of a nature justifying their inclusion: "In order to sustain impeachment under our Constitution I do not hold that it is necessary to prove a crime as an indictable offense, or any act *malum in se*. I agree with the distinguished gentleman from Pennsylvania on the other side of the House, who holds this to be a purely political proceeding. It is intended as a remedy for malfeasance in office and to prevent the continuance thereof. Beyond that, it is not intended as a personal punishment for past offenses or for future example."

He dwelt on the difference of impeachment proceedings under English law and under the American Constitution: "In England men in higher stations whom it was found difficult to convict before ordinary tribunals . . . were tried by impeachment or by bills of attainder. . . . The system soon degenerated into political and personal persecution, and men were tried, condemned and executed from malignant motives. . . . Here the whole punishment was made to consist in removal from office, and bills of attainder are wholly prohibited. We are to treat this question then as wholly political, in which, if an officer of the Government abuse his trust or attempt to pervert it to improper purposes, whatever might be his motives, he becomes subject to impeachment and removal from office."

He proceeded to show how this applied to the present case. Referring to Johnson's correspondence with General Grant he said: "If Andrew Johnson tells the truth then he is guilty of a high official misdemeanor, for he avows his effort to prevent the execution of the law. If the General commanding tells the truth then the President is guilty of a high misdemeanor, for he declares the same thing as the President, denying only his complicity. . . . If he and the General told the truth then he committed willful perjury by refusing to take care that the laws should be duly executed. . . . Indeed, to show his utter disregard for the laws of his country . . . he proclaims to the public that the laws of Congress are unconstitutional and not binding. . . . Who, after that, can say that such a man is fit to occupy the presidential chair, whose duty it is to inculcate obedience to those very laws?"

Yet far graver, in his opinion, were the following charges: "When the so-called Confederate States of America were conquered . . . the government and final disposition of the conquered country belonged to Congress alone. . . . Neither the Executive nor the judiciary had any right to interfere with it except so far as was necessary to control it by military rule until the sovereign power of the nation had provided for the civil administration. Andrew Johnson, with unblushing hardihood, undertook to rule them by his own power alone; direct them what government to erect and what constitution to adopt and to send Representatives and Senators to Congress according to his instructions. When admonished by express act of Congress . . . he disregarded the warning and continued his lawless usurpation. . . . In my judgment his conduct was a high-handed usurpation of power which ought long ago to have brought him to impeachment and trial. He has been lucky thus far in escaping through false logic and false law.

"I trust that when we come to vote upon this question we shall remember that although it is the duty of the President to see that the laws be executed the sovereign power of the nation rests in Congress, who have been placed around the Executive to enforce his obedience to the law and the Constitution."

He moved adoption of the impeachment resolution. It was adopted by a vote of 126 to 47. He then moved that two committees be appointed—a committee of two, to notify the Senate officially of the action taken by the House, and a committee of seven, to prepare Articles of Impeachment. He and Bingham were appointed on both committees.

9

The following day, at ten minutes past one, the doorkeeper of the Senate swung open both wings of the main entrance to the Senate chamber and announced: "A delegation from the House of Representatives!" Stevens and Bingham, dressed in black, walked slowly down the center aisle. The New York *Times* describes Stevens as "pale, emaciated, death-like in appearance," but his voice as "stern and vigorous." Addressing himself to Wade, president pro tempore of the Senate, he said:

"Mr. President, in obedience to the order of the House of Representatives, we appear before you, and in the name of the House of Representatives and of all the people of the United States we do impeach Andrew Johnson, President of the United States, of high crimes and misdemeanors in office; and we further inform the Senate that the House of Representatives will in due time exhibit particular articles of impeachment against him and make good the same; and in their name we demand that the Senate take order for the appearance of the said Andrew Johnson to answer said impeachment."

Wade gravely replied that the Senate would take order in the premises, and the two men withdrew.

The committee entrusted with the task of framing the Articles of Impeachment was confronted with an insurmountable obstacle. Innumerable were the times that Johnson had given encouragement to the Southern states to resist the national will. He had done so when the terms upon which the South could have been readmitted to participation in the national government were almost incredibly lenient. He had been doing so ever since. He had publicly insulted Congress over and over again. He had degraded the presidency. He had sacrificed the South to his ambition and megalomania and had been false to the North that had placed him in power. But he had not stolen a horse or even a chicken, so there was no way of impeaching him except by taking advantage of his violation of a law the constitutionality of which was doubtful. Handicapped by this limitation the ten Articles of Impeachment the committee managed to produce left much to be desired. Stevens was not satisfied with them and framed an eleventh article that gave more promise of success.

He artfully wove together some of Johnson's political offenses with the one criminal offense he had committed when dismissing Stanton. One of the most serious of the former was his statement on August 18, 1866, to a delegation that called on him at the White House, that "the Thirty-Ninth Congress was not a Congress of the United States authorized by the Constitution to exercise legislative power under the same; but on the contrary was a Congress of only part of the States." This, Stevens argued, was equivalent to "denying . . . that the legislation of said Congress was valid or obligatory upon him . . . except in so far as he saw fit to approve the same, and also thereby denying . . . the power of the Thirty-Ninth Congress to propose amendments to the Constitution of the United States." His flouting of the Tenure of Office Act thus appeared the natural consequence of this frame of mind.

10

The House chose seven of its ablest members to serve as managers of the impeachment. Since Stevens was too ill to take charge of the prosecution, Bingham was chosen chairman. The others were Stevens, Boutwell and Butler of Massachusetts, Wilson of Iowa, Williams of Pennsylvania, and Logan of Illinois. Counsel for the President were Attorney General Henry Stanbery, who had resigned from the cabinet so he could appear for the defense; Benjamin R. Curtis of Massachusetts, former associate justice of the Supreme Court, who had voluntarily left that tribunal after six years of service to devote himself to the practice of law; William M. Evarts, a famous New York lawyer; William S. Groesbeck of Cincinnati, a former Democratic representative; and Thomas A. R. Nelson of Tennessee, a personal friend of the President. As prescribed by law, Chief Justice Salmon P. Chase was to preside over the Senate while the trial was in progress.

Stevens took little active part in the trial. Once the rumor spread through the city that he had died. Yet he was the soul of the proceedings. There is a remarkable description of him in the Philadelphia *Press* as he appeared at the trial, seated at the managers' table:

He is seated in his cushioned chair, his elbows resting on the arms, and his long bony fingers interlaced. His voice has almost gone, and there is a strange huskiness about it, startlingly suggestive of the rattle in the throat of a dying man. His eyes are dim, and apparently the soft light of the chamber hurts them, for they are kept shut at long intervals. At times he leans his head forward, as if buried in deep contemplation, and thus raising it, unlaces his right hand from the other, and waving it majestically toward some one of his colleagues, makes a scarcely audible suggestion. There is something in his appearance which attracts the gaze with a strange, spellbound sensation, and the idea invariably suggests itself that something supernatural inhabits his weary frame. He is born to die, as he prays he will, in harness! He is the embodiment of all the principles involved in this mighty case; and while he does not absolutely lead or conduct the prosecution, because he is too feeble, no one imagines that it could be conducted without him.[16]

The trial opened officially on March 5, 1868, at one o'clock in the afternoon, when Chief Justice Chase, the personification of dignity, entered the Senate chamber accompanied by Associate Justice Nelson and a senatorial escort. He took the chair and said in his most solemn manner: "Senators, I attend the Senate in obedience to your notice, for the purpose of joining with you in forming a court of impeachment for the trial of the President of the United States. And I am now ready to take the oath." The senators, who had risen, remained standing while the oath was administered to him by Justice Nelson, after which the roll was called and all were sworn. The Senate then adjourned until one o'clock the following day.

The managers of the impeachment had already appeared in the Senate on March 4, and the Articles of Impeachment had been read. During the reading the managers had remained standing—all except Stevens who was physically unable to do so. On the thirteenth counsel for the President appeared and asked for forty days in which to prepare an answer. Butler remarked that this was "as long as it took God Almighty to destroy the world with a flood." Ten days was all that was allowed them. They presented their reply on the twenty-third. These and other preliminaries having been disposed of, the real trial began on March 30, when Butler opened for the prosecu-

[16] Cited by Alphonse B. Miller in *Thaddeus Stevens,* p. 353.

tion. His speech, which he read from printed slips, was long, learned, and fairly effective, but not what, considering his reputation, the public had expected. One reporter remarked that it was well for Butler to have *clipped* his own wings in arguing a case like this, but he should not have *shaved* them. Then followed a procession of some twenty-five witnesses for the prosecution.

On April 9 Judge Curtis opened for the defense and spoke for two days. Polished, suave, making few gestures, seldom raising his voice, he made what was generally considered the best of a bad case. Clemenceau, who had gone to see Stevens and had told him that he could not agree with his attacks on Johnson, and whose opinion therefore can be regarded as reasonably objective, was not impressed. He wrote concerning the speech:

> Mr. Curtis took up only two essential points. He contends that the law known as the Tenure-of-Office Bill does not apply in the case of Mr. Stanton, because the latter was appointed Secretary of War by Mr. Lincoln, and not by the present President. Whence he naturally concluded that the removal of Mr. Stanton was a perfectly legal act, and that Mr. Johnson violated none of the provisions of the Tenure-of-Office Bill. Then, after having established this point to his own satisfaction, he turns right around and seeks to prove that Mr. Johnson, in removing Mr. Stanton, violated the same law deliberately, with the plan of forcing the Supreme Court to give a decision on his action.
>
> I confess I cannot see how Mr. Curtis can reconcile his two lines of defense. I looked in vain all through his speech for anything which might serve as a transition between these two points of view. He merely says, in conclusion, that he realizes some people will think they see a contradiction in his double argument, but that he himself sees none. I doubt whether the Senate will be satisfied with this simple affirmation. The President either did or did not violate the Tenure-of-Office Bill. Mr. Curtis makes out that (1) he did not violate it, (2) he set out to violate it and did violate it, but that in doing so he acted with the best intentions in the world. I leave to someone more clever than I the task of finding some connection between these two propositions.[17]

11

Stevens spoke on April 27. Halfway down the official account of his speech, there appears this notation: "Mr. Manager Stevens read a portion of his argument standing at the Secretary's desk; but after

[17] *Op. cit.*, pp. 174-175.

proceeding a few minutes, being too feeble to stand, obtained permission to take a seat, and having read nearly half an hour from a chair until his voice became almost too weak to be heard, handed over his manuscript to Mr. Manager Butler, who concluded the reading."

Rhodes has said that Stevens made the ablest argument at the trial. Certainly it was the most concise. "Experience has taught me," he began by saying, "that nothing is more prolix than ignorance." But while the speech was logical and to the point it had none of that spontaneous eloquence that in the past had made his speeches so effective. He was old and ill and weary and somehow the speech reflected that condition. But he had not lost his cunning. Three of the Republican senators who were to vote for Johnson's acquittal—Grimes, Henderson, and Ross—later claimed that they did so because they felt the defense had not been fairly treated by the prosecution. Stevens must have sensed that Butler's bullying tactics were not calculated to advance the cause of impeachment. He tried the opposite tack. It cannot be said that he wholly succeeded, as for example when he referred to Johnson as "this offspring of assassination," but on the whole he kept the promise he made at the beginning of the speech when he said that he desired to "discuss the charges against the respondent in no mean spirit of malignity or vituperation, but to argue in a manner worthy of the high tribunal before which I appear, and of the exalted position of the accused." Since the speech contained nothing that has not been previously discussed, a short quotation must suffice:

"The President is sworn to take care that the laws be faithfully executed. In what part of the Constitution or laws does he find it to be his duty to search out for defective laws in order that he may advise their infraction? . . . If he were not willing to execute the laws passed by the American Congress and unrepealed, let him resign the office which was thrown upon him by a horrible convulsion and retire to his village obscurity. Let him not be so swollen by pride and arrogance, which sprang from the deep misfortune of his country, as to attempt an entire revolution of its internal machinery, and the disgrace of the trusted servants of his lamented predecessor." [18]

He had evidently sensed that the conviction of Johnson hinged

[18] *Op. cit.*, vol. II, pp. 219, 229.

on the ability of the prosecution to convince certain senators that Johnson had deliberately violated a law of Congress, for he said little about the grave political charges upon which he believed impeachment should primarily have been based. In accusing Johnson of wishing to revolutionize the internal machinery of the country by disobeying a law of Congress until its constitutionality had been tested, he seemed to have forgotten that he himself aimed to bring about an even profounder revolution by having the country change its presidential form of government to a parliamentary form.

12

It may be said that Johnson was tried before a jury composed of eleven senators. There were fifty-four, and thirty-six votes—two-thirds of the Senate—were necessary to convict. Twelve were Democrats and there never was the slightest doubt about how they meant to vote. Nor was there any doubt concerning thirty-one of the Republicans. As far as these forty-three were concerned the trial was a mere formality. They had made up their minds long ago and nothing could change them. Curtis might just as well have recited Shakespeare and Butler have intoned the "Star-Spangled Banner" for all the difference it would have made to them. There remained eleven about whom there existed uncertainty in varying degrees. If five of these could be convinced, persuaded, influenced, or bullied to vote guilty, Johnson would cease to be President. Whether or not they would vote for conviction depended more upon other considerations than upon the guilt or innocence of the accused. Some of these considerations were public, others private. The three principal ones were the personality of Johnson's successor, the fear of setting a precedent that might change the nature of the government, the fact that Johnson had less than a year to serve anyway and had done about all the damage he was capable of doing.

If Johnson was convicted his successor during the remainder of the term would be the president pro tempore of the Senate, Benjamin Franklin Wade, better known as Ben Wade or Old Ben Wade. He was a rough-hewn man of sixty-seven, had been an abolitionist long before the war, and was fearless and outspoken. There were few who did not respect him, but even fewer who agreed with him on questions of economics. He was a Greenbacker and had advanced ideas on the labor question. While somewhat at a loss about what to do about the matter, he felt that "that system of labor which degrades the poor and elevates the rich; which makes the rich richer and the poor poorer; which drags the very soul out of the poor man for a pitiful existence, is wrong. We must elevate the laborer and give him a share in the proceeds of his labor." [19] What worried Republicans most was that unlike Johnson, who could change his principles overnight, he would stick to them through thick and thin, as he had to his abolitionism, and would try to do something about the matter. It is therefore hardly surprising that a party which was strongly under the influence of the upper crust of society should have felt little enthusiasm about trading a political renegade for an economic radical.

Personal considerations likewise entered into the matter. It was generally believed that Fessenden, who had been defeated by Wade for the presidency of the Senate, would under no circumstances vote to elevate his successful rival even higher, thus giving him the opportunity of securing the Republican nomination at the forthcoming Republican National Convention.

So, with one thing and another, strategists decided that things narrowed down to how an obscure senator, Edmund G. Ross of Kansas, was going to vote. Mr. Ross, conscious of his own importance, refused to commit himself. He remained an enigma until his name was called by the chief clerk and in reply to the question put to him by the Chief Justice, he spoke the fateful words that determined the course of history.

In the afternoon of Saturday, May 16, 1868, a solemn and portentous scene took place in the Senate chamber. The Chief Justice occupied the chair. Below him, on his left, the managers of the impeachment sat at a table. On his right, at another table, sat the President's counsel. In front of him were the senators and the Committee of the Whole from the House of Representatives, with the committee chairman, the speaker, the chief clerk. In the diplomatic gallery sat the foreign ministers and other dignitaries. In the public gallery people were packed like sardines and there was a profusion of tally sheets. Over fifteen hundred people were crowded in a hall

[19] Interview in the New York *Herald,* July 8, 1867.

with a seating capacity of one thousand to watch the result of the trial of the century.

It had been agreed that Article XI would be the first to be submitted to a vote. That article—sometimes called the Omnibus Article—skillfully wove together the most serious charges contained in the other ten. The Chief Justice warned the gallery that any person creating a disturbance would be promptly arrested. Then the article was read, after which the chief clerk called the roll. As a senator's name was called he rose and the Chief Justice repeated the formula: "Mr. Senator, how say you? Is the respondent, Andrew Johnson, President of the United States, guilty or not guilty of a high misdemeanor, as charged in this article?" Finally the name of Ross was called and he said: "Not guilty." It is not recorded that Stevens gave any visible sign of disappointment. The final vote stood, 35 for conviction, 19 for acquittal. Johnson had won by one vote.

A motion was made to adjourn until May 26. It was hoped that the disapproval of their conduct expressed by the Republican press and letters from their constituents would make one or more of the recalcitrant Republicans relent. The press raged. An avalanche of telegrams and letters descended upon the unhappy men. All in vain. When on May 26 the Senate reconvened, the vote on Articles II and III was exactly as before. Adjournment was taken sine die. The trial was over.

CHAPTER XVIII

Last Days

Stevens felt angry and disappointed about the outcome of the trial. Others might consider the matter closed, he did not. He probably would have agreed that no immediate purpose would be served by removing Johnson, but he had been profoundly impressed by the inability of Congress to deal firmly with a situation that might, had a Frank Blair instead of a Johnson been in the White House, have resulted in renewed civil war. He believed advantage should be taken of this opportunity to set a precedent. Unless a broader construction was put on the constitutional right to impeach the President, the time might come when "the only resource will be found in the dagger of Brutus. God grant that it may never be used." [1]

So, soon after the Senate's adjournment sine die as a court, he set to work framing Additional Articles of Impeachment. He prepared five, as follows: The President had abused the patronage of the government for his personal ends; he had violated the Constitution by usurping legislative power belonging to Congress when he established provisional governments in the Southern states; he had resorted to corrupt practices when trying to induce senators from Colorado to pledge him their support in return for his approval of the act conferring statehood—likewise by pardoning deserters from the United States Army and restoring their right of suffrage on condition that they vote the Democratic ticket; he had, without authority from Congress, taken from the control of the United States Treasury

[1] *Globe,* July 7, 1868.

land and money confiscated from the rebels under the second Confiscation Act and had restored it to the former owners; he had sought to govern the rebel states by his own mere power, by forms unknown to the Constitution and without consulting Congress.

In support of the charges he wrote one of the longest speeches of his career, and on July 7 had it read in the House by the clerk. The following paragraph contains the essence of the argument: "Instead of alleging that impeachment can only be instituted where there is an indictable offense, I contend that the great object of impeachment was to punish for malfeasance in office—where there was no actual crime committed—no malfeasance against which an indictment would hold, and against which no allegation of evil intention need be made. In other words, that proceedings in impeachment should be had mainly where the true distinction was made between a charge against a party with malice aforethought in it, and a charge against a party with no evil intention, but with great injury to the country; in short, that they could be had mainly for political offenses."

Whether a change in the Constitution making this possible would be advisable need not be discussed here, but that such was the intention of the framers of the Constitution no constitutional authority has ever cared to affirm.

Toward the end of the speech, addressing himself to Speaker Colfax, whom the Republicans had nominated as Grant's running mate, Stevens said: "My sands are nearly run, and I can only see with the eye of faith. I am fast descending the downhill of life, at the foot of which is an open grave. But you, sir, are promised length of days and a brilliant career. If you and your compeers can fling away ambition and realize that every human being, however lowlyborn and degraded by fortune is your equal, that every inalienable right which belongs to you belongs also to him, truth and righteousness will spread over the land, and you will look down from the top of the Rocky Mountains upon an empire of one hundred millions of happy people."

Colfax must have known why Stevens made this appeal. He was dissatisfied with the platform the Republican National Convention had adopted. It failed to make provision for the extension of Negro suffrage to the Northern states by means of a constitutional amendment. Stevens considered this "tame and cowardly." In June he had written: "What did the bold men in Chicago mean by selling the right of suffrage? . . . We cannot maintain liberty by skulking." One can well understand why Chief Justice Chase should have told a visitor who said he meant to call on "Old Thad" who was ill in bed, "I wish you would say to Mr. Stevens for me that when he goes out of the House he will take with him more backbone than he will leave."

Stevens had meant to press the Additional Articles of Impeachment at the September session, but died before that time.

2

Frederick W. Seward, son of William H. Seward and assistant secretary of state during the administrations of Lincoln, Johnson, and Hayes, has written in his *Reminiscences:*

> One morning there was a buzz of excitement in the reporters' gallery and on the floor of the House of Representatives, occasioned by the sudden appearance of Secretary Seward, who calmly walked down the main aisle to the seat of Thaddeus Stevens, greeted him, and sat down for a chat. As Stevens was the especial leader of the opponents of the President, the evident cordiality between him and Seward was an enigma to both sides of the House. It grew more puzzling when Stevens went to dine and spend the evening with Seward. A day or two afterward he rose to propose an extra appropriation "for special service," to be expended under the direction of the Secretary of State. So strong and so implicitly trusted by his followers was Stevens that he had little difficulty in inducing them to vote for it, "though much they wondered why." The only information vouchsafed to them was that it was for a secret diplomatic mission, of which they would be informed as soon as compatible with the public interests.[2]

This incident, which took place in January, 1867, illustrates an important trait in Stevens's character: When it came to furthering a measure that might enhance the greatness of the United States, he made no distinction between friend or foe. Seward had reason to believe that the Bay of Samana might be leased or bought advantageously from Santo Domingo. This would provide the United States with a West Indian harbor, lack of which had been sorely felt during the war and which would be invaluable for defense in case

[2] *Op. cit.*, p. 345.

of attack by a maritime power. Although knowing that Stevens considered him Johnson's evil genius and had assailed him on numerous occasions, Seward felt certain that he would be able to count on him in a matter of that kind, and was not disappointed. Stevens got him the appropriation and the treaty was negotiated, but the Senate shortsightedly failed to approve it, not unlikely because the acquisition might reflect credit upon an administration with which it was at loggerheads.

It should be noted that Stevens's interest in projects that gave promise of promoting the nation's progress or power was sometimes taken advantage of by unscrupulous railway and other promoters. His friend Justin S. Morrill, who had been promoted to the Senate, alluded to this in his memorial address after Stevens's death. "Public treasures and public lands," he said, "were seldom too precious in his eyes to be scattered for objects national in scope; and he had no apprehensions, not being a jobber himself, that, so scattered, jobbers might harvest the major blessings from such dispensations." [3]

When the Russian government decided to sell "Russian America," now known as Alaska, to the United States because, as Frederick Seward put it, "the United States always had been and probably always would be a friend," [4] his father was eager to close the deal. The sum of $7,200,000 in gold was agreed on. As in the Samana affair Seward counted on Stevens to get the appropriation through the House. Stevens was as enthusiastic about the matter as Seward and put forth every effort to get the House to agree. On July 13, 1868, less than a month before his death, he made a speech in the House pleading with his colleagues to pass the appropriation. It passed the following day and the bill became law on July 27, 1868.

That any pleading should have been necessary may sound incredible to the present generation. The fact is, however, that while the treaty was promptly ratified by the Senate and proclaimed in force on June 20, 1867, more than a year was to pass before the House appropriated the purchase money. One reason was hostility toward anything emanating from the administration. Another was the administration's haste in taking possession after ratification of the treaty by the Senate, thus confronting the House with a *fait accompli*.

[3] *Globe,* Dec. 18, 1868.
[4] *Op. cit.,* p. 360.

Still another, the abysmal ignorance of the representatives concerning the character of the region. Some called it "Seward's folly," others "Johnson's Polar Bear Garden." One heard such expressions as "barren God-forsaken region," whose only products are "icebergs and polar bears," where the ground is "frozen six feet deep" and vegetation is "limited to mosses." It was conceded that there might be some "wretched fish" fit only for "wretched Eskimaux." To buy such a place was to squander millions. It is greatly to Stevens's credit that he should have exerted every effort to overcome this opposition. His only reward was calumny, for which Seward bears a large part of the responsibility.

3

On Sunday, September 6, 1868, when Stevens had been for several weeks in his grave, Seward and Johnson, wishing to escape the heat of Washington, went for a drive into the country. Some seven or eight miles from the city they stopped at a pleasant grove, had the servant unload the picnic basket, and partook of "refreshments." William A. Dunning, onetime professor of history and political philosophy, in Columbia University, concurs with the prevalent opinion among historians that "Seward was notoriously prone to narrative and reminiscence that were more conspicuous for picturesqueness than for strict accuracy . . . especially when the cheering cup was in circulation." To put it plainly, whatever his other qualities, he was an old gossip to whom the satisfaction of telling a sensational story meant more than a man's reputation. On that afternoon he indulged in gossip that was particularly pleasing to Johnson. No sooner had the President returned to the White House than he made a memorandum of what he had been told.

According to the memorandum, discovered in 1905, Forney, owner of the Philadelphia *Press,* had been paid $30,000 in gold by the Russian minister for his support of the appropriation. General Nathaniel P. Banks, chairman of the Foreign Relations Committee of the House, had received $8,000, and "the incorruptible Thaddeus Stevens received as his 'sop' the moderate sum of $10,000." Others, too, were mentioned, but since they do not particularly concern us will remain unnamed.

This was not the only time that the talkative Seward mentioned

Stevens's name in this connection. On September 22 he entertained at dinner John Bigelow, a Civil War diplomat. After dinner came a game of whist, during which Seward said: "Do you wish to know how the treaty was consummated?" He then related with some variations what he had told Johnson. Forney had received only $20,000, but Banks had received $10,000. As for Stevens, "one thousand more were to have been given to poor Thad Stevens, but no one would undertake to give that to him, so I undertook it myself. The poor fellow died, and I have it now." Bigelow, on returning to his hotel, jotted down in his diary what the Secretary had told him.

Whatever the truth about the matter, it is obvious from the variations that Seward possessed no firsthand information, but merely repeated what he had heard and even that inaccurately and perhaps with embellishments of his own. There were all sorts of rumors circulating about Washington concerning the treaty and the appropriation. One of these was that Seward himself had been bribed for the tidy sum of $250,000 and that Banks had received an equal amount. Seward may or may not have known this.

In December, 1868, the House ordered an investigation, which was made by the Committee on Public Expenditures. Witnesses were examined under oath. Among those who testified was Seward. He told the committee: "I know nothing whatever of the use the Minister made of the fund. I know of no payment to anybody, by him, or of any application of the funds which he received. In regard to all these allegations I have no knowledge."

How is this to be reconciled with the gossip he was retailing? If he was not telling the truth under oath, how could he be believed when not sworn to stick to facts?

Professor Dunning, after a careful weighing of the evidence (Bigelow's work had then not yet been published) reached the following conclusion: Forney, no longer connected with the Senate, may well have received $30,000 in gold for his support of the appropriation. As for Stevens and Banks—"it is quite possible that in the far-reaching gratitude of the Minister, he expressed a wish or a purpose to 'do something' for Banks and Stevens, whose support of the appropriation had been so effective. This *ex post facto* project of Stoeckl [the Russian minister] might easily have taken on, in the conversation of September 6, the form and implication that Johnson embodied in the memorandum. Whether the project was ever carried into effect or not, it is impossible with the available evidence, to say."

If such a distribution was made, Dr. Dunning is of the opinion that it could only have taken place between August 1 and September 16, in which case "it is hard to believe that Stevens got his share; for he was a very sick man on the first of August and he died on the 11th." Would he have accepted such an ex post facto gratuity had he been well? Seward's remark that "no one would undertake to give that to him," points to the contrary. His incorruptibility was too well known to make anyone willing to face his wrath in offering it to him. Moreover, what reason is there to believe that a man who in 1867 refused $100,000 freely offered him by his friends and admirers to reimburse him for losses suffered by him during the war, would in 1868 have accepted a bribe of $10,000? And why should the Russian minister have wasted such a sum on a man who from the beginning had been an enthusiastic supporter of the measure? How ardently he favored the Alaska purchase may be judged from the fact that on the afternoon of his death he told his nephew Thad and his friend Simon Stevens that it was the "biggest thing in Seward's life," and that if he could have purchased Samana it would have been the "crowning glory of his career."

Seward's son Frederick has tried to exonerate his father of being a malicious gossip by saying: "My own conjecture is, that he told Mr. Bigelow, who had recently arrived from Paris, the sort of news that he might expect to find flying around Washington and the lobbies of the Capitol, and that Mr. Bigelow, not fully comprehending that these were *canards,* went home and set them down in his diary as actual facts." This totally ignores Seward's statement to Johnson, similar to the one he made to Bigelow. Not Stevens's, but Seward's character has been damaged by the testimony.[5]

[5] Wm. A. Dunning, "Paying for Alaska," *Political Science Monthly,* vol. XXVII, Sept. 1912, No. 3, pp. 385-398; John Bigelow *Retrospections of an Active Life,* vol. IV, pp. 216-217; *H.R. Reports of Committees,* Fortieth Congress, Third Session, No. 35; Frederick Seward, *op. cit.,* p. 366. Professor Current in his *Old Thad Stevens* (pp. 315-316) gives just enough of the testimony to leave the implication that Stevens was bribed.

4

Horace Maynard of Tennessee, in his memorial address after Stevens's death, was to say: "All his life he held the outposts of thought!" He led, but seldom followed. If a question came up on which he and the party could not agree, he did not hesitate to say, as he did on one occasion: "In this case I do not act as a member of the Republican Party," and to go his own way.[6] Usually it was the party that offered to compromise, for he commanded a phalanx of devoted followers that made it dangerous to break with him. "He knows more than all of us put together," one of them, John Wentworth of Illinois, said on the floor of the House.[7]

Toward the end of his career Stevens and his party came violently to grips regarding fiscal policy.

There had been during the war some seven issues of government bonds. One had been floated in 1861, before the country went off the gold standard. Opinions concerning such matters being what they were at that time, all agreed that as far as that particular issue was concerned, principal as well as interest should be payable in specie. The remaining issues all carried the guarantee that the interest was to be payable in specie, but only two had the additional guarantee that the principal likewise was payable in gold. That the public fully understood the difference is evident from the fact that in 1864, when the country's credit was at its lowest ebb, one of the latter issues had been readily absorbed with a reduced interest rate because of the gold guarantee regarding the principal. It should furthermore be considered that now that the war was over, government revenues exceeded expenditures, so that the value of greenbacks, for which the various issues had been sold, had considerably risen in relation to gold. This meant that bondholders would have a profit on the principal anyway. But they were not satisfied with this. A movement was on foot to redeem all the bond issues in gold.

Stevens determined to oppose this. In October, 1867, he wrote a series of letters to his friend John Geiger in which he expressed his ideas on the subject. They were written for publication and quickly

[6] *Globe,* March 16, 1867.
[7] *Ibid.*

found their way into print. In one of the letters he pointed out that when it came to private debts, even an agreement clearly specifying that a debt was payable in gold had been declared invalid by the courts. Under these circumstances to demand that the government pay in gold when there was no agreement to that effect seemed to Stevens a conspiracy on the part of the bondholders against the country's taxpayers.

He had not been mistaken regarding the intentions of the "gold block," whose chief representatives in the House were Garfield and Blaine. No sooner had the Fortieth Congress assembled for its regular session, than Hugh McCulloch, Secretary of the Treasury, in his report of November 30, 1867, proposed that the principal of all government bonds should be paid in gold. He made this emotional argument: "How would the Government of the United States stand before the world—how would it stand in the estimation of its own people, if it should decline to pay, according to agreement, the money borrowed when its very existence was in peril, and without which it could not have prosecuted the war, on the ground that the lenders took advantage of its necessities and purchased its securities at less than their value." [8]

This was an amazing statement. Paying the loans "according to agreement" was precisely what Stevens wanted and the Secretary did not want. McCulloch had been president of an Indiana bank. One wonders how long the bank's board of directors would have allowed him to keep his post if he had proposed that all the bank's liabilities must be paid in gold when there was no agreement to that effect and gold was at a premium!

But the versatile McCulloch had some even more remarkable arguments. He claimed that the different classes of securities had been *"negotiated with the distinct understanding"* that they were to be paid in gold. The provision in two of the bond issues that principal as well as interest was payable in specie, *"if not accidental, attracted no attention at the time either in Congress or with the public."* Who was responsible for the "distinct understanding" about something not specified in the agreement? If the Treasury's agents, who sold the bonds to the public, had made such misstatements and

[8] *Globe,* Appendix, 1867-1868, p. 30.

the Treasury knew it, why had it not intervened? As for his second argument, are we to believe that when Congress lowered the interest on bonds of which the principal as well as the interest were payable in gold it did not know what it was doing? And are we to believe that agents who, according to McCulloch, had misrepresented bonds not redeemable in gold as being redeemable in that manner had failed to point out the gold guarantee in bonds paying a lower rate of interest?

5

It was not long before an attempt was made to translate McCulloch's proposal into legislation. Since in the House there would be Stevens to contend with, the gold conspirators decided to have the Senate take the initiative. The bond issue of February 25, 1862, came up for refunding. The bonds fell due in twenty years, but were callable in five, hence were known as the five-twenties. They bore 6 per cent interest payable in specie, but had no such guarantee regarding repayment of principal and were not exempt from taxation. Since the government's credit had vastly improved one would have expected that the Senate Finance Committee would have framed a refunding measure more favorable to the government. Yet here was what on December 17, 1867, John Sherman reported to the Senate on behalf of the committee:

The five-twenties were to be exchanged for forty-year bonds, callable in ten. The interest was to remain at 6 per cent and was as before payable in gold. But in addition to this the principal also was to be payable in gold and the bonds were to be exempt from taxation, state as well as federal! That a Senate committee should have had the audacity to make such a proposal was a sinister foreboding of what was to come under the Grant administration.

The impeachment proceedings temporarily halted what Stevens called a "shameful swindle." But although the Republican National Convention in the meantime endorsed McCulloch's views, a sufficient number of senators felt conscience-stricken at least to the extent of demanding a lowering of the interest to 5 per cent. When the bill reached the House, the Ways and Means Committee made some further changes. The measure came up for discussion on July 17, when Stevens, although barely able to stand, took the floor. The

Democrats had nominated Horatio Seymour for president, and for vice-president an old enemy of the Commoner, Frank Blair. Yet so great was his indignation that he said: "If I knew there was any party in this country would go for paying in coin what is payable in money, thus enhancing it by one half; if I knew there was such a platform and such a determination . . . I would vote for the other side, Frank Blair and all. I would vote for no such swindle upon the tax-payers of this country; I would vote for no such peculation in favor of the large bondholders, the millionaires, who took advantage of our folly in granting them coin payment of interest. And I declare—well, it is hard to say it—but if even Frank Blair stood upon the platform paying the bonds according to contract, and the Republican candidate stood upon the platform of paying bloated speculators twice the amount which we agreed to pay them, then I would vote for Frank Blair, even if a worse man than Seymour headed the ticket."

On July 21, Garfield, speaking in support of the measure, quoted a few isolated sentences from a speech Stevens had made at about the time the five-twenties were issued, which made it appear as if he had been in favor of payment of principal as well as interest in gold. Stevens replied the following day, saying: "I shall not now undertake to explain the whole of this matter, as I am too feeble, but I shall take occasion hereafter to expose the villainy of those who charge me with having said, on the passage of the five-twenty bill, that the bonds were payable in coin. The whole debate from which they quote, and all my remarks which they cited, were made upon an entirely different bill. . . . My speech was made upon the introduction of the 'legal tender bill,' on which the interest for twenty years was to be paid in currency."

The exposure he promised was never made. He was standing at death's portal and could not summon the strength to do so. His intervention, however, produced results. The interest was further lowered to 4 per cent. The weary warrior pronounced himself satisfied. "I shall die hurrahing," he had said once. Whether "hurrahing" or not, he needed his remaining strength to die in a manner worthy of him.

6

Congress adjourned on July 27 to meet again in September. Two weeks earlier the Washington *Chronicle* had reported that "the Honorable Thaddeus Stevens was preparing to leave for his farm in Adams County." Dr. Young, Stevens's Washington physician, forbade the journey. It was a great disappointment. Washington in August, with the heat worse than usual! It was not a pleasant prospect. When he realized that he would be unable to leave, he wrote his friend John Law, an Indiana Democrat, to come and keep him company for a few weeks. He promised to arrange with a couple of others so they could have a frequent game of euchre. "Don't forget to live yourself if I should die," he added. "A little of the old stock will be needed, whoever has the helm." [9]

His friend John Hickman called, and wishing to cheer him remarked how well he looked. Thad replied sardonically: "Ah, John, it is not my appearance but my disappearance that troubles me." He knew he was making his last stand. "You have changed my medicine?" he asked the doctor. "Yes." "Well, this is a square fight." [10]

He had to take to his bed. The press became aware of the seriousness of his condition, and so great was the public interest that many newspapers published daily bulletins. Biographical sketches were prepared. On August 4 the Philadelphia *Press* reported that he had said to a friend the contest with death could not last much longer. Suddenly he rallied and on August 6 was able to sit up. On the eighth he seemed to be convalescing. Lydia Smith, quiet and efficient, did not feel reassured. She wrote to his nephew Thad. On the ninth he had a relapse and had to go back to bed.

A short distance from Stevens's house on Capitol Hill was the Providence Hospital, a charity for colored people he had helped to found and for which he had secured an appropriation of thirty thousand dollars from Congress. It was in charge of colored nuns. Two of them, Sisters Lorette and Genevieve, often came to help Lydia take care of the sick man. By day or by night one of the three women was in the room. Stevens was often in great pain, but made no complaint. He could take but little nourishment, but it was a comfort to

[9] *Stevens MSS.* Stevens to Law, July 21, 1868.
[10] Woodburn, *op. cit.*, p. 590; McCall, *op. cit.*, p. 351.

have one of the women waft a little coolness over him with a palm-leaf fan or slip a piece of ice from a bowl on the night table between his parched lips. Lewis West, the manservant, was kept busy at the front door answering inquiries.

Young Thad and Simon Stevens arrived. In the afternoon of the eleventh the Commoner felt well enough to engage in conversation with them. He said Reconstruction, finances, and the extension of the country's railway system were the three great problems of the day. He praised Seward for the purchase of Alaska, and said that Evarts, the new attorney general, the ratification of whose appointment he had favored, was an excellent lawyer and statesman. He believed his influence on Johnson might be such that a September meeting of Congress might not be necessary. The conversation was a last flaring up of the candle. He felt utterly exhausted. Dr. Young came and warned against tiring him with talking. He promised to return in the evening.

At seven o'clock two colored ministers presented themselves and asked if Mr. Stevens would receive them. When asked if they should be admitted, he said, "Certainly, certainly." They went in, and one of them said: "Mr. Stevens you have the prayers of all the colored people in the country." The sick man turned over on his side and held out his hand to him. They asked if he would like them to sing a hymn. He nodded, and they sang, then prayed for his recovery, after which they withdrew.

He seemed to have fallen asleep. His breathing was labored and irregular. There was a rattle in his throat. Lydia and the two men waited anxiously for the doctor. At nine o'clock he came. Stevens opened his eyes for a moment, then closed them. The doctor thinking there might be something the sick man might wish to communicate to his relatives before the end came, leaned over and told him that he was dying. Stevens nodded in token that he understood, but did not open his eyes.

The nuns arrived and seeing that he was *in extremis* knelt down at the foot of the bed and prayed. Lydia joined them. One of the nuns who knew that Stevens had never been baptized asked if she could perform the ceremony. Stevens did not hear or could not answer, but his nephew raised no objection. The nun sprinkled a little water on his forehead and performed the rite. The bell of St.

Aloysius church began striking the hour of twelve. Stevens had ceased to breathe.

The Lancaster *Express* was to report: "His last hour was one of tranquility, and when death came he passed calmly and peacefully away as though falling into a sweet slumber." [11]

7

Stevens's body was embalmed, and in the forenoon of the thirteenth was borne to the Capitol by three white and five colored pallbearers. An honor guard of colored Zouaves accompanied the remains and was to continue to guard them until they were lowered into the grave. In the rotunda of the Capitol, in front of the statue of Lincoln, the catafalque on which the martyred President's casket had reposed, had been set up. On this the coffin was placed, and the flowery tribute piled around it. A seemingly endless procession filed past the coffin that day and the next.

After a short service at the Capitol the casket was put aboard a special train for Lancaster. At every station there was a crowd of mourners, and stops were made at Harrisburg and York. Darkness was falling when the train reached the black-draped railway station at Lancaster where an enormous crowd was waiting and bells tolled mournfully.

For the next three days the body lay in state in the front parlor of Stevens's house, the windows of which were shuttered against the August heat. In the dim light, past the banks of flowers, the curious and the mournful came to cast a last look at his emaciated features.

It has been estimated that no less than twenty thousand people poured into the city on the day of the funeral by special train and other conveyances. The eight protestant ministers joined forces for the simple but impressive ceremony, and the octogenarian Catholic priest, a special friend of Stevens, attended. The City Hall and many houses were draped in black and all business was at a standstill. Bells tolled as the procession moved slowly toward Schreiner's cemetery between rows of people standing six feet deep.

Throughout the North there was mourning, and in the South

[11] Lancaster *Express,* Aug. 12, 1868.

Negroes and loyalists grieved at his passing. In Republican strongholds newspapers appeared double-leaded in black and flags flew at half-mast. The reconstructed governments in the South paid him honor. The legislature of South Carolina voted that the desks of the president of the Senate and of the speaker of the House were to be draped in mourning for thirty days. The New York *Tribune* and the Philadelphia *Press* claimed that not since the death of Lincoln had there been such mourning in the land, and that before this only the passing of Clay and of Jackson had produced a similar display of popular grief.

Stevens himself had composed the following lines that appear on the simple monument that marks his last resting place:

> I repose in this quiet and secluded spot,
> not from any natural preference for solitude,
> but finding other cemeteries
> limited by charter rules as to race,
> I have chosen this that I might illustrate in death
> the principles which I advocated through a long life,
> Equality of man before his Creator.

The Commoner's death came four days before the Republicans of Lancaster County were to nominate their candidates for the fall election. The chairman of the Republican County Committee, after consulting party leaders, recommended that, "as a fitting tribute to the memory of our most able and distinguished champion of freedom and justice, the unanimous vote of the party be cast for the name of Thaddeus Stevens in the ensuing primary meetings and arrangements be made later for filling the vacancy." So it was done.

There have been times when men have been nominated for office and have died after their names were placed on the ballot; but it is doubtful if another example exists of a constituency nominating a dead man for office. Whether Stevens was right or wrong, he must have accurately represented the sentiments of his constituency to have evoked such a tribute. And there can be no doubt that those sentiments were shared by the majority of the people of the North. Unworthy those sentiments were not. Professor Woodburn has rightly remarked: "His hatreds were not personal, and the enemies whom he faced in heat and passion were, as he thought, not his own enemies, but the enemies of his country, the enemies of a righteous and noble cause." [12]

8

Stevens's passing was commented on widely by newspapers at home and abroad. He was not liked in Europe where holders of American bonds believed that but for him refunding would have been far more generous. Yet Clemenceau spoke of him with respect and admiration in his letter to *Le Temps,* and the London *Times,* pro-Southern during the war, declared: "America has lost one of its foremost men. . . . Mr. Stevens was fanatical, self-willed and most bitter in his animosities, but there was neither meanness nor deceit in his nature. . . . However great might be the chafing, he always controlled his party, and with an iron will drove them on in the road he had chosen."

Comments in most Republican newspapers were laudatory, notwithstanding his party's displeasure with his stand on refunding. The New York *Herald,* claiming to be independent, said in part: "Of him it can be truly said that, although throughout his life his political predilections were of the most extreme kind, he never concealed them from his bitterest enemy. . . . This rough, and at times uncouth candor will mark him as one of the most honest politicians the United States ever had."

The vindictive attitude of many present-day Southerners toward him finds no precedent in the press of Richmond, Virginia, after his passing. All acknowledged his sincerity, honesty, and lack of hypocrisy. Indeed there was an ill-concealed note of admiration. The *Examiner* said that while it was impossible for the South sincerely to mourn his death—"Yet we cannot withhold a tribute to his honesty, which placed him far above the mean acts of the mere politician and made him boldly avow the wickedness of his purpose." The *Whig,* while considering him "the very incarnation of sectional prejudice," conceded that "all will feel that a man, and a strong man has gone from the earth, and that his departure is an event in history." The *Dispatch* gave him credit for "the very great virtue of sincerity" and said that "he fought boldly and never resorted to hypocrisy."

[12] *Op. cit.,* p. 606.

Louisiana papers, however, spewed venom. The New Orleans *Bee* gave him credit for no virtue whatever, called him a "malignant old man" and rejoiced that "our sphere is rid of a pest and a marplot." The *Planter's Banner* expressed this charitable wish: "May his new iron works wean him from earth, and the fires of his new furnaces never go out."

Stevens's will contained a bequest of one thousand dollars in aid of the Library Association he had founded in the Caledonia County Academy more than half a century earlier, "if the same is still in existence." He bequeathed five hundred dollars to the trustees of the graveyard in Peacham, where his mother and brother were buried. The interest on the bequest was to be paid to the sexton "to keep the graves in good order and plant roses and other cheerful flowers at each of the four corners in the spring." If either of these legacies lapsed, the money was to be given to the Baptist church nearest the town of Danville, Vermont, the place of his birth. One thousand dollars was bequeathed to Pennsylvania College for the maintenance of Stevens Hall.

His faithful housekeeper Lydia Hamilton Smith was generously provided for, as described in the chapter devoted to her. The principal legatee was his nephew Thad, who was to receive eight hundred dollars a year or more if he needed it. The principal, however, was not to be turned over to him except in the following manner: If he abstained from intoxicating liquors for five years he was to receive one-fourth of the estate, and so forth, every five years, until the whole was in his hands. If he failed to live up to this then the money—which proved to be forty thousand dollars—was to be used for the founding of an orphanage and training school. No preference was to be shown to any child on account of race, color, religion, or nationality. All were to be taught in the same classes and were to eat at the same table. His nephew could not or would not live up to the condition specified, and the money was used to found Stevens Institute in Lancaster, an industrial school for boys and girls.

A codicil in the will bequeathed one thousand dollars to the Baptist church in Lancaster for a new building. "I do this," he wrote, "out of respect for the memory of my mother to whom I owe what little prosperity I have had on earth, and which, small as it is, I desire emphatically to acknowledge."

When Congress assembled in December, 1868, the seventeenth of that month was devoted by the House to memorial speeches in Stevens's honor, while the Senate did the same the following day. Democrats as well as Republicans spoke. In the House, William E. Robinson of New York—a Democrat who had frequently crossed swords with him and had voted against nearly every measure he had proposed, yet had a profound admiration for him—thus eloquently finished his memorial address:

"He seemed like an eagle, perched alone upon a blasted oak in sullen and defiant majesty, scorning alike the chatter and the scream of other birds around him; his eye sometimes seemingly covered with film as of down from the passing wing of death, but in a moment shooting into pinions on which he proudly soared to the sun.

"That proud and defiant spirit, often fierce, sometimes unforgiving, and always bold and honest, has passed away."

SELECTED BIBLIOGRAPHY

Adams, Alice D. *The Neglected Period of American Anti-Slavery, 1808-1831,* Boston, 1908.
Adams, Charles Francis, *An Autobiography, 1835-1915,* Boston, 1916.
Adams, John Quincy, *Letters on the Masonic Institution,* New York, 1847.
—, *Memoirs,* C. F. Adams, ed., Philadelphia, 1876, 12 vols.
Altee, Benjamin C., "Thaddeus Stevens and Slavery," *Lancaster County Historical Society Reports,* vol. XV, No. 6, Lancaster, Pa., 1911.
Armor, William C., *Lives of the Governors of Pennsylvania, with the Incidental History of the State from 1609 to 1872,* Philadelphia, 1872.
Bacon, George W., *Life and Speeches of President Andrew Johnson,* London, 1865.
Bancroft, Frederic, *William H. Seward,* New York, 1900, 2 vols.
Barnes, Thurlow W., *Memoirs of Thurlow Weed,* Boston, 1884, 2 vols.
Barnes, William H., *History of the Thirty-Ninth Congress of the United States,* Indianapolis, 1867.
Bates, Edward, *The Diary of Edward Bates, 1859-1866,* Howard K. Beale, ed., Washington, 1933.
Beveridge, Albert J., *Abraham Lincoln, 1809-1858,* Boston and New York, 1928, 4 vols.
Bigelow, John, *Retrospections of an Active Life,* New York, 1909-1913, 5 vols.
Biographical Annals of Lancaster County, Pa., Chicago, 1903.
Blaine, James G., *Twenty Years of Congress,* Norwich, Conn., 1884-1886, 2 vols.
Bolles, Albert S., *Financial History of the United States,* New York, 1896.

Boutwell, George S., *Reminiscences of Sixty Years in Public Affairs,* New York, 1902.

Bowers, Claude G., *The Tragic Era,* Cambridge, Mass., 1929.

Bradford, Gamaliel, *Lee the American,* London, 1912.

Bremer, Frederika, *America of the Fifties,* New York, 1924.

Browning, Orville H., *Diary,* Springfield, 1927.

Burgess, John W., *Reconstruction and the Constitution,* New York, 1902.

—, *The Civil War and the Constitution,* New York, 1901, 2 vols.

Butler, Benjamin F., *Butler's Book. Autobiography of Personal Reminiscences,* Boston, 1892.

—, *Private and Official Correspondence of General Benjamin F. Butler,* 1917, 5 vols.

Callender, E. B., *Thaddeus Stevens, Commoner,* Boston, 1882.

Carpenter, Francis B., *Six Months at the White House,* Boston, 1866.

Chase, Salmon P., *Diary and Correspondence,* Washington, 1903.

Chidsey, Donald Barr, *The Gentleman from New York: A Life of Roscoe Conkling,* New Haven, 1934.

Clarke, Grace Julian, *George W. Julian,* Indianapolis, 1923.

Clemenceau, Georges, *American Reconstruction, 1865-1870,* New York, 1928.

Collins, C. W., *The Fourteenth Amendment and the States,* New York, 1912.

Congressional Globe, 1849-1853, 1859-1868.

Cooper, Thomas V., *American Politics,* Chicago, n.d.

Coulter, E. Morton, *The South during Reconstruction 1865-1877,* Louisiana State University Press, 1947.

Cowan, Frank, *Andrew Johnson, Reminiscences of His Private Life and Character, by One of His Secretaries,* Greensburg, Pa., 1894.

Current, Richard Nelson, *Old Thad Stevens,* Madison, 1932.

Curtis, Francis, *The Republican Party,* New York, 1904, 2 vols.

Curtis, George Ticknor, *Life of James Buchanan,* New York, 1882, 2 vols.

Dana, Charles A., *Lincoln and His Cabinet,* New York, 1896.

—, *Recollections of the Civil War,* New York, 1898.

Davis, Susan Lawrence, *Authentic History of the Ku Klux Klan 1865-1877,* New York, 1924.

Dewitt, David M., *The Impeachment and Trial of Andrew Johnson,* New York, 1903.

Dewey, Davis Rich, *Financial History of the United States,* New York, 1922.

Du Bois, W. E. Burghardt, *Black Reconstruction in America,* New York, 1935.

Dunning, William A., *Reconstruction, Political and Economic, 1865-1877,* New York, 1907.

Eaton, John, *Grant, Lincoln and the Freedmen,* New York, 1907.

Elliot, Edward Graham, *Biographical Story of the Constitution,* New York, 1910.

Fessenden, Francis, *Life and Public Services of William Pitt Fessenden,* Boston, 1907, 2 vols.

Fleming, Walter L., *Documentary History of Reconstruction,* Cleveland, 1906, 1907, 2 vols.

Flower, Frank A., *Edward M. Stanton, Autocrat of Rebellion,* Akron, Ohio, 1905.

Forney, John W., *Anecdotes of Public Men,* New York, 1873-1881, 2 vols.

Free Masonry Unmasked, Gettysburg, Pa., 1835.

Garner, James Wilford, *Reconstruction in Mississippi,* New York, 1901.

Grant, Ulysses S., *Personal Memoirs of U. S. Grant,* New York, 1885, 2 vols.

Greeley, Horace, *Recollections of a Busy Life,* New York, 1868.

Gurowski, Adam, *Diary,* Boston, 1862, 3 vols.

Hamilton, J. G., *Reconstruction in North Carolina,* New York, 1914.

Hamlin, C. E., *Life and Times of Hannibal Hamlin,* Cambridge, 1899.

Harris, Alexander, *A Review of the Political Conflict in America . . . Comprising also a Résumé of the Career of Thaddeus Stevens,* New York, 1876.

Hart, Albert Bushnell, *Salmon Portland Chase,* Boston, 1909.

Hayes, Rutherford B., *Diary and Letters,* Columbus, Ohio, 1922, 5 vols.

Helper, Hinton Rowan, *The Impending Crisis of the South,* New York, 1858.

Hendrick, Burton J., *Lincoln's War Cabinet,* Boston, 1946.

Hensel, W. U., *Christiana Riot and the Treason Trials of 1851,* Lancaster, 1911.

—, *Thaddeus Stevens as a Country Lawyer,* Lancaster, 1906.

Herndon, William H., and Weik, Jesse W., *Life of Lincoln,* annotated by Paul M. Angle, Cleveland and New York, 1942.

Hoke, Jacob, *The Great Invasion of 1863; or General Lee in Pennsylvania,* Dayton, Ohio, 1887.

Hood, Alexander H., *Thaddeus Stevens. A Biographical History of Lancaster County,* Alexander Harris, ed., Lancaster, 1872.

Johnson, Richard M., *Alexander H. Stephens,* Philadelphia, 1878.

Jones, James S., *Life of Andrew Johnson,* Greenville, Tenn., 1901.

Julian, George W., *Political Recollections, 1840-1872,* Chicago, 1884.

Kendrick, Benj. B., *The Journal of the Joint Committee of Fifteen on Reconstruction,* New York, 1914.

Landis, Charles I., *Refutation of the Slanderous Stories against the Name of T. Stevens Placed before the Public by Thomas Dixon,* Lancaster, 1924.
Lee, R. E., *Recollections and Letters of General Robert E. Lee,* New York, 1909.
Lester, C. Edwards, *The Life and Public Services of Charles Sumner,* New York, 1874.
Lincoln, Abraham, *Complete Works,* Nicolay and Hay, eds., New York, 1905, 12 vols.
Longstreet, James, *From Manassas to Appomattox,* Philadelphia, 1876.
Lossing, Benson J., *Pictorial History of the Civil War,* Philadelphia, 1866-1874, 3 vols.
Lynch, John R., *The Facts of Reconstruction,* New York, 1915.
Maurice, Sir John Frederick, *Robert E. Lee, the Soldier,* New York, 1925.
Maverick, Augustus, *Henry J. Raymond and the New York Press,* Hartford, 1870.
McCall, Samuel W., *Thaddeus Stevens,* Boston, 1899.
McCarthy, Charles H., "The Anti-Masonic Party," *Annual Report of the American Historical Association 1902,* Washington, 1903, vol. II.
—, *Lincoln's Plan of Reconstruction,* New York, 1901.
McClure, Alexander K., *Lincoln and Men of War Times,* Philadelphia, 1892.
—, *Colonel Alexander K. McClure's Recollections of Half a Century,* Salem, 1902.
—, *Old Time Notes of Pennsylvania,* Philadelphia, 1905, 2 vols.
—, *Our Presidents and How We Make Them,* New York, 1900.
McCulloch, Hugh, *Men and Measures of Half a Century,* New York, 1888.
McElroy, Robert McNutt, *Jefferson Davis: The Unreal and the Real,* New York, 1937.
McPherson, Edward, *The Political History of the United States of America during the Period of Reconstruction,* Washington, 1871.
Memorial Addresses on the Life and Character of Thaddeus Stevens, Delivered in the House of Representatives, Washington, D. C., December 17, 1868, Government Printing Office, 1869.
Miller, Alphonse B., *Thaddeus Stevens,* New York, 1939.
Moore, Frank, *Life and Speeches of Andrew Johnson,* Boston, 1865.
Moore, John B., *Works of James Buchanan,* Philadelphia, 1911, 12 vols.
Moore, John T., and Foster, A. P., *Tennessee,* Chicago, 1923.
Morse, John T., Jr., *John Quincy Adams,* Boston, 1883.
Muller, Henry R., *Whig Party in Pennsylvania,* New York, 1922.
Nevins, Allan, *The Emergence of Modern America,* New York, 1927.
—, *The Emergence of Lincoln,* New York, 1950.

Nevins, Allan, *Ordeal of the Union,* New York, 1947, 2 vols.
—, *The Statesmanship of the Civil War,* New York, 1953.
Nicolay, John G., and Hay, John, *Abraham Lincoln,* New York, 1890, 10 vols.
Oberholtzer, Ellis P., *A History of the United States since the Civil War,* New York, 1917, 3 vols.
Owen, Robert Dale, "Political Results of the Varioloid," *Atlantic Monthly,* June, 1875.
Parton, James, *General Butler in New Orleans; History of the Administration of the Department of the Gulf in the Year 1862,* Boston, 1863.
Piatt, Donn, *Memories of Men Who Saved the Union,* New York, 1887.
Randall, J. G., *Constitutional Problems under Lincoln,* New York, 1926.
—, *Lincoln the President,* New York, 1946, 2 vols.
—, *Lincoln and the South,* Baton Rouge, 1946.
—, *Lincoln the Liberal Statesman,* New York, 1947.
—, *Mid-Stream,* New York, 1952.
Rhodes, James Ford, *History of the United States from the Compromise of 1850-1877,* New York, 1896-1919, 7 vols.
Rice, Allen Thorndike, ed., *Reminiscences of Abraham Lincoln by Distinguished Men of His Time,* New York, 1886.
Richardson, James D., *Messages and Papers of the Presidents, 1789-1897,* Washington, 1897.
Riddle, Albert G., *Life of Benjamin F. Wade,* Cleveland, 1886.
—, *Recollections of War Times,* New York, 1895.
Sandburg, Carl, *Abraham Lincoln: The War Years,* New York, 1939, 4 vols.
Schurz, Carl, *The Reminiscences of Carl Schurz,* F. Bancroft and W. A. Dunning, eds., New York, 1908, 3 vols.
Seitz, Don C., *Lincoln the Politician,* New York, 1931.
Seward, Frederick, *Reminiscences of a War Time Statesman and Diplomat,* New York, 1916.
Seward, William H., *William H. Seward: An Autobiography from 1801 to 1834 with a Memoir of His Life and Selections from His Letters 1831-1846, ed. by Frederick W. Seward,* New York, 1891.
Sherman, John, *Recollections of Forty Years in the House, Senate and Cabinet,* Chicago, 1895, 2 vols.
Singmaster, Elsie, *I Speak for Thaddeus Stevens,* Boston, 1947.
Skaggs, William H., *The Southern Oligarchy,* New York, 1924.
Smith, William Ernest, *The Francis Preston Blair Family in Politics,* New York, 1933, 2 vols.
Spinoza, Benedict de, *A Theologico-Political Treatise,* New York, 1951.

Stephens, Alexander H., *Constitutional View of the Late War between the States,* Philadelphia, 1868, 2 vols.

Stewart, Lucy Shelton, *The Reward of Patriotism,* New York, 1930.

Sumner, Charles, *Memoirs and Letters of Charles Sumner,* Edward L. Pierce, ed., Boston, 1877-1894, 4 vols.

Sydnor, Charles S., *The Development of Southern Sectionalism, 1918-1948,* Louisiana State University Press, 1948.

Taylor, A. A., *The Negro in South Carolina during Reconstruction,* Washington, 1924.

—, *The Negro in the Reconstruction of Mississippi,* Washington, 1926.

Thayer, William Roscoe, *The Life and Letters of John Hay,* Boston, 1915, 2 vols.

Trial of Andrew Johnson, Government Printing Office, 1868, 3 vols.

Villard, Henry, *Memoirs,* Boston, 1904, 2 vols.

Walpole, Sir Spencer, *Life of Lord Russell,* London, 1893.

Weed, Thurlow, *Autobiography,* Harriet A. Weed, ed., Boston, 1884.

Welles, Gideon, *Diary,* New York, 1911, 3 vols.

Whitney, Henry C., *Life on the Circuit with Lincoln,* Boston, 1892.

Williams, Wythe, *The Tiger of France,* New York, 1949.

Wilson, Henry, *History of the Antislavery Measures of the Thirty-Seventh and Thirty-Eighth Congresses,* Boston, 1865.

—, *History of the Rise and Fall of the Slave Power in America,* Boston, 1872-1877, 3 vols.

Winston, Robert W., *Andrew Johnson, Plebeian and Patriot,* New York, 1928.

Woodburn, James A., *The Life of Thaddeus Stevens,* Indianapolis, 1913.

Woodley, Thomas Frederick, *Great Leveler—The Life of Thaddeus Stevens,* New York, 1937.

—, *Thaddeus Stevens,* Harrisburg, 1934.

INDEX